Zwischen den Reichen:
Neues Testament und Römische Herrschaft

TANZ 36

Texte und Arbeiten zum neutestamentlichen Zeitalter

herausgegeben von Klaus Berger

Michael Labahn / Jürgen Zangenberg
(Hrsg.)

Zwischen den Reichen:
Neues Testament
und Römische Herrschaft

Vorträge auf der Ersten Konferenz der
European Association for Biblical Studies

Die Deutsche Bibliothek – *CIP-Einheitsaufnahme*

Zwischen den Reichen : Neues Testament und Römische Herrschaft : Vorträge auf der Ersten Konferenz der European Association for Biblical Studies / Michael Labahn/Jürgen Zangenberg (Hrsg.). – Tübingen ; Basel : Francke, 2002
  Texte und Arbeiten zum neutestamentlichen Zeitalter ; 36
  ISBN 3-7720-2828-4

© 2002 · A. Francke Verlag Tübingen und Basel
Dischingerweg 5 · D-72070 Tübingen

Das Werk einschließlich aller seiner Teile ist urheberrechtlich geschützt. Jede Verwertung außerhalb der engen Grenzen des Urheberrechtsgesetzes ist ohne Zustimmung des Verlages unzulässig und strafbar. Das gilt insbesondere für Vervielfältigungen, Übersetzungen, Mikroverfilmungen und die Einspeicherung und Verarbeitung in elektronischen Systemen. Gedruckt auf säurefreiem und alterungsbeständigem Werkdruckpapier.

Druck und Bindung: Hubert & Co., Göttingen
Printed in Germany

ISSN 0939-5199
ISBN 3-7720-2828-4

Vorwort

Die Entscheidung der Herausgeber, das Thema „Frühes Christentum und Römisches Reich" im Rahmen eines wissenschaftlichen Seminars zu beschäftigen, reifte im Laufe des Jahres 1999. Ziel war es, Vertreter und Vertreterinnen unterschiedlicher akademischer Disziplinen und wissenschaftlicher Traditionen in einem möglichst internationalen Rahmen mit einander ins Gespräch zu bringen, um das gestellte Thema im Lichte neuer Quellen und Fragestellungen zu beleuchten. Bei der Vorbereitung des Panels erwies es sich jedoch sehr schnell, dass mit befriedigenden Ergebnissen nur zu rechnen ist, wenn man die ungemein komplexe ursprüngliche Themenstellung in überschaubare Einheiten unterteilt. Daher entschlossen wir uns, unter der Überschrift „Zwischen den Reichen" zunächst die Wechselwirkung zwischen römischer Herrschaft und frühchristlicher Lebenswirklichkeit aufzugreifen. Dass dabei der eine oder andere in diesem Band gebotene Beitrag über das rein Politische hinausgreift, mag angesichts der Tatsache zulässig sein, dass römische Herrschaft neben im engeren Sinne rechtlichen und politischen Elementen stets auch einen weiter gefassten, kulturellen Horizont beinhaltete, mit dem sich das ausbreitende frühe Christentum auseinander zu setzen hatte. Weitere Teilaspekte des Themas werden in den kommenden Jahren in ähnlichem Rahmen aufgegriffen und jeweils gesondert veröffentlicht.[1]

Bei der ersten Konferenz der *European Association of Biblical Studies*, die vom 6.–9.8.2000 in Utrecht stattfand, wurde uns für das Seminar ein angenehmes Arbeitsklima geboten, das sich als sehr produktiv erwies. Hier wurden die Mehrzahl der Beiträge dieses Bandes vorgetragen und intensiv diskutiert; für die Drucklegung wurden auch Beiträge aufgenommen, die aus verschiedenen Gründen in Utrecht nicht gehalten werden konnten.

Zu danken haben wir den Verantwortlichen der *European Association of Biblical Studies* (allen voran Prof. Dr. Bob BECKING und Prof. Dr. Lester GRABBE), dass sie unseren Vorschlag so bereitwillig aufgegriffen und uns bei der Durchführung auf der Konferenz in Utrecht unterstützt haben. Auch Herrn Pfr. Andreas SCHMIDT, Dissen ATW, der an der Konzipierung des Seminars und in der Anfangszeit an der Vorbereitung mitwirkte, haben wir zu denken.

Herrn Prof. Dr. Klaus BERGER gilt unser Dank für die Aufnahme des Bandes in die Reihe „Texte und Arbeiten zum Neutestamentlichen Zeitalter", Herr Dr. Stephan DIETRICH betreute den Band im Francke-Verlag in gewohnt pro-

---

[1] Rom 2001: *Christians as a Religious Minority in a Multicultural City. Modes of Interaction and Identity Formation in Early Imperial Rome / Christen als Minderheit in einer multikulturellen Stadt. Formen der Begegnung und Identitätsfindung im frühkaiserzeitlichen Rom.* – Berlin 2002 (mit projektierter Fortsetzung 2003), in Verbindung mit Bert Jan LIETAERT PEERBOLTE: *The Purpose of Narrating Miracle Stories in the New Testament and Its Environment / Die Pragmatik von Wundergeschichten im Neuen Testament und seiner Umwelt.*

fessioneller Weise. Shane BERG von der Yale University Divinity School (New Haven, Connecticut) und Bethann BLACK vom Bangor Theological Seminary (Bangor, Maine) gebührt Dank dafür, dass sie die englischen Texte durchgesehen und den Herausgebern zahlreiche sprachliche Verbesserungsvorschläge unterbreitet haben, die wir in Abstimmung mit den Autoren gern berücksichtigt haben. Die endgültige Fassung der Beiträge liegt jedoch in der Verantwortung der Beiträger und Beiträgerinnen.

Unseren Referenten/Referentinnen und Autoren/Autorinnen gilt unser aufrichtiger Dank dafür, dass sie durch ihre Sachkenntnis und ihr großes Engagement das Panel und den vorliegenden Band erst ermöglicht haben.

Halle/Saale Michael LABAHN
Wuppertal Jürgen ZANGENBERG

Inhalt

Vorwort V

Michael Labahn / Jürgen Zangenberg
Einleitung 3

Hintergründe:
Aspekte römischer Herrschaft und Kultur

Hannah M. Cotton
Jewish Jurisdiction under Roman Rule:
Prolegomena 13

Werner Eck
Die Inschriften Iudäas im 1. und frühen 2. Jh. n. Chr. als
Zeugnisse der römischen Herrschaft 29

Markus Öhler
Römisches Vereinsrecht und christliche Gemeinden 51

Richard DeMaris
Cults and the Imperial Cult in Early Roman Corinth:
Literary Versus Material Record 73

Brechungen:
Reaktionen frühchristlicher Gruppen auf römische Herrschaft und Kultur

Marco Frenschkowski
Kyrios in Context
Q 6:46, the Emperor as "Lord", and the Political Implications of Christology in Q 95

Gudrun Guttenberger
Why Caesarea Philippi of all Sites?
Some Reflections on the Political Background and Implications of Mark
8:27–30 for the Christology of Mark 119

Outi Lehtipuu
The Imagery of the Lukan Afterworld in the Light of Some
Roman and Greek Parallels 133

Michael Labahn
‚Heiland der Welt'
Der gesandte Gottessohn und der römische Kaiser – ein Thema johanneischer Christologie? 147

Martin Meiser
Lukas und die römische Staatsmacht 175

Francois P. Viljoen
Song and Music in the Early Christian Communities
Paul's Utilisation of Jewish, Roman and Greek Musical
Traditions to Encourage the Early Christian Communities
to Praise God and to Explain his Arguments 195

Lauri Thurén
Jeremiah 27 and Civil Obedience in 1 Peter 215

Daria Pezzoli-Olgiati
Between Fascination and Destruction
Considerations on the Power of the Beast in Rev 13:1–10 229

Bert Jan Lietaert Peerbolte
To Worship the Beast
The Revelation of John and the Imperial Cult in Asia Minor 239

Anhang

Liste der Mitarbeiterinnen und Mitarbeiter 263

Stellenregister... 268

Einleitung

Michael Labahn / Jürgen Zangenberg

„Zwischen den Reichen"
Zur komplexen Interaktion von frühem Christentum und römischer Herrschaft

In der Erinnerung an die Verkündigung Jesu tradierte christliche Predigt die Vorstellung vom anbrechenden Reich Gottes; zugleich aber bildete ein anderes, ein politisches Reich die entscheidende Lebensbedingung der christlichen Bewegung. Jesu Leben und Sterben geschah unter und durch römisches Recht, die frühe Gemeinde lebte und gestaltete ihr theologisches Denken im römischen Reich, Mission und Ausbreitung geschahen unter den Bedingungen römischer Herrschaft. In all diesen geschichtlichen Prozessen markieren zwei Herrschaftsansprüche die Pole, zwischen denen sich Leben und Denken der frühen Christenheit abspielte. Es ist von einer komplexen Interaktion von frühem Christentum und römischer Herrschaft auszugehen, will man sich angemessen diesem spannungsvollen Verhältnis widmen. Im vorliegenden Band kann und soll dies nicht in enzyklopädischer Breite geschehen, vielmehr aber wurden interessante und zentrale Einzelaspekte des Themas aufgenommen und neu dargelegt.

Den „Hintergründen" widmen sich die vier Beiträge zu Beginn des Bandes und erhellen unterschiedliche Aspekte römischer Herrschaft und Kultur. Sie verdeutlichen in exemplarischer Weise, unter Massgabe welcher rechtlicher, politischer, sozialer und religiöser Gegebenheiten sich frühchristliches Leben entfalten konnte.

Hannah M. COTTONs Studie über Aspekte des Rechtswesens in Palästina unter römischer Herrschaft aufgrund der Papyri aus der judäischen Wüste und Werner ECKs Diskussion ausgewählter Inschriften des 1. und 2. Jh. n.Chr. aus Palästina greifen dabei auf zum Teil erst kürzlich entdecktes und von der neutestamentlichen Forschung noch weitgehend unbeachtetes Material zurück. Sowohl die Papyri als auch die zur Zeit systematisch gesammelten und analysierten Inschriften werfen ein hilfreiches Licht auf die tatsächliche Praxis und Selbstdarstellung römischer Herrschaft in einer Provinz wie Judäa und den Umgang der Menschen mit der vor allem in Rechtsfragen nur allzu präsenten Besatzungsmacht.

Hannah COTTONs Beitrag konzentriert sich auf die Frage der Reichweite lokaler jüdischer Rechtsinstitutionen in Judäa/Syria-Palaestina unter römischer Herrschaft und kann dabei zeigen, dass römische Praktiken und Institutionen in viel stärkerem Maße präsent waren und genutzt wurden, als man dies aufgrund der Lektüre späterer jüdischer Quellen wie der Mischna vermuten könnte. Lokale rabbinische Gerichte, die so oft in der Mischna begegnen, scheinen viel eher im Bereich privater Schlichtung als auf dem Feld formaler Rechtsprechung angesiedelt gewesen zu sein. Für alle weiter gehenden Rechtsfälle bis hin zur Kriminalgerichtsbarkeit bediente man sich römischer Institutionen. Mit dieser Praxis ähnelt Palästina dem zeitgenössischen Ägypten, wo eine ebenso alte und tief verwurzelte indigene Rechtskultur auf den Einfluss römischer Herrschaft stieß wie in Judäa.

In Werner ECKs Untersuchung ausgewählter Inschriften aus Palästina begegnen nicht allein Pontius Pilatus, der wohl bis heute bekannteste römische Präfekt der im Jahre 6 n.Chr. geschaffenen Provinz Judaea, sondern auch einzelne Personen aus dem Verwaltungsapparat. Mit dem Ausbruch des Jüdischen Krieges im Jahre 66 n.Chr. nimmt die römische Präsenz in der Region erwartungsgemäss dramatisch zu. Inschriften dokumentieren die Anwesenheit von Soldaten und ihrer Einheiten sowie den Bau von Straßen und militärischen Anlagen. Die neue Form der Herrschaft wird vor allem in Inschriften aus Caesarea deutlich wie der öffentlichen Ehrung eines in der Finanzverwaltung tätigen Freigelassenen oder eines Senators, zu dessen Laufbahn auch die Verwaltung der Provinz Judaea gehört hat. Von besonderer Bedeutung für die Art, wie römische Dominanz kommuniziert wurde, sind die Fragmente einer mehr als 10 m breiten monumentalen Inschrift, die anlässlich der Niederschlagung des Bar-Kochba-Aufstandes unweit südlich von Skythopolis an einem Siegesbogen angebracht wurde. Sorgfältig in ihrem baulichen und kulturellen Kontext interpretiert erweisen sich Inschriften trotz aller Zufälligkeit ihrer Erhaltung als wertvolle Schlaglichter mit durchaus programmatischer Spitze.

Markus ÖHLER widmet sich in seinem Beitrag juristischen Fragestellungen des römischen Vereinsrechts, um vor diesem Hintergrund christliche Gemeindebildung und ihr Bemühen um rechtliche Anerkennung in den Blick zu nehmen. Der leitende Gesichtspunkt des Vereinsrechts ist der Grundsatz, dass durch die Vereine die Staatsinteressen nicht berührt werden dürfen, mehr diesen nützen sollen. Nach diesen Grundsätzen wurden neben bestehenden ‚alten Vereinen' seit Augustus neue *collegia* vom Staat zugelassen oder bei Abweichungen aufgelöst. Vor diesem Hintergrund konnten christliche Gemeinden von den staatlichen römischen Stellen wahrgenommen und sowohl geduldet (1Petr) als auch aufgelöst werden (Plin Ep 10,96f).

Einsetzend bei Strabos berühmtem Zitat über die Tempelprostitution (Strab 8,6,20) und seiner Wirkung in neutestamentlicher Exegese und archäologischer Forschung mahnt Richard DEMARIS an, die materiellen Überreste der antiken Stadt Korinth im Interpretationsprozess gegenüber den literarischen Quellen Ernst zu nehmen. Die undifferenzierte Nutzung archäologischer Beobachtungen kann zu ebenso problematischen Ergebnissen führen wie eine zu starke Beeinflussung durch die literarischen Quellen, wie beispielsweise Pausanias, den archäologischen Befund missdeuten kann. DEMARIS entwirft so ein differenzierteres Bild der Religion des kaiserzeitlichen Korinth und bietet neue Perspektiven zum Verständnis der paulinischen Korrespondenz mit den Korinthern. Die Neugestaltung der Agora Korinths im 2. Jh. n.Chr., die im Hintergrund der Darstellung des Pausanias steht, führt zu einer Marginalisierung der traditionellen Verehrung von Heroen und chthonischen Gottheiten, während der Kult der olympischen Götter und der Herrscherkult an Bedeutung gewinnen, deren zentrale Bauten nunmehr das Weichbild der Stadt prägen. Die Verkündigung des Paulus setzt jedoch ein anderes kulturelles Profil der Stadt voraus. Sie knüpft noch an korinthisch-griechische Religiosität an und trägt damit Züge des Widerstands gegen den römischen Imperialismus.

Alle vier Beiträge unterstreichen die wachsende Bedeutung der Nachbardisziplinen Archäologie, Epigraphik und Papyrologie für die Interpretation neutestamentlicher Texte.[1] Ein umfassendes Verständnis des Neuen Testaments ist nur möglich, wenn dessen Kontextualisierung in den geistigen und sozialen Auseinandersetzungen während der Zeit seiner Entstehung gelingt. Dabei gilt es aber, die Befunde selbst zur Kenntnis zu nehmen ohne ihnen fremde Fragestellung auf zu oktroyieren. Daher ist die oft beschworene „Umwelt des Neuen Testaments" aus den Fesseln einer bloss nach „Parallelen" suchenden Sichtweise zu befreien; sie ist in ihren literarischen und nichtliterarischen Aspekten der ‚Kon-Text', der bei der Lektüre der neutestamentlichen Texte stets mitgelesen sein will.

Die folgenden neun Beiträge bilden den zweiten Hauptteil des Buches: sie beschäftigen sich mit einzelnen Aspekten der Reaktion frühchristlicher Gruppen auf römische Herrschaft und Kultur und damit ihres Agierens in dieser Welt. Diese Beiträge stellen eine keineswegs zufällige Auswahl dar, die allerdings in verschiedener Weise ergänzt werden könnte.[2]

---

[1] Mit Sicherheit verdienen auch weitere Felder Berücksichtigung wie beispielsweise die Numismatik; vgl. hierzu z.b. Larry J. KREITZER, Striking New Images. Roman Imperial Coinage and New Testament World, JSNTS 134, Sheffield 1996, Wolfram WEISER/Hannah M. COTTON, „Gebt dem Kaiser, was des Kaisers ist …" Die Geldwährungen der Griechen, Juden, Nabatäer und Römer im syrisch-nabatäischen Raum unter besonderer Berücksichtigung des Kurses von Sela'/Melaina und Lepton nach der Annexion des Königreiches der Nabatäer durch Rom, in: ZPE 114 (1996), 237–287, und Gudrun GUTTENBERGER in diesem Band.

[2] Gerade zum paulinischen Schrifttum wäre noch Weiteres zu den politischen Rahmenbedingungen der paulinischen Mission auszuführen (vgl. jetzt z.B. David ALVAREZ CINEIRA, Die Religionspolitik des Kaisers Claudius und die paulinische Mission, HBS 19, Freiburg im Breisgau et al. 1999), aber auch die Referenzen auf das Verhältnis zum Staat in den paulinischen und deuteropaulinischen Brief selbst sind zu beachten (vgl. z.B. Richard A. HORSLEY, Paul and Empire. Religion and Power in Roman Imperial Society, Harrisburg, PA, 1997). Zur Wahrnehmung der paulinischen Gemeinden im römischen Staat vgl. den Beitrag von Markus ÖHLER in diesem Band. – Auch das Matthäusevangelium ist hinsichtlich seines Verhältnisses zu politischen Herrschaftskonzeptionen untersucht und als Alternativentwurf interpretiert worden: Gerd THEISSEN, Vom Davidssohn zum Weltherrscher. Pagane und jüdische Endzeiterwartung im Spiegel des Matthäusevangeliums, in: Michael BECKER/Wolfgang FENSKE (Hrsg.), Das Ende der Tage und die Gegenwart des Heils. Begegnungen mit dem Neuen Testament und seiner Umwelt. FS Heinz-Wolfgang KUHN, AGJU 44, Leiden – Boston – Köln 1999, 145–164. – Eine wertvolle und willkommene Weiterführung des Themas bietet der Sammelband Raban VON HOEHLING (ed.), Rom und das himmlische Jerusalem. Die frühen Christen zwischen Anpassung und Ablehnung, Daramstadt 2001, der erst bei der Endredaktion des vorliegenden Bandes erschienen ist.

Die Überschrift „Brechungen" trägt der Tatsache Rechnung, dass nie die gesamte Bandbreite möglicher Bezugspunkte der Umwelt von einer Gruppe rezipiert bzw. durch Wort und Verhalten „kommentiert" wird. Wie sich Licht durch ein Prisma in mehrere farbige Strahlen zerlegen lässt, so zeigen die verschiedenen Entwürfe frühchristlichen Umgangs mit ihren Lebenskontexten eine beträchtliche Vielstimmigkeit in Bezug auf das konkrete Verhalten im Alltag wie auch hinsichtlich der theoretischen Begründung dieses Verhaltens im Rekurs auf das Alte Testament oder auf andere Quellen.

Ausgehend von der Verwendung von κύριος als Epitheton und als Titel im ersten nachchristlichen Jahrhundert zeichnet Marco FRENSCHKOWSKI anhand von Q 6,46 den komplexen Dialog nach, den die Trägergruppe der Logienquelle mit zeitgenössischen politischen Erwartungen und Ansprüchen geführt hat. Das weitgehende Fehlen des Begriffs „Messias" in Q spricht nach FRENSCHKOWSKI keinesfalls für eine „unpolitische" Theologie der Logienquelle. Die Verwendung des Begriffs κύριος (und des aramäischen Äquivalents *mare'*) unterstreicht den umfassenden Anspruch Jesu. Für Q ist Jesus weit mehr als nur ein Weisheitslehrer, er steht in klarer Konkurrenz etwa zu den politischen Ansprüchen eines Nero. In Treue zum erhöhten Jesus ordnet sich Q damit in den auch politischen Widerstand gegen das Imperium ein, auch wenn die Angehörigen der Trägergruppe von Q nicht offen zum Aufruhr aufgerufen haben.

Gudrun GUTTENBERGERs Untersuchung zu Mk 8,27–30 zielt in eine ähnliche Richtung. Durch die Verortung des Messiasbekenntnisses des Petrus bei Caesarea Philippi führt Markus Jesus als rechtmäßigen König Israels in Konkurrenz zur herodianischen Dynastie und als wahren Herrn der ganzen *oikumene* im Wettbewerb mit den Kaisern von Rom ein. GUTTENBERGERs Interpretation zeigt das große Potential einer genauen Analyse des Lokalkolorits und regt zur Diskussion über die Berechtigung einer größeren Beachtung von oft als „redaktionell" bezeichneten Einleitungswendungen synoptischer Erzählperikopen an.

Outi LEHTIPUU greift die in der Forschung verschiedentlich diskutierte Frage nach dem religionsgeschichtlichen Hintergrund der lukanischen Vorstellungen über das Jenseits, besonders in Lk 16,19–31, auf. Im Unterschied zur klassischen Verknüpfung mit demotischen Volkserzählungen über die Umkehrung des Geschicks des reichen und armen Mannes im Jenseits betont LEHTIPUU die Ähnlichkeit mit griechisch-römischen Vorstellungen vor allem bei Homer und Vergil. Letzten Endes sollte sich aber die Frage nach der „Herkunft" der in Lk 16,19–31 verarbeiteten Vorstellungen nicht zu sehr auf eine einzige Alternative beschränken. Vor allem die Darstellung der Erscheinungsweise der Toten in der Unterwelt deutet für die Autorin darauf hin, wie sehr bestimmte Vorstellungen über das Jenseits zum Allgemeingut der mediterranen Welt gehört haben.

Illustriert Lk 16,19–31 das kreative Anknüpfen neutestamentlicher Autoren bzw. ihrer Quellen an populäre Vorstellungen der griechisch-römischen Welt, so zeigt Michael LABAHN in seiner Untersuchung des Portraits Jesu in zentralen Texten des Johannesevangeliums (Joh 4,42; 20,28 sowie einzelne Wundergeschichten), dass sich der Verfasser des vierten Evangeliums mit Ansprüchen des römischen Staates, repräsentiert durch Kaiserpropaganda und Kaiserverehrung, auseinandersetzt. Freilich deutet die Erwähnung Jesu als „Heiland der Welt" nicht auf einen unmittelbaren Konflikt oder direkte Polemik zwischen johanneischer Gemeinde und Kaiserkult hin, ist sie doch Teil der johanneischen Sprach- und Erzählwelt. Berührungen mit Terminologie und Motivik der Herrscherverehrung bleiben auffällig und können zur Verdichtung der johanneischen Sprache geführt haben. Im Ergebnis spielt sich nach LABAHN die Auseinandersetzung im grundsätzlicheren Bereich konkurrierender Heilsangebote ab, zu denen die römische Herrscherverehrung gehört, deren Ansprüche für Leser und Leserinnen erkennbar begrenzt wird.

Martin MEISERs Untersuchung des Verhältnisses von Lukas zur römischen Staatsmacht führt über das oft behauptete Postulat einer „positiven Grundeinstellung" des Lukas *in rebus Romanis* hinaus, indem er ihren situativen Kontext aufzeigt. Nach „aussen" propagiert Lukas die Harmlosigkeit des Christentums für das Imperium, nach „innen" wirbt er darum, die politisch unbedenkliche Haltung der Christen durchzuhalten und den Mut zu besitzen, diese auch nach aussen hin offensiv zu vertreten. Die Pflicht zur Loyalität dem Staat gegenüber bedeutet für Lukas freilich keine kritiklose Hingabe an den Staat. Kritische Stellungnahmen erfolgen im Rahmen dessen, was auch antike Literatur an Kritik gegenüber dem Staat, vor allem verstorbenen Herrschern, belegt. Gott bleibt der eigentliche Herr der Geschichte, der über seine Gemeinde wacht, gerade wenn Vertreter des Staates den Angehörigen dieser Gemeinde Unrecht tun. Es überrascht nicht, dass dieses differenzierte Bild des Christentums als „loyale fremde Elite" für die Folgezeit von entscheidender Bedeutung war.

Francois P. VILJOENs knapper Überblick über die Rolle von Musik und Gesang in den paulinischen und nachpaulinischen Gemeinden greift ein selten behandeltes Feld der Interaktion von griechisch-römischer und jüdischer Tradition bei der Entwicklung des frühchristlichen Gemeindelebens auf. Texte wie Röm 15,9–12; 1Kor 14,15–17; Eph 5,19 und Kol 3,16 setzen nach VILJOEN dabei eine Vertrautheit mit griechischen, römischen und jüdischen musikalischen Traditionen ebenso voraus wie die konsequente Adaptation dieser Traditionen im Kontext des christlichen Bedürfnisses, Gott mit allen zur Verfügung stehenden Mitteln zu loben und die Gemeinde aufzubauen.[3]

Lauri THURÉN warnt in seiner Studie zur „politischen Theologie" des 1Petr vor anachronistischer Kritik an der vom Verfasser geforderten bedingungslo-

---

[3] Zur Vertiefung des Themas sind auch die bei der Abfassung des Beitrags noch nicht vorhandenen Darstellungen der synagogalen Liturgie bei Lee I. LEVINE, The Ancient Synagogue. The First Thousand Years, New Haven 2000, 501–560 und der Musik im frühen Christentum von James W. MCKINNON, Music, in: Philip F. ESLER (ed.), The Early Christian World Volume II, London – New York 2001, 773–790, zu Rate zu ziehen. Über Musik in griechischer und römischer Kultur informiert auch Giovanni COMETTI, Music in Greek and Roman Culture, Baltimore – London 1989.

sen Unterordnung unter den römischen Staat. Die Spannung zwischen kritischer Distanz zur römischen Kultur und der durchweg positiven Haltung den Vertretern römischer Macht gegenüber resultiert nicht aus opportunistischem Kalkül, sondern verdankt sich der Rezeption von Jer 27 mit einer spezifisch christologischen Spitze: Christi Beispiel der Erniedrigung und Duldung von Gewalt soll das Leben der Adressaten prägen, damit die Gemeindeglieder wie der Christus gerettet werden.

Die beiden abschliessenden Artikel wenden sich dem letzten Buch des Neuen Testament, der Johannesapokalypse, zu, dessen vielfältige Bezugnahmen auf das römische Reich und seine Herrschern die Auslegung seit langem beschäftigt.

Daria PEZZOLI-OLGIATI widmet sich der Vision des aus dem Meer steigenden Tieres, Apk 13,1–10. Die Bewunderung der ganzen Welt *hinter* (ὀπίσω) dem Tier (Apk 13,3b) entspricht einer Bewegung im Text selbst. Am Anfang des Textes – die horizontalen Perspektive – steht die Bewunderung der grandiosen Erscheinung des Tieres. Nach der Beschreibung seiner zerstörerischen Macht werden die wahren Verehrer Gottes und des Lammes denen des Tieres gegenüber gestellt, was die himmlische Perspektive des Sehers repräsentiert. Indem die Leser und Leserinnen durch den Seher aufgefordert werden, die Verbindung von historischem Kontext (die Verfasserin rechnet mit der Abfassung der Apk unter Domitian) und Vision zu ziehen, sollen sie in radikaler Opposition zur römischen Herrschaft die eigentlich handelnde Macht Gottes anerkennen.

Anders als PEZZOLI-OLGIATI beschäftigen sich Bert Jan LIETAERT PEERBOLTE nicht mit der Vorstellung eines Einzeltextes. Ausgangspunkt seiner Analyse ist die berühmte Plinius-Korrespondenz mit Kaiser Trajan über die Christen (Plin Ep 10,96f), der auf die Verweigerung jeglicher Verehrung griechisch-römischer Götter gehe. Der kurz nach der Apokalypse verfasste Briefwechsel entspricht weitgehend der des Sehers Johannes und seiner Gemeinden. Um zu klären, warum der Seher so scharf gegen den Herrscherkult polemisiert, werden zunächst die Passagen der Apokalypse vorgestellt, in denen sich die Auseinandersetzung spiegelt. Dem Konflikt stellt LIETAERT PEERBOLTE die soziale Wirklichkeit der römischen Provinz *Asia Minor* gegenüber, indem die politische Organisation der kleinasiatischen Städte untersucht und die Vorteile herausgestellt werden, die diese Städten erlangen, wenn sie den Herrscherkult fördern. Von diesem religiösen und politischen Rahmen grenzt die Polemik des Sehers sich und seine Anhänger aus. Mehr noch, er lehnt das gesamte Sozialsystem als solches ab.

Die Interpretationen zeigen ein Spektrum von relativer, auf den politischöffentlichen Raum begrenzter Akzeptanz des römischen Herrschaftssystems bis hin zu polemischer Abgrenzung und Ablehnung. Die Rolle, die die politischen Fragen für die Interpretation der untersuchten neutestamentlichen Schriften spielen, wird unterschiedlich bewertet. Mag sich die im Werden begriffene christliche Theologie auch im Einzelnen der Möglichkeiten des römischen Herrschaftssystem mit seiner relativen Sicherheit bedient haben und sucht man in kultureller und religiöser Hinsicht anschlussfähig zu bleiben, so ist eine grundlegende Differenz zum römischen Reich charakteristisch für das christliche Leben „zwischen den Reichen".

Auf der methodischen Seite wurden antike Quellen der griechisch-römischen Welt, vor allem der römischen Herrschaft aufgenommen – neben den klassischen antiken Literaturwerken in diesem Band vor allem Inschriftenbelege, aber auch Münzfunde – und für die Interpretation nutzbar gemacht. Ausser diesen antiken Texten und Materialien dienen auch alttestamentliche Referenzen als Modelle für die Ortsbestimmung frühchristlicher Autoren in der Gegenwart „zwischen den Reichen".

Anhand der in diesem Werk versammelten Beiträge wird allerdings auch deutlich, dass offene Fragen bleiben und zwar auf beiden Seiten der Dokumente. Die Interpretation der antiken Materialien kann ebenso unterschiedlich ausfallen wie ihre historische Einordnung. Auffällig ist dies vor allem bei der Bewertung der Dokumente über Kaiser Domitian und der Beurteilung ihrer Relevanz für die Interpretation der neutestamentlichen Schriften. Neben einer gegenüber der älteren, stark von der römischen und christlichen Polemik gegen diesen Kaiser beeinflussten Forschung sensibleren Auswertung der Nachrichten über Domitian changieren die Interpretationen über seine Rolle und seinen titularen Anspruch im Kaiserkult (vgl. die Beiträge von FRENSCHKOWSKI, LABAHN, MEISER, PEZZOLI-OLGIATI, und LIETAERT PEERBOLTE). Hier meldet sich weiterer Diskussionsbedarf an.[4] Auch die neutestamentlichen Schriften selbst bleiben – wie die Diskussion vor Ort gezeigt hat – für Rückfragen offen, wobei das Spektrum von Einzelfragen bis zur literarhistorischen Gesamtverortung reicht.

Die Beiträge des zweiten Hauptteils zeigen, dass die Lektüre der neutestamentlichen Schriften „zwischen den Reichen" erfolgversprechend ist und tiefere Einsichten in ihr Verständnis ermöglicht. Die solide Kenntnis des sozialen und politischen Rahmens der frühchristlichen Bewegung und ihrer Schriften bleibt eine wichtige Aufgabe, die nur im interdisziplinären Gespräch zu gewinnen ist. Nur so kann der komplexen Interaktion von frühem Christentum und römischer Herrschaft nachgegangen werden und der zweifelsohne stets neu zu präzisierende Diskurs über die Interpretation ständig präzisiert werden. Eine Interpretation neutestamentlicher Texte jenseits ihrer historisch-religiösen und sozial-politischen Mitwelt steht hingegen in der Gefahr zu kurz zu greifen.

---

[4] Nicht übersehen werden sollte, dass durch die keineswegs unumstrittenen Beiträge von Manfred CLAUSS zur römischen Herrscherverehrung (*Deus praesens*. Der römische Kaiser als Gott, in: Klio 78 [1996], 400–433; Kaiser und Gott. Herrscherkult im römischen Reich, Stuttgart – Leipzig 1999) auch in der Altphilologie ein für unser Thema wichtiges Fragestellung möglicherweise neu diskutiert wird.

Hintergründe

Aspekte römischer Herrschaft und Kultur

Hannah M. Cotton

Jewish Jurisdiction under Roman Rule:
Prolegomena

For my sister, Ruth, on her birthday

The study of the day-to-day aspect of Roman rule in a province has normally to rely on non-literary sources, mainly on epigraphy; sometimes, as in the case of Egypt, it can tap the rich resources of papyrology. The historian of the province of Judaea, later on Syria Palestina, on the other hand, is in the fortunate position of being able to draw on literary sources: above all Josephus, the New Testament and rabbinic literature. However, these literary sources have conspired to create the biassed notion of the special and unique status of the province of Judaea/Syria Palaestina within the Roman empire. Some corrective of this bias is supplied by the inscriptions, all of which – and their number has increased considerably recently – are now about to be collected for the first time in the comprehensive multi-lingual *Corpus Inscriptionum Iudaeae Palaestinae*.[1] The documentary papyri from the Judaean Desert supply yet another corrective to the traditional view – especially now that almost the entire evidence from the Judaean Desert has been published.[2] True, many of the documents were written in the Nabataean kingdom which in 106 became the province of Arabia. However, the patterns of the relationship between the Jews of Arabia and the Roman authorities documented in the papyri cannot be assumed to have been very different from those current in the province of Judaea/Syria Palaestina.

Elsewhere I have tried to determine the precise status of the province of Judaea within the Roman empire.[3] The following discussion, triggered off by the striking resemblance between the papyrology of the Judaean Desert and that of Egypt,[4] should be conceived as no more than preliminary remarks on the extent of local judicial autonomy in Judaea/Syria Palaestina under Roman rule. This issue has, I believe, suffered the greatest distortion under the overwhelming impact of rabbinic legal sources. The documents do not bear out many of the assumptions commonly held.

---

[1] See W. ECK, Inschriften, 47. On the *CIIP* see *ZPE* 127 (1999), 307–8 and *SCI* 18 (1999), 175–6.
[2] For an exhaustive survey see H.M. COTTON, Papyrusdokumente, to which add EAD., Documentary Texts.
[3] H.M. COTTON, Aspects. For a more detailed exposition see EAD., Provincia Iudaea.
[4] See H.M. COTTON, Guardianship, 94ff.

It has been observed[5]

> It is a remarkable fact that no court, Jewish or non-Jewish, other than that of the Roman governor of Arabia, is mentioned in any of the documents from the Judaean Desert, a great many of which ... are legal documents. We should not therefore conclude, however, that the governor's court was the only court in operation in a Roman province. Nonetheless, the absence of any reference to other courts is disturbing, especially in view of the host of references in rabbinic sources to courts of different sizes in towns and villages.[6]

The governor's court, it should be pointed out, is mentioned explicitly only in the Greek documents of the Babatha archive.[7] There we watch the provincials making use of the assize system prevailing in the Roman provinces[8] to make petitions to the governor[9] or summon their opponents to appear before his ambulatory tribunal, wherever that happened to be.[10] However, even when the Roman governor is not mentioned explicitly in the documents, certain elements present in them imply that these documents were intended for a Roman court of law. The following list does not attempt to be exhaustive but records the more salient features of Romanization in the documents:

- the use of the double document, probably under Roman influence[11] since elsewhere it was going out of fashion;[12]
- the use of *testatio*, a document signed by seven witnesses in front of whom the plaintiff makes his declaration;[13]
- the presence of three copies of a Roman instrument, namely the *actio tutelae* in the Babatha archive;[14]
- the use of Roman legal arguments in the documents;[15]

---

[5] H.M. COTTON in H.M. COTTON/A. YARDENI, Texts, 154.
[6] E. SCHÜRER/G. VERMES/F. MILLAR, History 2, 184–8; G. ALON, Jews 1, 553–7; A. GULAK, Study 1, 54ff; less sceptical is Z. SAFRAI, Jewish Community, 76ff.
[7] Edited by N. LEWIS, Documents. The papyri are referred to as *P.Yadin*.
[8] Cf. G.P. BURTON, Proconsuls; Ch. HABICHT, New Evidence; R. HAENSCH, Konventsordnung.
[9] E.g., *P.Yadin* 13.
[10] E.g. *P.Yadin* 26, lines 2–11: 'Babatha ... summoned Miriam ... to accompany her in person before Haterius Nepos ... ὅπου ἂν ᾖ ὑπ' αὐτοῦ ὑπαρχία ('wherever he happens to be exercising justice in the province') ... καὶ παρεδρεύιν ἐπὶ τὸν αὐτὸν Νέπωτα μέχρι διαγνώσεως. See H.M. COTTON, Guardianship, 106f. for a detailed survey of all references to summons to the governor's court in the Babatha archive.
[11] Roman military diplomas, copies made on bronze tablets of the constitutions granting privileges to individual soldiers which were displayed in Rome, are double documents, as are the deeds on wooden tablets from pre-Vesuvian Campania; on the latter see now the review article by G. ROWE, Trimalchio's World.
[12] See N. LEWIS, Documents, 6–10.
[13] *P.Yadin* 15 and 24, and probably also *P.Jericho* 16, as interpreted by R. HAENSCH, Verständnis.
[14] See D. NÖRR, Prozessuales; T.J. CHIUSI, Vormundschaft; EAD., Babatha.
[15] See above all Chiusi in the two papers cited in n. 14; cf. H.M. COTTON, Guardianship, 102–5.

- and finally the use of the stipulation.[16]

A strong argument for thinking that these documents were intended for a Roman court of law is the presence of a male guardian to represent a woman in the Greek documents and his total absence from the Semitic documents. The passive role of the guardian (in general it is merely his presence which is recorded συμπαρόντος αὐτῆς ἐπιτρόπου) makes it eminently clear that this is just a matter of form and procedure required by the courts for which the Greek contracts were intended, namely Roman courts of law where a woman could not appear without a male representative.[17]

Last but not least the use of the Greek language – the language used *par excellence* as means of communication between rulers and subjects in the Roman Near East – in legal documents strongly suggests that the court envisioned was that of the Roman governor; admittedly, the alternative explanation of a Greek-speaking court of a *polis* cannot be excluded.

As an aside one may observe that all this implies of course that non-citizens had recourse to Roman courts of law and Roman law long before 212, and that this does not seem to have required the grant of a special privilege.[18]

One can easily demonstrate the intimate connection between the advent of Roman rule (i.e. provincialiyation) and the recourse to using Greek in legal documents in the case of Nabataea, which in 106 became the Roman province of Arabia. Until 106 legal documents had been written in Nabataean, whereas from 106 onwards the Greek language takes over; as against two Nabataean contracts and four written in Jewish Aramaic we have altogether 32 Greek documents from the period between 106 and 132 in Arabia, that is in the first 25 years of the province.[19]

No such association can be made for the use of Greek in Judaea whose provincialization dates to 6 CE:[20] more than a hundred years elapsed before

---

[16] H.L.W. NELSON/U. MANTHE, Gai Institutiones III 88–181, 475ff.

[17] See H.M. COTTON, Guardian. The use of a single term – *epitropos* – for the two kinds of guardians is due to the influence of Roman law, where at least originally no legal distinction existed between the guardian of a minor and that of a woman, and, consequently, the same term, *tutor*, was used for both. Both, if they were not *sui iuris*, had to be represented by the *tutor*, see H.J. WOLFF, Provinzialrecht, 796–7.

[18] A choice between local courts and Roman courts, conferred on three Greek naval captains and their families – none of whom is a Roman citizen – is presented as a special privilege in the *SC de Asclepiade sociisque* of 78 BCE: R.K. SHERK, Roman Documents (= RDGE) no. 22. The same is true of the privileges bestowed by Octavian on Seleucus of Rhosus: Sherk, RDGE no. 58, lines 53–6.

[19] See H.M. COTTON, Languages, 225ff.

[20] See n. 3 above. With the exception of inscriptions on Jewish ossuaries, the first Greek documents from Jewish circles come from Masada, i.e. 66–73(4), see H.M. COTTON/J. GEIGER, Masada II, 9f.

Greek is first attested in legal documents from Judaea.[21] This could be a coincidence: our documentation is anything but complete; but it is probably not just a coincidence. Elsewhere I have suggested[22] that the same explanation could be offered for the immediate recourse to Greek in legal documents in Arabia and its somewhat delayed use in Judaea: in both provinces the recourse to Greek may well have been the corollary of the extent of local judicial autonomy granted by the Romans. The provincialization of Judaea in 6 CE left the Great Sanhedrin in Jerusalem with the high priest at its head a large measure of judicial independence in civil and criminal law alike.[23] There is much evidence for this in Josephus, Philo and the New Testament.[24] Even if officially the Sanhedrin's judicial competence did not extend beyond Judaea proper, its authority certainly did not know such bounds. Things must have changed drastically after the revolt (66–70). The destruction of Jerusalem and the Temple meant among other things the dissolution of the Great Sanhedrin. It is to be assumed that after 70 conditions in Judaea bore a strong resemblance to those current in Arabia in 106: these included a more limited local judicial autonomy under Roman rule.[25]

I have now come to realize that the argument which I offered in 1999 may be faulted on the ground of being circular: it would seem that I posit limited local judicial autonomy in order to explain the use of, or the transition to, the employment of the Greek language in legal documents; and, conversely, that I infer the existence of a limited local judicial autonomy from the use of Greek. We should, therefore cast our net wider and enquire about the extent of local judicial autonomy under Roman rule.

Theoretically all of Rome's subjects were *de iure* under the jurisdiction (*iuris dictio*) of Roman officials in the provinces. Judicial autonomy, that is the use of local courts of law, invariably called for a special grant by the Roman government. Of course some measure of judicial autonomy was almost always allowed, and very early on had become a tralatician part of the provincial edict, as we know from Cicero's provincial edict in Cilicia where he was governor in 50 BCE:

---

[21] This is if we accept 115 CE for *Mur* 114, dated by P. Benoit to 171 (P. BENOIT/J. T. MILIK/R. DE VAUX, Grottes de Murabbaʿat), but see H.M. COTTON and W. ECK in a forthcoming article on the papyrus; otherwise *P.Yadin* 12 of 125 CE would be the first safely dated legal document written in Greek from Judaea. See in general H.M. COTTON, Languages, 228f.

[22] In H.M. COTTON, Languages, 230f.

[23] See H.M. COTTON, Provincia Iudaea, for a discussion of autonomy under Roman rule in 6 CE based on Jos. *Bell* 2.22; *Ant* 17.227; *Bell* 2.80; *Ant* 17.300; *Bell* 2.91; *Ant* 17.314; *Ant* 17.303. See below Appendix 1, on criminal jurisdiction.

[24] See E. SCHÜRER/G. VERMES/F. MILLAR, History 2, 197f; 218ff.

[25] The Nabataean documents from the Babatha archive recently published by A. YARDENI, Textbook, imply to my mind limited local autonomy under the Nabataean kings; see also her new reading of *P.Starcky* in Decipherment. The Romans were likely to leave matters as they were, see H.M. COTTON, Guardianship, 107, Appendix I.

> *Multaque sum secutus Scaevolae, in iis illud in quo sibi libertatem censent Graeci datam, ut Graeci inter se disceptent suis legibus ... Graeci vero exsultant quod peregrinis iudicibus utuntur. 'Nugatoribus quidem' inquies. Quid refert? Ii se* αὐτονομίαν *adeptos putant* (Cic Att 6.1.15).
> Indeed I have followed many of Scaevola's provisions, including that one which the natives regard as their charter of liberty (*libertas*) that cases between natives should be tried under their own laws ... The natives are jubilant because they have foreign judges.[26] 'Triflers', you may say, well, what of it? They feel they have won *autonomia* just the same.

What was the extent of local judicial autonomy in the imperial period? Was it uniform or did it vary from one province to another, or even from one community to the next, depending on their status?

This is not the place to discuss the ancient evidence for uniformity and variation in local judicial autonomy – far less the vast array of modern opinions about the subject. I shall therefore claim for the views expounded here no more than the status of working hypotheses which may account for and explain the legal situation in Judaea and Arabia.

As a starting point we may take chapters 84 and 89 of the municipal charter of the city of Irni in Baetica which established the city as a Latin *municipium* subject to Roman law and legal procedure in the Flavian period.[27] In these two chapters it is explicitly stated that the magistrates in a Latin *municipium* (the *duoviri* and *aediles*) have jurisdiction (*iuris dictio*) in respect of any private dispute with a value up to 1,000 sesterces and no more, and that certain actions are altogether outside the competence of the local magistrates – unless both parties to the suit are willing to accept it. To the possibilities which are opened up by this derogation from the general rule I shall return later.

Should we argue *a minore ad maius* that if the judicial autonomy of Roman[28] and Latin communities was limited in such a way, there is all the more reason to believe that the judicial autonomy of peregrine communities was curtailed even further? In other words, did the provincials more often than not have to approach Roman courts of law (the governor's above all), for their own courts would not be competent to adjudicate cases exceeding a certain amount of money, or due to the character of the case? Or could it be argued that the limits set on the judicial autonomy of local courts in Roman and Latin communities are irrelevant for determining the scope of judicial autonomy in peregrine communities since the latter were so to speak outside the entire framework of the Roman legal system? If so, the local autonomy of peregrine

---

[26] See Ch. CROWTHER, Foreign Judges; D. NÖRR, Xenokriten; see now D. ROEBUCK, Arbitration, 269ff.

[27] For text and translation see J. GONZÁLES, Lex Irnitana. The bibliography has grown enormously since, but see on these two chapters A. RODGER, Jurisdictional Limits. See also U. LAFFI, Limiti.

[28] For Roman charters see Lex de Gallia Cisalpina in M.H. CRAWFORD (ed.), Roman Statutes I, no. 2, ch. 22, ll. 27–28, which stipulates a limit of 15,000 sesterces, and the Este Fragment, ibid. no. 16, ll. 4–7, which stipulates a limit of 10,000 sesterces on local jurisdiction.

communities might conceivably have been wider than that of Roman and Latin ones.

There are no cut and dried answers to these questions. A thorough examination of the relevant *documentary* evidence from the entire empire is necessary. This cannot be attempted here. However, we must also at all costs avoid a schematic legal approach which takes legal writings, both Roman and Jewish, as a reflexion of what happened in reality: such an approach removes us from the truth, and from reality. Perhaps an elucidation of the legal situation in Judaea and Arabia can be offered without taking a firm stand on the question of the scope of local judicial autonomy. After all, limited local judicial autonomy need not have been the only reason for approaching the Roman tribunals in the province. G.P. BURTON in his seminal article on the administration of justice in proconsular provinces rightly observes that 'whatever role we may finally ascribe to local courts', the evidence from different sources suggests that 'any governor was faced with an immense amount of possible work'.[29] The recourse to the Roman tribunals, which in Judaea and Arabia is attested in the use of Greek in documents[30] clearly meant for a Roman court of law, may not have been the corollary of limited local autonomy. In other words it may not have been a matter of necessity to go to a Roman court,[31] but a step taken out of choice. Rome's subjects could and would seek Roman justice whenever they believed that it would be more effective, more advantageous and more just than the local one.[32] This is clearly the impression one gets from the Babatha archive: 'Without coercion or attempts to impose uniformity, the very presence of the Romans as the supreme authority in the province invited appeals to their authority, to their courts as well as to their laws'.[33] Babatha seems to regard the Roman advent as the dawning of a new age; she wants her son 'to be raised in splendid style rendering thanks to *the[se] most blessed times* of the governorship of Julius Julianus'.[34] True, she needs to propitiate the

---

[29] G.P. BURTON, Proconsuls, 102.

[30] Of course an additional reason could be the need to deposit the deeds in a public archive, similar to what we know to have been the case in Egypt, where public archives were used to deposit private documents; having been registered there, these documents could later be produced in court as evidence.

[31] For officials other than the governor see W. ECK, Roman officials.

[32] The best example are marriage contracts: five out of eight (or nine) marriage contracts found in the Judaean Desert are written in Greek and cannot be said to be translations of Aramaic contracts, since they contain a different legal tradition (see H.M. COTTON, Marriage Contracts). However, the choice of Greek could hardly have been dictated by limited local judicial autonomy, for the Romans are unlikely to have interfered with peregrine marriage arrangements.

[33] H.M. COTTON, Guardianship, 107.

[34] ὅθεν λαμπρῶς διασωθῇ μου ὁ υἱὸς εὐχαριστῶν (εὐχαριστοῦντα) τοῖς μακαριωτάτοις καιροῖς ἡγεμωνίας Ἰουλίου Ἰουλιανοῦ ἡγεμῶνος (*P.Yadin* 15, ll. 10–11 = ll. 26–27); cf. *Acts* 24:2 (the rhetor Tertullus to Felix): πολλῆς εἰρήνης τυγχάνοντες διὰ σοῦ καὶ διορθωμάτων γινομένων τῷ ἔθνει τούτῳ διὰ τῆς σῆς προνοίας: 'Seeing that by thee we enjoy great quietness and that very worthy deeds are done unto this nation by thy providence'.

governor and her praise should be taken with a grain of salt, but it is not just empty phraseology either.

And yet the majority of documents from the Judaean Desert are written in Jewish Aramaic.[35] Moreover, contracts in Armaic continued to be written and used after the documents from the Judaean Desert dry up.[36] This we can infer from rabbinic sources, and above all from the Mishnah, where formulae taken from living Aramaic contracts are embedded in the legal discussion round about which is conducted in Hebrew.[37] Although, as pointed out before, no courts are ever mentioned in the Aramaic documents from the Judaean Desert,[38] the existence of legal contracts anticipates the possibilty of legal proceedings. Where would these legal proceedings be conducted? Where should one look for courts exercising *iuris dictio* (in the Roman sense of the word)[39] in Judaea/Syria Palaestina? Again we should look at patterns current everywhere in the empire.

The legal status of a city or *polis* in the Roman empire would normally go hand in hand with some measure of judicial autonomy, albeit occasionally quite limited as we have just seen in the Tabula Irnitana of the city of Irni in Spain. The city courts had jurisdiction over their own residents as well as over the city territory, the *chora*. However, this was not the principle of local organization in what is commonly called the 'Jewish region' of Palestine, where there are very few cities and the majority of cities that are there are on the fringes, and in any case are not likely to have controlled the entire Jewish region as their city-territories. Many settlements referred to as cities in the Jewish sources, and taken as such by scholars, would not pass the criteria of a *polis* in the Roman empire. The Jewish region as we know from Josephus, Pliny and now also from the documents from the Judaean Desert, was composed of villages of different sizes and divided into administrative units with central vil-

---

[35] For Hebrew see H.M. COTTON, Languages, 220–25.
[36] There are no safely dated contracts, either in Greek or in Aramaic, after 135 CE. The few Greek papyri mentioned in H.M. COTTON/W. COCKLE/F. MILLAR, Papyrology, as nos. 333ff. do not come from Jewish contexts, but either from Roman army circles or from the Greek *poleis*. They are irrelevant for my discussion here. But see N. LEWIS, Demise.
[37] See H.M. COTTON, Aramaic Legal Tradition.
[38] H. MISGAV, Jewish Courts, maintains that *Mur* 29–30 contain reference to the presence of four people before whom the contracts are written who are unlikely to constitute a court of law. Nevertheless, they seem to resemble the Egyptian *synchoresis*, and thus may well be described as something like notarized legal instruments. However these documents have now been predated to the time of the Great Revolt – see H.M. COTTON, Languages, 220–23 and H. ESHEL/M. BROSHI/T.A.J. JULL, Documents, 233ff – whereas I am concerned here mainly with jurisdiction under Roman rule. Thus those legal documents written at the time of the two revolts, i.e. at the time of Jewish independence, remain largely outside the scope of the present discussion – unless they too betray the use of what I shall designate here arbitration.
[39] A practical definition of a court of law with formal jurisdiction, meant for historians rather than for jurists, is a court of law whose decisions are binding and backed up by the powers that be – by the Roman government in our period – who will enforce them if the parties fail to do so themselves.

lages at their head. Only about Judaea proper can we be sure that these units were called *toparchiai*. There is no evidence for local officials at the head of these capital villages, nor for centrally appointed officials in charge of the *toparchiai* – but the existence of one or another kind of local officials must be assumed. There are some hints that the *toparchiai* were in charge of taxation. Above all it is hard to believe that nothing beyond a merely geographical relationship is intended by the description of the dependence of a village on a central village, especially since the dependence of the single village on the central village is described both in the papyri and in Josephus in terms identical to those describing the dependence of the *chora* on its *polis*. It is either here in the capital villages or in the smaller villages – which enjoyed a large measure of independence – that one should try to locate judicial autonomy in so far as it was allowed by the Romans.

However, we may be on the wrong track after all. Perhaps it is altogether misleading to think in terms of formal *iuris dictio* of a court of law. The restrictions on local judicial autonomy and the imperfections and deficiencies of the Roman assize system[40] – notwithstanding delegation of jurisdiction to lower officials (to *legati* in the public provinces and to *strategoi* and others in Egypt for example) – may well have led the provincials to seek other solutions, less cumbersome, less expensive and less time-consuming.[41] I should like to raise the option of private arbitration to account for the presence of contracts in Aramaic among the documents from the Judaean Desert and in the background of the Mishnaic legal discussion. It is worth recalling that the charter of Irni contained a derogation from the general rule, to wit that if both parties to a suit are willing, the local magistrates could adjudicate cases which go beyond their normal competence.[42] Whatever courts we hear about in the rabbinic sources, I suggest, may have been no more than forms of private arbitration, not backed by the powers that be, i.e. the Roman authorities in the province.[43] Thus you could not force your opponent to appear before an arbiter, nor – which is cru-

---

[40] See G.P. BURTON, Proconsuls, 99ff.

[41] One gets the impression that the Roman courts were simply blocked; the queue must have been enormous if one had to wait 8 months in Antioch to see the governor and then be sent packing with nothing achieved: see *P.Euphr.* 1 in D. FEISSEL/J. GASCOU, Documents.

[42] See Tabula Irnitana, ch. 84 and 89 (above, n. 27); cf. *Dig.* 50.1.28: *Inter convenientes et de re maiori apud magistratus municipiales agetur*. In the case of a Roman or Latin community such consent between the two parties may lead to that kind of arbitration recognised and provided for by the Roman lawyers. The parties could make a contract of arbitration (*compromissum*), in the form of a stipulation which (1) obliged the parties to follow the sentence of a private (non-official) *arbiter* and not to go to the public court, and (2) stipulated a *poena* (fine) for acting against the *compromissum*. The defendant could not be compelled to accept the sentence of the *arbiter*; if sued at court, he would merely forfeit the fine. The *compromissum* was valid only if the proposed *arbiter* committed himself to giving a sentence in a contract called *receptum arbitri*; see in general *Dig.* 4.8 and examples in G. CAMODECA, Tabulae Pompeianae Sulpiciorum (TPSulp.), nos. 34ff.

[43] Contra A. OPPENHEIMER, Jewish Penal Authority.

cial – enforce his verdict.⁴⁴ The one and only sanction would then have been the authority of the arbiter, that is the social and moral standing of the arbiter in the community and the social pressure exercised by the community in which one lived. The effectiveness of those should not be underestimated.

This could be an explanation for the absence of any mention of courts in the Aramaic documents; but far more importantly it could account for the fact that, as observed more than a hundred years ago by CHAJES and never refuted, when you examine the rabbinic sources closely, you never find people approaching a proper tribunal, but rather a single rabbi.⁴⁵ This would imply a private arbiter rather than a court of law.

Private arbitration must have played a much greater role in the Roman empire than is normally suspected, though it has left few traces.⁴⁶ It was, of its nature, rarely accompanied by documents, and thus in most cases the process and the results alike are hidden from our sight. But for all that I believe that we possess now three documents from the Judaean Desert which attest the results of private arbitration and the renunciation of further claims by the plaintiff: the Greek *P.Hever* 63 (127 CE) from the archive of Salome Komaïse daughter of Levi,⁴⁷ the Nabataean *P.Yadin* 9 (122 CE)⁴⁸ and the Aramaic *P.Hever* 13 (134 or 135 CE).⁴⁹ *P.Hever* 13 was written under Jewish rule at the time of the Bar Kokhba revolt, whereas my main concern here is with jurisdiction under Roman rule. *P.Yadin* 9 is badly damaged and its content is practically irretrievable.⁵⁰ I shall therefore give here only the text and translation of *P.Hever* 63, and refer to the other two in my discussion.

---

⁴⁴ As such it differs from that recognised in the late legislation of 398 CE (*Codex Theodosianus* 2:1:10): 'the governors of the provinces shall even execute their sentences as if they were appointed arbiters through a judge's award'. This is no longer pure private arbitration.

⁴⁵ H.P. CHAJES, Juges juifs. The one case I know of what might be a court of three is so confused and problematic that no sense can be made of it, although it is so often quoted; I refer of course to the case of Tamar in *yMegillah* ('scroll') 3.3 p. 74a. SH. ALBECK, *Law*, who also disputes the existence of formal Jewish courts, shows no awareness of the existence of Roman rule in Judaea/Syria Palaestina at the time when the rabbinic sources were written.

⁴⁶ Cf. R. BAGNALL, Egypt, 161: 'Actual litigation is only the tip of the iceberg; most disputes were handled (not necessarily "settled" or "resolved") in other ways'.

⁴⁷ First published in H.M. COTTON, Archive, as no. III; final publication in H.M. COTTON/A. YARDENI, Texts, 195ff. The papyri in H.M. COTTON/A. YARDENI, Texts, are referred to as *P.Hever*; for the reference see now H.M. COTTON, Documentary Texts.

⁴⁸ See A.YARDENI, Textbook vol I, p. 297; vol. 2, p. 97 for an English translation. For commentary see Y. YADIN/J.C. GREENFIELD/A. YARDENI/B. LEVINE, Documents II.

⁴⁹ Published in H.M. COTTON/A. YARDENI, Texts, 65ff. Its claim to fame rests though on the fact that the wife seems to refer in it to a deed of divorce she had given her husband, cf. H.M. COTTON/E. QIMRON, XHev/Se ar 13. Contra, A. SCHREMER, Divorce.

⁵⁰ Thus the editors of the commentary, see n. 48 above.

Mahoza, Arabia   between 25 April and 31 December, 127 CE

1 [ἐξωμολο]γήσατο καὶ συνεγρ[άψατο Σαλ]ωμη Αηουει τ̣ο̣υ̣[... συμπαρόντος αὐτῇ ἐπιτρόπου]
2 [c.7 letters]υ̣ Σιμωνος ἀνδρὸς α[ὐτῆ]ς τοῦδε τοῦ {...}π̣ρ̣[άγματος χάριν πρὸς Σαλωμην τὴν]
3 [καὶ Γραπτ]ην Μαναημο[υ c.6 letters]λου θυγατέρα, ἰ̣δ̣ί̣α̣ν̣ [δὲ μητέρα αὐτῆς c.13 letters]
4 [πάντες Μα]ω̣ζηνοι· καὶ ἡ [Σαλωμη Λ]ηουει μηδένα λ[όγον ἔχειν c.17 letters]
5 [c.8 letters].α̣ ἐξ ὀνόματος αὐ[τῆς πρὸς Σ]α̣λωμην τὴν καὶ [Γραπτην c.19 letters]
6 [c.3 letters περὶ τ]ῶν καταλειφθέντῳ[ν ὑπὸ Λ]ηουει γενομένου σ̣υ̣[μβίου αὐτῆς c.13 letters καὶ]
7 [ὑπὸ c.4 letters]λου γενομένου αὐ[τῆς υἱοῦ] ἀδελφοῦ δὲ τῆς ὁμ[ολογούσης c.17 letters]
8 [c.7–8 letters]α̣ ἔτι δὲ ὁμολογεῖ ἡ [Σαλωμ]η Αηουει μηδένα λ[όγον ἔχειν c.17 letters]
9 [πρὸς Σαλωμη]ν̣ τὴν καὶ Γραπτην[c.4–5 letters]η κληρονόμους αὐ[τῆς περὶ c.19 letters]
10 [c.7–8 letters]. παρῳχημέν[ης ἀμφισβ]ητήσεως ὅρκου ἐπ[ιδοθέντος c.17 letters]
11]....[.]. ..[..... ....].ε.. πρὸς αὐτὴν̣ [c.26 letters]
12 [c.26 letters   ]υμενης στᾶσα δ[ὲ c.25 letters]
13 [πίστει ἐπηρωτήθη καὶ ἀνθωμολογήθη ο]ὕτως καλῶς γενέσ[θαι vacat?]
14 [vacat?   ] vacat
15 m. 2. [ἐπὶ ὑπάτων Μάρκου Γαουίου Γαλλικανο]ῦ̣ καὶ Τίτ[ου Ἀτιλίου Ῥούφου Τιτιανοῦ vacat?]
16 [day and month? place?]   vacat

Translation:

[Sal]ome daughter of Levi, the son of X (or: son of Tou[)? – [present with her as her guardian for the purpose] of this matter, her husband [Sammou]os son of Shim'on – [acknow]ledged and agreed in w[riting], vis-á-vis Salome also (called) [Grapt]e daughter of Menahem, [son of]los (or]las), her own [mother . . . – all of them living in Ma]hoza: 'and also [(she) Salome] daughter of Levi has no [claims . . .] in her name [towards S]alome who is also (called) [Grapte . . . regarding] the properties left [by L]evi, her late hus[band . . . and by]los (or]las), her late [son] and brother of her who ag[rees . . .]. Likewise [Salom]e daughter of Levi agrees that she has no [claims . . . vis-á-vis Salom]e also (called) Grapte ... her heirs [regarding ..., the cont]roversy which has now been solved, an oath having been gi[ven] ... towards her ... while standing firm (?) [... In faith[51] the formal question was asked and it was agreed in reply] that this was thus rightly done. [vacat] (second hand) [In the consulate of Marcus Gavius Gallican]us and Tit[us Atilius Rufus Titianus] vacat? [day and month? place?] vacat.

---

[51] I stand corrected by U. Manthe: πίστει means of course *fide* not *bona fide*, see H.L.W. NELSON/U. MANTHE, Gai Institutiones III 88–181, 477.

The recent death of Salome's brother[52] – perhaps also of her father – was the likely occasion for writing this deed. We cannot be certain about the nature of the controversy – (line 10) – which preceded the deed, but it is likely to have concerned the property left after the death of both father and son: περὶ τ]ῶν καταλειφθέντω[ν ὑπὸ Λ]ηουει γενομένου συ[μβίου αὐτῆς ... καὶ] [ὑπὸ ...]λου γενομένου αὐ[τῆς υἱοῦ] ἀδελφοῦ δὲ τῆς ὁμ[ολογούσης (lines 6–7). The καὶ ἡ [Σαλωμη Λ]ηουει, '*and* also Salome daughter of Levi' (line 4), implies that there was a separate deed of renunciation of claims by the mother, Salome Grapte, who, for her part, had written a deed of renunciation in favour of the daughter. The settlement of the dispute (παρῳχημέν[ης ἀμφισβ]ητήσεως) accompanied by the taking of the oath (ὅρκου ἐπ[ιδοθέντος]) preceded the act of writing down the deed, and are likely to have taken place before a private arbiter. The waiver of all claims expressed by the formula μηδένα λόγον ἔχειν πρὸς αὐτήν, repeated twice (or even three times) in the present document (lines 4, 8, 11) cannot but call to mind the parallel Aramaic formula כל מדעם לא איתי לי עמך: 'I have no claim against you' which is repeated in three variations in *P.Hever* 13, where the wife renounces all claims against her former husband. The same formula recurs also in the fragmentary Nabataean *P.Yadin* 9, lines 6–7: ‎ולא... עמך מנדעם לא זעיר ‎[ולא שגיא].

The fact that the deed was written down in Greek and the use of the *stipulatio* imply to my mind that the parties left themselves the option of going to court – to a Roman court – in case one of them did not stand by the terms of the arbitration.[53]

---

[52] He was still alive on the 25th of April 127, see *P.Hever* 61.
[53] See detailed commentary and comparison with the Egyptian evidence in H.M. COTTON/A. YARDENI, Texts, ad no. 63 with bibliography on this type of deed. Derek Roebuck suggests to me that 'the use of *stipulatio* and Greek could just be borrowings by a legalistic arbitrator'; hence hardly 'good evidence of the parties' intentions to resort to another tribunal'.

Appendices:

1) Judicial autonomy in the Diaspora

Evidence for judicial autonomy in the Jewish Diaspora could be used as an *argumentum ex minore ad maius* for the existence of judicial autonomy in Judaea/Syria Palaestina. I do not find this argument very compelling. Not even in Egypt, where documents do exist, do we possess any proof that Jews used their own courts (or their own laws for that matter), despite evidence to the contrary in the rabbinic sources. In fact the editors of the *Corpus Papyrorum Iudaicarum* expressed their surprise at the absence of any documents reflecting the existence of Jewish courts in Egypt and the exercise of Jewish law there. As for the famous charters mentioned in Josephus, *Ant* 14.185–267 which contain privileges successfully sought and granted to Jews in the diaspora by the Roman government permitting them to live according to their ancestral laws or customs (νόμοι or ἔθη), it should be observed that an explicit grant of judicial autonomy is attested only for Sardis (Jos *Ant* 14.235), and might well be unique to this city, as suggested by Tessa RAJAK.[54] Otherwise we hear only of religious privileges, namely the freedom to observe the Sabbath, the right not to appear in court on the Sabbath (which must refer to a non-Jewish court of course), the right to collect and despatch the Temple Tax until 70 etc. The evidence in the newly published archive from Herakleopolis in Egypt dated to the middle of the second century BCE[55] suggests that under the Ptolemies there existed real autonomous Jewish jurisdiction, and we may well ask whether it disappeared in Roman times.[56]

2) Criminal jurisdiction

It must be clear that so far as criminal jurisdiction is concerned, it was much curtailed, if not altogether removed. However, even from the Jewish sources themselves one could demonstrate Roman 'total monopoly' so to speak in the sphere of criminal law. This is precisely what Saul Lieberman did in an important article published in 1944.[57] In that article Lieberman shows convincingly that the rabbinic sources faithfully describe the legal procedure in Roman courts in Judaea/Syria-Palaestina in penal cases. The very terminology betrays the non-Jewish context. The judge is the 'king', the ἔπαρχος (*eparchos*), the

---

[54] See T. RAJAK in another context: 'Was There a Roman Charter for the Jews?', 116 and n. 35.
[55] J.M.S. COWEY/K. MARESCH (eds.), Urkunden.
[56] An exhaustive discussion of Jewish rights and privileges under Roman rule is now available in Miriam Pucci Ben Zeev's *Jewish Rights in the Roman World*.
[57] S. LIEBERMAN, Roman legal institutions in early rabbinics and in the Acta Martyrum.

ἡγεμών (*hegemon*), the ἄρχων (*archon*) and the Hebrew equivalent 'government' (*shilton*). The place of judgement is the *basilica* or the βῆμα (*bema*) and the defendant was put on a *gradus* (*gardom*). The sources are familiar with the interrogation during the trial, the tortures applied, the speech of the lawyer for the defendant, the *elogium* of the συνήγορος or the ῥήτωρ, the sentence (ἀπόφασις *apophasis* or *periculum* – *pericula*) and finally the execution. The picture which emerges seems highly authentic. But, so far as I am aware, there are no similar scenes describing criminal procedure in Jewish courts. And as for the later period, the famous letter of Origen to Julius Africanus (*Ad Africanum de Historia Susannae* 14, *PG* XI, 81–3) shows, as I read it, the opposite of what A. Oppenheimer claims for it in 'Jewish Penal Authority in Roman Judaea'. If anything, it shows that, as late as the first half of the third century CE, the right to try in criminal cases was usurped by Jews, not granted them by the Roman government. Anyone familiar with the principles of Roman provincial administration could hardly have expected anything different to take place in a province. And Judaea/Syria Palaestina was no exception.[58]

---

[58] I am very grateful to Peter EICH of the University of Köln for an ongoing dialogue on the issues discussed in this paper, and also to Werner ECK (Köln), Ulrich MANTHE (Passau), and Derek ROEBUCK (Oxford) for useful suggestions; and, as always, to David WASSERSTEIN.

Bibliography

ALBECK, Shalom, Law Courts in Talmudic Times, Jerusalem 1980.
ALON, Gedalyahu, The Jews in Their Land in the Talmudic Age, 70–640 C.E. vol. 1, Jerusalem 1980.
BAGNALL, Roger S., Egypt in Late Antiquity, Princeton 1993.
BENOIT, Pierre/MILIK, József Tadeusz /DE VAUX, Roland, Les Grottes de Murabba'at, DJD II, Oxford 1961.
BURTON, Graham P., Proconsuls, Assizes and the Administration of Justice under the Empire, in: JRS 65 (1975), 92–106.
CAMODECA, Giuseppe, Tabulae Pompeianae Sulpiciorum (TPSulp.) Edizione critica dell' achivio Puteolano dei Sulpicii, Vetera 12, Rome 1999.
CHAJES, Hirsch Perez, Les juges juifs en Palestine de l'an 70 à l'an 500', in: REJ 39 (1899), 39ff.
CHIUSI, Tiziana J., Zur Vormundschaft der Mutter, in: Zeitschrift d. Savigny-Stiftung für Rechtsgeschichte. Rom.Abt. 111 (1994), 155–194.
EAD., Babatha versus the Guardians of her Son: A Struggle for Trusteeship – Legal and Practical Aspects of P.Yadin 12–15, 27, in: Ranon KATZOFF (ed.), Proceedings of the Judaean Desert Documents Workshop held in Bar Ilan University, 3–5 June 1998 (forthcoming).
COTTON, Hannah M./GEIGER, Joseph, Masada II: The Latin and Greek Documents, The Masada Reports, Jerusalem 1989.
EAD., The Guardianship of Jesus son of Babatha: Roman and Local Law in the Province of Arabia', in: JRS 83, (1993), 94–113.
EAD., The Archive of Salome Komaïse Daughter of Levi: Another Archive from the "Cave of Letters", in: ZPE 105 (1995), 171–208.
EAD./COCKLE, Walter/MILLAR, Fergus, The Papyrology of the Roman Near East: A Survey, in: JRS 85 (1995), 214–35.
EAD., The Guardian (ἐπίτροπος) of a Woman in the Documents from the Judaean Desert', in: ZPE 118 (1997), 267–273.
EAD./YARDENI, Ada, Aramaic, Hebrew and Greek Texts from Nahal Hever and Other Sites with an Appendix Containing Alleged Qumran Texts (The Seiyâl Collection II), DJD XXVII, Oxford 1997.
EAD./QIMRON, Elisha, XHev/Se ar 13 of 134 or 135: a wife's renunciation of claims, in: JJS 49 (1998), 108–118.
EAD., The Languages of the Legal and Administrative Documents from the Judaean Desert, in: ZPE 125 (1999), 219–231.
EAD., Die Papyrusdokumente aus der judäischen Wüste und ihr Beitrag zur Erforschung der jüdischen Geschichte des 1. und 2. Jh. n. Chr., in: ZDPV 115 (1999), 228–247.
EAD., Some Aspects of the Roman Administration of Judaea/Syria-Palaestina, in: Lokale Autonomie und römische Ordnungsmacht in den kaiserzeitlichen Provinzen vom 1.–3. Jh., Kolloquien des Historischen Kollegs, ed. Werner ECK, Munich 1999, 75–91.
EAD., 'Marriage Contracts from the Judaean Desert', in: Materia Judaica, Bolletino dell'associazione italiana per lo studio del giudaismo 6 (2000), 2–6.
EAD., 'The Documentary Texts from the Judaean Desert: A Matter of Nomenclature', in: SCI 20 (2001), 113–119.

EAD., The Aramaic Legal Tradition in Roman Judaea/Syria Palaestina, in: David WASSERSTEIN (ed.), Proceedings of the Conference on Synchysis and Polyglossia: Multiplicity of Tongues from the Ancient Near East to Medieval Europe held in Tel Aviv University on 23 February 1999 (forthcoming).

EAD., *Provincia Iudaea*: Epigraphical versus Literary Evidence (forthcoming).

COWEY, James M.S./MARESCH, Klaus (eds.), Urkunden des Politeuma der Juden von Herakleopolis (144/3–133/2 v. Chr.) (P.Polit.Iud.). Papyri aus den Sammlungen von Heidelberg, Köln, München und Wien, Papyrologica Coloniensia 29, Opladen – Wiesbaden 2001.

CRAWFORD, M.H. (ed.), Roman Statutes I, London 1996.

CROWTHER, Charles, Foreign Judges from Priene: Studies in Hellenistic Epigraphy, PhD thesis, King's College, London 1990.

ECK, Werner, 'Die Inschriften Iudäas im 1. und frühen 2. Jh. n. Chr. als Zeugnisse der römischen Herrschaft', in this volume 29–50.

ID., Roman officials in Judaea and Arabia and civil jurisdiction', in: Ranon KATZOFF (ed.), Proceedings of the Judaean Desert Documents Workshop held in Bar Ilan University, 3–5 June 1998 (forthcoming).

ESHEL, Hanan/BROSHI, Magen/JULL, T.A.J., Documents from Wadi Murabba'at and the Status of Jerusalem during the Bar Kokhba Revolt in: Refuge Caves of the Bar Kokhba Revolt, eds. Hanan ESHEL and David AMIT, Tel Aviv 1998, 233ff (Hebrew).

FEISSEL, Denis/GASCOU, Jean, Documents d'archives romains inédits du Moyen Euphrate, IIIe siècle après J.–C., 1. Les pétitions, P.Euphr. 1 à 5, in: *Journal des Savants* 1995, 65–119.

GONZÁLES, Julián, The lex Irnitana: A New Copy of a Roman Municipal Law, in: JRS 76 (1986), 147–243.

GULAK, Asher, Towards a Study of the History of Jewish Law in the Talmudic Period, vol. 1. Jerusalem 1929 (Hebrew).

HABICHT, Christian, New Evidence on the Province of Asia, in: JRS 65 (1975), 64–91.

HAENSCH, Rudolf, Zur Konventsordnung in Aegyptus und den übrigen Provinzen des römischen Reiches', in: Akten des 21. Internationalen Papyrologenkongresses Berlin, 13.–19.8.1995. Eds. KRAMER, Bärbel/LUPPE, Wolfgang/MAEHLER, Herwig/ POETHKE, Günter. Band I, Archiv fuer Papyrusforschung und verwandte Gebiete. Beiheft 3, Stuttgart – Leipzig 1997, 320–391.

ID., Zum Verständnis von P.Jericho 16, in: SCI 20 (2001), 155–167.

LAFFI, U., I limiti della competenza giurisdizionale dei magistrati locali, in: Estudios sobre la tabula siarensis, eds. Julián GONZÁLEZ and J. ARCE, Anejos de Archivo español de arqueología 9, Madrid 1988, 141ff.

LEWIS, Naphtali, The Documents from the Bar Kokhba Period in the Cave of Letters: Greek Papyri, Judean Desert Studies 2, Jerusalem 1989.

ID., The Demise of the Aramaic Document in the Dead Sea Region, in: SCI 20 (2001), 179–181.

LIEBERMAN, Saul, Roman legal institutions in early rabbinics and in the Acta Martyrum, in: JQR 35 (1944), 1–55).

MISGAV, Hagai, Jewish Courts of Law as Reflected in Documents from the Dead Sea, in: Cathedra 82 (1996), 17–24 (Hebrew).

NELSON, Hein L.W./MANTHE, Ulrich, Gai Institutiones III 88–181. Die Kontraktsobligationen. Text und Kommentar, Freiburger Rechtsgeschichtliche Abhandlungen NF 35, Studia Gaiana 8, Berlin 1999.

NÖRR, Dieter, Prozessuales aus dem Babatha-Archiv, in: Michel HUMBERT (ed.), Mélanges de droit romain et d'histoire ancienne. Hommage à la mémoire de André Magdelain, Paris 1998, 317–341.

ID., Xenokriten in der römischen Provinzialgerichtsbarkeit', in: Lokale Autonomie und römische Ordnungsmacht in den kaiserzeitlichen Provinzen vom 1.–3. Jh., Kolloquien des Historischen Kollegs, ed. Werner ECK, Munich 1999, 257–301.

OPPENHEIMER, Aharon, Jewish Penal Authority in Roman Judaea, in: The Jews in a Graeco-Roman World, ed. Martin GOODMAN, Oxford 1998, 181–191.

PUCCI BEN-ZE'EV, Miryam, Jewish Rights in the Roman World. The Greek and Roman Documents Quoted by Josephus Flavius, TSAJ 74, Tübingen 1998.

RAJAK, Tessa, Was There a Roman Charter for the Jews?, in: JRS 74 (1984), 107–123.

RODGER, Alan, Jurisdictional Limits in the Lex Irnitana and the Lex de Gallia Cisalpina, in: ZPE 110 (1996), 189–206.

ROEBUCK, Derek, Ancient Greek Arbitration, Oxford 2001.

ROWE, Gregory, Trimalchio's World, in: SCI 20 (2001), 225–245.

SCHREMER, Adiel, Divorce in Papyrus Se'elim 13 Once Again: A Reply to Tal Ilan', in: *HTR* 91 (1998), 193–202.

SAFRAI, Zeev, The Jewish Community in the Talmudic Period, Jerusalem 1995 (Hebrew).

SCHÜRER, Emil/VERMES, Geza/MILLAR, Fergus, The History of the Jewish People in the Age of Jesus Christ, 175B.C.–A.D.135 vol. 2, Edinburgh 1979.

SHERK, Robert K., Roman Documents from the Greek East. Senatus consulta and Epistulae to the age of Augustus, Baltimore 1969.

WOLFF, Hans Julius, Römisches Provinzialrecht in der Provinz Arabia, in: ANRW II.13 (1980), 763–806.

YADIN, Yigael/GREENFIELD, Jonas C./YARDENI, Ada/LEVINE, Baruch, The Documents from the Bar Kokhba Period in the Cave of Letters, Vol. II: Hebrew, Aramaic and Nabatean Documents, forthcoming.

YARDENI, Ada, Textbook of Aramaic, Hebrew and Nabataean Documentary Texts from the Judaean Desert and Related Material, 2 vols., Jerusalem 2000.

EAD., The Decipherment and Restoration of Legal Texts from the Judaean Desert: A Reexamination of *Papyrus Starcky* (*P.Yadin* 36), in: SCI 20 (2001), 121–137.

Werner Eck

Die Inschriften Iudäas im 1. und frühen 2. Jh. n. Chr. als Zeugnisse der römischen Herrschaft

Jede Herrschaft braucht Zeichen, in denen sie sich ausdrückt. Bis heute sind die klassischen Ausdrucksmittel der römischen Herrschaft über Italien und die Mittelmeerwelt die *fasces*, die Rutenbündel, die von den Amtsdienern der Magistrate, den Liktoren, zusammen mit den Beilen als Zeichen der unumschränkten Macht den Konsuln und Prätoren, ebenso aber auch den Statthaltern senatorischen Ranges und schließlich den Kaisern vorangetragen wurden.[1] Wenn die syrischen Provinzlegaten in den ersten Jahren der römischen Herrschschaft über Iudaea als die eigentlichen Statthalter dieses Gebietes von Ptolemais aus hinauf nach Jerusalem zogen, dann waren sie ebenfalls von ihren Liktoren begleitet. Diese Symbole römischer Macht waren dabei freilich nicht genug, es bedurfte der Absicherung durch die militärische Stärke. Auch Pilatus demonstrierte diese Stärke, als er sich zu einem der großen Feste mit seinen Auxiliarkohorten nach Jerusalem begab. Doch während die kaiserlichen Legaten, die aus der syrischen Hauptstadt Antiochia in das ihnen ebenfalls unterstellte Iudaea zogen, bei der Demonstration der römischen Suprematie Rücksicht auf die Vorstellungen der jüdischen Bevölkerung nahmen, provozierte Pilatus deren Gefühle, indem er die Kaiserbilder, religiöse Symbole für die höchste Macht der Kaiser über die Welt, nicht von den Feldzeichen abnehmen ließ.[2] Die Reaktion von seiten der Juden war ähnlich wie bei der Forderung Caligulas, der Statthalter Syriens, P. Petronius, solle das Bild des Kaisers im Tempel von Jerusalem aufstellen.[3] Solch ungeschminkte, rücksichtslose Demonstration von Herrschaft konnte nur Widerstand hervorrufen und die Herrschaft selbst gefährden.

Doch es gab auch andere Wege, um Dominanz mitzuteilen, ohne doch Beherrschte unmittelbar und bewußt zu provozieren. So erwies Augustus in Jerusalem gegenüber dem Gott der Juden seine Verehrung. Er stiftete Brandopfer, die täglich im Tempel in seinem Namen dargebracht werden sollten.[4] Ob dies in irgendeiner öffentlich sichtbaren und über den aktuellen Moment hinausweisenden Form dokumentiert wurde, etwa durch eine Inschrift, ist bei Philo, der von dieser auf Dauer angelegten Stiftung berichtet, nicht überliefert.[5] Doch

---

[1] Umfassend zu den *fasces* Th. SCHÄFER, Insignia, 19. 209.
[2] Jos Ant 18,55ff; Bell 2,169ff.
[3] Siehe zuletzt zu P. Petronius E. DĄBROWA, Governors, 42f, sowie PIR² P 269.
[4] Philo Leg Gai 157.317.
[5] Vergleichbar ist das, was Augustus gegenüber dem Heiligtum der Artemis von Ephesus tat. Er gab Teile der heiligen Ländereien wieder zurück; die so wieder erworbenen Gebiete wurden durch zahlreiche Grenzsteine markiert. Der inschriftliche Text war in latei-

wäre solches auch im jüdischen Kontext wohl nicht unmöglich. In einer solchen Inschrift hätte sich direkt zunächst nur die Devotion des mächtigen Herrschers gegenüber der Gottheit der Juden manifestiert. Doch tatsächlich hätte auch die Herrschaft, die bereits damals von Rom faktisch über das Volk der Juden ausgeübt wurde, ihren Ausdruck gefunden, freilich in zurückhaltender Form.

Inschriften als Medium der Kommunikation im römischen Iudaea[6]

Alle diese Möglichkeiten, Herrschaft zu demonstrieren, sind uns für den jüdisch-palästinensischen Raum nur noch durch literarische Berichte zugänglich. Die konkreten Formen, in denen sich dies ausdrückte, sind für uns zumeist nicht mehr direkt zu erkennen oder gar zu erleben. Doch eines der seit augusteischer Zeit überall in der römischen Welt immer häufiger angewandten Medien, um den Untertanen Botschaften zu übermitteln, um zu demonstrieren, daß Herrschaft existierte und präsent war, ist uns auch heute noch unmittelbar zugänglich, nämlich Inschriften, epigraphische Denkmäler.[7] Auch das Neue Testament berichtet von einer Inschrift, die in besonders eklatanter Weise als Medium für die Botschaft von der Verfügung der Macht über Leben und Tod wirkte: dem *titulus crucis*, auf dem Pontius Pilatus in Ἑβραϊστί, Ῥωμαϊστί, Ἑλληνιστί, auf Hebräisch, Lateinisch und Griechisch, den Grund für die Hinrichtung Jesu verkünden ließ.[8] Vergleichbar ist die inschriftliche Warnung an alle Nichtjuden, den heiligen Bezirks des Tempels in Jerusalem nicht zu betreten; denn wer diese Anordnung übertrat, mußte mit dem Leben bezahlen.

---

nischer und griechischer Sprache abgefaßt. Auf diese Weise erwies Augustus der Göttin gegenüber seine Devotion, gleichzeitig dokumentierte er aber auch, wie durch ihn die Ordnung in den Provinzen wieder hergestellt wurde. Die Ordnung war Ausfluß der römischen Herrschaft. Siehe I.Ephesus VII 2, 3501.3502. Vgl. I.Ephesus II 459 = G. ALFÖLDY, Notizen, 157ff

[6] Zu der hier behandelten Problematik siehe die partiell ähnlichen Gedanken bei W. ECK, Spiegel.

[7] Siehe als kurze Einführung in die Epigraphik W. ECK, Epigraphik, 92–111; G. PETZL, Epigraphik, 72–83. Die Trennung nach den Sprachen Latein und Griechisch ist oft nicht sachadäquat, da sich inhaltlich in lateinischen und griechischen Inschriften nicht selten dasselbe findet. Der zutreffendere Begriff ist deshalb: Römische Epigraphik, womit ausgedrückt wird, daß sich die Texte auf Sachverhalte beziehen, die sich unter römischer Herrschaft abgespielt haben. Zur Frage eines Corpus Inscriptionum Iudaeae/Palaestinae, das Inschriften in allen damals in diesem Raum gesprochenen Sprachen umfaßt, siehe am Ende des Beitrags: Appendix.

[8] Mt 27,37: Οὗτός ἐστιν Ἰησοῦς ὁ βασιλεὺς τῶν Ἰουδαίων = *Hic est Iesus rex Iudaeorum*; Mk 15,26: ὁ βασιλεὺς τῶν Ἰουδαίων = *Rex Iudaeorum*; Lk. 23,38: ὁ βασιλεὺς τῶν Ἰουδαίων οὗτος = *Hic est rex Iudaeorum;* Joh. 19,19: Ἰησοῦς ὁ Ναζωραῖος ὁ βασιλεὺς τῶν Ἰουδαίων ... καὶ ἦν γεγραμμένον Ἑβραϊστί, Ῥωμαϊστί, Ἑλληνιστί = *Iesus Nazarenus, rex Iudaeorum*. Zum *titulus crucis* siehe zuletzt J. GEIGER, Titulus, 202–207; P.L. MAIER, Inscription, 58–75.

Auch sie war in zwei Sprachen geschrieben, in Griechisch und Lateinisch;[9] die lateinische Form zielte wohl vor allem auf Angehörige des römischen Militärs in Iudaea.

Inschrift und Monument

Während uns diese beiden historisch so wichtigen epigraphischen Texte real nicht erhalten geblieben sind,[10] läßt uns eine wachsende Zahl von Dokumenten immer deutlicher erkennen, daß Inschriften auch im Land der Bibel ein wichtiges Medium waren, in dem sich römische Herrschaft einst ausgedrückt hat und das uns vor allem heute noch konkret erfahrbar ist, zumindest partiell.[11] Denn es ist sogleich zu betonen, daß Inschriften zumeist nur in ihrem konkreten Kontext voll verständlich werden.[12] Hätten wir nur den Text des *titulus crucis* erhalten, nicht jedoch das konkrete Wissen darum, daß es sich um die Aussage über einen zum Tod am Kreuz Verurteilten handelt, würden wir aus den wenigen Worten über den „König der Juden" völlig falsche Schlußfolgerungen ziehen. Die meisten Inschriften sind eben nur Teil eines größeren Ganzen. Sie stehen z.B. über dem Eingang von Gebäuden, zeigen, wer ein Bauwerk geplant und finanziert hat; die volle Aussagekraft haben wir notwendigerweise aber erst dann, wenn wir auch das Gebäude kennen, seine Größe, seine Ausstattung, seine topographische Lage. Grabinschriften lassen alleine nur erkennen, wer gestorben ist; vielleicht sprechen sie zusätzlich noch über das Lebensalter, die sozio-politische Stellung des Verstorbenen und erwähnen manchmal die Angehörigen, die den Toten bestattet haben. Aber wenn das Grab selbst noch erhalten ist, dann sagt sowohl seine Größe wie seine Ausstattung, aber auch seine Lage in der Nähe einer Stadt oder weit entfernt von jeder größeren menschlichen Siedlung Zusätzliches über den Verstorbenen und seine Familie aus.[13] Sogenannte Ehreninschriften sind ausschließlich die geschriebene Erklärung für die eigentliche Ehre, die einer Person erwiesen wurde, zumeist durch die Errichtung einer Statue. Diese sind zwar in den meisten Fällen nicht mehr erhalten oder zumindest nicht mehr der zugehörigen Inschrift zuweisbar. Doch die Statuen müssen in ihrer Vielfalt mitgedacht werden, um ermessen zu können, was das Verdienst des Geehrten wirklich gewesen ist. Denn es war nicht gleichgültig, ob einer Person eine der zahlreichen einfachen Statuen, lateinisch gesprochen eine *statua pedestris*, dediziert wurde, oder eine überlebensgroße Reiterstatue oder gar ein Gespann mit zwei oder vier Pferden aus Bronze,

---

[9] Jos Bell 5,194; 6,125f.
[10] Von der lateinisch-griechischen Version ist kein epigraphisches Zeugnis erhalten, wohl aber von einer nur griechischen Version. Siehe die letzte zusammenfassende Behandlung bei L. BOFFO, Iscrizioni, 283–290.
[11] Siehe dazu im Überblick W. ECK, Rom, 237–263; DERS., Spiegel, im Druck. Vgl. auch allgemein zu Inschriften als Kommunikationsmedium G. ALFÖLDY/S. PANCIERA, Denkmäler, und W. ECK, Latein, 641–660.
[12] Siehe dazu grundsätzlich W. ECK, Öffentlichkeit, 55–75.
[13] Vgl. unten zum Grab der Goliathfamilie.

wobei der Geehrte auf dem Wagen den Zeitgenossen präsentiert wurde. Darin konnte sich soziale Wertschätzung ausdrücken, aber auch politischer Einfluß und anderes.[14] Das Monument, dessen Teil eine Inschrift einst war, ist also immer mitzudenken, auch wenn es uns häufig heute nicht mehr erhalten ist und wir es nur gedanklich dem Szenario zuordnen können. Die Inschrift bietet immer nur einen Teil der Information. Dies gilt überall im römischen Kontext, wie auch viele der folgenden Beispiele zeigen.

Zur Inschrift des Pontius Pilatus aus Caesarea

Gerade das früheste epigraphische Zeugnis in Iudaea für die direkte Präsenz Roms,[15] die sogenannte Pilatusinschrift aus Caesarea, beweist dies in eindrucksvoller Weise. Der Stein, auf den die Inschrift gemeißelt ist, war 1961 in Zweitverwendung im Theater in Caesarea gefunden worden und hat, vor allem da sie nur fragmentarisch erhalten ist, eine heftige Diskussion über die möglichen Ergänzungen und damit über die inhaltliche Bedeutung ausgelöst.[16] Dies war engstens damit verbunden, welches Gebäude man sich vorstellte, an dem das Zeugnis einst angebracht war. Dies soll hier nicht im Detail besprochen werden, da G. Alföldy zuletzt eine sehr überzeugende Lösung vorgelegt hat.[17] Vor allem hat er die konkrete Form des Steins und den maximal für den Text verfügbaren Platz bei seiner Rekonstruktion berücksichtigt, was sonst zumeist nicht geschehen ist. Er schlägt folgenden Text vor:

[Nauti]s Tiberieum
[.Po]ntius Pilatus
[praef]ectus Iudae[a]e
[ref]é[cit].

Während man bisher generell davon ausging, der Text dokumentiere ein von Pontius Pilatus errichtetes Gebäude, das in irgendeiner Form der Verehrung, vermutlich sogar der kultischen Verehrung des Herrschers dienen sollte, versetzt Alföldy die Inschrift in einen weit prosaischeren, allerdings für die Präsenz Roms in Iudaea sehr wichtigen Zusammenhang. Zum einen hat Pontius Pilatus kein neues Gebäude errichtet, sondern nur ein schon bestehendes erneuert; das ergibt sich aus dem erhaltenen Textrest in Zeile 4 und der zwingenden Tatsache, daß der Text auf den Stein völlig symmetrisch gemeißelt

---

[14] Siehe z.B. G. ALFÖLDY, Statuen; DERS., Pietas, 11ff; W. ECK, Ehrungen, 359–376; D. ERKELENZ, Ehrungen.
[15] Einige noch frühere lateinische Inschriften, nämlich Graffiti auf Amphoren, die bereits im Jahr 19 v. Chr. geschrieben und bei den Ausgrabungen auf Masada gefunden wurden, sind kein Zeugnis für Iudaea, da diese *tituli picti* nicht im Land, sondern bereits in Italien geschrieben wurden. Siehe H.M. COTTON/J. GEIGER, Documents, 149–160 Nr. 804–818.
[16] Zur Dokumentation der Forschungssituation zu diesem Text siehe L. BOFFO, Iscrizioni, 217ff; C. M. LEHMANN/K.G. HOLUM, Inscriptions, 67ff Nr. 43.
[17] G. ALFÖLDY, Pilatus, 85ff, wo auch die gesamte frühere Literatur zu finden ist; vgl. auch C. M. LEHMANN/K.G. HOLUM, Inscriptions, Nr. 43.

wurde. Dazu paßt aber nur das Verbum *[ref]é[cit]* und nicht *[f]é[cit]*. Zum andern parallelisiert er das Wort Tiberieum mit dem bei Josephus für Caesarea überlieferten Δρουσεῖον, womit bei dem Historiker einer der beiden Leuchttürme bezeichnet wird, die Herodes an der Einfahrt zu dem von ihm erbauten Hafen hatte erbauen lassen.[18] Von daher kommt dann auch seine sehr plausible Ergänzung zu Beginn von Zeile 1: *[Nauti]s*, also den Seefahrern, denen das Feuer des Leuchtturms, des Tiberieums, die Einfahrt in den Hafen erleichtern sollte. Mit dieser prosaischen Erklärung stimmt nunmehr auch endlich die Form des Steins, auf den die Inschrift geschrieben war, sowie die Qualität des Steines überein. Denn es handelt sich um einen nicht sehr hochwertigen Stein, wie er für ein Gebäude mit kultischem Zweck kaum verwendet worden wäre. Zudem müßte man in diesem Zusammenhang eine ganz andere Form des Steines erwarten. Dann müßte der Text nach dem, was man für einen Kultbau erwarten kann, auf einem Architrav gestanden haben. Hier aber liegt ein einfacher Quader vor, der 81 cm hoch, 68 cm breit und 21 cm tief ist. Solche Blöcke ohne jede Rahmung aber begegnen vor allem bei großen Nutzbauten, die insgesamt aus Quadern errichtet sind. Der Unterschied zwischen dem normalen Mauerwerk und dem Inschriftenstein ist allein durch die Farbe und vielleicht auch durch die Form des Quaders bestimmt.[19] Einen vergleichbaren Unterschied zwischen Inschrift und umgebendem Mauerwerk kann man in Caesarea selbst etwa an dem Aquädukt beobachten, den Hadrian durch Vexillationen, die aus verschiedenen Legionen abgeordnet worden waren, hat errichten lassen. Auch dort heben sich die Bauinschriften durch das hellere Steinmaterial von den dunkleren Steinen des Bauwerks selbst deutlich ab.[20]

Obwohl damit die Inschrift eines vielleicht erregenderen Inhalts, gerade unter dem Aspekt der religiösen Situation im Iudaea der damaligen Zeit, entzaubert ist, bleibt ihre Bedeutung, auch unter dem Blickpunkt der römischen Herrschaft, voll erhalten. Denn die römische Dominanz wurde ja nicht erst mit der Übernahme der direkten Herrschaft durch Rom in Iudaea spürbar, sondern längst vorher. Herodes nannte seine neue Stadt anstelle von Stratonsturm nach Caesar Augustus eben Caesarea, er errichtete dort einen Tempel für den Kult der Roma und des Augustus direkt über dem inneren Hafen, dessen Fundamente inzwischen bei den neuesten Ausgrabungen gefunden wurden.[21] Hinzu aber kamen auch die Ehrungen für Mitglieder der Familie des Princeps, für Drusus und Tiberius, wie Josephus und die neu ergänzte und neu verstandene Pilatusinschrift zeigen.

Die Bedeutung der Inschrift geht jedoch weit über den lokalen Bezug zu Caesarea hinaus. Denn er bringt die definitive Lösung des lange diskutierten Problems, wie denn die römische Herrschaft in Iudaea ab dem Jahr 6 n.Chr. an

---

[18] Jos Ant 15,336; Bell 1,412. Zur handschriftlichen Überlieferung und der Variante Δρουσεῖον siehe G. ALFÖLDY, Pilatus, 94 Anm. 27.
[19] G. ALFÖLDY, Pilatus, 102ff.
[20] Vgl. etwa die Beschreibung der Inschriften bei C.M. LEHMANN/K.G. HOLUM, Inscriptions, 71ff Nr. 45ff.
[21] Vgl. K.G. HOLUM, Temple Platform.

organisiert war. Während man aus Tacitus und teilweise aus Josephus (wenn man sich nur auf einzelne Aussagen stützte) immer wieder den Schluß gezogen hatte, Iudaea müßte bereits ab dem Jahr 6 n.Chr. eine eigenständige Provinz gewesen sein, zeigt dieser Text in Verbund mit vielen Aussagen bei Josephus eindeutig, daß Iudaea zumindest bis zum Jahr 41 n.Chr., als Agrippa nochmals die Königsherrschaft über das Land übernahm, nur ein Teil der großen, umfassenden Provinz Syria gewesen ist. Das Land aber unterstand einem Unterstatthalter des konsularen Legaten von Syrien, der wie auch in anderen Gegenden des Reiches (z.B. in Rätien, Nordspanien oder in Mösien) die Bezeichnung *praefectus* trug. Die Amtsbezeichnung, die Tacitus Pontius Pilatus gibt, nämlich *procurator*, ist dagegen nur eine anachronistische Übertragung eines Titels, der im Jahr 6 n.Chr. für die Funktion eines normalen Provinzstatthalters noch gar nicht existierte.[22] Allerdings hatte dieser *praefectus* das Recht der Kapitalgerichtsbarkeit, die er jedenfalls gegenüber den peregrinen Bewohnern der Provinz ohne Befragung des ihm übergeordneten Statthalters der Gesamtprovinz, der in Antiochia in Syrien residierte, ausüben konnte.[23]

Vertreter Roms in Iudaea vor dem jüdischen Aufstand

Von Anfang an waren im provinzialisierten Iudaea auch noch andere Personen als der *praefectus Iudaeae* anwesend, die als direkte Vertreter der kaiserlichen Macht angesehen wurden oder werden konnten. Dazu gehörten vor allem die, die für den Kaiser von den Bewohnern Geld in Form von Steuern, Zöllen oder Pacht eingetrieben haben. Vermutlich war die Erhebung der regelmäßig zu leistenden Steuern zunächst die Aufgabe des Prokurators von Syrien, nicht etwa des Präfekten von Iudaea.[24] Diese Abgaben hat der Prokurator aber sicher nicht selbst eingezogen, er hat vielmehr nur die vereinbarten Summen von den Gemeinden oder den Steuerpächtern in Empfang genommen. Dabei haben ihn aber ohne Zweifel auch einige Sklaven und Freigelassene des Kaisers unterstützt.[25] Solche sind bisher in den epigraphischen Quellen der Zeit vor dem Jüdischen Aufstand nicht erschienen, wohl aber innerhalb der Verwaltung des kaiserlichen Privatbesitzes, des Patrimonium. Salome, Herodes' Schwester, hatte von ihrem Bruder u.a. Iamnia mit den dortigen Palmenhainen geerbt. Bei ihrem Tod um das Jahr 10 n.Chr. vererbte sie all dies an Livia, Augustus' Frau.[26] Dies hatte zur Folge, daß in der üblichen römischen Manier ein Prokurator für die Verwaltung bestimmt wurde. Einen dieser Funktionsträger kennen wir, einen C. Herrenius Capito, der als *proc(urator) Iuliae Augustae,*

---

[22] Der *praefectus Aegypti*, der durch Octavian erst nach einem eigens verabschiedeten Gesetz eingesetzt wurde, war kein Modell, das von Augustus weitergeführt wurde.
[23] Zu diesem Gesamtkomplex siehe zuletzt H. M. COTTON, Aspects, 75ff; DIES., Josephus, (in Vorbereitung).
[24] Darauf hat H. M. COTTON, Josephus, zu Recht hingewiesen.
[25] Vgl. Jos Ant 20,113: Ein kaiserlicher Sklave wird auf dem Weg von Emmaus nach Jerusalem ausgeraubt.
[26] Jos Ant 18,31.

proc(urator) Ti. Caesaris Aug(usti), proc(urator) G(ai) Caesaris Aug(usti) Germanici in Iamnia gewirkt hat; allerdings ist er nicht aus einer Inschrift aus Iudaea, sondern aus dem italischen Teate Marrucinorum bekannt.[27] Wohl aber ist durch einen epigraphischen Text aus Iamnia ein Ti. Iulius Mellon bezeugt, der ein Freigelassener von Kaiser Tiberius war und ebenfalls den Titel *proc(urator)* trägt. Er bestattete innerhalb der Grenzen der kaiserlichen Domäne von Iamnia seine Frau Iulia Grata in einem Sarkophag.[28] Da er vermutlich gleichzeitig mit Herennius Capito in Iamnia tätig war, muß er als dessen Stellvertreter angesehen werden. Obwohl er weit von Rom entfernt weilte und bei der Bestattung seiner Frau natürlich einen rein privaten Akt durchführte, unterläßt er es nicht, auf seinen Status als *libertus* und *procurator* des Princeps Tiberius hinzuweisen. Das zeigt nur, wie wichtig dieser Status in seiner gesamten Existenz, bei seinem öffentlichen Auftreten war. Insofern ist die Benennung auf der Grabinschrift auch ein Reflex seiner Lebenswirklichkeit in Iudaea. Dies wird noch deutlicher bei einem zweiten Beispiel, ebenfalls einem kaiserlichen Freigelassenen. Ein Theodotus wird auf seiner Grabinschrift ἀπελεύθερος βασιλίσσης 'Αγριππείνης genannt. Seine Freilasserin war somit Agrippina die Jüngere, die Frau von Kaiser Claudius. Theodotus wurde in Jericho im Grab der Goliath Familie, zu der er gehörte, bestattet. Während fast alle anderen Grabinschriften in dem Mausoleum in hebräischer Sprache abgefaßt sind, wird bei ihm das Griechische verwendet.[29] Das weist zusammen mit der Benennung als Freigelassener der „Königin" Agrippina darauf hin, wie wichtig beides, seine Stellung und die Sprache, für seine soziale Position während seines Lebens gewesen sind. Fragt man, warum ein Freigelassener Agrippinas in Jericho bestattet ist, dann drängt sich die Antwort direkt auf: In Jericho lag ein Teil der Balsamhaine, die in kaiserlichen Besitz übergegangen waren; es ist recht wahrscheinlich, daß Agrippina ihren Gatten dazu brachte, ihr diesen Besitz ganz oder zumindest zum Teil zu überschreiben.[30] Sie hat dann wie Livia oder Tiberius und Gaius in Iamnia auch in Jericho ihre eigenen Sklaven und Freigelassenen eingesetzt, die die Besitztümer für sie zu verwalten hatten. An solchen Orten wie Jericho, aber wohl auch schon in Engedi oder in Iamnia begegneten die Bewohner Iudaeas somit Rom in einer sehr konkreten Form.

Die Präsenz Roms in Inschriften seit dem jüdischen Aufstand von 66

Die Schaffung von Sicherheit war für Rom und seine Vertreter in den Provinzen eine der vordringlichsten Aufgaben. Soweit diese betroffen war, entschloß

---

[27] AE 1941, 105.
[28] AE 1948, 141; vgl. dazu W. ECK, Rom, 252f Anm. 70.
[29] R. HACHLILI, Family, 31ff = SEG 31, 1405–1407.
[30] Dazu W. ECK, Rom, 252f; zu den Balsamhainen H.M. COTTON/W. ECK, Staatsmonopol, 153–161.

man sich auch zu Baumaßnahmen, die sonst, soweit sie im Interesse der Bewohner waren, vornehmlich die Aufgabe der einzelnen Gemeinden war. Doch vor allem für die schnelle Kommunikation der römischen Amtsträger mit den in der Provinz dislozierten Truppen und auch zum Verkehr mit den Gemeinden schuf die römische Seite sehr oft recht schnell ein überregionales Straßensystem, das wie weniges sonst zeigte, wer die Macht in der Provinz ausübte und wie durchsetzungsfähig diese Macht war. Frühzeitig wurden an Straßenbauten auch Meilensteine errichtet, die nicht nur eine praktische Funktion hatten, sondern stets auch mit ihrem knappen Text, aber oft monumentalen Buchstaben die Träger der Macht benannten. Das kann man beispielsweise bald nach der Einrichtung der Provinz Asia im Jahr 133 v. Chr. sehen, als dort durch Aquilius eine Straße ausgebaut wurde, um Roms Herrschaft leichter durchsetzen zu können; Meilensteine säumten diese Straße.[31] In Iudaea brauchte es, wenn wir von den bisher bekannten Straßenbaumaßnahmen und den damit verbundenen Meilensteinen ausgehen, jedoch relativ lange, bis Rom umfassende Maßnahmen ergriff. Erst als Vespasian von Nero als Sonderlegat zur Niederkämpfung des jüdischen Aufstandes nach Iudaea gesandt wurde und dort am 1. Juli 69 zum Kaiser akklamiert wurde, scheinen umfassendere Straßenbauprojekte unternommen worden zu sein, die dann auch ihren Niederschlag in der Aufstellung von Meilensteinen gefunden haben.[32]

Schon aus dem Jahr 69 stammt ein Meilenstein, der nahe der heutigen Stadt Afula gefunden wurde.[33] Die Inschrift führt neben Vespasian, der im Nominativ genannt ist, auch den damaligen, bereits aus Josephus, Bell 3,289ff. bekannten Legaten der legio X Fretensis, M. Ulpius Traianus, den Vater des späteren Kaisers, an; er war für die Durchführung der Straßenbauarbeiten von Caesarea über Caparcotna nach Scythopolis verantwortlich. Die eigentlichen Straßenbauarbeiten wurden in diesem Fall aller Wahrscheinlichkeit nach von den Soldaten der Legion, die Traian kommandierte, durchgeführt. Das geschah sicher nicht, um die Verkehrsbedingungen für die Bevölkerung zu verbessern, vielmehr war hier das einzige Motiv, die Beweglichkeit der Armee in diesem Land zu verbessern. Vermutlich galt das auch für die Straße, deren Erbauung oder zumindest Reparatur durch die beiden Meilensteine bezeugt ist, die in Jerusalem nahe dem Tempelberg gefunden wurden. Sie wurden nur wenige Jahre später aufgestellt, nämlich erst als Titus, Vespasians Sohn bereits Teilhaber an der Herrschaft war. Denn er wird im Text der beiden Inschriften neben dem Vater genannt. Beide erscheinen wieder im Nominativ, worauf der Statthalter der Provinz folgt, dessen Name jedoch später eradiert wurde.[34] Bis heute ist es nicht gelungen, zu klären, wer dieser Statthalter der Provinz Iudaea

---

[31] Siehe z.B. DESSAU 5814.
[32] Zu den Meilensteinen in der Provinz Iudaea/Syria Palaestina siehe vor allem B. ISAAC/I. ROLL, Roads I; M. FISCHER/B. ISAAC/I. ROLL, Roads II.
[33] B. ISAAC/I. ROLL, Milestone, 36–45 = AE 1977, 829.
[34] B. ISAAC/M. GICHON, Inscription, 117ff = R. SYME, Antonius, 12ff = AE 1978, 825 = W. ECK, Lucilius Bassus, 109–120. Vgl. Appendix: Lucilius Bassus oder L. Antonius Saturninus auf einem Meilenstein aus Jerusalem, 119–120.

war. Lange Zeit hat man geglaubt, der Senator L. Antonius Saturninus, der im Winter 88/89 gegen Domitian in Obergermanien revoltiert hat, sei zuvor prätorischer Statthalter in Iudaea gewesen. Nach der fehlgeschlagenen Revolte in Obergermanien aber sei sein Name reichsweit eradiert worden. Allerdings ist der eradierte Raum auf der Inschrift so kurz, daß alle seine Namen in abgekürzter Form, nämlich als L. [Ant. Sat.] oder nur als L. [Antonio] hätten geschrieben sein müssen. Das aber ist nicht so wahrscheinlich, eher sogar unwahrscheinlich. Deshalb ist vor kurzem als Name L[ucilio Basso] vorgeschlagen worden, also der Name des Statthalters, der nach Josephus' Bericht die Festung Herodium, die von Resten der aufständischen Juden besetzt war, im Jahr 72 erobert hat. Wie auch immer dies gewesen sein mag, in dem Text der beiden Meilensteine drückt sich die neue Form der römischen Herrschaft in der Provinz in aller Kürze, aber auch Klarheit aus: Vespasian und sein Sohn Titus sind diejenigen, die den Befehl zur Errichtung der Meilensteine und das heißt dann natürlich auch zur Erbauung der Straße gegeben haben; die Durchführung der Aufgabe fällt auf den senatorischen Statthalter, der als Vertreter des Kaisers im proprätorischen Rang die eben in der Provinz stationierte legio X Fretensis kommandierte und gleichzeitig auch für alle sonstigen Angelegenheiten der Provinz verantwortlich war.[35] Dies ist die ganz übliche Form der Darstellung der kaiserlichen Herrschaft in jeder Provinz des Reiches, so auch in Iudaea. Gleiches läßt sich, ebenfalls gleich zu Beginn der neuen Ordnung in der Provinz nach der Niederschlagung des Aufstandes, auf einem sehr fragmentarischen Zeugnis ablesen, das an der Straße von Jerusalem nach Lydda gefunden wurde. Nur wenige Buchstaben sind in vier Zeilen einer Inschrift auf einer Tafel erhalten, die nach der äußeren Form zu einer Bauinschrift gehört haben muß.[36]

IMP CAES[---]
IMP T[--]
SEX LV[--]
COH[---]

Doch der Vergleich mit strukturell gleichartigen Texten aus anderen Provinzen läßt eine fast vollständige Ergänzung der Inschrift zu, deren Text etwa folgendermaßen lauten muß:

---

[35] Seine genaue Amtsbezeichnung ist der Inschrift nicht zu entnehmen; er könnte *leg(atus) Aug(usti) pr(o) pr(aetore) leg(ionis) X Fr(etensis)* genannt sein; doch ist es genauso möglich, daß seine Titel nur *leg(atus) Aug(usti) pr(o) pr(aetore)* lautete und dann *leg(io) X Fr(etensis)* aufzulösen ist, d.h. die Legion stand im Nominativ, weil sie den Straßenbau durchzuführen hatte. Wenn die erste Variante richtig wäre, dann hieße dies nicht, daß er nicht Statthalter war, sondern daß das Kommando über die Legion betont werden sollte. Bereits Flavius Silva wird in seinem Cursus honorum *[legatus Aug. pr. pr. pr]ovinc(iae) Iudaeae* genannt; vgl. W. ECK, Senatoren, 93–111. Vgl. dazu auch M. F. FENATI, Flavio Silva.

[36] Ursprünglich publiziert von H. VINCENT, Église, 414ff.

Imp(erator) Caes(ar) [Vespasianus Augustus]
Imp(erator) T(itus) [Caesar Vesp(asiani) Aug(usti) fil(ius)]
Sex(to) Lu[cilio Basso leg(ato) Aug(usti) pr(o) pr(aetore)]
coh(ors) [---].

Wiederum geben die beiden Herrscher, Vespasian und sein Sohn Titus, den Befehl, etwas zu erbauen; der Legat Lucilius Bassus führt den Befehl aus und die Durchführung oblag einer Militäreinheit, deren Name allerdings nicht ergänzt werden kann. Was in diesem konkreten Fall erbaut wurde, läßt sich, da der Text nicht in situ gefunden wurde, nicht mehr feststellen. Da es sich jedoch nach dem Fundort um ein Bauwerk an einer auch für die Truppen und die Provinzialverwaltung wichtigen Straße handelte, sind die Möglichkeiten nicht sehr groß. Entweder stand die Bauinschrift über dem Eingang eines militärischen Stützpunktes, etwa einer Abteilung der legio X Fretensis oder einer Auxiliareinheit, oder es war dort eine Straßenstation zum Wechseln der Zugtiere und zum Übernachten der Reisenden erbaut worden. Das Bauwerk diente jedenfalls der römischen Herrschaft, so wie die Inschrift über dem Eingang es verkündete.

Auch in der Hauptstadt der neuen Provinz, in der schon vorher der Präfekt Iudaeas seinen Sitz gehabt hatte, zeigte sich die neue Form, die die Herrschaft nunmehr angenommen hatte. Neben dem Statthalter, der freilich nicht mehr aus dem zweiten Stand des Reiches, den Rittern, sondern aus dem *ordo senatorius* genommen wurde, erschien jetzt ein Finanzprokurator, der für den Einzug der Steuern und die Besoldung des Heeres zuständig war. Er wurde vom Kaiser, wie der frühere Präfekt, aus den Reihen der Ritter gewählt. Natürlich mußte er wie der senatorische Gouverneur einen eigenen Verwaltungssitz erhalten, und zwar auch in Caesarea. Dieses Praetorium des Prokurators konnte durch die großflächigen Ausgrabungen an der Seeseite der Stadt in den 80er und 90er Jahren des 20. Jahrhunderts ausgegraben und durch die Auswertung der Inschriften einwandfrei identifiziert werden.[37] Natürlich stand dem Prokurator von Anfang an ein größeres Personal zur Ausübung seiner Aufgaben zur Verfügung; neben Soldaten, die aus den Truppen der Provinz abgeordnet wurden, waren dies vor allem kaiserliche Sklaven und Freigelassene – wie in allen anderen Reichsteilen auch. Welche Stellung manche von diesen einnehmen konnten, zeigt eine der frühesten lateinischen Inschriften, die während der neueren Ausgrabungen in Caesarea entdeckt wurde. Der Text ist auf eine runde Basis geschrieben, auf der einst die Statue des Geehrten, eines kaiserlichen *libertus*, gestanden hatte:[38]

---

[37] Siehe dazu in Kürze den abschließenden Ausgrabungsbericht von Joseph PATRICH; darin W. ECK, Inscriptions.
[38] C. M. LEHMANN/K.G. HOLUM, Inscriptions, 35f Nr. 2.

T(ito) Flavio Aug(usti) liber(to)
Callisto
G(aius) Aurunculeius amico suo
h(onoris) c(ausa).[39]

Diese Basis mit der Statue wurde im Bereich des Prokuratorenpraetoriums gefunden, das einst auch der Ort der Aufstellung gewesen war. Das Monument zeigt einen typischen Zug der kaiserzeitlichen römischen Herrschaft, der sich in vielen Bereichen bemerkbar machte. Es ist klar, daß jedem in der römischen Gesellschaft, auch der Gesellschaft der römischen Kolonie Caesarea, bewußt war, daß ein Freigelassener, ein *libertus*, ursprünglich ein Sklave gewesen war. Diesen ‚Makel' konnte niemand ganz vergessen machen. Zumindest aber war dieses Faktum für Gegner eines *libertus*, wenn es nötig oder nützlich erschien, jederzeit funktionalisierbar. Dennoch gab es Freigelassene, die es zeitweise geschafft haben, daß die Mitwelt die Herkunft vergaß, oder, richtiger gesagt, zumindest zu vergessen schien. Dies waren insbesondere *liberti* des Kaisers, die durch den Bezug zu ihrem Patron, den sie deutlich in der Bezeichnung *Aug(usti) libertus* zur Schau trugen, an dessen Prestige und Macht partizipierten. Sie konnten dann auch in der Öffentlichkeit in einer Form auftreten oder sogar Auszeichnungen entgegennehmen, die einem Freigelassenen eines normalen römischen Bürgers verwehrt gewesen wären. Dazu gehörte auch die öffentliche Ehrung mit einer Statue, wie es in diesem Fall mit T. Flavius Callistus geschah. Er war, wie sein Name *T(itus) Flavius* zeigt, Freigelassener eines der flavischen Kaiser, also von Vespasian, Titus oder Domitian. Noch unter ihnen oder bald danach war er in Caesarea in der prokuratorischen Verwaltung tätig, möglicherweise war er derjenige, der den ritterlichen Prokurator vertrat. Bei seiner Tätigkeit hat er sich offensichtlich Freunde geschaffen, von denen einer sich entschloß, Callistus in einer Form zu ehren, wie sie für führende freigeborene Mitglieder der lokalen und überlokalen römischen Gesellschaft üblich war, mit einer Statue. Sie wurde, was der Fundort anzeigt, innerhalb des prokuratorischen Praetoriums errichtet, was aber nicht bedeutete, daß sie mit ihrer Wirkung nur auf die beschränkte Öffentlichkeit des administrativen Stabes des Prokurators abzielte und nicht auf die allgemeine Öffentlichkeit. Denn der Verwaltungskomplex des Prokurators war aus sachlichen Gründen natürlich für alle Bewohner der Provinz zugänglich. Somit konnten auch alle wahrnehmen, wie durch die Nähe zur kaiserlichen Macht ein inferiorer juristischer Status und übliche soziale Vorurteile, wie sie sonst für Freigelassene zu beobachten waren, überspielt werden konnten. Der Platz, an dem sich dies manifestierte, nämlich ein Gebäudekomplex der Provinzadministration, machte dies noch deutlicher. Auch das war eine Wirkung des römischen Herrschaftssystems.

---

[39] Diese beiden letzten Worte flankieren in der Inschrift in Zeile 2 in Abkürzung das Cognomen Callistus. Sie sind hier um der besseren Verständlichkeit des Textes willen ans Ende gesetzt, so wie sie ja auch inhaltlich gelesen werden müssen.

Die Bedeutung der öffentlichen Ehrung von Personen hoher soziopolitischer Stellung ist für uns dank epigraphischer Zeugnisse auch im Palast des Statthalters der Provinz zu verifizieren. Es war der Gebäudekomplex, in dem nach Apostelgeschichte 23, 35 Felix, der Vertreter Roms in Iudaea in der spätclaudisch-frühneronischen Zeit, den Apostel Paulus in Haft halten ließ: ἐν τῷ πραιτωρίῳ τοῦ Ἡρῴδου. Durch die neuesten Ausgrabungen ist, allerdings für eine weit spätere Zeit, eine Amtsstube in diesem Statthalterpalast aufgedeckt worden, die speziell für das Wachpersonal des Gefängnisses vorgesehen war.[40]

Nicht nur die Präfekten, sondern auch die späteren Statthalter hatten in diesem Palast des Herodes, der später noch wesentlich erweitert wurde, ihren Sitz und benutzten die Portiken, Innenhöfe und Zugänge, um dort die gesellschaftliche Rangordnung durch statuarische Monumente und Inschriften abzubilden. Obwohl die meisten bis heute erhaltenen Zeugnisse erst aus dem späteren zweiten und vor allem dem dritten Jahrhundert stammen, hat ein Neufund gezeigt, daß ähnlich wie im Praetorium des Prokurators so auch in dem des Statthalters frühzeitig diese Form der Ehrung geübt wurde. Der recht fragmentarische Text lautet in Abschrift folgendermaßen:

ONIO L·F·S
IO·CRIS.INO·MA
ELLINO NVMI
I VIR EPUL·
R PR .ROVIN
H V

Dies läßt sich dank einer weiteren Inschrift aus Antiochia im kleinasiatischen Pisidien[41] zu einem fast vollständigen Text rekonstruieren:[42]

[L(ucio) Coss]onio L(ucii) f(ilio) S[tel(latina) Gallo]
[Vecil]io Cris[p]ino Ma[nsuanio]
[Marc]ellino Numi[sio Sabino]
[co(n)s(uli), VI]I vir(o) epul(onum) [leg(ato) Imp(eratoris) Hadri-]
[ani Aug(usti) p]r(o) pr(aetore) [p]rovin[ciae Iudaeae]
[--]

Die Inschrift steht auf dem Fragment einer Marmorsäule, auf der ursprünglich die Statue des Geehrten errichtet worden war. Geehrt wurde der Senator L. Cossonius Gallus Vecilius Crispinus Mansuanius Marcellinus Numisius Sabinus, der im Jahr 116 zum Konsulat gekommen war und kurz danach, spätestens um 120 n.Chr., die Leitung der Provinz Iudaea übernommen hatte, also kurz nach der großen Revolte der Juden in der Diaspora, von der aber auch die

---

[40] H.M. COTTON/W. ECK, Governors. Wenn in einigen englischen und amerikanischen Zeitungen bald nach Bekanntwerden des Fundes davon gesprochen wurde, das Gefängnis des Apostels Paulus sei gefunden, so ist dies allerdings haltlos, da der Raum mit dem Mosaik aus weit späterer Zeit stammt.
[41] CIL III 6813 = DESSAU 1038.
[42] Siehe H.M. COTTON/W. ECK, Governors, 219ff.

Provinz Iudaea betroffen worden war. Wer diesen Statthalter geehrt hat, ist nicht bekannt, da der Text nur fragmentarisch auf uns gekommen ist, so daß das Ende des Textes, wo der Dedikant erwähnt war, fehlt. Doch zeigt die Inschrift genug, um erkennen zu lassen, daß die typische Form der Ehrung eines römischen Senators hier Verwendung fand, indem nämlich alle Stationen seiner Laufbahn bis zu der aktuellen in der Provinz Iudaea aufgeführt wurden. Der allgemeinen Öffentlichkeit wurde somit gezeigt, welchen Rang der Geehrte erreicht hatte, wie er in die führende Elite des Reiches eingebunden war.

Die Spitze der politischen und sozialen Hierarchie nahm der Kaiser ein. Man muß voraussetzen, daß gerade die aufeinander folgenden Herrscher in zahlreichen Bildnisstatuen den Untertanen auch in der Provinz Iudaea sichtbar gemacht wurden. Bisher hat man allerdings keine frühen epigraphischen Zeugnisse dafür nachweisen können. Vor kurzem aber wurde in dem Corpus der Inschriften von Caesarea ein Text in Erinnerung gerufen, der bereits 1971 publiziert worden war und eine Dedikation an Vespasian darstellen soll; welche genauere Funktion die Inschrift gehabt haben soll, wird nicht erörtert.[43] Folgender Text wird geboten:

[Imp(eratori) Caesa(ri) Ves(pasiano) A]ug(usto) pon[t(ifici) max(imo)]
[---p(atri) p(atriae) co(n)]s(uli) VIII, cen[sori]
[---imp(eratori) XVI]I oder [XVII]I trib(unicia) pot(estate) V[I] oder V[III].

Sobald man das Photo des Fragments mit der Rekonstruktion vergleicht, wird deutlich, daß diese unmöglich zutreffen kann. Denn da die Buchstaben der ersten Zeile viel größer sind als die in den Zeilen 2 und 3, ist mit dem, was in diesen beiden Zeilen rekonstruiert werden muß, der vorhandene Platz nicht zu füllen.[44] Die Inschrift hat in Wirklichkeit ganz anders ausgesehen und zwar, ohne dies hier im Detail zu begründen,[45] etwa folgendermaßen:

[Imp.Caesar Vespasianus A]ug. pon[tif.max.]
[trib.potest VII imp.XVII co]s. VIII cen[sor p.p.]
[T. Caes. Aug. f. Vespasianus imp. XI]I trib. pot. V[cos. VI]
[censor]
[---].

Tatsächlich handelt es sich also nicht um eine Dedikation an Vespasian; vielmehr waren in dem Text Vespasian und Titus zusammen angeführt, jeweils mit der zugehörigen Titulatur. Sie erschienen auch nicht im Dativ, sondern im Nominativ, weil die Inschrift an einem Bauwerk angebracht gewesen war, dessen Errichtung die Kaiser angeordnet hatten, womit auch verbunden war, daß die kaiserliche Kasse die Finanzierung übernahm. Daß sich in Caesarea

---

[43] A. NEGEV, Inscriptions, 260f; C. M. LEHMANN/K. G. HOLUM, Inscriptions, Nr. 27.
[44] Dabei ist zu berücksichtigen, daß man den Namen Vespasianus in einer Ergänzung nicht so stark abkürzen darf, da dies in den erhaltenen Zeugnissen auch nicht geschieht oder zumindest nicht so stark. Man muß also Vespasianus ergänzen, wodurch die Zeile noch breiter wird.
[45] Siehe dazu meine Rezension des Buches in der Zeitschrift Topoi (in Vorbereitung).

ein solcher Inschriftentyp findet, ist auch gar nicht erstaunlich; waren doch durch Vespasian in der Stadt wesentliche Veränderungen eingetreten. Zum einen war, wie schon erwähnt, neben den neuen senatorischen Statthalter nunmehr ein ritterlicher Prokurator getreten, dessen Amtssitz erbaut werden mußte.[46] Zum andern war durch Vespasian Caesarea zu einer römischen Kolonie geworden, in der nach aller Wahrscheinlichkeit auch zahlreiche römische Veteranen angesiedelt wurden, wodurch überhaupt erst das lateinisch-römische Element in der Stadt so stark geworden ist, daß es sich überall im Leben der Kolonie bemerkbar machen konnte. Denn eine Kolonie sollte ja, wie Gellius, ein römischer Autor des 2. Jh. n. Chr., bemerkt, ein verkleinertes Abbild des römischen Volkes sein.[47] Für ein solches Abbild Roms haben die Gründer zumeist auch finanzielle Mittel bereit gestellt, um das neue Gemeinwesen mit allen notwendigen Einrichtungen auszustatten. So könnte das Gebäude, auf dessen Bauinschrift Vespasian und sein Sohn gemeinsam als die Urheber erscheinen, auch zur Erstausstattung der Kolonie gehört haben.[48]

Eine Ehrung des Kaisers mit einer Statue ist mit dem epigraphischen Dokument also nicht bezeugt. Die früheste, die wir in Caesarea, aber wohl auch in ganz Iudaea nachweisen können, stammt vermutlich aus dem Jahr 130, als Hadrian die Provinz besuchte und dabei durch eine Gruppe von Soldaten, die zum besonderen Dienst um den Statthalter abgeordnet waren, die sogenannten *beneficiarii consularis*, mit einer überlebensgroßen Statue geehrt wurde, wie wiederum eine fragmentarische Inschrift aus Caesarea beweist:[49]

[Imp. Caes(ari) divi Traiani Parth(ici) f(ilio), divi Nervae nep(oti) Traiano Hadriano] / Aug(usto) pont(ifici) ma[x(imo), tr(ibunicia) pot(estate) XIV(?), co(n)s(uli) III, p(atri) p(atriae)] / b(eneficiarii) Tinei Rufi [leg(ati) Aug(usti) pr(o) pr(aetore) --] / [---].

Später finden sich solche einfachen ehrenden Texte dann doch recht häufig auch im epigraphischen Material Iudaeas. Sie waren stets mit einer bildlichen Darstellung des Herrschers verbunden und stellten damit die unmittelbarste und direkteste Form der Repräsentation der römischen Herrschaft dar, versinnbildlicht in der Gestalt des Kaisers.

Für die meisten Provinzialen war der Kaiser eine weit entfernte Macht, deren Wirkung nur durch die Vermittlung seiner Repräsentanten erfahren wurde. Doch immer wieder kamen auch direkte Weisungen der kaiserlichen Majestät bis zu den Ohren und Augen der Untertanen. Solches kann man sich etwa beim ersten Census im provinzialisierten Iudaea im Jahr 6 n.Chr. vorstellen, als der kaiserliche Legat von Syrien, Sulpicius Quirinius, die sicherlich von Augustus direkt gegebene Anordnung zur Durchführung eines Census in der Provinz

---

[46] Siehe oben S. 30.
[47] Gell 16,13,9: *propter amplitudinem maiestatemque populi Romani, cuius istae coloniae quasi effigies parvae simulacraque esse quaedam videntur.*
[48] Später finden wir dann beispielsweise die Bauinschriften aus der Zeit Hadrians, die an dem Aquädukt angebracht waren, den Hadrian durch verschiedene Legionsvexillationen hatte erbauen lassen; siehe C.M. LEHMANN/K.G. HOLUM, Inscriptions, Nr. 45–54.
[49] Siehe H.M. COTTON/W. ECK, Governors, 235ff.

auch auf das eben an Syrien angeschlossene Gebiet von Iudaea ausdehnte. Vermutlich hat er den Erlaß des Caesar Augustus, wie es im Lukasevangelium heißt,[50] zusammen mit seinem Begleitbrief im Wortlaut ins Land der Juden gesandt,[51] wo er sodann durch Verlesen in allen Orten oder durch Veröffentlichung auf Papyrus bzw. auf geweißten Holztafeln bekannt gemacht wurde.[52] Diese Form der Publikation bedingt freilich, daß außerhalb Ägyptens solche Dokumente bis in unsere Zeit nur in verschwindend geringer Zahl erhalten geblieben sind. Nur wenn aus besonderem Grund, und zwar zumeist auf Initiative von einzelnen interessierten Leuten, ein kaiserlicher Erlaß auf dauerhaftes Material, d.h. im Osten auf Stein, im Westen häufiger auf Bronze, übertragen wurde, ergab sich die Chance, daß er die Zeiten überdauerte.[53] Dieses Prinzip galt für die Provinz Iudaea nicht weniger als für andere Reichsteile. Entsprechend ist uns bis heute nur ein einziger Erlaß eines römischen Herrschers in den ersten drei Jahrhunderten erhalten. Caesarea, die Provinzhauptstadt, in der zahllose Edikte der verschiedenen Kaiser publiziert worden sein müssen, hat bisher kein einziges Zeugnis dafür erbracht. Der erhaltene Erlaß, das Διάταγμα Καίσαρος ist auf eine Marmortafel geschrieben, die der Archäologe Froehner im Jahr 1878 in Nazareth erhalten hatte.[54] Wenn die Inschrift antik und nicht gefälscht ist, wovon man heute im allgemeinen ausgeht, dann fassen wir hier eine Regelung eines Kaisers zur Unverletzlichkeit aller Gräber. Wer dieser Caesar gewesen ist, konnte bis heute nicht definitiv geklärt werden. Doch wer auch immer das gewesen sein mag, das Edikt ist dann ein winziger, aber gewichtiger Reflex eines Mediums, durch das immer wieder die kaiserliche Macht mit den Provinzialen in Verbindung trat. Ein solches kaiserliches Wort lud freilich nicht zur Diskussion ein; es war vielmehr autoritative Anordnung, die absoluten Gehorsam forderte. Wer gegen das handelte, was in dem genannten Edikt vorgeschrieben wurde, mußte mit der Todesstrafe rechnen: Εἰ δὲ μή, τοῦτον ἐγὼ κεφαλῆς κατάκριτον ὀνόματι τυμβωρυχίας θέλω γενέσθαι = „Wer gegen meine Anordnung handelt, soll nach der Vorschrift über die Verletzung eines Grabes die Todesstrafe erleiden."

---

[50] Lk 2,1: δόγμα παρὰ Καίσαρος Αὐγούστου wird generell als Kaiser Augustus übersetzt, so wie es schon Luther getan hatte. Diese Übersetzung ist falsch und anachronistisch. Denn Caesar Augustus sind zwei *Namenselemente* aus dem Gesamtnamen des ersten Princeps: das *nomen gentile* Caesar und das *cognomen* Augustus; es handelt sich aber nicht um den Titel Kaiser. Man muß also schlicht übersetzen: „ein Gebot von Caesar Augustus".
[51] Vgl. H.M. COTTON, Ἐπαρχεία, 204–208.
[52] Siehe zu diesem Phänomen W. ECK, Inschriften, 203–217; DERS., Einleitung, 1–15 bes. 9ff.
[53] Siehe W. ECK, Documenti, 359–381.
[54] Siehe die letzten zusammenfassenden Arbeiten zu dem Text bei L. BOFFO, Iscrizioni, 319–333 und M. SORDI/E. GRZYBEK, Edit, 279–291; die beiden zuletzt genannten Autoren sehen in dem Caesar der Inschrift Kaiser Nero.

Das Militär als machtpolitischer Faktor

Was hier dem einzelnen Gesetzesbrecher angekündigt wurde, galt noch mehr dem gegenüber, der sich gegen die römische Macht insgesamt stellte. Kaum eines der vielen Völker im Imperium Romanum hat in so kurzer Zeit so oft gegen Rom revoltiert wie das jüdische: 66, 117 und 132 n. Chr. Die Folgen waren im Endeffekt verheerend. Denn die militärische Potenz Roms war zu groß für das kleine Volk der Juden. Seit dem Jahr 70 lag eine Bürgerlegion, die X Fretensis, in Jerusalem. Ihre Spuren finden sich im Land an vielen Stellen. Zahllos sind die Ziegel, die bei Ausgrabungen zu Tage kommen und mit ihrem Namen gestempelt sind.[55] In Abu Gosh ist eine große Steintafel mit dem Text:[56]

Vexillatio /leg(ionis) X Fretensis

in die Wand eines Brunnens vor der Kreuzfahrerkirche eingelassen. Wozu diese Tafel einst gehörte, ist bisher noch nicht erkannt. Doch hat die Legion sicher eine Baumaßnahme durchgeführt und dort ihren Namen verewigt. Möglicherweise war es ein Außenposten der Legion, der wie andere, die über das Land verstreut waren, für die Sicherheit der Provinz sorgen sollte. Neben der Legion standen eine ganze Reihe von Hilfstruppeneinheiten aus Kohorten von Fußsoldaten und berittenen Alen, so wie sie auch schon den Präfekten zur Verfügung gestanden hatten. Die Soldaten, die im Zusammenhang der Passionsgeschichte im Neuen Testament erwähnt werden, stammten aus solchen Hilfstruppeneinheiten. Nach dem Jahr 70 wurde die Zahl dieser Auxiliarformationen erhöht; ein Militärdiplom, das für einen Soldaten der *cohors II Thracum* ausgestellt wurde und mit dem ihm der Erhalt des römischen Bürgerrechts nach 25 Jahren Dienst bestätigt wurde, bezeugt für das Jahr 86 insgesamt sechs solcher Einheiten.[57] Ein neues, noch unpubliziertes Diplom aus dem Jahr 90 führt insgesamt neun Truppenteile an, zwei Alen und sieben Kohorten.[58]

Nicht immer haben freilich die Truppen in der Provinz genügt, um die Ruhe und Sicherheit zu gewährleisten. So war im Jahr 116/117 eine Abteilung der legio III Cyrenaica, deren Standquartier damals in Arabia oder noch in Ägypten lag,[59] in Jerusalem anwesend, wo sie *[I]ovi O(ptimo) M(aximo) Sarapidi pro salute et victoria* Kaisers Traians und des römischen Volkes einen Altar errichtete.[60] Möglicherweise war sie nach Iudaea gesandt worden, um dort die Auswirkungen des jüdischen Aufstandes in der Diaspora, der sich so verheerend auch für den Partherkrieg Traians erwiesen hatte, im Kernland des Ju-

---

[55] D. BARAG, Brick Stamp.
[56] AE 1902, 230 = 1926, 136.
[57] CIL XVI 33
[58] Dankenswerte Mitteilung von Ben Isaac und David MacDonald.
[59] Siehe zu dieser umstrittenen Frage jetzt P.-L. GATIER, Legio, 341–349 und H.M. COTTON, Legio, 351–357.
[60] CIL III 13587.

dentums zu bekämpfen. Nur diese Inschrift, die später in einer Wand im Lions-Gate in Jerusalem eingemauert wurde, hat die Überlieferung von diesem Einsatz bewahrt.

Ein Triumphbogen als Monument des Sieges

Kurze Zeit später, im Jahr 132, explodierte dann die innere Spannung, die sich in der Provinz angestaut hatte, erneut. Der Aufstand unter Führung von Bar Kochba war die schlimmste Herausforderung, die Rom von seiten des jüdischen Volkes zu bewältigen hatte. Der Statthalter, unter dem die Revolte ausbrach, war Tineius Rufus, der spätestens seit dem Jahr 130 bereits im Amt war.[61] Er hatte auch Frau und Tochter mit in die Provinz genommen, obwohl das nicht so gerne gesehen wurde. Beide Frauen wurden in Scythopolis mit Statuen geehrt;[62] es sind die ersten Statuenehrungen für Angehörige eines Statthalters, die bis jetzt aus Iudaea bekannt wurden. Inwieweit man daraus etwas für die allgemeine Stimmung in der Provinz schließen darf, kann erst die Publikation der Texte zeigen.

Ob Tineius Rufus der Aufstandsbewegung nicht Herr wurde oder ob er während der Kämpfe starb, läßt sich bisher nicht sagen. Sein Nachfolger bei der Niederkämpfung des Aufstandes wurde Sex. Iulius Severus, der aus Britannien nach Iudaea versetzt wurde, was ein deutliches Zeichen einer Notmaßnahme ist. Er erscheint bisher auf keinem epigraphischen Zeugnis aus der Provinz, obwohl er mindestens für zwei Jahre das große, aus allen Teilen des Reiches zusammengeholte Heer kommandierte. Ebensowenig sind bisher zwei andere Römer, die an der Niederschlagung des Aufstandes beteiligt waren, in den inschriftlichen Dokumenten aus der Provinz genannt: Q. Poblicius Marcellus, der damalige Statthalter von Syrien, und T. Haterius Nepos, Statthalter der östlich anschließenden Provinz Arabia. Sie nahmen so erfolgreich an den Kämpfen teil, daß Hadrian ihnen wie auch Iulius Severus die Triumphalabzeichen, die höchste militärische Auszeichnung Roms, verliehen hat. Schon diese völlig ungewöhnlichen Auszeichnungen für drei Kommandeure gleichzeitig zeigen, wie umfassend die Herausforderung für Rom war. Den eigentlichen Beweis dafür aber bietet ein außerordentliches epigraphisches Zeugnis, das in Fragmenten südlich von Scythopolis bei Tel Shalem entdeckt wurde. Eine Rekonstruktion der Inschrift ergibt folgenden Text:[63]

---

[61] Siehe oben den epigraphischen Text zu Anm. 49.
[62] Unpublizierte Texte.
[63] W. ECK/G. FOERSTER, Triumphbogen, 294–313.

IMP. CAE[S. DIVI T]RA[IANI PAR-]
TH[I]CI F. D[IVI NERVAE NEP. TR]AIANO [HADRIANO AUG.]
PON[T]IF. M[AX., TRIB. POT. XX ?, IMP. I]I, COS. [III, P. P. S. P. Q. R. ?].

Imp(eratori) Cae[s(ari) divi T]ra[iani Par-]/th[i]ci f(ilio) d[ivi Nervae nep(oti) Tr]aiano [Hadriano Aug(usto)]/pon[t]if(ici) m[ax(imo), trib(unicia) pot(estate) XX ?, imp(eratori) I]I, co(n)s(uli) [III, p(atri) p(atriae) S(enatus) P(opulus)q(ue) R(omanus) ?].

Der Text erstreckt sich über eine Breite von mehr als 10m. Eine Inschrift dieser Größe ist überhaupt nur bei einem Monumenttyp üblich, nämlich bei einem Bogen. Am Ende des Textes wurden *S(enatus) P(opulus)q(ue) R(omanus)*, also Senat und Volk von Rom als diejenigen ergänzt, die das monumentale Bauwerk errichten ließen. Wenn diese Ergänzung zutrifft, dann beweist der Text, daß für Hadrian südlich von Scythopolis, auf dessen Territorium sich sonst nur griechische Inschriften finden, ein gewaltiger Bogen erbaut wurde, mit einer lateinischen Inschrift, deren Buchstaben größer sind als alles, was man sonst in dieser Region kennt. Selbst die meisten Inschriften in Rom, der Hauptstadt des Reiches, können in der Monumentalität der Lettern nicht mithalten. Das aber sagt dann, daß man auch in Rom die Schwere des Aufstandes sehr wohl erkannt hat und dann nach der Überwältigung des Gegners diesem Triumph auch einen monumentalen Ausdruck zur Erinnerung an den Sieg gegeben hat. Beides, Inschrift und monumentaler Bogen, sind ein erneuter Beweis für die Einheit von Monument und Inschrift; nur zusammen können sie die Botschaft, die sie verkünden sollen, dem Publikum überbringen: Rom und sein Kaiser sind siegreich. Die Opfer des Triumphes wurden nicht einmal erwähnt. Sie konnten vergessen werden, so wie es auch die Inschrift auf dem Triumphbogen von Tel Shalem getan hat. Auch das Verschweigen war eine Botschaft.[64]

---

[64] W. ECK, Öffentlichkeit, 55–75.

Appendix

In diesem Beitrag wurde nur auf epigraphische Zeugnisse in lateinischer und griechischer Sprache verwiesen. Bei der Thematik, nämlich Inschriften als Zeugnisse der römischen Herrschaft, ist dies kaum anders zu erwarten. Denn beide Sprachen wurden von den Herrschenden selbst verwendet. Die Provinz Iudaea ist allerdings ein besonders klares Beispiel, wie unter römischer Herrschaft die lokalen und regionalen Sprachen nicht verdrängt wurden, sondern ihr Eigenleben führen konnten. Das gilt auch für die Verwendung dieser Sprachen in inschriftlichen Äußerungen. Neben lateinischen und griechischen Inschriften finden sich im regionalen Bereich der römischen Provinz Iudaea auch solche in hebräischer, aramäischer, samaritanischer, syrischer, nabatäischer und thamudischer Sprache. Will man Leben und kulturelle Äußerungen dieser Region in allen ihren Aspekten erfassen – jedenfalls soweit man sich dazu des Mediums der Inschriften bediente – dann genügt es also nicht, sich allein mit den Inschriften in den beiden Reichssprachen zu befassen, vielmehr müssen dann alle Texte, in welcher Sprache auch immer abgefaßt, eingeschlossen werden. Ein solcher Versuch scheitert bisher daran, daß es keine zusammenfassenden Sammlungen der einschlägigen Texte gibt, nicht einmal für Texte in einer der genannten Sprachen.

Deshalb hat sich eine Gruppe von israelischen und deutschen Forschern daran gemacht, diesem Manko für die Wissenschaft abzuhelfen. In Arbeit ist ein Corpus Inscriptionum Iudaeae/Palaestinae (CIIP), das von der Zeit Alexanders, also dem 4. Jh. v. Chr., bis zur Eroberung Palaestinas durch die Araber im 7. Jh. n. Chr. alle Texte erfassen soll, die in einer der angeführten Sprachen abgefaßt sind. Da kein Wissenschaftler alle diese Sprachen in der gleichen Kompetenz für die epigraphische Überlieferung beherrscht, haben sich bisher die folgenden Personen zusammengetan, um dieses Corpus zu erstellen: Hannah Cotton, Leah Di Segni, Werner Eck, Benjamin Isaac, Jonathan Price, Israel Roll, Alla Stein, Vasilios Tzaferis, Nurit Tsafrir, Yoram Tsafrir, Ada Yardeni. An der Hebrew University in Jerusalem und an der Universität zu Köln sind Archive im Aufbau, um das gesamte Material zu erfassen. Das Projekt wird von der German Israeli Foundation gefördert.[65]

---

[65] Siehe dazu auch: H.M. COTTON/L. DI SEGNI/W. ECK/B. ISAAC, Corpus, 307f. Um mit den Bearbeitern des Corpus Kontakt aufzunehmen, bediene man sich folgender e-mail Adressen: Für Jerusalem: corpus@h2.hum.huji.ac.il; für Köln: Werner.Eck@uni-koeln.de.

Literatur

ALFÖLDY, Geza, Römische Statuen in Venetia et Histria. Epigraphische Quellen, AHAW.PH 3. Abh., Heidelberg 1984.

DERS., Epigraphische Notizen aus Kleinasien I. Ein beneficium des Augustus in Ephesos, in: ZPE 87 (1991), 157–162

DERS., Pontius Pilatus und das Tiberieum von Caesarea Maritima, in: SCI 18 (1999), 85–108.

DERS., *Pietas immobilis erga pricipem* und ihr Lohn: Öffentliche Ehrenmonumente von Senatoren in Rom während der Frühen und Hohen Kaiserzeit, in: Geza ALFÖLDY/Silvio PANCIERA, Inschriftliche Denkmäler als Medien der Selbstdarstellung in der römischen Welt, Heidelberg 2001, 11ff.

DERS./PANCIERA, Silvio, Inschriftliche Denkmäler als Medien der Selbstdarstellung in der römischen Welt, Heidelberg 2001.

BARAG, D., Brick Stamp Impressions of the Legio X Fretensis, in: BJ 167 (1967), 244–267.

BOFFO, L., Iscrizioni Greche e Latine per lo studio della bibbia, Brescia 1994, 283–290.

COTTON, Hannah M./GEIGER, Joseph, The Latin and Greek Documents. Masada II. The Yigael Yadin Excavations 1963–1965. Final Reports, Jerusalem 1989, 149–160 Nr. 804–818.

DIES./ECK, Werner, Ein Staatsmonopol und seine Folgen. Plinius, Naturalis Historia 12, 123 und der Preis für Balsam, in: RhM 140 (1997), 153–161.

DIES., Ἡ νέα ἐπαρχεία ’Αράβια: The New Province of Arabia in the papyri from the Judaean Desert, in: ZPE 116 (1997), 204–208.

DIES./DI SEGNI, Leah/ECK, Werner/ISAAC, Ben, Corpus Inscriptionum Iudaeae/Palaestinae, in: ZPE 127 (1999), 307f.

DIES., Some Aspects of Roman Administration of Judaea/Syria Palestina, in: Werner ECK (Hg.), Lokale Autonomie und römische Ordnungsmacht in den kaiserzeitlichen Provinzen vom 1. bis 3. Jahrhundert, München 1999, 75–91.

DIES., La *Legio VI Ferrata*, in: Les Légions de Rome sous le Haut-Empire. Actes du congres de Lyon 17–19 sept 1998. 2 vols, hg. Yann LE BOHEC/C. WOLFF, Lyon 2000, 351–357.

DIES./ECK, Werner, Governors and their Personnel on Latin Inscriptions from Caesarea Maritima, in: The Israel Academy of Sciences and Humanities. Proceedings vol. VII no. 7, Jerusalem 2001, 215–240.

DIES., Josephus and the Representatives of the (Roman) Ruling Power in Judaea, (in Vorbereitung).

DĄBROWA, Edward, The Governors of Roman Syria from Augustus to Septimius Severus, Bonn 1998.

DESSAU, Hermann, Inscriptiones Latinae Selectae, ND Berlin 1962.

ECK, Werner, Senatoren von Vespasian bis Hadrian. Prosopographische Untersuchungen mit Einschluß der Jahres- und Provinzialfasten der Statthalter, München 1970.

DERS., Ehrungen für Personen hohen soziopolitischen Ranges im öffentlichen und privaten Bereich, in: Die römische Stadt im 2. Jh. n.Chr., Koll. in Xanten vom 2. Mai bis 4. Mai 1990, hg. Hans-Joachim SCHALLES/Henner VON HESBERG/Paul ZANKER, Köln 1992, 359–376.

DERS., Lateinische Epigraphik, in: Fritz GRAF (Hg.), Einleitung in die lateinische Philologie, Stuttgart – Leipzig 1997, 92–111.

DERS., Documenti amministrativi: Pubblicazione e mezzo di autorappresentazione, in: Epigrafia Romana in Area Adriatica, Actes de la IXe rencontre franco-italienne sur l'épigraphie du monde Romain, Macerata 1995, hg. von Gianfranco PACI, Ichnia 2, Pisa u.a. 1998, 343–366 = in: DERS., Die Verwaltung des römischen Reiches in der Hohen Kaiserzeit. Ausgewählte und erweiterte Beiträge, Bd. 2, hg. Regula FREI-STOLBA und Michael A. SPEIDEL, Basel 1998, 359–381.

DERS., Inschriften auf Holz. Ein unterschätztes Phänomen der epigraphischen Kultur Roms, in: Imperium Romanum. Studien zu Geschichte und Rezeption, FS Karl Christ zum 75. Geburtstag. Hg. Peter KNEISSL u. Volker LOSEMANN, Stuttgart 1998, 203–217.

DERS., Rom und die Provinz Iudaea/Syria Palaestina: Der Beitrag der Epigraphik, in: Jüdische Geschichte in hellenistisch-römischer Zeit. Wege der Forschung: Vom alten zum neuen Schürer, hg. von Aharon OPPENHEIMER, München 1999, 237–263.

DERS., Zur Einleitung. Römische Provinzialadministration und die Erkenntnismöglichkeiten der epigraphischen Überlieferung, in: DERS., Lokale Autonomie und römische Ordnungsmacht in den kaiserzeitlichen Provinzen vom 1. bis 3. Jahrhundert, München 1999, 1–15.

DERS., Sextus Lucilius Bassus, der Eroberer von Herodium, in einer Bauinschrift aus Abu Gosh, in: SCI 18 (1999), 109–18; 119–120.

DERS., Öffentlichkeit, Monument und Inschrift, in: Akten des 11. Intern. Kongresses für Griech. u. Lat. Epigraphik, Rom 1997, hg. von Silvio PANCIERA, Rom 1999, 55–75.

DERS., Latein als Sprache politischer Kommunikation in Städten der östlichen Provinzen, in: Chiron 30 (2000), 641–660.

DERS., Ein Spiegel der Macht. Lateinische Inschriften römischer Zeit in Iudaea/Syria Palaestina, in: ZDPV 117 (2000), 47–63.

DERS., New Inscriptions from Caesarea Maritima in Iudaea/Syria Palaestina Final Report, hg. J. Patrick (in Vorbereitung).

DERS./FOERSTER, Gideon, Ein Triumphbogen für Hadrian im Tal von Beth Shean bei Tel Shalem, in: JRA 12 (1999), 294–313.

ERKELENZ, Dirk, Ehrungen der Amtsträger römischer Provinzen vom 2 Jh. v. Chr. bis ins 3. Jh. n. Chr., Diss. Köln 2000 (in Druckvorbereitung).

FENATI, M. F., Lucio Flavio Silva Nonio Basso e la Città di Urbisaglia, Macerata 1995.

FISCHER, Moshe/ISAAC, Ben/ROLL, Isaac, Roman Roads in Judaea II. The Jaffa-Jerusalem Roads, Oxford 1996.

GATIER, P.-L., La *Legio III Cyrenaica* et l'Arabie, in: Les Légions de Rome sous le Haut-Empire. Actes du congres de Lyon 17–19 sept 1998. 2 vols, hg. Yann LE BOHEC/C. WOLFF, Lyon 2000, 341–349.

GEIGER, Joseph, Titulus crucis, in: SCI 15 (1996), 202–207.

HACHLILI, Rachel, The Goliath Family in Jericho: Funerary Inscriptions from a First-Century A.D. Jewish Monumental Tomb, Bull. of the Americ. School of Orient. Research 235, (1979), 31ff.

HOLUM, Kenneth G., The Temple Platform. Progress Report on the Excavations, in: Kenneth G. HOLUM/Avner RABAN/Joseph PATRICH (eds.), Caesarea Papers 2. Herod's Temple, The Provincial Governor's Praetorium and Granaries, the Later Harbor, a Gold Coin Hoard and Other Studies, Journal of Roman Archaeology, Supplement Series 35, Portsmouth 1999, 12–34

ISAAC, Benjamin H./ROLL, Israel, A Milestone of A.D. 69 from Judaea: The Elder Trajan and Vespasian, in: JRS 66 (1976), 15–19 = in: ISAAC, Benjamin H., The Near East under Roman Rule: Selected Papers, Leiden 1998, 36–45.

DIES., Roman Roads in Judaea I. The Legio - Scythopolis Roads, London 1982.

ISAAC, Benjamin H./GICHON, Mordechai, A Flavian Inscription from Jerusalem, in: IEJ 24 (1974), 117f.
LEHMANN, Clayton M. – HOLUM, Kenneth G., The Greek and Latin Inscriptions of Caesarea Maritima, Boston 2000 (Manuskriptabschluß 1995, mit einigen späteren Zusätzen).
MAIER, P. L., The Inscription on the Cross of Jesus of Nazareth, in: Hermes 124 (1996), 58–75.
NEGEV, Avraham, Inscriptions hébraiques, grecques et latines de Césarée Maritime, in: RB 78, (1971), 247–263.
PETZL, Georg, Griechische Epigraphik, in: Heinz-Günther NESSELRATH (Hg.), Einleitung in die griechische Philologie, Stuttgart – Leipzig 1997, 72–83.
SCHÄFER, Thomas, Imperii Insignia: Sella curulis und fasces. Zur Repräsentation römischer Magistrate, Mainz 1989.
SORDI, M/GRZYBEK, E., L'Edit de Nazareth et la politique de Néron à l'égard des chrétiens, in: ZPE 120 (1998), 279–291.
SYME, Ronald, Antonius Saturninus, in: JRS 68 (1978), 12–21.
VINCENT, H., Église Byzantine et inscription Romaine à Abou-Ghoch, in: RB 4 (1907), 414ff.

Markus Öhler

Römisches Vereinsrecht und christliche Gemeinden

1   Römische Bestimmungen über Vereine im 1. und 2. Jahrhundert

Grundsätzlich bestand in republikanischer Zeit das Recht zu freier Vereinsgründung bzw. Vereinsautonomie bei gleichzeitiger Beachtung allgemein gültigen Rechts. Im Zwölftafelgesetz wird bezüglich Vereinen festgehalten (8,27):

> His (*sodalibus*) *autem potestatem facit lex pactionem quam velint sibi ferre, dum ne quid ex publica lege corrumpant* (Gaius, Dig 47,22,4).
> Vereinsmitglieder haben das Recht (die Macht), sich selbst jede Regel zu geben, vorausgesetzt es widerspricht nicht öffentlichem Recht.[1]

Da sich aus dieser frühen Zeit kein Verbot von Vereinen o.ä. findet, ist wohl anzunehmen, daß generell Vereinsfreiheit bestand.[2] Die tolerante Haltung der Staatsführung änderte sich allerdings, als während des Bürgerkriegs auch politische Vereine und vereinsähnliche Schlägertrupps eine wichtige Rolle spielten.[3] Sie wurden sämtlich aufgelöst durch ein *senatus consultum* aus dem Jahr 64 v.Chr.:[4]

---

[1] Gaius setzt voran eine Erklärung des Sprachgebrauchs: *Sodales sunt, qui eiusdem collegii sunt: quam Graeci ἑταιρείαν vocant.* Cf. dazu v.a. F.M. AUSBÜTTEL, Untersuchungen, 16ff: „Für die römischen Vereine sind rund fünfzig verschiedene Bezeichnungen überliefert – eine Tatsache, die nicht zu erstaunen braucht, wenn berücksichtigt wird, daß den Römern ein allgemeinverbindlicher Vereinsbegriff fehlte" (17); ähnlich J.S. KLOPPENBORG, Collegia, 18ff. Es ist daher auch nicht zielführend, aufgrund der Terminologie verschiedene Vereine zu unterscheiden; so etwa auch O.M. VAN NIJF, World, 9f.

[2] Die Stelle bei Dionysius Halicarnassus, wonach der letzte König Tarquinius Superbus die Versammlungsfreiheit aufgelöst habe (Ant Rom 4,43,2; cf. auch Liv 39,15,11), ist nicht auf Vereine zu beziehen und gewiß auch nicht als historisch zutreffend zu werten (cf. etwa E. KORNEMANN, Collegium, 404; M. RADIN, Legislation, 69f). Sie zeigt aber immerhin, daß die Aufhebung dieser grundlegenden republikanischen Freiheit für einen Autor während des beginnenden Prinzipats (Dionysius veröffentlichte seine röm. Geschichte im Jahr 7 v.Chr.) eine typisch tyrannische Handlung war. Auch die sicherlich unhistorische – wenn auch wohl traditionelle – Konstruktion, wonach Numa (Plut Num 17,1ff) bzw. Servius Tullius (Flor 1,6,3) die Handwerkerkollegien eingerichtet hätten (cf. schon Plin Nat Hist 34,1,1; 35,46,159), demonstriert die Hochschätzung zumindest des beruflichen Vereinswesens; cf. dazu insgesamt M. COHN, Vereinsrecht, 21ff; W. LIEBENAM, Geschichte, 3ff; M. RADIN, Legislation, 63ff.

[3] Zuvor waren schon im Jahr 186 v.Chr. die Bacchusvereine rigoros eingeschränkt worden (CIL I² No. 581); cf. dazu M. RADIN, Legislation, 72ff; G. KRÜGER, Rechtsstellung, 11ff; F.M. DE ROBERTIS, Storia I, 56ff. Die Darstellung bei Livius (39,8,3ff) wird allerdings

Senatus consulto collegia sublata sunt, quae adversus rem publicam videbatur esse.[5]

Auf Beschluß des Senats sind alle Vereine aufgelöst, die als gegen den Staat gerichtet erscheinen.

Der Grundsatz, daß Staatsinteressen durch Vereine nicht gefährdet werden dürften, blieb auch für die folgende Zeit grundlegend.[6] Einem späteren Senatsbeschluß bzw. einer Reihe von Beschlüssen[7] läßt sich zusätzlich die Bestimmung entnehmen, daß die Vereine dem öffentlichen Nutzen dienen sollten (*quae utilitas civitatis desiderasset*).[8] Nach einer Zwischenphase genereller Vereinsfreiheit unter Clodius (Dio Cass 38,13,1f),[9] kam es zu neuen Verboten im Jahr 56 v.Chr.[10] sowie in der *lex Licinia de sodaliciis* (55 v.Chr.).[11] Dabei

---

jetzt bezüglich ihres historischen Wertes kritischer beurteilt, sie gibt aber zumindest einen Einblick in die Einschätzung von Vereinen, deren kultische und ethische Praxis Anstoß erregte (cf. dazu zuletzt H. CANCIK-LINDEMAIER, Diskurs, 77ff; siehe dazu auch unten Anm. 23 und 52). Die Einschränkung bezüglich der Bacchusvereine ist m.E. nicht im Zusammenhang mit einer generellen Vereinsregelung zu sehen. Zu überlegen ist allerdings, ob die Darstellung des Livius aus Augusteischer Zeit sich als Folie für die Beurteilung der Christen bei Tacitus oder Plinius verstehen läßt; cf. dazu u.a. W.H.C. FREND, Martyrdom, 109ff; H. CANCIK-LINDEMAIER, Diskurs, 93f.

[4] Cf. dazu M. COHN, Vereinsrecht, 39ff; W. LIEBENAM, Geschichte, 20ff; M. RADIN, Legislation, 76ff; F.M. DE ROBERTIS, Storia I, 83ff; J. LINDERSKI, Senat, 94ff; F.M. AUSBÜTTEL, Untersuchungen, 87 Anm. 11. Cf. auch die Erwähnungen dieses Beschlusses bei Cic Piso 9 (dazu unten Anm. 9).

[5] Asconius zu Cicero Piso 8 (ed. CLARK 7). Zur Datierung cf. W. LIEBENAM, Geschichte, 21f.

[6] Cf. etwa J. LINDERSKI, Senat, 97; F.M. AUSBÜTTEL, Untersuchungen, 88; U. FELLMETH, Vereine, 33. Ein besonderer Dorn im Auge waren dabei die so genannten *collegia compitalicia*, die aus Sklaven und Freigelassenen bestanden und unter anderem als Schlägertrupps dienten. Mit ihnen gemeinsam wurden auch die entsprechenden Feiern zu Ehren der *Laren* verboten. Cf. dazu etwa W. LIEBENAM, Geschichte, 24f; J. LINDERSKI, Senat, 101ff; F. BÖMER, Religion I, 35ff; F.M. AUSBÜTTEL, Untersuchungen, 89f; U. FELLMETH, Vereine, 34. Augustus führte die Feiern der *Compitalia* – wenn auch in veränderter Form (cf. D. KIENAST, Augustus, 196f) – wieder ein (Suet Aug 31,4). Daß die entsprechenden Kollegien auch schon vor Augustus belegt sind (F. BÖMER, Religion I, 37f), läßt manches über die laxe Anwendung von Vereinsverboten erahnen, die sich in der späteren Kaiserzeit fortsetzte.

[7] So J. LINDERSKI, Senat, 97f; F.M. AUSBÜTTEL, Untersuchungen, 88 Anm.17; anders etwa W. LIEBENAM, Geschichte, 23.

[8] Asconius zu Cicero, Corn 67 (ed. CLARK 75). Asconius führt als Beispiele dafür zwei Berufskollegien – *(collegia) fabrorum fictorumque* „Handwerker und Bildhauer" – an.

[9] Cf. auch Asconius zu Cicero, Piso 8. Cicero polemisierte ausdrücklich dagegen: *Conlegia non ea solum quae senatus sustulerat restituta, sed innumerabilia quaedam noua ex omni faece urbis ac seruitio concitata* (Piso 9; ed. GRIMAL 97). „Es wurden nicht nur die Vereine, die der Senat verboten hatte, wiedererrichtet, sondern unzählige neue gegründet mit Hilfe des städtischen Gesindels jeder Art und der Sklaven."; cf. auch Sest 34.55; Red Sen 13,33; Red Quir 5,13. Cicero hatte freilich auch selbst erfolgreich Vereine für seine Wahl zum Konsul mobilisiert; cf. F.M. AUSBÜTTEL, Untersuchungen, 85ff.

[10] Bei Cic Quint Fr 2,3,5: *senatus consultum factum est ut sodalitates decuriatique discederent lexque de iis ferretur, ut qui non discessissent ea poena quae est de vi tenerentur* (ed. BAILEY 44) „Es erging ein Senatsbeschluß, die Vereinigungen und politi-

ging es jeweils um politische Vereine, die als Gefahr für den Frieden verstanden wurden. Das grundsätzliche Verbot führte aber dazu, daß in weiterer Folge alle Vereinigungen mit Skepsis betrachtet wurden. Stets standen sie unter dem Verdacht der politischen Umtriebe, was sich in der Kaiserzeit fortsetzte.[12]

Von *Julius Cäsar* sind mehrere Bestimmungen zu Vereinen überliefert:

Cuncta collegia praeter antiquitus constituta distraxit (Suet Caes 42,3; ed. ROLFE 58).
Er hat alle Vereine aufgelöst, ausgenommen die von Alters her bestehenden.

Aus dieser knappen Notiz wird deutlich, daß es zwei Kategorien von Vereinen gab: alte und neue. Unter die *collegia antiqua* sind wohl jene Vereine zu zählen, die trotz der mit dem *senatus consultum* aus dem Jahr 64 v.Chr. beschlossenen Vereinsbeschränkung weiter bestanden, weil sie politisch nicht gefährlich waren.[13] Bei jenen, die von Cäsar aufgelöst wurden, handelte es sich dann wohl um Vereine, die aufgrund der Wiederzulassung unter Clodius und später entstanden waren und politische Unruheherde bilden konnten.[14]

Unter den weiterhin bestehenden Vereinen waren auch die jüdischen Synagogen. In einem Brief an die Parianer bei Jos Ant 14,213–216, heißt es:[15]

καὶ γὰρ Γάιος Καῖσαρ ὁ ἡμέτερος στρατηγὸς [καὶ] ὕπατος ἐν τῷ διατάγματι κωλύων θιάσους συνάγεσθαι κατὰ πόλιν μόνους τούτους οὐκ ἐκώλυσεν οὔτε χρήματα συνεισφέρειν οὔτε σύνδειπνα ποιεῖν (Ant 14,215; ed. NIESE III 279).
Denn auch Gajus Cäsar, unser Konsul und Prätor, verbot in einem Edikt den Vereinen in der Stadt zusammenzukommen, allein diesen (den Juden) verbot er es nicht, auch nicht das Einsammeln von Geld oder gemeinsame Mahlzeiten.

---

schen Abteilungen sollten sich auflösen und ein Gesetzesantrag eingebracht werden des Inhalts, daß diejenigen, die sich nicht auflösten, mit der auf Gewalttat stehenden Strafe belegt werden sollten"; ähnlich Plan 18,45; cf. dazu W. LIEBENAM, Geschichte, 25f; F.M. DE ROBERTIS, Storia I, 116ff; E.S. GRUEN, Generation, 229; U. FELLMETH, Vereine, 35.

[11] Bei Cic Plan 15,36; cf. dazu W. LIEBENAM, Geschichte, 26f; F.M. DE ROBERTIS, Storia I, 129ff; E.S. GRUEN, Generation, 230f; F.M. AUSBÜTTEL, Untersuchungen, 91f. E.S. GRUEN, Generation, 228ff, gibt zu bedenken, daß das Vereinsverbot, auch wenn es nur staatsgefährdende Gruppen treffen sollte, auch als Einschränkung der bürgerlichen Rechte interpretiert werden konnte.

[12] F. BÖMER, Religion I, 36: Die „Tendenz zur Unterwanderung und zum politischen Mißbrauch der *collegia* argwöhnten die Behörden seit dem Bacchanalienskandal, und dieser Argwohn bestand unvermindert noch zur Zeit Trajans."

[13] Man wird vor allem an die alten religiösen Vereinigungen zu denken haben, die für die römischen Sakralfeierlichkeiten von Bedeutung waren (cf. den Überblick bei J.H. WASZINK, Genossenschaft, 102f).

[14] So schon M. COHN, Vereinsrecht, 70f; cf. auch U. FELLMETH, Vereine, 37. Anders etwa M. RADIN, Legislation, 91, der meint, es wären bei Sueton die Dionysosvereine gemeint.

[15] Zu dem Brief cf. etwa auch E. SCHÜRER, History III/1, 116; E.M. SMALLWOOD, Jews, 134f; T. RAJAK, Charter, 113f; W. COTTER, Collegia, 77f; L.V. RUTGERS, Policy, 94.

Der Josephustext spricht von einem Edikt, in dem Cäsar die Zusammenkunft von Vereinen – nicht nur religiösen – in der Stadt Rom verboten habe.[16] Lediglich den Juden waren weitere Zusammenkünfte sowie das Sammeln von Geld und gemeinsame Mähler erlaubt.[17] Ihnen war also Freiheit in der Ausübung ihres Vereinswesens gegeben. Für unsere Fragestellung ist neben den besonderen Privilegien, die Cäsar den Juden aus politischen Gründen gewährte,[18] von Bedeutung, daß er sie als Ausnahme betrachtete. Für die römischen Behörden galten die jüdischen Gemeinden in Rom offensichtlich als *collegia antiqua*.[19] Der bei Sueton verwendete Plural weist freilich darauf hin, daß die Juden – entgegen dem Text bei Josephus – beileibe nicht die einzigen geduldeten Vereine waren.

Ebenfalls bei Sueton finden wir einen Text, der von Regelungen unter *Augustus* berichtet:

Plurimae factiones titulo collegi novi ad nullius non facinoris societatem coibant. igitur grassaturas dispositis per opportuna loca stationibus inhibuit, ergastula recognovit, collegia praeter antiqua et legitima dissolvit (Aug 32,1; ed. ROLFE 172ff.).

Es bildeten sich auch viele Vereinigungen unter dem Namen eines neuen Vereins zu dem Zweck, alle denkbaren Verbrechen gemeinschaftlich zu begehen. Daher gebot er (Augustus) durch die Aufstellung von Wachen an geeigneten Orten der Wegelagerei Einhalt, er kontrollierte die Arbeitshäuser, er löste die Vereine mit Ausnahme der alten und rechtmäßigen auf.

Vereine werden in diesem Text im selben Atemzug mit Räuberbanden genannt, woraus m.E. deutlich wird, daß es sich bei den von Augustus aufgelösten *collegia* nicht um religiöse oder beruflich motivierte Zusammenschlüsse handelte, sondern um staatsgefährdende Verbindungen, die sich unter dem Schutzmantel des Vereinsrechtes konstituierten.[20] Die „neuen" Vereine, die nicht aufgelöst wurden, scheinen nun aber nicht unkontrolliert gegründet worden zu sein, sondern sind in diesem Text unter den *collegia legitima* zu verste-

---

[16] Es handelt sich mithin nicht um ein Edikt, das die jüdischen Vereine bestätigte (so etwa T. RAJAK, Charter, 113). Auch von einer Geltung dieser Erlaubnis im gesamten Imperium (so E.M. SMALLWOOD, Jews, 134) ist nicht die Rede, sondern lediglich von einer Regelung in Rom, die vom mysischen Parion übernommen werden soll.

[17] Der Zweck der Sammlungen ist nicht eindeutig: Handelt es sich um die Tempelabgabe oder um Gelder für den Aufwand gemeinsamer Mahlzeiten? Die drei genannten Elemente des jüdischen Lebens – regelmäßige Treffen, Geldsammlungen und Gemeinschaftsmähler – sind im Übrigen gerade nicht typisch jüdisch, sondern entsprechen den Gebräuchen in den meisten Vereinen.

[18] Die Juden hatten im Krieg mit Pompeius auf Cäsars Seite gestanden und zählten daher zu denen, die er als seine Verbündeten wußte. Cf. dazu etwa E.M. SMALLWOOD, Jews, 135; K.L. NOETHLICHS, Judentum, 15f.

[19] Cf. P. RICHARDSON, Synagogues 93. Die Frage, ob die verschiedenen jüdischen Gemeinden einzeln lizensiert wurden, ist wohl zu verneinen (so auch H. BOTERMANN, Judenedikt, 119f Anm. 373), dennoch galten sie wohl als einzelne Kollegien.

[20] Die Maßnahmen des Augustus werden allerdings nicht ausdrücklich als Wiederaufnahme der Bestimmungen Cäsars beschrieben, cf. W. COTTER, Collegia, 78; anders J. LINDERSKI, Bericht, 328.

hen. Einen Hinweis auf das entsprechende Gesetz[21] finden wir in einer Inschrift aus Augusteischer Zeit:

> Dis manibus. | Collegio symphonia|corum qui sacris publi|cis praestu sunt, quibus | senatus c(orpus) c(oire) c(onvocari) permisit e | lege Iulia ex auctoritate | Aug(usti) ludorum causa.[22]
> Den göttlichen Manen. Dem Verein der Musiker, die sich für die heiligen öffentlichen Feiern zur Verfügung stellen und denen der Senat die Erlaubnis gegeben hat, sich als Verein zu versammeln und zusammengerufen zu werden, aufgrund der *lex Iulia* auf Geheiß des Augustus, wegen der Spiele.

Wesentlich ist an diesem Text für unsere Frage vor allem, daß der Verein eine formale Zulassung erhalten hatte und zwar durch den Senat im Auftrag des Augustus.[23] Ein weiteres wichtiges Element war die Feststellung eines öffentlichen Nutzens (*ludorum causa*), ein Aspekt, der auch schon in republikanischer Zeit offenbar eine Rolle gespielt hatte (siehe Seite 52). Die wesentlichen Grundlagen der Vereinsgesetzgebung waren damit geschaffen. Die *lex Iulia* galt allerdings entsprechend der Notiz bei Sueton für neu gegründete Vereine, da die älteren ja aufgrund ihres Alters Legitimität gewonnen hatten und nur bei staatsgefährdenden Aktivitäten von Auflösung betroffen waren. Die jüdischen Gemeinden, die sowohl als landsmannschaftliche wie als religiöse Vereinigungen betrachtet werden konnten, blieben von den Bestimmungen daher unberührt, zumal Augustus die jüdischen Vorrechte, die Cäsar gewährt hatte, bestätigte (Jos Ant 16,162ff).[24] Problematischer war dies aber sicherlich im Blick auf etliche neue Kulte, die sich in Rom als Vereine organisierten.[25] Augustus war entsprechend seiner Religionspolitik hier besonders vorsichtig.[26]

---

[21] Für die Bezugnahme auf ein besonderes Vereinsgesetz cf. u.a. J. LINDERSKI, Bericht, 324f; F.M. DE ROBERTIS, Storia I, 212; anders etwa M. RADIN, Legislation, 93f, der auf die *lex Iulia de vi publica* verweist.

[22] CIL VI No.2193 (= No.4416 bzw. ILS No.4966). Zur Auflösung von CCC cf. F.M. DE ROBERTIS, Storia I, 197f Anm.6.

[23] Bewilligung durch den Senat war schon 186 v.Chr. für die Abhaltung von Bacchusfeiern vorgeschrieben worden (CIL I² No. 581). Der Verweis auf ein Julisches Gesetz meint wohl eine Bestimmung, die auf Cäsar selbst zurückgeht; so etwa D. KIENAST, Augustus, 104 Anm. 80 (mit Datierung des Durchführungserlasses des Augustus auf 23/22 v.Chr.); W. COTTER, Collegia, 78; anders z.B. M. KASER, Privatrecht, 308; F.M. AUSBÜTTEL, Untersuchungen, 92. Mir scheint der Bezug bei Sueton auf die zur Zeit des Augustus bereits bestehenden legitimen Vereine darauf hinzuweisen, daß das Zulassungsgesetz älter ist.

[24] Zu kaiserlichen Privilegien bei Vereinen cf. auch BGU IV No.1074 (= P.Agon No.1; Oxyrhynchos, 273/274 n.Chr.; cf. dazu auch M. SAN NICOLÒ, Vereinswesen II/1, 15): Dem weltweiten Verein der Künstler (Techniten) hatte, wie diese stolz anführen, bereits Augustus Privilegien gewährt, die von den folgenden Kaisern wie Claudius, Hadrian und den Severern bestätigt wurden (ähnlich P.Lond III No.1178 = P.Agon No.6). Künstler- und Athletenvereine hatten schon im 1. Jhd. v. Chr. eine besondere Stellung.

[25] Cf. etwa M. COHN, Vereinsrecht, 75f; G. LA PIANA, Groups, 225ff; W.H.C. FREND, Martyrdom, 108f. Zur Attraktivität orientalischer Kulte in Rom cf. u.a. F. CUMONT, Religionen, 18ff; H.S. VERSNEL, Religion, 41ff. Das beste Beispiel dafür sind die Maßnahmen gegen den Isis und Serapis-Kult, der sich auch in Kollegien organisierte (cf. dazu S.A. TAKÁCS, Isis, 75ff).

Von *Tiberius* sind zwar keine ausdrücklichen vereinsrechtlichen Bestimmungen überliefert, er setzte aber wohl die kritische Linie seines Vorgängers fort. Gegenüber fremden Religionen verhielt er sich feindlich, ließ sie verbieten sowie viele Anhänger aus Rom exilieren.[27] Dies bedeutete gleichzeitig auch die Auflösung der verschiedenen *collegia*, in denen sich die Anhänger organisiert hatten.

Für die Zeit des Tiberius haben wir allerdings aus Ägypten den Bericht des Philo, wonach der Statthalter Flaccus die Genossenschaften und Vereine – nach Philo Orte der Trunkenheit und des Aufruhrs – auflöste und hart gegen ihre Mitglieder vorging.[28] Daß von diesen Vereinen eine politische Gefahr ausging, beschreibt der Alexandriner später ausführlicher (Flacc 136ff). Isidorus bediente sich nämlich jener Vereine, die eine große Mitgliederzahl hatten, und führte in den meisten selbst den Vorsitz. Auf seinen Befehl hin hätten diese Vereine stets seine Anliegen unterstützt, bis Flaccus dem Treiben seines Widersachers ein Ende bereitet habe. Damit haben wir einen ersten Bericht über das Vorgehen gegen politisch gefährliche Vereine in den Provinzen.

Gaius Caligula ließ offenbar eine so große Anzahl von Vereinsgründungen zu, daß *Claudius* dies (wohl im Jahr 41) wieder rückgängig machte (Dio Cass 60,6,6). Typischerweise führt Dio Cassius dies im Zusammenhang mit der Untersagung jüdischer Zusammenkünfte an.[29] Beides, die Auflösung der Kollegien sowie das Versammlungsverbot für die jüdischen Gemeinden, war dadurch motiviert, daß diese die Ordnung des Staates störten bzw. sogar politisch gefährlich werden konnten.[30] Daß deshalb religiösen Bedürfnissen unter Um-

---

[26] Cf. W. COTTER, Collegia, 79. Dio Cassius läßt daher Maecenas dem Augustus den Rat geben, jene zu verfolgen, die mit neuen Gottheiten die alten ersetzen wollen, so daß Verschwörungen, Zusammenschlüsse und Vereine (συνωμοσίαι καὶ συστάσεις ἑταιρεῖαί τε) entstünden (52,36,1f).

[27] Suet Tib 36; Tac Ann 2,85. Das Vorgehen gegen den Isis und Serapis-Kult (Jos Ant 18,66ff) illustriert dies augenfällig; cf. S.A. TAKÁCS, Isis, 83ff. Die Maßnahmen waren freilich nicht von allzu langer Gültigkeit, da sich sowohl Juden wie Isisverehrer bald wieder in Rom fanden.

[28] Philo Flacc 4: τὰς τε ἑταιρείας καὶ συνόδους, αἳ ἀεὶ ἐπὶ προφάσει θυσιῶν εἰστιῶντο τοῖς πράγμασιν ἐμπαροινοῦσαι, διέλυε τοῖς ἀφηνιάζουσιν ἐμβριθῶς καὶ εὐτόνως προσφερόμενος (edd. COHN/REITER 121). „Die Genossenschaften und Vereine, die stets Gelage feierten unter dem Vorwand des Opfers, wobei sich ihre Trunkenheit in politischen Intrigen Luft machte, löste er auf und ging hart und mit Nachdruck gegen Aufständische vor." Unter Berücksichtigung der Tugendhaftigkeit hält Philo allerdings Mitgliedschaft in Vereinen durchaus für möglich (Ebr. 20f).

[29] Cf. auch H. BOTERMANN, Judenedikt, 103 Anm. 325; R. RIESNER, Frühzeit, 151; anders zuletzt D. ALVAREZ CINEIRA, Religionspolitik, 199f, der μὴ συναθροίζεσθαι m.E. zu Unrecht nur auf politische Versammlungen bezieht.

[30] Ein Versammlungsverbot muß allerdings nicht mit einer Vereinsauflösung gleichgesetzt werden. Zur Annahme, Claudius oder ein anderer Kaiser habe eine generelle Erlaubnis einfacher Begräbnisvereine (*coll. tenuiorum sive funeraticia*) gegeben, siehe unten Seite 59–55.

ständen nicht mehr nachgekommen werden konnte, etwa was den Sabbatgottesdienst betrifft, war für den Kaiser und seine Beamten unwesentlich.³¹
Die Politik des Claudius bezüglich der Vereine war freilich nicht der Art, daß sie sämtlich verboten waren. Es ist vielmehr damit zu rechnen, daß die seit Augustus herrschenden Regeln vielen Vereinen die weitere Existenz gewährten und lediglich die neuen Vereine, die unter Gajus möglicherweise gar nicht lizensiert worden waren, aufgelöst wurden.³² Doch dort, wo staatsgefährdende Aktivitäten vorlagen oder vermutet wurden, ging Claudius rigoros vor. Mitglieder der jüdischen Gemeinden, in denen sich die Konflikte mit den Christen zu Tumulten auswuchsen, wurden aus Rom vertrieben (Suet Claud 25,4).³³

Unter *Nero* ereignete sich 59 n.Chr. ein Zwischenfall in Pompei (Tac Ann 14,17): Nach Gladiatorenspielen kam es zu Tumulten, die u.a. zur Folge hatten, daß die Kollegien, *quae contra leges instituerant,* aufgelöst wurden.³⁴ Mit der widerrechtlichen Gründung ist gemeint, daß sie nicht den Anforderungen der *lex Iulia* entsprachen, also nicht vom Senat konzessioniert worden waren.³⁵ Vereine, denen diese öffentliche Zulassung fehlte, wurden offenbar erst im Anlaßfall verboten.³⁶ Zudem gehört die Kontrolle dieser Vereine in den Verantwortungsbereich der Städte, die damit durchaus unterschiedlich verfahren konnten. Nicht offiziell zugelassene Vereine lebten aber stets unter der Gefahr, plötzlich aufgelöst zu werden, entweder aufgrund strengerer Durchsetzung der Vereinsgesetze oder wegen tatsächlicher oder behaupteter staatsgefährdender Vergehen ihrer Mitglieder. In den meisten Fällen werden solche Ereignisse nicht vorgekommen sein, da die *collegia* zumeist harmlose Zusammenschlüsse waren, in denen sich religiös, sozial und/oder beruflich Gleichgesinnte trafen. Viele der Vereinigungen übernahmen gerade aufgrund ihrer sozialen Tätigkeiten (Begräbnisse, aber auch zinsfreie Kredite) Aufgaben, die der Staat für nützlich halten konnte. In den Provinzen wie Ägypten zeigte sich gerade bei den Berufsgenossenschaften, daß die Besteuerung aufgrund der Vereinsorgani-

---

[31] Die Bestimmung gegen die jüdischen Versammlungen war nicht judenfeindlich: Die väterlichen Sitten (Sabbatobservanz, Reinheitsgebote) einzuhalten, wurde ausdrücklich gestattet.
[32] Zur Privilegierung von Berufsvereinen durch Claudius cf. F.M. AUSBÜTTEL, Untersuchungen, 101; V. WEBER, Kollegienwesen, 114f, sowie oben Anm.24.
[33] Zur Diskussion, wer von dieser Vertreibung betroffen war, sowie zur Datierung (wohl 49, also nach den Vorkehrungen gegen jüdische Versammlungen), cf. H. BOTERMANN, Judenedikt, 50ff; D. ALVAREZ CINEIRA, Religionspolitik, 206ff. Sollten alle Juden betroffen gewesen sein, dann wären wohl auch die Synagogen aufgelöst worden, doch ist eine vollständige Vertreibung unwahrscheinlich.
[34] Zur Vereinssituation in Pompei cf. W. LIEBENAM, Geschichte, 35ff; F.M. AUSBÜTTEL, Untersuchungen, 20ff. 36f.
[35] Dies kann auch als Hinweis darauf gewertet werden, daß die zunächst nur stadtrömischen Bestimmungen auch für die italischen Städte galten; cf. M. COHN, Vereinsrecht, 82f.
[36] Cf. etwa G. KRÜGER, Rechtsstellung, 60: „Solange eine nichtautorisierte Gemeinschaft nicht gegen die Strafgesetze verstösst, kann sie durch Unterlassung eines Verbots toleriert werden." Ähnlich auch R. MACMULLEN, Enemies, 247; J.H. WASZINK, Genossschaft, 112f.

sation erleichtert wurde.[37] Zudem hatten einige Vereine wie auch die Juden bereits von Augustus Privilegien zugesprochen bekommen. Die überwiegende Mehrzahl der überaus zahlreichen Vereine im römischen Imperium existierte auf diese Weise ohne ausdrückliche Erlaubnis durch den Senat.[38]

Bis zu *Trajan* haben wir keine Zeugnisse über besondere vereinsrechtliche Maßnahmen, so daß wohl angenommen werden darf, daß die bis dahin eingeschlagene Politik fortgeführt wurde: Anerkennung von politisch ungefährlichen Vereinen durch den Senat bzw. Tolerierung auch ohne Anerkennung, wenn keine besonderen Umstände zum Einschreiten zwangen. Bei Trajan wird die Sache nun schärfer, wie in einem Reskript an den Statthalter Bithyniens deutlich wird. Plinius hatte im Jahr 109 angefragt, ob es nicht klug wäre, als Feuerwehr in Nikomedien ein *collegium fabrorum* von 150 Mann ins Leben zu rufen (Ep X 33).[39] Die Antwort Trajans ist eindeutig (Ep X 34): Die Provinz Bithynien habe unter solchen Vereinen schon zu leiden gehabt und es sei allein schon deshalb nicht anzuraten, sie zuzulassen.

Quodcumque nomen ex quacumque causa dederimus iis, qui in idem contracti fuerint, hetaeriae eaeque breui fient (ed. MYNORS 308).
Egal welchen Namen wir ihnen geben und aus welchem Grund wir es jenen erlauben, die zu einem bestimmten Zweck versammelt werden, es werden in ganz kurzer Zeit Vereine daraus.

Die griechische Bezeichnung *hetaeria* soll wohl speziell den politisch agierenden Verein meinen.[40] Auch die Versicherung des Plinius, ein *collegium fabrorum* wäre ja leicht zu kontrollieren, wog Trajans Bedenken nicht auf.[41]

Anders urteilte Trajan freilich dort, wo eine Stadt die *libertas* besaß, ihre inneren Angelegenheiten selbst zu bestimmen (Ep X 92f). Den Amisenern wird gestattet, entsprechend der Gesetze ihrer Polis ἔρανοι zu gründen, was allerdings nicht zu *turbas et inlicitos coetus* führen dürfe (X 93). Die beabsichtigte Versorgung der *tenuiores*, also der einfachen Leute,[42] müsse aber der einzige Zweck bleiben. In Städten, die völlig dem römischen Recht unterstün-

---

[37] Cf. dazu A.C. JOHNSON, Egypt, 393.
[38] So besitzen wir nur wenige inschriftliche Belege, die eine ausdrückliche Konzessionierung dokumentieren (siehe dazu Anm. 54).
[39] Zu den Handwerkerkollegien als Feuerwehren cf. F.M. AUSBÜTTEL, Untersuchungen, 71ff. F.M. AUSBÜTTEL zählt 105 *collegia fabrorum* im Westen des Reiches (72 Anm.7).
[40] Cf. F.M. AUSBÜTTEL, Untersuchungen, 17. Gleichzeitig privilegierte Trajan Berufsverbände in Rom, was ein deutliches Licht auf die lokal völlig unterschiedliche Praxis wirft; cf. W. LIEBENAM, Geschichte, 37; F.M. AUSBÜTTEL, Untersuchungen, 102f; V. WEBER, Kollegienwesen, 112.
[41] Zur Kontrolle von Vereinen unter Trajan cf. auch den Brief der Hieroglyphenschreiber (107 n.Chr.), in dem sie versichern, daß ihr Verein aus nicht mehr als den angeführten fünf Personen bestehe (P.Oxy No.1029).
[42] Die Diskussion über *collegia tenuiorum*, die man entweder primär als Vereine von Armen (so zuletzt mit Emphase wieder U. FELLMETH, Vereine, 52ff) oder als sozial gemischte Vereine versteht, in denen die Ärmsten keinen Platz hatten (F.M. AUSBÜTTEL, Untersuchungen, 25ff; F. VITTINGHOFF, Gesellschaft, 210f), muß hier nicht entscheiden werden.

den, wären freilich auch solche Einrichtungen zu verbieten. Die Publikation der Pliniusbriefe bedeutete einen wichtigen Schritt zur Allgemeingültigkeit dieses Verbots, da das Kaiserreskript ausdrücklich von allen Orten spricht, die römischer Jurisdiktion unterstanden. Da sich dieser Bereich in weiterer Folge immer mehr erweiterte,[43] ist mit einem zumindest formal gültigen Vereinsverbot im gesamten Imperium zu rechnen, von dem lokal bedingte Ausnahmen gemacht werden konnten.[44] Diese rigorosen Einschränkungen änderten an der Blüte des Vereinswesens freilich nichts.

Plinius setzte schließlich die Anweisung zum Vereinsverbot um, wie er im sogenannten „Christenbrief" berichtet (X 96). Sein Edikt wurde offenbar auch von unpolitischen Vereinen befolgt wie etwa von den Christen. Sie hätten, so Plinius, es unterlassen, sich nach den religiösen Versammlungen zum gemeinsamen Mahl zu treffen, wie es in den Vereinen allgemein üblich war.[45]

Eine Inschrift des Vereins der Verehrer Dianas und des Antonius in *Lanuvium* in der Nähe Roms aus dem Jahr 136 n.Chr. ist vielfach (zuerst von THEODOR MOMMSEN) so gedeutet worden, daß hier eine generelle staatliche Erlaubnis für Begräbnisvereine zitiert worden wäre.[46] Der darin zitierte Senatsbeschluß lautet:[47]

---

[43] Cf. D. NÖRR, Imperium, 64; J. BLEICKEN, Verfassungsgeschichte I, 177f. Es ist zudem zu beachten, daß die Erlaubnis aufgrund des *foedus* ein *beneficium* war, und auch im Blick auf das Verhältnis des Imperiums zu verbündeten Städten ein Einzelfall blieb; D. NÖRR, Imperium, 61. Cf. auch A.H.M. JONES, Civitates, 112ff, zur Gewährung von Freiheiten (neben der Beibehaltung der eigenen Verfassung v.a. Tribut- und Garnisonsfreiheit) in der Kaiserzeit (114 zu Amisus).

[44] Zur restriktiven Vereinspolitik Trajans cf. auch F. VITTINGHOFF, Gesellschaft, 209.

[45] Die nächtliche Versammlung zum Gesang für Christus (... *soliti stato die ante lucem conuenire, carmenque Christo*) ist nicht in diesem Zusammenhang zu sehen; anders W. COTTER, Collegia, 83. Aus der Unterlassung der Mahlfeier wird deutlich, daß es der staatlichen Autorität nicht um ein Religionsverbot ging, sondern um die Untersagung von Vereinstreffen. Ähnlich waren schon die Maßnahmen anläßlich des Bacchanalienskandals. Zu konkreten Auswirkungen des Vereinsverbotes auf die Christen siehe unten S.62f.

[46] Cf. besonders F.M. DE ROBERTIS, Storia I, 275ff. 341ff. mit Darstellung der älteren Forschung (etwa T. MOMMSEN, Lex Iulia, 116f.; A. MÜLLER, Sterbekassen, 187; G. LA PIANA, Groups, 242; G. KRÜGER, Rechtsstellung, 64), aber auch J.H. WASZINK, Genossenschaften, 106; J. BLEICKEN, Verfassungsgeschichte II, 91; W. DAHLHEIM, Geschichte, 62; J.E. STAMBAUGH/D.L. BALCH, Umfeld, 122; K.L. NOETHLICHS, Judentum, 35; U. FELLMETH, Vereine, 42ff; T. SCHMELLER, Hierarchie, 28f. Zur Bestimmung von Vereinen als Begräbnisvereine, wie sie ausführlich schon bei A. MÜLLER, Sterbekassen, 183ff, beschrieben sind, ist anzumerken, daß diese Ansicht heute allgemein als veraltet gilt: Vereine kümmerten sich *auch* um Begräbnisse, wurden aber nicht primär bzw. singulär für diesen Zweck gegründet. Allerdings wird durch die gemeinsame Finanzierung von Begräbnissen immerhin deutlich, daß diese vor allem jenen zugute kam, die sich ein eigenes Begräbnis – zumindest mit der gewünschten Ausstattung – nicht leisten konnten. Zur allgemeinen Klassifizierung von Vereinen und der damit verbundenen Problematik cf. auch J.S. KLOPPENBORG, Collegia, 16ff.

[47] Der Wortlaut der Inschrift CIL XIV No.2112 p.I l.10–13 (= ILS II/2 No.7212) ist unsicher; cf. dazu auch A.E. GORDON, Album II, 61ff. Tafeln 87f. Ich zitiere eine veränderte Fassung, die sich nach den Ergänzungen von F.M. AUSBÜTTEL, Untersuchungen, 26ff,

Kaput ex s(enatus) c(onsulto) p(opuli) R(omani)| Quib[us permissum est, co]nvenire collegiumq(ue) habere liceat. Qui stipem menstruam conferre vo|len[t ad facienda sa]cra, in it collegium coeant, ne(que) sub specie eius collegii nisi semel in men|se c[oeant stipem co]nferendi causa, unde defuncti sepeliantur.

Ein Abschnitt aus einem Senatsbeschluß des römischen Volkes: Diesen ist es erlaubt, zusammenzukommen und einen Verein zu haben. Sie wollen monatliche Beiträge einheben zur Ausübung der Sakralfeierlichkeiten, zu denen sich dieses Kollegium versammelt, und sie sollen sich nicht unter dem Anschein des Vereins mehr als einmal im Monat versammeln, um den Beitrag einzusammeln, aus dem die Verstorbenen bestattet werden sollen.

FRANK M. AUSBÜTTEL hat darauf hingewiesen, daß eine generelle Erlaubnis aus diesem Text nicht entnommen werden kann. Einerseits bezieht sich der Senatsbeschluß nur auf diesen einen Verein (*quibus ... in it collegium*), andererseits sind die Textlücken gegenüber CIL anders zu ergänzen.[48] Es ist daher wohl nicht mehr anzunehmen, daß eine generelle Erlaubnis für bestimmte Arten von Vereinen in dieser frühen Zeit gegeben worden war.

Ein abschließender Blick sei noch auf die *Digesten* geworfen, in denen sich wohl Bestimmungen finden, die bis in das 2.Jhd. zurückreichen. Auf das Referat des Gaius zum Zwölftafelgesetz, das mit einem Hinweis auf Solon verbunden ist (Dig 47,22,4),[49] sind wir oben schon eingegangen, doch Gaius nennt auch spätere Bestimmungen (Gesetze, Senatsbeschlüsse und kaiserliche Konstitutionen), aus denen das Vereinsrecht bestand (Dig 3,4,1). Typischerweise geht es ihm dabei aber nur um Berufsvereine, da diese für den Staat von besonderer Bedeutung waren. Die Dig 3,4,1 erwähnten Bestimmungen über Vereinseigentum und Rechtsvertretung sind wohl ebenfalls auf jene *collegia* zu beziehen (cf. auch Dig 50,6,6,12). Der Anfang des 3.Jhds. wirkende Jurist Aelius Marcianus hält bezüglich religiöser Treffen fest (Dig 47,22,1,1), daß jene nicht verboten sind, wenn sie nicht gegen das Verbot ille-

---

richtet; so auch V. WEBER, Kollegienwesen, 109f; anders zuletzt wieder T. SCHMELLER, Hierarchie, 100. In CIL (ed. DESSAU) lautet der Text:
Kaput ex s c p r| Quib[us coire co]nvenire collegiumq habere liceat. Qui stipem menstruam conferre vo|len[t in fun]era in it collegium coeant neq sub specie eius collegi nisi semel in men|se c[oeant co]nferendi causa unde defuncti sepeliantur.

[48] Cf. F.M. AUSBÜTTEL, Untersuchungen, 25ff; V. WEBER, Kollegienwesen, 110; ähnlich schon M. COHN, Vereinsrecht, 139ff. J.S. KLOPPENBORG, Collegia, 20ff, datiert die generelle Erlaubnis erst in die Zeit Hadrians (so auch J.H. WASZINK, Genossenschaft, 107). Mit der Widerlegung der Annahme, es gäbe eine generelle Erlaubnis für Begräbnisvereine, ist auch jene These aufzugeben, wonach sich die christlichen Gemeinden als *collegia funeraticia* konstituierten, um eine Bewilligung zu erhalten (cf. v.a. G.B. DE ROSSI, Roma I, 101. III, 507ff; cf. auch E. RENAN, Apostel, 242; W. LIEBENAM, Geschichte, 267ff; zuletzt wieder bei F.M. DE ROBERTIS, Storia I, 338ff. II 72ff.; J.S. JEFFERS, Conflict, 41; E. DASSMANN, Kirchengeschichte I, 241). Zwar kümmerten sich die Gemeinden sicherlich auch um ihre Toten („Totentaufe" 1 Kor 15,29), doch erwuchs ihnen daraus keine Konzession.

[49] Zu griech. Vereinsbestimmungen, die für unseren Zeitraum unwesentlich sind, cf. P. HERRMANN, Genossenschaft, 98f, der „von einer grundsätzlichen u. weitgehenden Freizügigkeit der griech. Staaten gegenüber Vereinsbildungen" spricht. Man kann wohl diese Freiheiten auch für jene griechischen Städte annehmen, die wie Amisus nicht unter röm. Jurisdiktion standen. Ähnlich auch M. SAN NICOLÒ, Vereinswesen II/1, 10ff, für Ägypten.

galer Vereine (*illicita collegia*) verstoßen.⁵⁰ Marcianus berichtet auch von der Auflösung nicht gestatteter Vereine (47,22,3) sowie von der Bestimmung, daß Sklaven nur mit Erlaubnis ihres Herrn einem Verein beitreten dürfen (47,22,3,2). Man dürfe auch nicht Mitglied in zwei Vereinen sein (47,22,1,2), was wohl gegen die unlautere Inanspruchnahme von Privilegien, die Vereinsmitgliedern zugestanden wurden, gerichtet ist. Doch alle diese Bestimmungen sind nach 150 zu datieren und daher für unsere Fragestellung nicht heranzuziehen.

Strafrechtliche Maßnahmen konnten sich gegen den Verein als Ganzes richten, wenn er z.B. politisch gefährlich war.⁵¹ Es konnten aber auch Vergehen einzelner Mitglieder für die Strafverfolgung ausschlaggebend sein.⁵² Ansonsten wurden illegale Vereine aufgelöst (cf. etwa Philo Flacc 4) und ihr Besitz eingezogen.⁵³

Zusammenfassend ist also festzuhalten: Spätestens seit Augustus gab es eine genaue Regelung bezüglich der Vereinszulassung: Ein *collegium* konnte beim Senat um Bewilligung ansuchen⁵⁴ und erhielt diese, wenn keine staatsgefährdenden Aktivitäten zu erwarten waren und ein öffentlicher Nutzen vorlag.⁵⁵ Bestimmte alte Vereine wie z.B. auch die jüdischen Synagogen waren aufgrund ihrer Tradition immer schon lizensiert. Daneben gab es aber eine Unzahl von nicht konzessionierten Vereinen, die so lange geduldet wurden, bis sie durch Straftaten oder andere Vergehen auffielen.

---

⁵⁰ Cf. T. MOMMSEN, Strafrecht, 877 Anm.2. Es geht wohlgemerkt nur um religiöse Treffen von Vereinen, die bereits bewilligt sind. Zu dem Abschnitt cf. auch F.M. DE ROBERTIS, Storia I, 341ff; F.M. AUSBÜTTEL, Untersuchungen, 23ff.

⁵¹ Cf. schon Cic Quint Fr 2,3,5 (*vis*; siehe auch oben Anm. 10); zum *crimen maiestatis* cf. Dig 48,4 (Ulpian).

⁵² Zieht man das Vorgehen der Behörden gegen die Bacchusvereine in Rom und Italien als Parallele heran, so ist auffällig, daß Livius unterscheidet zwischen jenen, die sich Verbrechen (Unzucht, Mord, Fälschung von Dokumenten) zuschulden kommen ließen – sie wurden mit dem Tod bestraft, und jenen, die nur Mitglieder und damit Mitwisser waren – diese kamen ins Gefängnis (39,18,3–6). Der entsprechende Senatsbeschluß (CIL I² No.581) sieht es weiters als Kapitalverbrechen an, wenn gegen die rigorosen Beschränkungen des Bacchuskultes verstoßen wurde (Zwang zur Bewilligung durch den Senat, Verbot von Vereinsbildung, Beschränkung der Teilnehmerzahl bei Feiern auf fünf Personen – zwei Männer und drei Frauen). Im Vergleich dazu harmlos erscheint die wohl in die Zeit Mark Aurels gehörende Bestimmung, daß die Mitgliedschaft in einem (illegalen oder zweiten?) Verein mit einer Geldbuße von 500 Drachmen zu ahnden sei (BGU V No.1 §108). Für die Zeit des Severus Alexander nennt Ulpian wieder die Todesstrafe (Dig 47,22,2).

⁵³ Cf. dazu insgesamt T. MOMMSEN, Strafrecht, 662f. 877; G. KRÜGER, Rechtsstellung, 61f; F.M. DE ROBERTIS, Storia I, 390ff.

⁵⁴ Cf. auch die Formel *quibus ex senatus consulto coire liceat* (Belege bei J.-P. WALTZING, Étude I, 125ff. F.M. DE ROBERTIS, Storia I, 218f Anm. 60), die für die Zeit vom 1.Jhd. n.Chr. bis Severus Alexander belegt ist (anders bezüglich der Datierung J.S. KLOPPENBORG, Collegia, 20). In späterer Zeit werden die Vereine v.a. Zwangskollegien von Berufen, die der Staat selbst einrichtete (cf. aber schon Plinius, Ep 10,33); dazu auch V. WEBER, Kollegienwesen, 108ff.

⁵⁵ Jene Vereine, von denen kaiserliche Dedikationsinschriften u.ä. überliefert sind (Beispiele bei P.A. HARLAND, Honouring, 111ff), demonstrieren ihre Loyalität besonders augenfällig.

2. Die christlichen Gemeinden als *collegia*

Unabhängig davon, ob sich eine christliche Gemeinde selbst als Verein verstand, ist doch mit einiger Gewißheit anzunehmen, daß sie von ihrer Umgebung – also sowohl staatlich wie gesellschaftlich – als *collegium* wahrgenommen wurde.[56] Für die Christen lassen sich unter vereinsrechtlichem Aspekt verschiedene Möglichkeiten erwägen, wie sie auf diese Einschätzung reagieren konnten:
1. Sie konnten als lizensiertes *collegium* auftreten.
 * Dies war als innerjüdische Bewegung möglich, mit der zunehmenden Entfremdung zwischen Juden und Christen aber immer schwieriger. Spätestens seit Nero wurden die Christen als eigene Gruppierung unabhängig vom Judentum wahrgenommen.
 * Die Anerkennung als *collegium* war aber vielleicht unter Berücksichtigung lokaler Unterschiede möglich. Die Bezeichnung als Χριστιανοί (Apg 11,26; 26,28; 1Petr 4,16) könnte als Hinweis darauf gewertet werden, daß die Christen in Antiochien von staatlicher Seite – die Form spricht eher für die römische Verwaltung – als eigener Verein erkannt, vielleicht sogar anerkannt, worden waren.[57]
2. Die Christen konnten andererseits als nicht lizensierter Verein ähnlich wie viele pagane *collegia* unbehelligt bleiben, so lange ihre politische Unbedenklichkeit feststand.
3. Es bestand schließlich aber auch die Möglichkeit, daß die Gemeinde als illegales *collegium* angeklagt wurde und ihre Mitglieder entsprechend bestraft wurden.

Im Folgenden möchte ich zwei dieser möglichen Alternativen näher erläutern. Einerseits soll die staatliche Reaktion am Beispiel des Pliniusbriefes erörtert werden, in dem das Vereinsverbot auf die Christen bezogen wird. Andererseits zeigt m.E. der 1Petr, wie die Gemeinde nach Wegen zur staatlichen und gesellschaftlichen Anerkennung suchen konnte.

a) Anklage als illegales Kollegium

Der „Christenbrief" des Plinius (Ep X 96) gibt einen gewissen Anhaltspunkt für die Möglichkeit, daß die christlichen Gemeinden zu Beginn der illegalen Vereinsbildung verdächtigt wurden.[58]

---

[56] Cf. etwa Luc Peregr Mort 11; Origenes, c.Cels 1,1; Minucius Felix, Octav 8,4.
[57] Cf. dazu M. HENGEL/A.M. SCHWEMER, Paulus, 342. Über die Vereinspraxis in der syrischen Metropole wissen wir allerdings mangels Inschriften nur sehr wenig.
[58] Cf. zum Folgenden W. LIEBENAM, Geschichte, 269f; W.H.C. FREND, Martyrdom, 221f; A. WLOSOK, Rechtsstellung, 282f. 292ff; B. REICKE, Diakonie, 336f; F. BÖMER, Religion I, 39f; R. FELDMEIER, Fremde, 123; P. ACHTEMEIER, 1Petr, 26; allgemein M. RADIN, Legislation, 126ff; erwogen u.a. auch von P. LAMPE, Christen, 314. Gegen eine Bezugnahme auf das Vereinsverbot sind etwa W.M. RAMSAY, Church, 214f; A.N. SHERWIN-

Der Brief gibt zunächst nach der Einleitung zu erkennen, daß Plinius über Prozesse gegen Christen wußte, nicht aber, wie die Anklage lautete und welche Strafen verhängt wurden. Der Vf. beschreibt im Fortgang zwei Phasen seines Vorgehens gegen die Christen.[59] Zunächst (*interim*) habe er es nur mit überzeugten Christen zu tun gehabt, die er aufgrund ihrer Halsstarrigkeit zum Tode verurteilte (2–4). Erst im Laufe der Zeit (*mox*), als die Zahl der Angeklagten gewachsen war, hatte Plinius genauere Nachforschungen angestellt (5f). Die Aussagen ehemaliger Christen, die durch die Folter zweier Diakonissen bestätigt wurden, hätten schließlich ergeben, daß die Christen sich nicht zu Verbrechen verabredeten, bei ihren Mählern ganz normale Speise essen würden, und auch das Hetärienverbot eingehalten hätten (7).[60] Es handle sich aber um *superstitio prava* (8).

Mir scheint der Fall hier so zu liegen, daß Plinius zu Beginn von tatsächlichen Vergehen ausging, die sich aber sämtlich bei späterer genauerer Nachprüfung nicht bewahrheiteten.[61] Einer dieser Vorwürfe, ja vielleicht sogar der entscheidendste, wäre dann die Beteiligung an einem illegalen *collegium* gewesen. Der Name *Christianus* besagte ja schon diese Mitgliedschaft und ein weiteres Festhalten daran stellte einen glatten Verstoß gegen das Hetärienverbot dar.[62] Widerstand aber jemand dem römischen Statthalter in dieser Angelegenheit, bedeutete dies ein Kapitalverbrechen.[63] Erst später hatte sich herausgestellt, daß die Christen auch das Vereinsverbot eingehalten hätten, weshalb Plinius dann auch auf den primitiven Aberglauben (*superstitio prava*) verweist. Es läßt sich daher nicht behaupten, die Anklage wegen unerlaubter Vereinsbetätigung wäre insgesamt die Begründung für das römische Vorgehen gegen die Christen gewesen. Der Pliniusbrief befreit die Christen von diesem

---

WHITE, Letters, 779f; R. FREUDENBERGER, Verhalten, 158; R. KLEIN, Christentum I, 322 Anm.12; P. KERESZTES, Rome, 284.

[59] Cf. A.N. SHERWIN-WHITE, Letters, 694: „The affair came to a head fairly quickly, in two main stages, marked by *interim* (s.2) and *mox* (s.4)."

[60] Die Liste in §7 ist m.E. ein Reflex auf die Vorwürfe von *flagitia*, mit denen der Legatus durch die Ankläger der Christen konfrontiert gewesen war. Die Einhaltung des Versammlungsverbots kann auch nur auf die Apostaten bezogen werden, die sich aus Furcht vor strafrechtlichen Konsequenzen von der Eucharistie- und Agapefeier fernhielten, doch ist die Aufgabe der Mahlgemeinschaft wohl generell auf alle Christen Bithyniens zu beziehen.

[61] Die Darstellung, wonach sich verschiedene Fälle erst im Laufe der Verhandlungen ergeben hätten (4), verstehe ich entsprechend so, daß Plinius es zunächst tatsächlich nur mit bekennenden Christen zu tun hatte, die seiner Aufforderung zum Abfall nicht Folge leisteten.

[62] M.E. ist auch die Leidensformel διὰ τὸ ὄνομά μου (Mk 13,13 par; Mt 24,9; Joh 15,21; Apk 2,3) ebenfalls auf die Mitgliedschaft bei den Χριστιανοί zu beziehen. Cf. v.a. 1Petr 4,16: μὴ γάρ τις ὑμῶν πασχέτω ὡς φονεὺς ἢ κλέπτης ἢ κακοποιὸς ἢ ὡς ἀλλοτριεπίσκοπος· εἰ δὲ ὡς Χριστιανός, μὴ αἰσχυνέσθω, δοξαζέτω δὲ τὸν θεὸν ἐν τῷ ὀνόματι τούτῳ.

[63] Cf. die Hinweise bei A.N. SHERWIN-WHITE, Letters, 699. 784ff, betreffend des Tatbestandes der *contumacia* (bei Plinius: *pertinacia certa et inflexibila obstinatio*).

Vorwurf (7): Sie haben sich nicht mehr als Hetärien versammelt!⁶⁴ Die Bestrafung erfolgte in der Folgezeit vielmehr aufgrund des sturen Festhaltens an dieser Religion.

Die Antwort Trajans (Ep X 97) ist im Grunde eine Bestätigung für das Vorgehen des Plinius mit der Ergänzung, nicht aktiv nach Christen zu forschen und anonyme Anzeigen nicht zu beachten. Gerade die Unterlassung der aktiven Ausforschung könnte auch im Rahmen der Vereinspolitik der römischen Kaiser verstanden werden: gesetzliches Legitimierungsgebot und tatsächliche Toleranz bei politischer Unbedenklichkeit entsprechen sich auch hier. Von einer etablierten Norm, die Trajan im Umgang mit Christen nicht anführen kann, ist bezüglich der Vereine in der Kaiserzeit zwar formal die Rede, nicht aber in der Praxis.

Die Christen waren also in zweierlei Hinsicht vom Vereinsrecht betroffen:
1. Einerseits repräsentiert §7 des Pliniusbriefes eine Aufzählung jener Anklagepunkte, die gegen die Christen vorgebracht worden waren. Vergehen gegen das Vereinsverbot gehörten wohl dazu. Diese Anklage hielt solange, als das Bekenntnis *Christianus sum* als illegale Vereinsbetätigung interpretiert werden konnte. Plinius hält freilich ausdrücklich fest, daß sich in einem späteren Stadium herausstellte, daß die Christen auch in dieser Hinsicht unschuldig waren.
2. Andererseits mußten die Christen auch ihre religiösen Feiern ändern. Die Mahlgemeinschaft konnte nicht mehr durchgeführt werden, wahrscheinlich war davon sogar das Herrenmahl selbst betroffen. Die religiöse Versammlung selbst war weiterhin gestattet, vereinsähnliche Treffen waren aber verboten.⁶⁵

b) Auf der Suche nach Duldung und Anerkennung

Als ein christliches Zeugnis, das auf dem Hintergrund vereinsrechtlicher Bestimmungen gut verständlich ist, möchte ich den 1.Petrusbrief heranziehen.

---

[64] Spuren dieses naheliegenden Vorwurfs finden sich allerdings noch in der literarischen Kritik am Christentum. Celsus wirft den Christen vor, darin gegen das allgemeine Gesetz zu verstoßen, daß sie geheime Verbindungen errichten (... ὡς συνθήκας κρύβδην πρὸς ἀλλήλους ποιουμένων Χριστιανῶν παρὰ τὰ νενομισμένα; Origenes, c.Cels 1,1 [SC 132, ed. BORRET 78]; der Einwand bei R. KLEIN, Christentum I, 330f Anm. 1, ist m.E. unzutreffend, weil zirkulär). Origenes antwortet darauf, daß ein barbarisches Gesetz auch nicht eingehalten werden muß, er bestreitet also die Rechtmäßigkeit des Vereinsverbots. Es sei daher nicht unvernünftig, um der Wahrheit willen Verbindungen einzugehen (οὐκ ἄλογον οὖν συνθήκας παρὰ τὰ νενομισμένα ποιεῖν τὰς ὑπὲρ ἀληθείας). Ähnlich Minucius Felix, Octav 8,4; cf. dazu u.a. W. SCHÄFKE, Widerstand, 605ff; R.L. WILKEN, Christen, 58ff (mit weiteren Hinweisen auf Tertullians Versuch, die christlichen Gemeinden im Gegensatz zu den paganen Vereinen als politisch und moralisch vorbildliche Vereinigungen darzustellen [Apol 39; dazu auch G. KRÜGER, Rechtsstellung, 91ff; B. KÖTTING, Genossenschaft, 146f; E. DASSMANN, Kirchengeschichte I, 243]).

[65] Wie bei der Regelung der Bacchanalien wurde der Kult selbst nicht verboten, die Vereinsbildung aber ausgeschlossen.

Aus den verschiedenen Themen dieses pseudonymen Schreibens, das wohl in die Zeit Trajans gehört,[66] aus Rom stammt (5,13) und sich an Christen in Kleinasien richtet,[67] möchte ich das Verhältnis zu der die Christen umgebenden Gesellschaft und den staatlichen Autoritäten herausgreifen. Der Vf. behandelt dies besonders ausführlich in 2,11–17. Der Abschnitt gibt ganz konkrete Anweisungen für das „exoterische" Verhalten der Christen, zum einen allgemein ἐν τοῖς ἔθνεσιν (vv.11f), zum anderen in Bezug auf die Obrigkeit (vv.13–17).

Was den Wandel unter den Heiden angeht, sollen die Christen, die in ihrer Gesellschaft als Beisassen und Fremdlinge eigentlich keine Heimat haben, sich auch von allem fernhalten, was moralisch verwerflich ist.[68] Ihr Verhalten sollte vielmehr tadellos (καλός) sein, voller guter Werke (καλὰ ἔργα), um die feindlich gesinnten Menschen zu überzeugen, so daß diese den wahren Gott im Eschaton anbeten (cf. Mt 5,16).[69] Dabei ist impliziert, „daß ein Konsens zwischen Christen und Heiden über das besteht, was ein ‚gutes Leben' ist, was ‚gute Taten' sind."[70] Dies kann so verstanden werden, daß das individuelle sittliche Benehmen dem entsprechen soll, was sich Heiden von „ordentlichen Leuten" erwarteten. Man sollte m.E. allerdings nicht vorschnell auf eine rein individualistische Privatethik schließen, sondern den korporativen Charakter der christlichen Gemeinden ernst nehmen.[71] Gemeinschaftliche gute Werke können nun z.B. darin bestehen, Bedürftige zu versorgen. Allerdings richtete sich diese wichtige Aktivität frühchristlicher Gemeinden nur auf die eigenen Mitglieder (wie auch bei Vereinen), was schwerlich dazu dienen konnte, die

---

[66] Cf. A. REICHERT, Praeparatio, 94f; anders K.H. SCHELKLE, 1Petr, 9; N. BROX, 1Petr, 41; R. FELDMEIER, Fremde, 199.

[67] Pontus und Bithynien – die Gebiete des Plinius – stehen an Beginn und Ende der Adressatenangabe. Möglicherweise stehen dahinter die tatsächlichen Empfänger; cf. P. LAMPE/U. LUZ, Christentum, 198; zum Problem auch N. BROX, 1Petr, 25f; R. FELDMEIER, Fremde, 199 Anm.40.

[68] Die Formulierung ἀπέχεσθαι τῶν σαρκικῶν ἐπιθυμιῶν αἵτινες στρατεύονται κατὰ τῆς ψυχῆς warnt grundsätzlich vor allem, was das Leben als Heilige (1,15f; 2,5.9) gefährdet. In 4,3 erläutert der Autor dies genauer in einem Lasterkatalog, der mit den allgemeinen Vorwürfen der Trunksucht und Völlerei an die Adresse der Heiden auch Eigenheiten des Vereinslebens aufs Korn nimmt (cf. Philo Flacc 136).

[69] Zur Bedeutung von ἡ ἡμέρα ἐπισκοπῆς cf. N. BROX, 1Petr, 114f; A. REICHERT, Praeparatio, 126ff Anm. 2.

[70] N. BROX, 1Petr, 113; cf. auch K.H. SCHELKLE, 1Petr, 71; H. GIESEN, Lebenszeugnis, 113.

[71] Die Aufforderung in 1Petr richtet sich an alle Adressaten. Der Vf. spricht entsprechend auch betont von der Bruderschaft (ἀδελφότης: 2,17; 5,9), und auch im vorhergehenden Abschnitt waren die Adressaten als γένος ἐκλεκτόν, βασίλειον ἱεράτευμα, ἔθνος ἅγιον, λαὸς εἰς περιποίησιν (2,9) bezeichnet worden. Die Bezeichnung ἐκκλησία verwendet er hingegen nicht, während sich ἀδελφότης wiederum nur in 1Petr findet. Letzteres läßt sich möglicherweise sogar auf den spezifisch westlichen Sprachgebrauch in Vereinen zurückführen, wo geschwisterliche Bezeichnungen eine wichtige Rolle spielten (cf. W. LIEBENAM, Geschichte, 185. 273; F. BÖMER, Religion I, 178). Kann dies als zusätzlicher Hinweis auf eine Abfassung in Rom gewertet werden?

Heiden positiv zu stimmen. Möglicherweise konnten sich Christen in einem gewissen Maß auch an öffentlichen Veranstaltungen, bei denen Vereine eine wichtige Rolle spielten,[72] beteiligen. Dies war auch Juden durchaus möglich gewesen, wie ihre Beteiligung an Cäsars Begräbnis (Suet Caes 84,5) oder ihre festen Plätze in Theatern (z.B. I.Mil VI,2 No.940 f.g.h) demonstrieren. Dabei war freilich stets die Frage, wie weit diese Veranstaltungen aufgrund der Warnung, die Seele nicht zu gefährden (1Petr 2,11) und Götzendienst zu meiden (4,3; cf. auch 1,14; 2,11.25), nicht völlig ausgeschlossen waren. Doch es gab auch andere Möglichkeiten, die christliche Gemeinschaft als positives Element in der antiken Gesellschaft darzustellen: So konnten einzelne, in der Gesellschaft angesehene Christen[73] zu Ehren der Gemeinde Stiftungen vornehmen, so daß diese am Ansehen ihrer Wohltäter partizipieren konnte.[74] Dies war für antike Vereine durchaus erstrebenswert: Sie gewannen Patrone und Wohltäter auch deshalb, weil ihre Stellung in der Stadt damit abgesichert werden konnte.

Vv.13–17 bestätigen m.E. die hohe Bedeutung, die der Vf. des 1Petr dem öffentlichen Wirken der Christen als Wohltäter zuspricht.[75] Der Abschnitt beginnt mit der Aufforderung, sich jeder menschlichen Autorität unterzuordnen um des Herrn willen (διὰ τὸν κύριον).[76] Dabei denkt der Vf. an den Kaiser und seinen Statthalter bzw. an alle kaiserlichen Beamten. Jene wären gesandt, um die Übeltäter zu bestrafen, die Wohltäter aber zu belohnen. Ἀγαθοποιός bzw. das Verbum oder Nomen verwendet der Autor auffallend oft in seinem Schreiben (2,20; 3,6.17; 4,19; cf. auch 3,11).[77] Die Terminologie nimmt dabei den Sprachgebrauch antiker Ehreninschriften für Wohltäter auf.[78] Der Vf. rechnet zwar einerseits mit der Einsicht der feindlich gesinnten Umgebung, erhofft sich aber vor allem staatliche Auszeichnung.[79] Es handelt sich nämlich bei der ἀγαθοποιΐα um mehr als um bloße Einhaltung der Gesetze, denn letzteres würde von den staatlichen Autoritäten gewiß nicht ausdrücklich gelobt.[80]

---

[72] Cf. für den griech. Osten dazu ausführlich O. M. VAN NIJF, World, 131ff.
[73] Auf deren Existenz weist auch Plinius hin, der davon berichtet, daß Menschen jedes Standes sich zum Christentum bekehrt hätten (Ep X 96,9).
[74] Cf. allgemein O. M. VAN NIJF, World, 110. Weitere Beispiele bei B.W. WINTER, Welfare, 37; ähnlich F.W. DANKER, Benefactor, 359; anders etwa P. ACHTEMEIER, 1Petr, 184. Die Apostelgeschichte demonstriert die hohe Bedeutung von Patronen für die Christen auffällig (z.B. Apg 13,7ff; 17,4.12).
[75] Dies gilt selbstverständlich auch dann, wenn eine traditionelle Vorlage für den Abschnitt angenommen wird (so etwa N. BROX, 1Petr, 116f).
[76] Zur Bedeutung des Themas „Unterordnung" in 1Petr cf. etwa N. BROX, 1Petr, 117f.
[77] Im NT sonst nur noch Lk 6,9.33.35; 3Joh 11. Auch Paulus hatte bereits die Obrigkeit beschrieben als Instanz, die jene lobe, die Gutes tun (Röm 13,3: τὸ ἀγαθὸν ποίει, καὶ ἕξεις ἔπαινον).
[78] Cf. dazu B.W. WINTER, Welfare, 34ff; anders R. FELDMEIER, Fremde, 152, der ἀγαθοποιός als Synonym zu ὑποτάσσεσθαι versteht.
[79] Cf. F.W. BEARE, 1Petr, 117; K.H. SCHELKLE, 1Petr, 74; anders H. GIESEN, Lebenszeugnis, 138.
[80] Cf. dazu u.a. F.W. BEARE, 1Petr, 117; W.C. VAN UNNIK, Teaching, 91f; B.W. WINTER, Welfare, 33ff; B.L. CAMPBELL, Honor, 112ff; P.A. HARLAND, Honouring, 116; anders L. GOPPELT, 1Petr, 185; N. BROX, 1Petr, 120 Anm. 397. N. BROX, 1Petr, 118f, hält den

Vielmehr geht es um öffentliches Auftreten einzelner Wohltäter, die als Christen bekannt sind oder sich als solche deklarieren. Sich als *benefactor* zu betätigen, sei, so 2,15, Gottes Wille, um die gesellschaftlichen Vorurteile zu überwinden.[81] Dazu gehört auch die Ehre für den Kaiser, zu der am Abschluß dieses paränetischen Abschnittes aufgefordert wird (2,17). Wiederum kann hier individuelle Ehrbezeugung gemeint sein, ob im persönlichen Gespräch oder gar bei öffentlicher Anklage. Aber antike Vereine verstanden es als Gemeinschaft, sich durch Kaiserdedikationen, durch Glückwünsche zum *Dies imperium* oder Geburtstag, Privilegien zu erwerben und Staatsloyalität öffentlich zu demonstrieren.[82] Auch der Vf. des 1Petr hat dies m.E. im Sinn, um auf diesem Weg zu erreichen, die christlichen Gemeinden als geduldete Vereine zu etablieren. Er fordert zu dem auf, was von Vereinen als verbreitete Praxis dokumentiert ist.

Hinsichtlich vereinsrechtlicher Regelungen ist für diesen Aspekt frühchristlichen Gesellschaftsbezugs vor allem von Bedeutung, daß in Zeiten der Bedrängnis, die offensichtlich unorganisiert von seiten des Volkes erfolgte, die Christen alles tun mußten, um sich als positiver Teil der Gemeinschaft zu präsentieren. Sie waren Fremde, weil sie sich nicht länger an den vielen kultisch konnotierten Aktivitäten beteiligen konnten. Sie standen aber auch als *collegium* stets im Verdacht, politisch gefährlich zu werden. In dieser Situation suchten sie Wege, um wenigstens einige, vor allem aber die staatlichen Autoritäten, davon zu überzeugen, daß sie bereit waren, als Einzelpersonen und als Gemeinschaft den Erwartungen der Gesellschaft zu entsprechen.[83]

Gedanken einer „demonstrativen Loyalität" zwar für nicht nachweisbar (so aber F.-R. PROSTMEIER, Handlungsmodelle, 398), für den Gesamtduktus des 1Petr aber immerhin für passend. Theologisch gewendet erscheint der Gedanke der guten Werke als Überbietung der Gebotseinhaltung bei Hermas, Sim 5,3 (=56,3f).

[81] Der Vf. sagt in v.15 nicht, daß Gottes Wille bestimmen würde, was gut ist (auch wenn dies selbstverständlich implizit vorhanden ist), sondern daß es Gottes Wille sei, durch ἀγαθοποιία die Heiden zur Einsicht zu bewegen; anders H. GIESEN, Lebenszeugnis, 138. Dies gelingt freilich nur, wenn die Christen ihre Freiheit als Knechte Gottes nicht so verstehen, daß ihnen alles gestattet sei (v.16). Cf. dazu u.a. K. NIEDERWIMMER, ἐλεύθερος, 1058, mit Hinweis auf Gal 5,13; Röm 6,18.22; L. GOPPELT, 1Petr, 187f; K.H. SCHELKLE, 1Petr, 75f; N. BROX, 1Petr, 122. Oder wäre es tatsächlich möglich, daß ἐλευθερία hier die Versammlungsfreiheit meint, die einige für Schlechtes ausnützen, während die Christen sich darin als vorbildlich erweisen sollen? Ähnliche Vorwürfe erhob, wie wir gesehen haben, Flaccus gegen Isidorus (oben Seite 56), und die Tarnung als Collegium für Verbrechen wird auch bei Suetons Erörterung der Vereinseinschränkungen unter Augustus thematisiert (oben Seite 54).

[82] Cf. für Ephesus z.B. P.A. HARLAND, Honours, 328ff.

[83] Das Konzept der Vf. des 1Petr hatte freilich wenig Erfolg, zumindest zunächst. Cf. etwa auch Diog. 5,16: Ἀγαθοποιοῦντες ὡς κακοὶ κολάζονται.

Literatur

ACHTEMEIER, Paul J., 1 Peter, Hermeneia, Minneapolis 1996.
ALVAREZ CINEIRA, David, Die Religionspolitik des Kaisers Claudius und die paulinische Mission, Herders Biblische Studien 19, Freiburg u.a. 1999.
AUSBÜTTEL, Frank M., Untersuchungen zu den Vereinen im Westen des römischen Reiches, Frankfurter Althistorische Studien 11, Kallmünz 1982.
BEARE, Francis Wright, The First Epistle of Peter. The Greek Text with Introduction and Notes, Oxford ²1958.
BLEICKEN, Jochen, Verfassungs- und Sozialgeschichte des Römischen Kaiserreiches, 2 Bde., UTB 838+839, Paderborn u.a. ²1981.
BÖMER, Franz, Untersuchungen über die Religion der Sklaven in Griechenland und Rom, I: Die wichtigsten Kulte und Religionen in Rom und im lateinischen Westen, AAWLM.G 7, Wiesbaden 1958.
BOTERMANN, Helga, Das Judenedikt des Kaisers Claudius. Römischer Staat und *Christiani* im 1. Jahrhundert, Hermes 71, Stuttgart 1996.
BROX, Norbert, Der erste Petrusbrief, EKK 21, Zürich u.a. 1979.
CAMPBELL, Barth L., Honor, Shame, and the Rhetoric of 1 Peter, SBL.DS 160, Atlanta 1998.
CANCIK-LINDEMAIER, Hildegard, Der Diskurs Religion im Senatsbeschluß über die Bacchanalia von 186 v.Chr. und bei Livius (B.XXXIX), in: Geschichte – Tradition – Reflexion. FS Martin Hengel. Hg. v. Hubert CANCIK, Hermann LICHTENBERGER u. Peter SCHÄFER, II, Tübingen 1996, 77–96.
COHN, Max, Zum römischen Vereinsrecht. Abhandlungen aus der Rechtsgeschichte, Berlin 1873.
COTTER, Wendy, The Collegia and Roman Law. State restrictions on voluntary associations, 64 BCE – 200 CE, in: Voluntary Associations in the Graeco-Roman World, hg. v. John S. KLOPPENBORG, London u.a. 1996, 74–89.
CUMONT, Franz, Die orientalischen Religionen im römischen Heidentum, Leipzig u. Berlin ³1931.
DAHLHEIM, Werner, Geschichte der römischen Kaiserzeit, Oldenbourg-Grundriß der Geschichte 3, München ²1989.
DANKER, Frederick W., Benefactor: Epigraphic Study of a Graeco-Roman and New Testament Semantic Field, St. Louis 1982.
DASSMANN, Ernst, Kirchengeschichte I. Ausbreitung, Leben und Lehre der Kirche in den ersten drei Jahrhunderten, Kohlhammer Studienbücher Theologie 10, Stuttgart u.a. 1991.
DE ROBERTIS, Francesco M., Storia della corporazioni e del regime associativo nel mondo Romano, 2 Bde., Bari 1971.
DE ROSSI, Giovanni B., La Roma Sotterranea Cristiana, 3 Bde., Rom 1864–77 (ND Frankfurt 1966).
FELDMEIER, Reinhard, Die Christen als Fremde. Die Metapher der Fremde in der antiken Welt, im Urchristentum und im 1.Petrusbrief, WUNT 64, Tübingen 1992.
FELLMETH, Ulrich, Die römischen Vereine und die Politik. Untersuchungen zur sozialen Schichtung und zum politischen Bewußtsein in den Vereinen der städtischen Volksmassen in Rom und Italien, Diss. Stuttgart 1987.
FREND, W.H.C., Martyrdom and Persecution in the Early Church. A Study of a Conflict from the Maccabees to Donatus, Oxford 1965.

FREUDENBERGER, Rudolf, Das Verhalten der römischen Behörden gegen die Christen im 2. Jahrhundert dargestellt am Brief des Plinius an Trajan und den Reskripten Trajans und Hadrians, MBPF 52, München 1967.

GIESEN, Heinz, Lebenszeugnis in der Fremde. Zum Verhalten der Christen in der paganen Gesellschaft (1 Petr 2,11–17), in: SNTU 23 (1998), 113–152.

GOPPELT, Leonhard, Der Erste Petrusbrief, KEK 12/1, Göttingen 1978.

GORDON, Arthur E., Album of Dated Latin Inscriptions. II: Rome and the Neighborhood, A.D.100–199, Berkley u. Los Angeles 1964.

GRUEN, Erich S., The Last Generation of the Roman Republic, Berkeley u.a. 1974.

HARLAND, Philipp A., Honouring the Emperor or Assailing the Beast: Participation in Civic Life among Associations (Jewish, Christian and Other) in Asia Minor and the Apocalypse of John, in: JSNT 77 (2000), 99–121.

DERS., Honours and worship: Emperors, imperial cults and associations at Ephesus (first to third centuries C.E.), in: SR 25 (1996), 319–334.

HENGEL, Martin/SCHWEMER, Anna Maria, Paulus zwischen Damaskus und Antiochien. Die unbekannten Jahre des Apostels. Mit einem Beitrag von Ernst Axel KNAUF, WUNT 108, Tübingen 1998.

HERRMANN, Peter, Genossenschaft A. Griechisch, in: RAC 10 (1978), 84–97.

JEFFERS, James S., Conflict at Rome. Social Order and Hierarchy in Early Christianity, Minneapolis 1991.

JOHNSON, Allan Chester, Roman Egypt to the Reign of Diocletian, An Economic Survey of Ancient Rome II, Baltimore 1936.

JONES, Arnold H.M., Civitates Liberae et Immunes in the East, in: Anatolian Studies. FS William H. Buckler. Hg. v. William M. CALDER u. Josef KEIL, PUM 265, Manchester 1939, 103–117.

KASER, Max, Das römische Privatrecht, I: Das altrömische, das vorklassische und klassische Recht, HAW X 3.31, München ²1971.

KERESZTES, Paul, Rome and the Christian Church I, in: ANRW II 23.1 (1979), 247–315.

KIENAST, Dietmar, Augustus. Prinzeps und Monarch, Darmstadt ³1999.

KLEIN, Richard/GUYOT, Peter, Das frühe Christentum bis zum Ende der Verfolgungen. Eine Dokumentation, 2 Bde., Darmstadt 1997.

KLOPPENBORG, John S., Collegia and Thiasoi. Issues in function, taxonomy and membership, in: Voluntary Associations in the Graeco-Roman World. Hg. v. John S. KLOPPENBORG, London u.a. 1996, 16–30.

KÖTTING, Bernhard, Genossenschaft D. Christlich, in: RAC 10 (1978), 142–152.

KORNEMANN, Ernst, Collegium, in: PRE 4 (1901), 380–480.

KRÜGER, Gerda, Die Rechtsstellung der vorkonstantinischen Kirchen, KRA 115/116, Stuttgart 1935.

LA PIANA, George, Foreign Groups in Rome during the First Centuries of the Empire, in: HThR 20 (1927), 183–403.

LAMPE, Peter, Die stadtrömischen Christen in den ersten beiden Jahrhunderten. Untersuchungen zur Sozialgeschichte, WUNT II/18, Tübingen ²1989.

DERS./LUZ, Ulrich, Nachpaulinisches Christentum und pagane Gesellschaft, in: Die Anfänge des Christentums. Alte Welt und neue Hoffnung. Hg. v. Jürgen BECKER u.a., Stuttgart u.a. 1987, 185–216.

LIEBENAM, Wilhelm, Zur Geschichte und Organisation des römischen Vereinswesens. 3 Untersuchungen, Aalen 1964 (ND v. 1890).

LINDERSKI, Jerzy, Der Senat und die Vereine, in: Gesellschaft und Recht im griechisch-römischen Altertum, Bd. I. Hg. v. M.N. Andreev u.a., AAWDDR. Altertumswissenschaft 52, Berlin 1968, 94–132.

DERS., Suetons Bericht über die Vereinsgesetzgebung unter Caesar und Augustus, in: ZRG 79 (1962), 322–328.

MACMULLEN, Ramsay, Enemies of the Roman Order. Treason, Unrest, and Alienation in the Empire, Cambridge, Mass. 1966.

MOMMSEN, Theodor, Die *lex Iulia de collegiis* und die lanuvische *lex collegii salutaris*, in: Gesammelte Schriften III: Juristische Schriften III, Berlin 1907, 113–120.

DERS., Römisches Strafrecht, Leipzig 1899.

MÜLLER, Albert, Sterbekassen und Vereine mit Begräbnisfürsorge in der römischen Kaiserzeit, NJKA 8 (1905), 183–201.

NIEDERWIMMER, Kurt, ἐλεύθερος κτλ., in: EWNT I ([2]1992), 1052–1058.

VAN NIJF, Onno M., The Civic World of Professional Associations in the Roman East, Dutch Monographs on Ancient History and Archaeology 17, Amsterdam 1997.

NÖRR, Dieter, Imperium und Polis in der hohen Prinzipatszeit, MBPF 50, München [2]1969.

NOETHLICHS, Karl Leo, Das Judentum und der römische Staat. Minderheitenpolitik im antiken Rom, Darmstadt 1996.

PROSTMEIER, Ferdinand-Rupert, Handlungsmodelle im ersten Petrusbrief, FzB 63, Würzburg 1990.

RADIN, Max, The Legislation of the Greeks and Romans on Corporations, Diss. Columbia o.J. (um 1905).

RAJAK, Tessa, Was there a Roman Charter for the Jews?, in: JRS 74 (1984), 107–123.

RAMSAY, William Mitchell, The Church in the Roman Empire before A.D. 170, London [8]1904.

REICHERT, Angelika, Eine urchristliche Praeparatio ad Martyrium. Studien zur Komposition, Traditionsgeschichte und Theologie des 1.Petrusbriefes, BET 22, Frankfurt a.M. u.a. 1989.

REICKE, Bo, Diakonie, Festfreude und Zelos in Verbindung mit der altchristlichen Agapenfeier, UUÅ 5, Uppsala-Wiesbaden 1951.

RENAN, Ernest, Die Apostel, Geschichte der Anfänge des Christenthums II, Berlin o.J. (Paris 1868).

RICHARDSON, Peter, Early Synagogues as Collegia in the Diaspora and Palestine, in: Voluntary Associations in the Graeco-Roman World, hg. v. John S. KLOPPENBORG, London u.a. 1996, 90–109.

RIESNER, Rainer, Die Frühzeit des Apostels Paulus. Studien zur Chronologie, Missionsstrategie und Theologie, WUNT 71, Tübingen 1994.

RUTGERS, Leonard Victor, Roman Policy toward the Jews: Expulsions from the City of Rome during the First Century C.E., in: Judaism and Christianity in First-Century Rome. Hg. v. Karl P. DONFRIED/Peter RICHARDSON, Grand Rapids u. Cambridge 1998, 93–116.

SAN NICOLÒ, Mariano, Ägyptisches Vereinswesen zur Zeit der Ptolemäer und Römer, I: München 1913, II/1: MBPF 2, München 1915.

SCHÄFKE, Werner, Frühchristlicher Widerstand, in: ANRW II 23.1 (1979), 460–723.

SCHELKLE, Karl Hermann, Die Petrusbriefe. Der Judasbrief, HThK 13/2, Freiburg u.a. [5]1980.

SCHMELLER, Thomas, Hierarchie und Egalität. Eine sozialgeschichtliche Untersuchung paulinischer Gemeinden und griechisch-römischer Vereine, SBS 162, Stuttgart 1995.

SCHÜRER Emil, The History of the Jewish People in the Age of Jesus Christ (175 B.C.–A.D. 135). A New English Version, III/1. Hg. v. Geza VERMES, Fergus MILLAR u. Martin GOODMAN, Edinburgh 1986.
SHERWIN-WHITE, Adrian N., The Letters of Pliny. A Historical and Social Commentary, Oxford ²1968.
SMALLWOOD, E. Mary, The Jews under Roman Rule from Pompey to Diocletian. A Study in Political Relations, Leiden 1981.
STAMBAUGH, John E./BALCH, David L., Das soziale Umfeld des Neuen Testaments, GNT 9, Göttingen 1992.
TAKÁCS, Sarolta A., Isis and Sarapis in the Roman World, EPRO 124, Leiden u.a. 1995.
VAN UNNIK, Willem C., The Teaching of Good Works in I Peter, in: Sparsa Collecta II, NT.S 30, Leiden 1980, 83–105.
VERSNEL, Hendrik S., Römische Religion und religiöser Umbruch, in: Die orientalischen Religionen im Römerreich. Hg. v. Marten J. VERMASEREN, EPRO 93, Leiden 1981, 41–72.
VITTINGHOFF, Friedrich, Gesellschaft, in: Europäische Wirtschafts- und Sozialgeschichte in der römischen Kaiserzeit. Hg. v. Friedrich VITTINGHOFF, Handbuch der Europäischen Wirtschafts- und Sozialgeschichte I, Stuttgart 1990, 161–369.
WALTZING, J.-P., Étude historique sur les corporations professionnelles chez les Romains depuis les origines jusqu'à la chute de l'Empire d'Occident, 4 Bde., Leuven 1895–1900.
WASZINK, Jan Hendrik, Genossenschaft B. Römisch, in: RAC 10 (1978), 97–117.
WEBER, Volker, Zum Kollegienwesen: Die Berufsvereine in Handwerk und Handel, in: Gesellschaft und Wirtschaft des Römischen Reiches im 3. Jahrhundert. Hg. v. Klaus-Peter JOHNE, Berlin 1993, 101–134.
WILKEN, Robert L., Die frühen Christen. Wie die Römer sie sahen, Graz u.a. 1986.
WINTER, Bruce W., Seek the Welfare of the City. Christians as Benefactors and Citizens, First Century Christians in the Graeco-Roman World, Grand Rapids u. Carlisle 1994.
WLOSOK, Antonie, Die Rechtsgrundlagen der Christenverfolgungen der ersten zwei Jahrhunderte, in: Das frühe Christentum im römischen Staat. Hg. v. Richard KLEIN, WdF 267, Darmstadt 1971, 275–301.

Richard E. DeMaris

Cults and the Imperial Cult in Early Roman Corinth:
Literary Versus Material Record

> The temple of Aphrodite was so rich that it owned more than a thousand temple-slaves, courtesans [*hetairas*], whom both men and women had dedicated to the goddess. And therefore it was also on account of these women that the city was crowded with people and grew rich; for instance, the ship-captains freely squandered their money, and hence the proverb, "Not for every man is the voyage to Corinth." (Strab 8.6.20 [#378])[1]

When the geographer Strabo wrote these words, not long before the beginning of our era (29 B.C.E.),[2] he was not describing the Corinth that he had visited but the Corinth of a fabled past. As a result, modern scholarship has raised questions about the accuracy of Strabo's account. Devotion to Aphrodite or Venus in Strabo's day, in the early years of the Roman colony at Corinth, would certainly *not* have included cult prostitution. Such practices were unknown to earlier Greek religion as well, so that many scholars have concluded that Strabo probably indulged in fabrication about Corinth's past, continuing, intentionally or not, the character assassination that classical Athenian writers had carried out against their arch rivals, the Corinthians.[3] The Athenian playwright Philetaerus, for instance, entitled one of his plays *Corinthiast*, by which he meant whoremonger or fornicator (Athen XIII 559a), and Aristophanes coined the term *korinthiazomai*, which evidently meant "to associate with courtesans" or "to be a pimp."[4] Even Plato could refer to a courtesan as a Corinthian girl (Resp 404d). If Corinth and sexual vice were synonymous in Greek literature, it is understandable why Strabo characterized the Corinthian cult of Aphrodite, the goddess of love, as he did.

Though scholars have challenged this characterization, Corinth's reputation as a city of sexual immorality remains surprisingly intact. One contemporary interpreter takes Paul's mention of a prostitute in 1 Cor 6:15 as a reference to prostitution at the Temple of Aphrodite, since Paul introduces the subject of the temple four verses later.[5] Another sees no need to cite Strabo, but simply accepts his description as fact: "We can imagine that in a city where sacred

---

[1] LCL transl., STRABO, Geography 4, 191.
[2] Scholars assign this date to the visit based on Strabo's comments in 10.5.3 (#485). See STRABO, Geography 1, xx; J. WISEMAN, Corinth, 509.
[3] H. CONZELMANN, Korinth, 247–261; R.E. OSTER, Jr., Use, 70, n. 94; J. MURPHY-O'CONNOR, Corinth, 56, 125–128; V.P. FURNISH, Corinth, 25.
[4] R. KASSEL/C. AUSTIN, Aristophanes, fragment 370.
[5] R.H. GUNDRY, *Sôma*, 75.

prostitution was practiced many men and women did not have a healthy attitude toward sex."[6] Other scholars, aware of the challenge to Strabo's claim, defend his accuracy.[7] John MCRAY goes so far as to use the archaeological record of Corinth to verify its depravity.[8]

The uncritical acceptance of Strabo is becoming less frequent in scholarship, but even among those inclined to dismiss Strabo, the reputation of Corinth that he and others fostered lingers. For instance, C.K. BARRETT's well-known commentary on 1 Corinthians expresses ambiguity on the subject. He opens the book with the comment, "In Paul's day, Corinth was probably little better and little worse than any other great sea port and commercial centre of the age."[9] Yet later, in underscoring the dire situation in Corinth that called for Paul's insistence to flee *porneia* – sexual immorality (1 Cor 6:18) – BARRETT claims, "Temptations to fornication were so common in Corinth that mere disapproval was likely to be inadequate; strong evasive action would be necessary."[10] Likewise, on the very page in his 1 Corinthians commentary where he dismisses Strabo's description as erroneous, Gordon FEE perpetuates Corinth's reputation for sexual vice in a gratuitous remark about the votive objects recovered in huge numbers from the Temple of Asklepios and now on display at the Corinth Museum: "here on one wall are a large number of clay votives of human genitals that had been offered to the god for the healing of that part of the body," then FEE adds, "*apparently ravaged by venereal disease*" (italics added).[11] New Testament scholarship does not seem ready to set aside the image of Corinth as a Mediterranean Hamburg, Amsterdam, or San Francisco.

Why does Corinth's reputation for sexual vice persist, even when scholarship has discredited the writers that created it? The texts of those writers survived, unlike any rebuttal to the Athenian opinion about Corinth. As for biblical scholars, they listen to another voice from antiquity, namely, the apostle Paul's, which seems to confirm the Corinthian reputation for sexual indulgence and degradation. In the course of 1 Corinthians, Paul warns his readers (and listeners) about visiting prostitutes (6:15–18); reminds them of their former ways as fornicators, adulterers, male prostitutes, and sodomites (6:9–11); and scolds them for their toleration of illicit sexual relations in their midst (5:1–8). Clearly, Strabo's slander persists, at least in part, because it agrees with what scholars have gathered about the Corinthians from Paul's correspondence to them, such as BARRETT's deduction that they are libertines.[12]

A generous estimate of New Testament scholarship on this issue, such as Richard OSTER's,[13] concludes that scholars now largely recognize Strabo's

---

[6] S.E. JOHNSON, Paul, 64.
[7] E.g., B. WITHERINGTON III, Conflict, 13–14.
[8] J. MCRAY, Archaeology, 315–317.
[9] C.K. BARRETT, Commentary, 3.
[10] C.K. BARRETT, Commentary, 150.
[11] G.D. FEE, Epistle, 2.
[12] C.K. BARRETT, Commentary, 121, 144.
[13] R.E. OSTER, Jr., Use, 70, n. 94.

description and the Athenian characterization of Corinth as jaundice, and they have freed Corinth from its tarnished reputation.[14] There are too many counter examples, I believe, to be so optimistic. Yet whatever judgment we reach about New Testament scholarship, the point of these opening paragraphs should be clear: ancient texts have exercised an inordinate and largely unchecked influence on the study of antiquity, on reconstructions of the past, and on characterizations of peoples and places in the ancient world. Certain texts carry so much authority that they have even controlled scholarly interpretation of archaeological data. As a case in point, an example mentioned above, we have John MCRAY's marshaling of Corinth's material record to support Strabo.[15] With regard to Corinth generally, such textual tyranny has often resulted in misinterpretation of the material record.

Unmasking text-induced misreadings of the archaeological data is a primary task of this study, and doing so will set the table for accomplishing a second major goal: once we have identified and set aside distortions fostered by the literary record, we can ask what the material record reveals about the religious climate of early Roman Corinth. What emerges, I will argue, is a picture of Corinth and a profile of religion there that differs from the one commonly accepted. Moreover, this archaeologically-informed picture suggests new and different ways of approaching Paul's correspondence to the Corinthians and the fledging Christian movement in Corinth.

I. Tyranny of Texts and Misreading the Material Record

Comparing and coordinating the literary and material records of the ancient Mediterranean world is crucial to our reconstruction of the past. In the case of biblical studies, such comparative work was once motivated by the desire to verify the accuracy of the text, or, in other words, to prove that the Bible was true. Yet most biblical scholars nowadays simply want to place the text in context, that is, to locate the New Testament in the picture of the world we construct from the archaeological data. Victor FURNISH, for example, notes the architectural evidence for a massive civic building program underway in Corinth in the mid-first century C.E., and he suggests such activity may have prompted the language of 1 Cor 3:10–15, where Paul compares his founding of the church at Corinth to the work of a skilled master builder laying a foundation.[16]

The effort to tie text to archaeology is admirable, but it sometimes goes astray. FURNISH proposes that the well-attested bronze and ceramic industries of Corinth may have inspired the metaphors Paul uses in his correspondence when he refers to mirrors (highly polished bronze; 1 Cor 13:12; 2 Cor 3:18) –

---

[14] So, for example, J. MURPHY-O'CONNOR, 1 Corinthians, 49; B.D. EHRMAN, New Testament, 290.
[15] J. MCRAY, Archaeology, 315–317.
[16] V.P. FURNISH, Corinth, 17.

as in the phrase "for now we see in a mirror, dimly"[17] – and when he refers to clay jars (2 Cor 4:7) – "but we have this treasure in clay jars."[18] While this suggestion is inviting, there is a problem with it. Corinth had been a preeminent bronze and pottery producer centuries before Paul, but the Corinth of Paul's day was still recovering from the devastation of the city in 146 B.C.E., when the Romans sacked it. Corinthian archaeologist James WISEMAN notes, for instance, that Corinth's bronze production saw some revival in the early life of the Roman colony (first century C.E.).[19] But would this reemerging bronze industry have reached sufficient scale to impress Paul? Would Paul have known about the city's famous ceramic industry, whose apogee had come before the classical period, some seven hundred years before Paul? FURNISH's suggestion about what inspired Paul depends on a reputation the city had *long* before Paul, but to assume that Paul knew about Corinth's distant past may not be warranted. Still, this is a fairly harmless mistake: FURNISH makes no major interpretive claim, only a suggestion. Moreover, this attempt at connecting the New Testament text with the realities of the day, while probably anachronistic, is not flagrantly so.

Other misuses of the archaeological record are more glaring. Andrew HILL, for instance, has argued that Paul's body illustration in 1 Cor 12:12–26 took its inspiration from the terracotta representations of human body parts that grateful visitors dedicated at the Temple of Asklepios in Corinth in recognition of the cure the healing god had brought them.[20] According to HILL, when Paul saw the collection of votive body parts on a supposed visit to the Asklepios Temple, it triggered his reflection on the church as the body of Christ and on individual members as parts of that body.[21]

This correlation of material and textual record stumbles, however, on the fact that the votives under discussion were recovered from deposits that can be firmly dated to a time well before Paul's stay in Corinth. Coins, lamps, and pottery found with the votives point to a range of dates from the last quarter of the fifth to the end of the fourth century B.C.E.[22] HILL's argument rests, therefore, on an obvious anachronism. Paul could not possibly have seen the votives in question, for they would have long been buried in his day.[23]

HILL's misinterpretation has minor repercussions, however, compared to the problems caused when archaeologists yield to the influence of a text and interpret the material record according to it. If we fault New Testament scholars for misusing the material record in the interpretation of Paul's letters, we have a more troublesome situation when classicists and classical archaeologists

---

[17] NRSV transl. for this and all other biblical quotations in the chapter.
[18] V.P. FURNISH, Corinth, 18.
[19] J. WISEMAN, Corinth, 512.
[20] A.E. HILL, Temple, 437–439; the votives are described and pictured in C. ROEBUCK, Asklepieion, 114–128, plates 29–46.
[21] See also J. MURPHY-O'CONNOR, Corinth, 165, 167.
[22] C. ROEBUCK, Asklepieion, 113, 128–131.
[23] R.E. OSTER, Jr., Use, 71–73.

force the material record of Corinth through the filter of Pausanias. Doing so has resulted in the neglect or misuse of the archaeological record at crucial points. Moreover, New Testament scholars and others have relied on that flawed scholarship and disseminated those errors in their own work.

An example will illustrate the misinformation this chain of transmission can spread. If the educated reader knows nothing else about the ancient city of Corinth it is that the landmark of the archaeological site, the few remaining columns of a massive archaic temple, was dedicated to Apollo. Yet some archaeologists are quick to point out that that identification rests almost entirely on an interpretation of Pausanias's visit to Corinth (2.3.6), an account full of imprecision.[24] Nevertheless, so great has been Pausanias's influence that references to the Archaic Temple as the Temple of Apollo fill both scholarly and popular literature. The archaeological record does not corroborate such an identification, however.

Such misinformation is not always the fault of popularizers who garbled or misreported the findings of experts. Rather, the excavators themselves have been ready to put their trust in Pausanias and marshal the material record of their excavations to support him. In the case of Corinth's eastern seaport, Kenchreai, we have the following brief report from Pausanias (2.2.3): "In Cenchreae are a temple and a stone statue of Aphrodite, after it on the mole running into the sea a bronze image of Poseidon, and at the other end of the harbour sanctuaries of Asclepius and of Isis."[25] Following Pausanias's lead, chief excavator of Kenchreai, Robert SCRANTON, identified an Aphrodision in a section of the port called Area C, on the northern side of the harbor, and a Sanctuary of Isis in a site called Area A, on the southern mole of the harbor (see figure 1).[26] The New Testament scholar Dennis SMITH relied in turn on reports from SCRANTON's excavation in his Harvard Theological Review article of 1977 on the Egyptian cults at Corinth, in which he described the Isis Sanctuary at Kenchreai in some detail.[27]

How warranted are these identifications? SCRANTON admits that neither the buildings nor the objects found in them point explicitly to Isis or Aphrodite sanctuaries. Rather, the material record, he claims, is compatible with the Pausanias-inspired identifications.[28] Yet this assertion belies how forced SCRANTON's interpretation of the material record is. Nothing the excavators labeled an Aphrodision has any architectural connection with a temple or sanctuary. On the contrary, the buildings of Area C look domestic. Accord-

---

[24] J. WISEMAN, Corinth, 475, 530.
[25] LCL transl., PAUSANIAS, Description 1, 255.
[26] R.L. SCRANTON/J.W. SHAW/L. IBRAHIM, Topography, 53–90, figures 31, 34. Figure 1 from B. ADAMSHECK, Pottery, figure 14.
[27] D.E. SMITH, Cults, 201–210. Smith relied primarily on a preliminary report by R.L. SCRANTON/E.S. RAMAGE, Investigations, since the final report had not yet appeared.
[28] R.L. SCRANTON/J.W. SHAW/L. IBRAHIM, Topography, 74–78, 89–90.

ingly, SCRANTON wrote about residences for priestesses and cult prostitutes – an unacknowledged reference to Strabo's characterization![29]

Recently, another Corinthian archaeologist has reviewed the findings of the University of Chicago-Indiana University excavation of Kenchreai and taken issue with its conclusions. To Richard ROTHAUS, the large brick building excavators consider the strongest candidate for belonging to an Aphrodision looks very much like a Roman villa, as evidenced by its peristyle courtyard (see figure 2).[30] SCRANTON considered but rejected this possibility because of the proximity of Area C to the center of the port. He could not picture a villa in a "plebian and commercial atmosphere,"[31] but ROTHAUS notes that urban villas were not uncommon in the port cities of the Roman empire, such as Ostia.

ROTHAUS also raises questions about the so-called Isieion. He notes that the key architectural features of the structure in question, an apsidal building with fountain joined to an unroofed rectangular courtyard, mark it as a Roman nymphaeum, similar both in form and setting to the imperial nymphaeum at Baia (Baiae), on the Campanian coast, just north of the bay of Naples (see figure 3).[32] Whether or not ROTHAUS's alternative interpretations arc convincing, his reexamination of the final reports of the Kenchreai excavations reveals how dependent SCRANTON and others were on Pausanias and how ambiguous the archaeological record actually is.

Excessive reliance on Pausanias has caused the same distortion of the archaeological record in the case of Corinth and resulted in a misleading picture of the civic center of that city. For instance, when Pausanias reached the city fountain associated with Glauke in his travel account of Corinth, he mentioned a cluster of other related monuments he found nearby, immediately northwest of the Roman forum (2.3.6–11). At this point, Pausanias interrupted his travel report to introduce the legends and figures of the rich Greek tradition surrounding Glauke: Jason, Medea, and Hera. This emphasis in Pausanias's narrative suggested to excavators that Glauke Fountain marked a section of the city devoted to her memory, a devotion with a long Greek heritage that the Romans had preserved and revitalized. Accordingly, Temple C, built by the Romans in the late Augustan or Tiberian period, was identified with Hera Akraia, and was thought to be a replacement for an earlier Greek temple also dedicated to her (see figure 4).[33] The final report admits, however, that no data from the site support this identification.[34] Instead, the identification of the temple and the positing of an earlier Greek-period temple derives solely from

---

[29] R.L. SCRANTON/J.W. SHAW/L. IBRAHIM, Topography, 90.
[30] R.M. ROTHAUS, Corinth, 66, 68–69. Figure 2 from R.L. SCRANTON/J.W. SHAW/L. IBRAHIM, Topography, figure 38.
[31] R.L. SCRANTON/J.W. SHAW/L. IBRAHIM, Topography, 88.
[32] R.M. ROTHAUS, Corinth, 69. See G. TOCCO SCIARELLI, Baia, which Rothaus refers to under the name Fausto Zevi. Figure 3 from R.L. SCRANTON/J.W. SHAW/L. IBRAHIM, Topography, figure 31.
[33] R. STILLWELL/R.L. SCRANTON/S.E. FREEMAN, Architecture, 131–165, especially 157–165. Figure 4 from M.E.H. WALBANK, Evidence, 205, figure 2.
[34] R. STILLWELL/R.L. SCRANTON/S.E. FREEMAN, Architecture, 149.

Pausanias, who does not explicitly refer to a Hera Temple near Glauke Fountain. Consequently, the current generation of Corinthian archaeologists distances itself from such speculation: they reserve judgment about the identity of the Roman-era temple and largely dismiss the hypothesis about an earlier Greek temple as "highly conjectural."[35]

As for Glauke Fountain, Pausanias is explicit about its identity and location (2.3.6), and the architectural remains at the site are clearly those of a fountain. Unfortunately, the original excavators of the site were convinced, under Pausanias's spell, that the Romans did little more than preserve the Greek legacy that Pausanias described in his travelogue. As a result, until recently archaeologists were convinced that Glauke Fountain was originally a Greek structure carved from living rock, which the Romans saved and modified.[36] But the current opinion is that the Romans thoroughly imitated Greek architectural form in producing a building that highlighted Greek heritage. Charles WILLIAMS, for many years director of the Corinth Excavations, offers this interpretation of the structure:

> With Glauke we have, then, an example of deliberate architectural eclecticism within Laus Julia Corinthiensis. ... I would suggest that the design was determined by the literary spirit of the educated Roman colonist, who wanted to be able to show a monument of ancient Corinth fitting, as he saw it, the myth of Medea as it was passed down, ...[37]

WILLIAMS saw Hellenistic influence at work here in the incredibly close mimicry of Greek architecture by the Roman colonists.

A different motivation may lie behind the construction of the fountain, however. Not to slight WILLIAMS's very important correction of how Corinth's material record should be interpreted, but his suggestion about why the Romans built the fountain is, in my opinion, too Pausanian. Had the fountain been built under the philhellenic Hadrian, his suggestion would make sense, but not earlier in the history of the colony, when the fountain was constructed.

Glauke Fountain's location in relation to the plan of central Roman Corinth suggests a political rather than literary motivation for building it. The fountain stood beside the route that led to the sole entrance to the Archaic Temple precinct in the Roman era. One former access to the temple had been from the south, but that was blocked by the Northwest Stoa. A grand stairway had once given access to the temple precinct from the southeast, but that access was obliterated when the Romans quarried the eastward extension of the ridge on which the temple sat.[38] The Archaic Temple now had an axial entrance to the west, which meant that the temple and entry to it were oriented toward Rome.

The new configuration meant that Glauke Fountain served as a source of water as one approached the Roman forum from the north and west and as one

---

[35] J. WISEMAN, Corinth, 473, n. 132.
[36] B.H. HILL, Springs, 200–228; H.S. ROBINSON, Corinth, 10.
[37] C.K. WILLIAMS II, Refounding, 35.
[38] C.K. WILLIAMS II, Refounding, 31.

came to the entry of a prominent temple precinct in Roman Corinth. The arrangement was, therefore, similar to other important sanctuaries in the Greek east that underwent Roman reshaping. The Roman remodeling of the Demeter Sanctuary at Pergamon, for instance, included construction of a nymphaeum in the sanctuary's forecourt.[39] Likewise, the Greater (or Outer) Propylaia at Eleusis, which replaced the older North Pylon and served as the main gate to the walled sanctuary precinct, was flanked by a well.[40]

WILLIAMS may be right that eclecticism was at work in the construction of Glauke Fountain, and not of a random or unintended sort. By imitating Greek architecture in their reconfiguring of a central Corinthian religious site, the Romans were dressing Romanization in Greek clothing. In so doing, were they artfully ingratiating themselves with the local Greeks by presenting themselves as preservers of the past? If so, such insinuation was not the expression of literary spirit or philhellenism. Anthropologists of colonialism would call it cultural imperialism in the form of indigenization: exercising hegemony by the conscious adoption and manipulation of native elements. Glauke Fountain may well represent cultural eclecticism, but it was an eclecticism according to Roman taste and under Roman control.[41]

II. A New Picture of Religion in Roman Corinth

Pausanias, because of his own preoccupation with the Greek past, left us a distorted picture of Corinth and other Greek cities and places under the Roman empire. His text, more than any other, has caused scholars to miss the fact that Corinth in his day was a Roman city and an expression of Roman culture and ideology on Greek soil. As Corinthian archaeologist Mary WALBANK notes,

> For long there was an implicit assumption by scholars that *Colonia Laus Iulia Corinthiensis* was not a conventional Roman colony, but rather a re-foundation and continuation of the Greek city destroyed a hundred years earlier. Today most scholars accept that Corinth was a traditional Roman colony.[42]

What does it mean that Corinth was a traditional, conventional Roman colony? In terms of the heart of Corinth, its central marketplace, it meant profound discontinuity between the Greek and Roman periods. The survival of the massive South Stoa from Hellenistic through late Roman times once signaled to modern interpreters that the Roman forum was essentially a continuation of the Greek agora, which matched the impression of the city Pausanias gave. Yet excavators have found no evidence for a Greek agora under the Roman forum, so they now surmise that archaic and classical Greek Corinth had its central market elsewhere, somewhere to the north of the Archaic Temple or Peirene

---

[39] C.H. BOHNTZ, Demeter-Heiligtum, 15–16.
[40] K. CLINTON, Contribution, 59; D. GIRAUD, Propylaia, plate 13, figure 1; plate 23, figure 14.
[41] C. STEWART/R. SHAW, Introduction, 7, 12.
[42] M.E.H. WALBANK, Foundation, 95.

Fountain.⁴³ The forum is, therefore, a purely Roman creation, built over a Greek-period race track, not a reestablishment of the Greek agora.⁴⁴

A dramatic change in cultic orientation accompanied this geographical shift in city center. Scholars have determined that a number of small cults, local in scope, devoted to heroes, and chthonic or funerary in orientation, occupied the civic center of Corinth in the Greek period.⁴⁵ At the same time, the Olympian deities appear to have been insignificant there. As WILLIAMS notes, "none of them was housed in an elaborate building nor given an elaborate architectural setting."⁴⁶ Yet quite the reverse was so in the Roman era. None of the hero cults survived into the Roman period. Rather, shrines and temples to the Olympian gods populated the Roman forum. Capturing that striking discontinuity in city center, WILLIAMS says, "Few, perhaps none, of the Roman temples ... were constructed over the remains of ... cults of the Greek period."⁴⁷ In contrast to the relative continuity in cults outside city center – the Romans reestablished the Asklepieion and the Demeter and Persephone (Kore) sanctuary on the slope of Acrocorinth – there was little or no religious continuity from the Greek to Roman periods in the center of Corinth.⁴⁸

The new civic center created by the Romans featured an impressive row of monuments and temples at the western end of the forum, which would have attracted the attention of anyone entering it. When Pausanias described this end of the forum, he was not entirely clear (2.2.6–8), and the archaeological remains have not shed much additional light (see figure 4). Archaeologists generally agree about a fountain to Poseidon or Neptune in the middle of the row, later replaced by a temple in honor of emperor Commodus.⁴⁹ The current wisdom identifies Temple F with Aphrodite, that is, Venus Genetrix, mother of the Roman people and, of course, the Roman colony of Corinth.⁵⁰ WILLIAMS suggests that the other building with strong ties to Rome was Temple G, immediately next to Temple F. He identifies it as dedicated to Clarian Apollo, a nod no doubt to Augustus, who claimed Apollo as progenitor.⁵¹ The identification of each specific temple remains subject to dispute, but it is clear the Olympian gods were well represented in the row of monuments that defined the western end of the Roman forum.

---

[43] J. WISEMAN, Corinth, 488–489.
[44] C.K. WILLIAMS II, Cults, 163.
[45] C.K. WILLIAMS II, Cults, 65–66, 77–78, 86–87, 169; A. STEINER, Pottery, 385–408, especially 402–405; O. BRONEER, Hero, 128–161, especially 132, 142–145, 156.
[46] C.K. WILLIAMS II, Cults, 162.
[47] C.K. WILLIAMS II, Cults, 164.
[48] C.K. WILLIAMS II, Cults, 19, 169; M.E.H. WALBANK, Pausanias, 383.
[49] C.K. WILLIAMS II, Refounding, 29; C.K. WILLIAMS II/J.E. FISHER, Corinth, 25; R.L. SCRANTON, Monuments, 69.
[50] C.K. WILLIAMS II, Re-evaluation, 157; C.K. WILLIAMS II/J.E. FISHER, Corinth, 27; J. WISEMAN, Corinth, 529.
[51] C.K. WILLIAMS II, Re-evaluation, 158. The original excavator connected Clarian Apollo with another temple nearby (R.L. SCRANTON, Monuments, 71–72).

However we sort these small temples out among the Olympians, another, much larger temple overshadowed them all, namely Temple E, which most archaeologists assign to Octavia or Gens Julia.[52] Pausanias mentioned the temple only in passing (2.3.1), but numismatic evidence supports his identification.[53] An axis projected from Temple E divided the forum temples, left and right. As one approached the west end of the forum, the temple to the imperial cult stood above a monumental set of stairs, elevated by a podium, and flanked by the smaller forum temples below it. This cluster of forum temples drew the eye to the west end of the forum, but they also pointed beyond themselves to the larger, higher temple looking down on the forum.[54] If Olympian deities dominated the center of Corinth in the Roman era, they did so in the service of the imperial cult.[55]

Pausanias's tour of Corinth's civic center may have masked the importance of the imperial cult in Corinth, but the architecture and city plan revealed by excavation underscore its centrality. If the Archaic Temple had once dominated city center because of its elevation and size, the Romans undid its dominance by blocking it off from the forum and turning its face westward, as noted above.[56] Now Temple E, a Roman creation, controlled the forum. The imperial cult was, therefore, the new religious focal point of Roman Corinth. In this way, Corinth did indeed conform to what we would expect of a traditional Roman colony. It was not, as Pausanias presented the city, a museum of the glorious Greek past.

With this new topography of cultic Roman Corinth in mind, what can we say about Paul and the Christians of Corinth? The picture of Corinth emerging from a more critical reading of Pausanias and a more careful reading of the archaeological record presents us with a city that was the very opposite of the static picture Pausanias gave us. It was dynamic not only in the palpable sense that Corinth was undergoing a construction boom, intense economic development, and a tremendous population growth in Paul's day. The Romanization of Corinth also brought with it the dynamics typical of any colonial setting. Roman historian Susan ALCOCK describes the situation well, when she asserts that Roman Greece must be regarded not as a "cultural haven, an imaginary world, or a museum locked in spiritual twilight," but rather as "a society in the process of change, adapting and assimilating itself to a new position within an imperial system – just as countless other subordinate societies have been forced to do throughout the centuries."[57] The cultural imperialism at work in the forum no doubt triggered a response; we should expect to see native re-

---

[52] J. WISEMAN, Corinth, 522; C.K. WILLIAMS II, Refounding, 29.
[53] M.E.H. WALBANK offers a useful survey of the evidence, but few accept her conclusion that Temple E was a Capitolium (Pausanias, 361–394; Evidence, 201–213). See C.K. WILLIAMS II, Refounding, 35–36, n. 6, 7.
[54] R. STILLWELL/R.L. SCRANTON/S.E. FREEMAN, Architecture, 233.
[55] C.K. WILLIAMS II, Refounding, 29–30.
[56] M.E.H. WALBANK, Pausanias, 365.
[57] S. ALCOCK, Graecia, 230.

sponses to Romanization, either in the form of adaptation and assimilation or resistance and subversion, and most likely both.

New Testament scholars have typically defined the ethnic differences that divided early Christian communities in terms of Jew versus Gentile. The factions at Corinth, however, may have had a different basis. Perhaps we should reconceive of tensions between Christians there as conflict between Romans and Greeks, or more to the point, as conflict between colonists and natives. Evidence for such ethnic diversity comes in the form of Greek and Latin names that Paul mentions.[58] I have explored elsewhere the implications of the difference in burial practices between the Roman colonists and the local Greek population of Corinth.[59] Cultural difference and the conflict it engendered, especially in a colonial situation, may account for other disputes among the Corinthians, masked until now by the tendency of New Testament scholars to lump Greek and Roman together under the rubric of Gentile or Greco-Roman.

The ethnic diversity reflected in Paul's letters was not only a result of the mixed population that colonized Roman Corinth. The Roman colonists evidently encountered a residual Greek population, descendents of those surviving the sack of the city in 146 B.C.E. While some reports from antiquity describe a completely devastated and abandoned Corinth, such as Cassius Dio's (21 [=Zonaras 9.31]), scholars detect hyperbole at work in them. The archaeological record confirms the reports of eyewitnesses like Cicero who encountered local inhabitants living among the ruins of Corinth (Tusc 3.22 #53). The material record indicates that parts of the city, like the South Stoa, survived the sack relatively intact. Moreover, ceramic and numismatic data point to habitation and commercial activity between 146 and the founding of the Roman colony in 44 B.C.E.[60] We can be certain, therefore, there was a residual local and regional population that preserved the traditions of the past. Accordingly, I am inclined to agree with a comment voiced sixty years ago by Corinth archaeologist Oscar BRONEER concerning the hero cults of Greek-period Corinth:

> During the interval of a century, between the destruction of the city under Mummius and its rebuilding by Caesar, many of the lesser sanctuaries fell into decay and some of them may have been abandoned. But religious beliefs lie too deeply rooted in the human consciousness to disappear during the course of three generations, and the cult is likely to have been revived in some form after the rebuilding of the city, even if its original nature and significance was no longer apparent.[61]

Among the surviving Greek-period traditions was a religious disposition toward hero cults and, concomitantly, a chthonic and funerary orientation. Rome's alteration of Corinth's civic center obliterated cultic places given over to hero devotion, but elimination of place did not necessarily mean the end of

---

[58] G. SELLIN, Hauptprobleme, 2997. G. THEISSEN provides a full discussion in Schichtung, 232–272.
[59] R.E. DEMARIS, Religion, 671.
[60] J. WISEMAN, Corinth, 494–495; R.E. DEMARIS, Religion, 670, n. 52.
[61] O. BRONEER, Hero, 153.

orientation and practice. Instead, it may have meant their displacement from center to periphery.

Where and in what fashion did this religious orientation reemerge in Roman Corinth? One answer to this question comes from the change in devotion to Demeter and Persephone between the Greek and Roman periods. At their sanctuary, located well away from the civic center of Corinth, a chthonic orientation came to prominence in the Roman era.[62]

Corinthian Christianity may have provided another outlet for the religious impulse that Rome pushed out of city center. If 1 Corinthians is an accurate indicator, Christianity there had a decidedly chthonic tone. Two key Christian rites, the common meal and baptism, had a funerary cast. What Paul writes about the Corinthians' dining ritual places the common meal squarely in a mortuary context (11:17–34): "For as often as you eat this bread and drink the cup, *you proclaim the Lord's death* until he comes" (v. 26; italics added).[63] Similarly, the Corinthians gave baptism a funerary application by practicing it on behalf of their dead (15:29).[64]

In this light, perhaps we should consider Paul's christological emphasis at Corinth, what he called a foolish proclamation (1:21–25), an indication of how Paul tailored his gospel to his audience. When Paul wrote, "I decided to know nothing among you except Jesus Christ, and him crucified" (2:2), stress fell on the tragic death of the movement's hero. Did Paul accent this aspect of the gospel in order to capitalize on the Corinthian disposition, at least among the Greek population, toward the heroic, funerary, and chthonic?[65] If so, we can then begin to locate Christianity in the religious topography of early Roman Corinth: It took root in Corinth because of its ability to shelter and express a Greek religiosity that Rome had suppressed. Consequently, we should consider the elements of Corinthian and Pauline Christianity just mentioned as a form of resistance to Roman imperialism on Greek soil.

This understanding of Paul and the Christians of Corinth is certainly not beyond dispute, but space does not permit me to make a full argument for what I have suggested. Besides, I may revise this interpretation as my research on the material record continues and as the archaeologists of ancient Corinth refine their analyses. What cannot be disputed, however, is this: The archaeological record of Corinth generates a new profile of early Roman Corinth, different from one based largely or solely on ancient literature, and it promises to be a continuing source of fresh insight into Paul's Corinthian correspondence. As archaeology further informs our picture of religious life in ancient Corinth, we will have to make additional adjustments to our picture of the Christian community there.

---

[62] R.E. DeMaris, Demeter, 105–117.
[63] C.K. Barrett, Commentary, 267, 270. H. Lietzmann, Mass, xviii, 182.
[64] R.E. DeMaris, Religion, 661–682.
[65] R.S. Nash, Death; G.J. Riley, Jesus, 69–74.

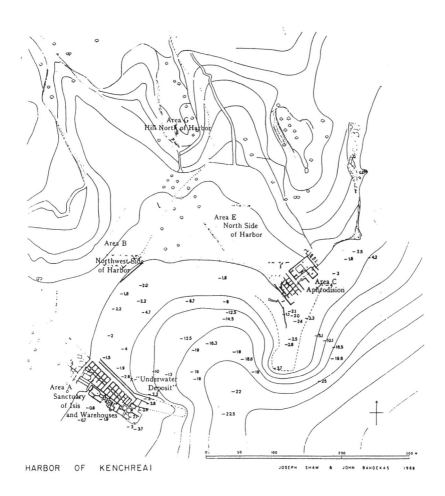

Figure 1. Kenchreai, Eastern Port of Corinth

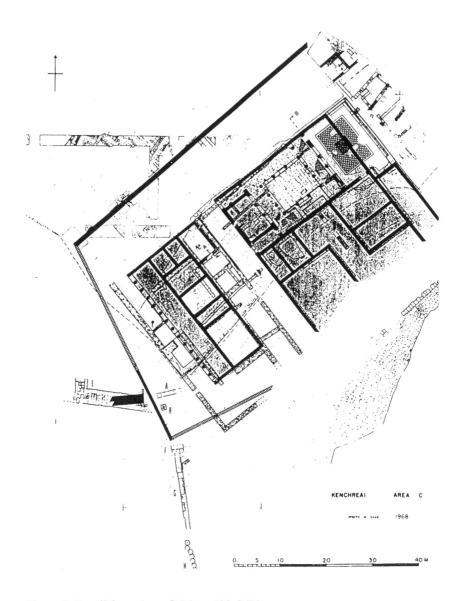

Figure 2. Detail from Area C (circa 100 C.E.)

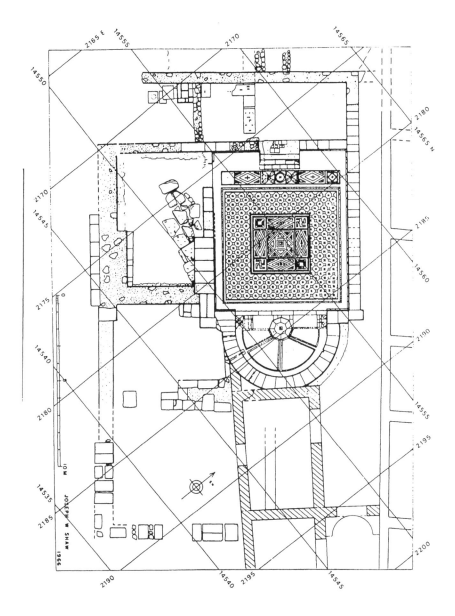

Figure 3. Detail from Area A: Fountain Court and Temple of Isis

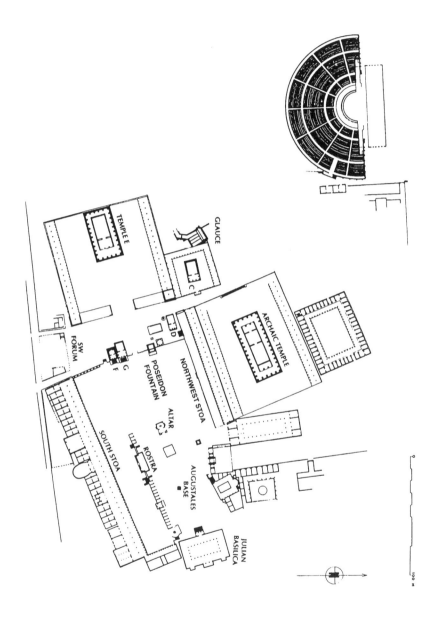

Figure 4. Corinth's Civic Center (circa 50 C.E.)

Bibliography

ADAMSHECK, Beverley, Kenchreai, Eastern Port of Corinth, vol. 4, The Pottery, Leiden 1979.
ALCOCK, Susan E., Graecia Capta. The Landscapes of Roman Greece, Cambridge 1993.
BARRETT, Charles Kingsley, A Commentary on the First Epistle to the Corinthians, Harper's New Testament Commentaries, New York 1968.
BOHTZ, Carl Helmut, Das Demeter-Heiligtum, Deutsches Archäologisches Institut, Altertümer von Pergamum 13, Berlin 1981.
BRONEER, Oscar, Hero Cults in the Corinthian Agora, in: Hesp. 11 (1942), 128–161.
CLINTON, Kevin, Hadrian's Contribution to the Renaissance of Eleusis, in: The Greek Renaissance in the Roman Empire. Papers from the Tenth British Museum Classical Colloquium. Ed. by Susan WALKER/Averil CAMERON, Institute of Classical Studies Bulletin Supplement 55, London 1989, 56–68.
CONZELMANN, Hans, Korinth und die Mädchen der Aphrodite. Zur Religionsgeschichte der Stadt Korinth, in: NAWG.PH 8 (1967), 247–261.
DEMARIS, Richard E., Corinthian Religion and Baptism for the Dead (1 Corinthians 15:29). Insights from Archaeology and Anthropology, in: JBL 114 (1995), 661–682.
ID., Demeter in Roman Corinth. Local Development in a Mediterranean Religion, in: Numen 42 (1995), 105–117.
EHRMAN, Bart D., The New Testament. A Historical Introduction to the Early Christian Writings, Oxford [2]2000.
FEE, Gordon D., The First Epistle to the Corinthians, NICNT, Grand Rapids 1987.
FURNISH, Victor Paul, Corinth in Paul's Time: What Can Archaeology Tell Us?, in: BArR 15/3 (May/June 1988), 14–27.
GIRAUD, Demosthenis, The Greater Propylaia at Eleusis, a Copy of Mnesikles' Propylaia, in: The Greek Renaissance in the Roman Empire. Papers from the Tenth British Museum Classical Colloquium. Ed. by Susan WALKER/Averil CAMERON, Institute of Classical Studies Bulletin Supplement 55, London 1989, 69–75 and plates 13–26.
GUNDRY, Robert H., Sôma in Biblical Theology, with Emphasis on Pauline Anthropology, MSSNTS 29, Cambridge 1976.
HILL, Andrew E., The Temple of Asclepius. An Alternative Source for Paul's Body Theology, in: JBL 99 (1980), 437–439.
HILL, Bert Hodge, Corinth, vol. 1,6, The Springs. Peirene, Sacred Spring, Glauke, Princeton 1964.
JOHNSON, Sherman E., Paul in the Wicked City of Corinth, in: LexTQ 17 (1982), 59–67.
KASSEL, Rudolph/AUSTIN, Colin (eds.), Poetae Comici Graeci vol. 3,2. Aristophanes, Testimonia et Fragmenta, Berlin 1984.
LIETZMANN, Hans, Mass and Lord's Supper. A Study in the History of the Liturgy (with Introduction and Further Inquiry, by Robert D. RICHARDSON), transl. with app. by D.H.G. REEVE, Leiden 1979.
MCRAY, John, Archaeology and the New Testament, Grand Rapids 1991.
MURPHY-O'CONNOR, Jerome, 1 Corinthians, NTMes 10, Wilmington 1979.
ID., St. Paul's Corinth. Texts and Archaeology, GNS 6, Wilmington 1983.

NASH, R. Scott, Death Becomes Him. Memorializing Untimely Death in the Ancient Korinthia and Paul's Foolish Preaching of the Cross. Presidential address, National Association of Baptist Professors of Religion, Southeast Region (USA) March 2000.
OSTER, Richard E., Jr., Use, Misuse and Neglect of Archaeological Evidence in Some Modern Works on 1Corinthians (1Cor 7,1–5; 8,10; 11,2–16; 12,14–26), in: ZNW 83 (1992), 52–73.
PAUSANIAS, Description of Greece, transl. by W.H.S. JONES, H.A. ORMEROD, and R.E. WYCHERLEY, LCL, 6 vols., London 1918–1935.
RILEY, Gregory J., One Jesus, Many Christs. How Jesus Inspired Not One True Christianity, But Many, New York 1997.
ROBINSON, Henry S., Corinth. A Brief History of the City and a Guide to the Excavations, Athens 1964.
ROEBUCK, Carl, Corinth, vol. 14, The Asklepieion and Lerna, Princeton 1951.
ROTHAUS, Richard M., Corinth. The First City of Greece. An Urban History of Late Antique Cult and Religion, Religions in the Graeco-Roman World 139, Leiden 2000.
SCRANTON, Robert L., Corinth, vol. 1,3, Monuments in the Lower Agora and North of the Archaic Temple, Princeton 1951.
SCRANTON, Robert L./RAMAGE, Edwin S., Investigations at Corinthian Kenchreai, in: Hesp. 36 (1967), 124–186 and plates 33–54.
SCRANTON, Robert L./SHAW, Joseph W./IBRAHIM, Leila, Kenchreai, Eastern Port of Corinth, vol. 1, Topography and Architecture, Leiden 1978.
SELLIN, Gerhard, Hauptprobleme des Ersten Korintherbriefes, in: ANRW II 25,4 (1987), 2940–3044.
SMITH, Dennis E., The Egyptian Cults at Corinth, in: HThR 70 (1977), 201–231.
STEINER, Ann, Pottery and Cult in Corinth. Oil and Water at the Sacred Spring, in: Hesp. 61 (1992), 385–408 und plate 87.
STEWART, Charles/SHAW, Rosalind, Introduction. Problematizing Syncretism, in: Syncretism/Anti-syncretism. The Politics of Religious Synthesis. Ed. by Charles STEWART/Rosalind SHAW, European Association of Social Anthropologists, London 1994, 1–26.
STILLWELL, Richard/SCRANTON, Robert L./FREEMAN, Sarah Elizabeth, Corinth, vol. 1,2, Architecture, Cambridge 1941.
STRABO, The Geography of Strabo, transl. by H.L. JONES (based in part upon the unfinished version of J.R.S. STERRETT), LCL, 8 vols., London 1917–1932.
THEISSEN, Gerd, Soziale Schichtung in der korinthischen Gemeinde. Ein Beitrag zur Soziologie des hellenistischen Urchristentums, in: ZNW 65 (1974), 232–272.
TOCCO SCIARLLI, Giuliana (ed.), Baia: il ninfeo imperiale sommerso di punta Epitaffio. N.p. 1983.
WALBANK, Mary E. Hoskins, Evidence for the Imperial Cult in Julio-Claudian Corinth, in: Subject and Ruler. The Cult of the Ruling Power in Classical Antiquity. Ed. by A. SMALL, Journal of Roman Archaeology Supplementary Series 17, Ann Arbor 1996, 201–213.
ID., The Foundation and Planning of Early Roman Corinth in: JRA 10 (1997), 95–130.
ID., Pausanias, Octavia and Temple E at Corinth, in: ABSA 84 (1989), 361–394.
WILLIAMS, Charles K., II, Pre-Roman Cults in the Area of the Forum of Ancient Corinth, Ph.D. Diss., University of Pennsylvania 1978.
ID., A Re-evaluation of Temple E and the West End of the Forum of Corinth, in: The Greek Renaissance in the Roman Empire. Papers from the Tenth British Museum

Classical Colloquium. Ed. by Susan WALKER/Averil CAMERON, Institute of Classical Studies Bulletin Supplement 55, London 1989, 156–162.
ID., The Refounding of Corinth. Some Roman Religious Attitudes, in: Roman Architecture in the Greek World. Ed. by Sarah MACREADY/F.H. THOMPSON, Occasional Papers (N.S.) 10, London 1987, 26–37.
ID./FISHER, Joan E., Corinth, 1974. Forum Southwest. in: Hesp. 44 (1975), 1–50 und plates 1–11.
WISEMAN, James, Corinth and Rome I. 228 B.C.–A.D. 267, in: ANRW II 7,1 (1979), 438–548.
WITHERINGTON, Ben, III, Conflict and Community in Corinth. A Socio-Rhetorical Commentary on 1 and 2 Corinthians, Grand Rapids 1995.

Brechungen

Reaktionen frühchristlicher Gruppen auf römische Herrschaft und Kultur

Marco Frenschkowski

Kyrios in Context
Q 6:46, the Emperor as "Lord", and the Political Implications of Christology in Q

The Christology of Q[1] seems to be a topic of never ending fascination. It is not so much the strange ambivalencies of the Son of Man-passages, but more what is often seen as an archaic and conspicuous lack of other more advanced christological interpretations and titles. Research during the last decades has concentrated on these aspects, e.g. on what at first sight seems to be an absence of explicit messianic allusions. Q became something of a principal witness to non-mainstream (non-Pauline!) and radically alternative reconstructions of Christian beginnings. Much less attention has been given to *kyrios* though as far as I can see we have good reason to assume that metonymic *kyrios* was to Q as important as *maran* was to those early Christians who first formulated the Maranatha. David CATCHPOLE calls *kyrios* "the dominant christological category of Q",[2] whereas on the other side Christopher TUCKETT – another major voice in recent Q-research – says: "Thus kyrios for Q does not appear to be a term of great christological significance".[3] These contradicting statements form the starting point of my inquiry: how can the limited material we have form the basis of theories that vary to such a degree?

This article will briefly address three topics. After some general remarks on *kyrios* in 1st century religious and secular contexts I endeavor to give as a second part an overview of the different uses of *kyrios* in Q (laying some emphasis in Q 6:46), and as a short third part will attempt to define more clearly the political background of the Q-group between imperial Rome on the one side and the uprising rebellion in Jerusalem on the other side, for which *kyrios* – as I hope to show – gives some minor indications. Many points are only briefly addressed here, but will be more fully discussed in my forthcoming (German language) monograph "*Q-Studien*". I take for granted that Q was a Greek language document roughly identical with the text we can reconstruct from Matthew and Luke, and that it was compiled in the late 60's (which means I date it a bit later than is usually assumed). All the reasons for my chronology of the Q-tradition are discussed extensively in the before-mentioned monograph. Also I do not presuppose any special theory on the

---

[1] Generally the text presupposed is the one grown and developed from the reconstuctions of the International Q Project (IQP) and given in the 'Critical Edition' (abbr.: CE). My own reconstruction that differs in some details – which are of no importance for the questions discussed here – is given in my "Q-Studien'.
[2] D. CATCHPOLE, Quest, 161.
[3] C.M. TUCKETT, Q, 218.

stratigraphy of Q – like the one connected with the name of John KLOPPENBORG[4] – though I do believe that we have earlier and later layers in the Sayings Source, and that composition history is possible and necessary. I do not agree with Jens SCHRÖTER[5] and others who prefer a synchronic approach or even rule out the possibility of a diachronic approach. Concerning the question of *Gattung* it will suffice to say Q was a sayings collection combining elements from older wisdom literature (instructions), apophthegms, chriae collections and to a much lesser degree also prophetic books and oracle collections. Q does not seem to have been a finished product, but was, so to say, a work still in progress. It is not named Sayings Gospel here as has been fashionable for some time, because I see no indication that it ever formed something like a complete expression of the kerygma or theology of a group or an individual writer; being quite unfinished, it still had left many arbitrary elements and never can be taken as expressing everything a compiler or author might have to say on any given topic.[6]

I. *Kyrios* as Metonym, Epithet and Title in the 1st Century AD

It is necessary first to give a rough sketch of the development of *kyrios* as an metonym, epithet and title in the background of early Christianity. An epithet accompanies a name (as when we say 'Lord Jesus'), a metonym takes the place of a name (as when we say 'the Lord' for Jesus), whereas a title is not just a mode of speech but a social reality: a title is formally bestowed by someone (a person or an institution), and its use usually has a strict temporal starting point from which on it becomes legitimate. In Rom 1:3–4 Jesus is inaugurated 'Son of God' (ὁρισθέντος υἱοῦ θεοῦ) on the day of his resurrection by God: so 'Son of God' here is a formal title. *Kyrios* sometimes is a title, as in Phil 2:11 (where it is explicitly given by God on the occasion of the ascension), but mostly it is not. Nevertheless it is a central term of honor.

The following remarks are a by-product of my forthcoming article on *kyrios* for the *Reallexikon für Antike und Christentum*.[7] Contrary to popular misconception, *kyrios* is not particularly important in the mystery religions. Though it is true that Isis, Serapis and other deities, especially the Egyptian ones, are often called *kyrios* and *kyria*, this is not a distinguishing trait of mystery religions. Many deities can be called *kyrios*, and the more often the

---

[4] J.S. KLOPPENBORG, Formation; ID., Excavating Q, *passim*.
[5] J. SCHRÖTER, Erinnerung, 60. 483–484 and *passim*.
[6] This is discussed at great length in my Q-Studien. For another approach see e.g. J.S. KLOPPENBORG, Excavating Q, 398 and 401–407. Arland Jacobson calls his important study on Q "The first Gospel".
[7] See also W. FOERSTER ET AL., κύριος; M. HENGEL/A.M. SCHWEMER, Paulus, 98–99, 169, 194–208, 323 n. 1335, 416–418, 419 n. 1738, 430 and especially D. ZELLER, Kyrios.

more they are somehow seen as "oriental". Classical Greek tradition quite rarely refers to Zeus and others as *kyrios*. Pindar is an early instance, who calls Zeus "Lord of all" (Isth 5:53), but this is not yet a regular epithet. The triumph of *kyrios* as a mode of honoring the Gods only comes with Hellenism, and for Greeks always kept something of oriental sycophancy. Nevertheless it is possible to address gods as *kyrioi*, – not indiscriminately, however, but in well-defined contexts. Egyptian deities,[8] Syrian deities[9] and Thracian ones regularly are called *kyrioi*, irrespective of any mystery connections. Of course not every cult of Isis is a mystery cult and in fact most are not. When covering a Greek God *kyrios* usually means the *interpretatio Graeca* of an oriental deity. This is all well known and needs no elaboration.

Kyrios in paganism never has any exclusiveness; as Paul says: ὥσπερ εἰσὶν θεοὶ πολλοὶ καὶ κύριοι πολλοί (1 Cor 8:5). Not just calling Jesus Lord is something special; the uniqueness of Christianity lies already in the very act of saying "There is one and only one Lord". Even philosophical monotheism that could agree to many Christian ideas about God never could join in this exclusiveness.

More important because less well-known is the political use, which will have a major place in my argument. Aramaic *mare'*, mostly in the form *maran* "our lord" is the regular way of addressing the king in all Aramaic speaking nations and cultures. We have many 1ˢᵗ century epigraphic examples from the Nabataean realm,[10] and also from later Rabbinic literature. A biblical example would be Dan 4:16. Also in Biblical Hebrew the king is addressed as *adoni* "my lord" (1 Sam 24:9; 26:17,19; 29:8; 2 Sam 3:21; 4:8; 9:11; 1 Kgs 1:2; 2:38; 20:4,9; Dan 1:10; 1 Chr 21:3,23 etc.; cf. also "our Lord" as in 1 Kgs 1:43), whereas *adonay* is reserved for God. The semantic difference is still a matter of some debate. A recent study by Martin RÖSEL[11] gives a complete new analysis of the evidence, but this is not our topic now. In Aramaic inscriptions *mare'* can be "lord" in a secular sense, whereas *maran* or (with article) *marana'* "our lord" in the overwhelming number of instances is exclusively the king. Inscriptions of Aretas IV, who of course also plays a minor role in the biography of Paul, are important examples. This applies also to the tetrarchs in Palestine who – as it is well known – were popularly seen as kings though they did not officially have that epithet (examples see below). It has been Ptolemaic tradition to speak of the king and his wife – who is often also his sister – as *kyrios* and *kyria*. In Hellenistic Greek *kyrios* to a small degree lost its original

---

[8] See G. RONCHI, Lexicon Theonymon 3, 600–639; L. BRICAULT, Myrionimi, 37–42, 82, 108–113, 124, 132. Ronchi gives e.g. 85 instances for Isis as kyria, 87 for Serapis as kyrios, 8 for Pauthnuphis, 6 for Bes, 5 for Ammon, 13 for Hermes-Thot.
[9] Easily accessible examples from OGIS are 589:1; 606; 607:2. Dozens of instances are discussed in H. DREXLER, Kyrios; M. HENGEL/A.M. SCHWEMER, Paulus; M. FRENSCHKOWSKI, Kyrios.
[10] Nabatean Mare-Inscriptions have already been used for comparison with early christology by H. MERKLEIN, Marānā.
[11] M. RÖSEL, Adonaj – Warum Gott 'Herr' genannt wird.

social connotations describing the owner of a slave and became a way of describing other relations as well: the Ptolemaic king in relation to his subjects, oriental gods (more rarely Greek ones) in relation to men, the husband in relation to his wife, and similar cases.

In *traditional* Greek and Roman society it would have been quite unheard of to address the king as *kyrios*. This would have been seen as servile flattery, as *kyrios* never entirely lost the basic meaning of slave-holder. A *kyrios* is not just a Lord, it's a Lord of slaves. *Kyrios* always describes a relationship, it is part of an interrelated word-pair, and this word-pair still mostly is slave-Lord. It has sometimes been said in theological literature that *kyrios* expresses lawful Lordship, whereas *despotes* describes effective power regardless of whether it is legal or not. This is not entirely true. Mostly the words are synonymous, as also Philo explicitly says they are (Rer Div Her 22); Josephus indeed prefers *despotes*, as do the later Christian emperors.

The emperors in the early years of the empire only reluctantly were called *kyrioi*. Augustus had even forbidden to be called *dominus* (Suet Aug 53:1), similarly Tiberius who also did not want to be addressed as *despotes* (Suet Tib 27; cf. Tac Ann 2:87). According to Dio Cassius Tiberius declared: "I am *despotes* only of slaves, but *autokrator* (emperor) of the army and simply *prokritos* of normal people" (57.8.2). *Prokritos* is a less common Greek translation of princeps, a word that more often is rendered as *hegemon*. In poetic diction similar appellations are possible: Augustus is *terrarum dominus* (Ovid Pont 2.8.26). But in another passage Ovid makes a contrast between Romulus who is said to have had *domini nomen* and Augustus, the second founder of Rome, who only wanted to be called *princeps* (Fast 2.142). Tiberius also explicitly declined to be called "lord". We have here once again a result of Roman reluctance to define the empire as a monarchy, which in fact it was and as which it has always been perceived by Greek authors. Fergus MILLAR in his famous study on the emperor in the Roman world has made this fact abundantly clear.[12]

When one of the assassins of Caesar, Cassius, was formally addressed as "king and lord" by the population of the island of Rhodes, in biting irony he replied:

"οὔτε βασιλεὺς οὔτε κύριος, τοῦ δὲ κυρίου καὶ βασιλέως φονεὺς καὶ κολαστής"
"neither king nor lord but chastiser and slayer of lord and king" (Plut Brut 30,3f).

This is the older Roman attitude, and it survives well into the empire.

All this changes dramatically at a very fixed point in Roman history, during the reign of Nero. We have very few Egyptian instances of *kyrios* for emperors earlier than that, but they are left-overs from Ptolemaic monarchic language. We can mention one instance for Augustus in 12 BC and perhaps one or two instances for Caligula and Claudius, but after that we encounter a veritable

---

[12] F. MILLAR in a later study even calls the Roman Empire "a personal monarchy of a strikingly primitive type" (The Roman Near East, 44).

explosion of *kyrios*-piety.[13] All of a sudden literally hundreds of ostraca and papyri use κύριος ἡμῶν "our lord" as an abbreviated way of referring to the emperor, mostly in places where some years earlier the more official αὐτοκράτωρ would have been used. As almost all our papyri and private letters come from Egypt, the spread of this piece of imperial piety can only be partially documented. In the famous declaration of independence for Greece as proclaimed by Nero in 67 AD the emperor is ὁ τοῦ παντὸς κόσμου κύριος (Syll³ 814:32). Particularly telling is the extent of ostraca from all levels of society, in which we often also find simply ὁ κύριος for *Neron*. We do not have any evidence whether this terminology was systematically supported by the authorities who apparently did not use it often. As far as I can see, it is rather a revitalization of older Hellenistic (Ptolemaic) piety that quickly spread through the empire. A famous New Testament example whose true importance has not generally been recognized is Acts 25:26, where Festus calls Nero *kyrios*.

After Nero we can observe a stabilization and further increase in the use of *kyrios* for the emperor. In the reign of Galba (in 68 AD) we have the first instance of it on a Jewish tax declaration, a second one comes from the era of Titus. Jews would have had to comply to this fashion. Josephus even says that the Romans now are κύριοι τῆς οἰκουμένης ("lords of inhabited earth") (Ap. 2:41). Jews somehow had to deal with this reality, only the rebels of 66 AD denied the word *despotes* to the emperor which must have included *kyrios* as well (Jos Bell 2.118; 7:418 cf. Hippolyt, Ref. IX 12:9).

On ostraca and in formulas dating private letters κύριος ἡμῶν "our Lord" as metonym or as an epithet becomes very regular (often anarthrous), as it seems also in other parts of the empire where of course we have much less evidence than in Egypt. Both a deity and the emperor can be called *kyrioi* in the same text; in Ephesus e. g. the one great *kyria* is Artemis, but the emperor remains the *kyrios* on earth par excellence (as in I.Eph 27, inscription of Vibius Salutaris from 104 AD). Though an expression of personal devotion, *kyrios* does not mean "god": instances of κύριος καὶ θεός are no ἓν διὰ δυοῖν (cf. John 20:28).[14]

Kyrios for the emperor or for kings is also not exactly a title, and neither is *dominus et deus* for Domitian a few years later (which never had any official character).[15] It is never formally bestowed or awarded, and it never becomes part of imperial or senatorial decrees. In 1st century imperial ideology it never is part of the official way of addressing the emperor, which means it is also never used on coins, in official correspondence or in State inscriptions. On the other side it is used literally hundreds of times in documents of a more private

---

[13] Cf. P. BURETH, Titulatures impériales, 33–35, with many examples.
[14] Cf. e.g. Diod S III 61:6. P.Tebtunis II 248:6 (1st century BCE) has ὁ Σεκνεβτῦνις ὁ κύριος θεός; here κύριος is adjective. On *dominus et deus* see M. FRENSCHKOWSKI, Kyrios.
[15] See also A. MARTIN, Titulature épigraphique.

character, on papyri and ostraca. It can also be used for other Roman officials (as for the Egyptian prefect Tiberius Alexander: OGIS 669), but the most impressive number of examples is exclusively devoted to the emperor, and so it remains through much of the 2nd and 3rd centuries AD. In a later Rabbinical midrash we find a parable where the emperor driving by in his chariot is acclaimed as *domine, domine* (the Semitic text GenR 8:10, the parallel QohR 6:10 even has the phrase in Latin).[16] This is an important, because circumstantial example of the acclamatory nature of *kyrie* and *domine*.

The conclusion seems clear: *kyrios* for the emperor is part of personal piety – it is a way of expressing a personal relation to the far-away *basileus* who is seen as saviour, Lord, supreme judge and guardian of public prosperity. We know that Nero in the Greek speaking world had devoted followers;[17] in general he was not seen nearly so critically as by the Roman nobility. Tacitus who is mainly responsible for our popular Hollywood picture of Nero as youthful tyrant only gives the point of view of the Roman senatorial class which was violently opposed to Nero. Indeed, in the Greek-speaking part of the empire he was quite a popular figure. His declaration of releasing Greece from political dependency in 67 AD (Syll^3 814) where he spoke of Greece as εὐγενεστάτη Ἑλλάς "most noble Hellas" was taken very seriously, and even Josephus still mentions many writers who saw Nero as quite a good ruler. Also the *Nero redivivus* legend that we mostly know as part of the Antichrist myth definitely posed Nero originally as hero, as a king returning from hiding and bringing back the good old times. Though we do not really know why this explosion, this sudden spread of *kyrios*-piety occurred in Nero's time, the phenomenon as such is an important fact that has to be taken notice of. Anybody who used *kyrios* in Nero's later years would have been aware of it. In Acts 25:26 Festus speaks of Nero as ὁ κύριος, a passage that we already referred to above and which is important because it does not come from Egypt.

Once *kyrios* became established in imperial piety it remained a means of expressing personal devotion to the emperor all during the following two centuries. For reasons not entirely clear – but not connected with the rise of Christianity – in the late 3rd century *despotes* almost completely takes the place of *kyrios*, once again starting in Egypt. The Christian emperors lay claim to the address *dominus* as well as the pagan ones. It is of course one of the many surprising facts of Roman history that when the empire became Christian almost no changes took place in imperial ideology and its symbolic expressions. Coming back to the 1st century, we are insufficiently informed to draw clearcut conclusions for other parts of the empire, but I believe the development of calling the emperor "our lord" started in Egypt and in very few years spread all over the Eastern part of the empire. Jews joined the general chorus, though our evidence comes only from later years. Many interesting 2nd century instances

---

[16] See on this text C. THOMA/S. LAUER, Gleichnisse 2, 111–116.
[17] Generally on Nero, the Nero redivivus legend etc. see my overview in: M. FRENSCHKOWSKI, Nero.

come from the Judean Desert documents, not those from Qumran but from somewhat later mostly Greek letters.[18]

As is well known, *kyrios* is also a part of common every-day language. The spouse calls her husband *kyrios*, but he can also write to her as his *kyria*. Our main source for such patterns of address are, as expected, letters. In polite language the elder brother can write in this way to his younger brother or even a mother to her son and address him with *kyrie*. In many cases *kyrie* increasingly comes to mean no more than our "mister", it can also be used ironically. Greek, Latin and Aramaic usage coincides here. In the Vindolanda writing tablets, the largest collection of Latin private letters form the 1st century presently extant, written by soldiers of the Roman army on wood, found some years ago on Hadrian's Wall in Great Britain and for the main part published only in 1994, *domine* is the common way to address the recipient.[19] The Greek instances are well known, but also Aramaic *mare'*, in later Syriac often simply *mar*, can be used exactly like *kyrie*. This is the lowest social level of the use of the word. Its higher levels (as in imperial piety) have to be discerned from the context (was heisst 'lower' and 'higher'?.

Of the general ranges of use of the word *kyrios* three are of immediate importance to Q: The slave-owner is called *kyrios* by his slave. Slave labor in Galilee is not all-important, but of course it is a social reality. It is also a main source of imagery in the parables. We also find *kyrios* as secular address in letters; and we have royal language. We will see in what way these observations may be helpful for understanding Q.

There is no need here to say more about *kyrios* as a metonym or metaphor for God. It is still not quite certain how old *kyrios* for YHWH in the Septuagint is. Older manuscripts have very different ways of rendering the tetragrammaton. P.Fouad 266 from the 1st century BC uses YHWH in Aramaic letters in the Greek text, the 12-Prophets-Scroll from Nahal Hever has Palaeo-Hebrew letters, others have Greek IAΩ and so on. It is interesting to note that in some manuscripts the substitute for the tetragrammaton is inserted by other hands. On the other side, Philo presupposes *kyrios* as being the normal way of translating the tetragrammaton, and more recent research (I am referring here mainly to Martin Rösel[20]) has put good arguments forward for supposing that *kyrios* after all was the original Septuagint rendering of YHWH and only was avoided when more archaizing styles became fashionable like in Qumran. The use of *kyrios* for YHWH in the Septuagint is a major element in redefining the God of Israel in Greek terms. It should not be overlooked that YHWH is a name whereas *kyrios* is not. To continuously interpret YHWH as *kyrios* means completely concentrating the concept of God on one single aspect, that of

---

[18] See e.g. H.M. COTTON/A. YARDENI (eds.), DJD 27, 169 no. 60 (from 125 AD); 177 no. 61ab (127 AD); 246 no. 67:2; 209s; 221 no. 64a:10 and 64b:29 (both from 129 AD); or N. LEWIS (ed.), no. 43:13 (124 AD); no. 66–67:24 and 34 (127 AD), and many other examples from the quickly increasing number of Palestinian papyri.

[19] A.K. BOWMAN/J.D. THOMAS (ed.), Vindolanda Writing Tablets.

[20] M. RÖSEL, Adonaj, *passim*.

sheer will power. If God is mainly Lord, he is defined as expressing an ethical and historical will. This is much less self-evident than it might seem, because Christianity only comes into the picture after this fundamental and far-reaching decision of Hellenistic Judaism had already been taken.

II. *Kyrios* in Q[21]

The one major achievement in the last decade of Q research certainly is the publication of two critical texts of Q that make use of everything we know about the style and redaction history of the gospels. The International Q Project – founded by James M. Robinson – has dedicated more than a decade's work of a large team of scholars to the production of these texts. We have to speak of two texts, as by now be have both the IQP text as published in the Journal of Biblical Literature between 1990 and 1997 (quoted as IQP) and the "Critical Edition" (quoted as CE), published simultaneously by Peeters Publishers, Leuven, and by Fortress Press, Minneapolis 2000. These two texts share a common background of research and yet differ considerably. The IQP text is a very restrained reconstruction, leaving open many points where Matthew and Luke disagree. This has the advantage of providing a text about which many scholars can agree. On the other side IQP uses many ellipses and has many cases in which a general meaning is given but no reconstruction of the text which neither Matthew nor Luke seem to preserve reliably. The IQP text is also the result of the discussions of a large group that has voted on a majority opinion.

The Critical Edition (CE) on the other side is much more confident defining a final (that is, original) text. Where IQP gives only dots, CE now often decides what has to be regarded as the oldest text. The responsibility for this text is taken by only three scholars, James Robinson, Paul Hoffmann and John KLOPPENBORG. So what we have now are two texts, similar to one another but not identical. My own study on Q also gives a complete reconstruction of the Greek Q text, but this relies mainly on the IQP text and differs in only a few passages. Both texts are rather conservative in the way they define the extent of Q. Scholars like Alan Kirk and David Catchpole have been more open-handed with assigning texts from the special traditions of Matthew or Luke to Q. Others on the opposite of the spectrum – like Albrecht Scriba in an unpublished paper – have tried to restrict the texts that can be attributed to Q radically. But the majority of scholars would probably agree about IQP's definition of the approximate extent of Q.

---

[21] The question of Matthew's and Luke's special use of *kyrios* is not discussed here. On Luke see J. JEREMIAS, Sprache, 23–24, 57–58; G. SCHNEIDER, Gott; J.C. O'NEILL, Use; I. DE LA POTTERIE, Le titre κύριος; D.L. JONES, The Title ΚΥΡΙΟΣ; J.D.G. DUNN, ΚΥΡΙΟΣ; G. STRECKER, Theologie, 424–425. On Matthew see: W. SCHENK, Sprache, 285–288. 307–308; J.D. KINGSBURY, The Title "Kyrios"; G. STRECKER, Theologie, 394–395.

A most admirable by-product of the work of the IQP is the series Documenta Q of which 5 volumes have appeared so far. This series gives a reliable and complete overview of the discussion on the text of Q in the 19th and 20th century. It is especially valuable as all references are given in verbatim quotations. We now have easy access to all observations on the probable text of the Sayings Source, especially cherished by those who like the present author have only a small university library at hand. After these general remarks we can return to our main topic.

Kyrios in Q either refers to God, to a human slave-owner, or to Jesus as Lord. I first give a general overview before turning to Q 6:46, the most important text.

In a majority of instances, *kyrios* is God: Q 4:12,8; 10:2,21; 13:35; 16:13 cf. 3:4 (not from Q according to IQP and CE). Quoting the Septuagint, the pericope of the temptation has two attestations (4:8 and 12), both of which are from Deuteronomy 6.[22] Another more traditional use is in Q 10:21 (Thanksgiving for Revelation): "I praise you, Father, Lord of Heaven and Earth". This is traditional prayer language. More interesting is Q 10:2 (Lord of the Harvest): "The harvest is plentiful, but the workers are few. So ask the Lord of the harvest to dispatch workers into his harvest." (CE 160–161). The imagery is obvious: the missionary work of the Q community is seen as harvesting (which is more generally a picture for judgment), but success is not as obvious and overwhelming as Q Christians had hoped for. So becoming a missionary is strongly encouraged. This, by the way, is one of the few sayings which Matthew and Luke give in complete verbal agreement. *Kyrios* with a genitive is common in polytheistic contexts;[23] but here it is derived from the metaphorical background of the designation.

For Q, God is mainly the heavenly Father. Paternal imagery abounds, as in Q 6:36 ("Be merciful, even as your Father is merciful"), where God's fatherhood – a quite novel idea – is an example of ethical conduct, or as in Q 12:6,30, in the Lord's Prayer 11:2,13 and so on. But he is also the Lord: Q 10:21 combines both fundamental ideas about God, like many Jewish prayers do as well. Seeing any tension or contradiction here would be inappropriate. Q 12:53 in singular contrast envisions an eschatological breach of filial bonds that must have raised strong emotions when first promulgated, but the apoca-

---

[22] For a detailed discussion, see now D.C. ALLISON, Jesus, 25–29.
[23] Apollo is "Lord of the Sun" (Plut Def 7 [413c]), Helios is "Lord of the Fire", Poseidon "Lord of Water" (Dio Chrys Or. 37,11), Dionysos "Lord of the Vine" (Plut Is 35 [365a]). We especially encounter this kind of attribution referring to Isis, as in the famous "I-am speech" of which we have 4 textual witnesses and which seems to have been some kind of sacred text of Isis spirituality. Isis here is "Lady of rivers, winds and the Sea", "Lady of war", "Lady of navigation", "Lady of thunder" and so on. A critical text is provided in M. TOTTI, Texte, no. 1. But also in a polytheistic context a deity can be "Lord of everything" (Plut Is 12 [355e], of Osiris). Many more instances are given in M. FRENSCHKOWSKI, Kyrios. Diod S III 61:4 says the same about the God of the Jews; cf. PGM 13:201f of Iao.

lyptic destruction of family ties does not immediately concern the fatherhood of God. Q 4:8,12 stresses the basic tenets of monotheism.

In parables *kyrios* is part of the story-world. Q 14:16–23 (The Great Supper) depicts a slave-owner who by his slave invites all kind of people to his great banquet. Whatever the parable originally is about, for Q the meaning is clear: the missionaries are the slaves who invite in the name of their Lord, who is God or perhaps Christ, though in the light of the saying about the lord of the harvest more probably God is meant. Q 19:12–27 is the parable of the talents (which, by the way, are *mina* in Luke which I suppose to have been the original version. Matthew likes to adapt the parables to more royal imagery as also the Rabbis do with their parables).[24] Once again God is the slave-holder, and men are his slaves which is a concept not special to Q nor to older Jewish Christianity. We should bear in mind that Paul essentially employs the same kind of symbolism: he virtually defines himself as a slave of Christ. Many oriental religions use the slave/slave-owner imagery describing man's relation to the deity. These parables show – and this may be a very important observation – that *kyrios* never really looses its basic social background in the world of slavery. *Kyrios* makes sense as a metaphor when slavery is a predominant factor of social life. This will become clearer when we consider Q 16:13 (see below).

We have the same basic social reality presupposed in Q 12:42–46, where "lord" means Jesus. I quote the translation in CE: "Who then is the faithful and wise slave whom the master put over his household to give them food on time? Blessed is the slave whose master, on coming, will find him so doing. Amen, I tell you, he will appoint him over all his possessions. But if that slave says in his heart: My master is delayed, and begins to beat his fellow slaves, and eats and drinks with the drunkards, the master of that slave will come on a day he does not expect and at an hour he does not know, and will cut him to pieces and give him an inheritance with the faithless." (CE 366–375). The coming of the Lord is obviously essentially the same as the coming of the Son of Man, which forms a focus of Q's eschatology (Q 12:39–40; 17:23–35). In Q's parables "Lord" is an open metaphorical expression vacillating between God (14:21) and Jesus (12:43,45,46; 19:15–16,18,20). Q 13:25 is not quite clear in this respect.

God is *kyrios* in 13:5, too: "Look, your house is forsaken! ... I tell you, you will not see me until the time comes when you say: Blessed is the one who comes in the name of the Lord!". No use seems to be made in Q of Ps 110:1, the main inspiration for early Christian *kyrios* christology and the most frequently quoted Old Testament text in the New Testament.[25] Q 16:13 is of some

---

[24] A full discussion of numismatic matters pertaining to Q is given in M. FRENSCHKOWSKI, Q-Studien.
[25] Cf. D.C. ALLISON, Jesus, 157–171; M. FRENSCHKOWSKI, Q-Studien, excursus "Schriftgebrauch in Q". On Ps 110:1 in early Christianity see M. HENGEL, "Setze Dich zu meiner Rechten!".

importance for making clear the semantics of the metaphorical field (see below).

We also have some secular instances, where *kyrios* at first view seems simply to mean "mister"[26] and only coincidentally is a metonym for Jesus (Q 7:6; 9:59 cf. 13:25), but it immediately implies some movement towards a more religious meaning. Even the secular address *kyrie* will in Christian ears immediately take on new connotations, an ambivalence that Matthew makes some use of (where usually only followers call Jesus "Lord"). In Q 7:1–10 the centurion twice says *kyrie* when addressing Jesus. It has been suggested that the pericope of the centurion's servant boy (that is what παῖς here means) is connected to the inaugural sermon Q 6:20–49 by catch-word connection, and that the catch-word is *kyrios*.[27] If this were true it might mean that the centurion is mentioned as an example of faith and courage. His coming to Jesus in a situation of personal distress is the beginning of being a follower of the Lord Jesus. But this would be something quite different from what Q 6:46 in its context is all about: "Why do you call me 'Lord, Lord' and do not what I tell you?" (So the older Lukan version). "Doing the word of Jesus" in the composition of Q obviously has the inaugural sermon as a whole in view, which is virtually a first step to Jesus as a new Moses, giver of a new Torah, which in Matthew he actually becomes.[28] Yet no ethical qualification is given for the centurion besides belief, and since that is exactly what Q 6:46 is not referring to (instead patterns of ethical behavior), it seems that this compositional idea is problematic.[29] Q 7,1–10 was not added as an illustration of calling Jesus Lord, but has a very different point of interest. *Kyrios* here may well be simply the secular mode of an honorable address, an interpretation impossible for Q 6:46.

Not so clear is Q 9:59–60: "But another said to him: Master, permit me first to go and bury my father. But he said to him: Follow me, and leave the dead to bury their own dead." (CE 154). This unheard of breach of filial piety is one of the stronger arguments of those who see in Q some affinity to some

---

[26] For a documentation of the secular use of *kyrios* as a way of adressing superiors or (politely) persons on the same social level see M. FRENSCHKOWSKI, Kyrios, drawing mainly from papyrological epistolographic evidence. Rather surprisingly Greek, Latin, Hebrew and Aramaic undergo exactly the same development. As Mommsen already saw, we have in each case a de-familiarization of an older household expression. Especially Suet Aug 53 clearly illustrates "dass die Redensart im häuslichen Verkehr von den unfreien Hausgenossen (...) abusiv überging auf die freien, zuerst auf die abhängigen, dann auch auf die gleich oder gar höher stehenden Familienglieder. (... Wo) es den häuslichen Kreis überschreitet (...) geschieht dies mit Affectation der häuslichen Vertrautheit." (T. MOMMSEN, Staatsrecht II 2, 761 n. 1). Old-fashioned writers like Aulus Gellius did not like the address *domine* or *kyrie*.

[27] For a full listing of catch-word connections in Q and Thomas and a general history of composition by using catch-words see M. FRENSCHKOWSKI, Q-Studien.

[28] On Jesus as a new Moses already in Q see now especially Dale C. Allison in a forthcoming article.

[29] See also C.M. TUCKETT, Q, 215.

kind of Jewish cynicism. It remains undecided in what sense Jesus is here called "Lord".

The main instance that gives some color to what the metonym *kyrios* for God and Jesus is all about is Q 16:13: "Nobody can serve two masters (*kyrioi*); for a person will either hate the one and love the other, or be devoted to the one and despise the other. You cannot serve God and Mammon" (CE 462).[30] *Mammon*, which is originally a Phoenician word that was adopted by Aramaic and Hebrew (in Greek it is hapax legomenon in Q and only taken over into a few passages derived from Q), means "riches, wealth" in a strictly neutral sense, and here in early Christian usage almost (but only almost) seems hypostacised into a kind of demon. The social reality of slave-ownership still strictly defines the meaning of *kyrios*, but there is also an undercurrent of absolute loyalty that cannot easily be explained from that context alone. The Hellenistic religious world using *kyrios* for different deities at the same time is here at least far away.[31] God owns man as a slave owner owns his slaves. Appropriate behavior is δουλεύειν. This is so self-evident that the social reality of slavery can be made into an ethical argument about loyalty.

Matt 10:24b has twice a surplus complementing the "master-pupil"-imagery of the original Q text Q 6:40 by mentioning the "master-slave"-correlation. As no reason can be adduced why this should have been left out by Luke it is probably Matthew's redactional addition.

Then we have Q 13:25–27: "When the householder has arisen and locked the door, and you begin to stand outside and knock on the door, saying: Master, open for us, and he will answer you: I do not know you, then you will begin saying: We ate in your presence, and it was in our streets you taught. And he will say to you: I do not know you! Get away from me, you who do lawlessness!" (CE 408–413). The householder (οἰκοδεσπότης) who is addressed as *kyrie* here clearly means Jesus himself. Only he (not God!) "taught in the streets". Οἰκοδεσπότης is used as a parabolic metaphor both for the hearers of Jesus' words (12:39) and for God (14:21). Jesus is *kyrios* also in Q 19:12–26 (The Entrusted Money), where the original parable already acquires levels of allegorical meaning, the "Lord" being God or more probably Jesus. Very strikingly *kyrios* does not turn up in Q's eschatological sermon Q 17:? – 35: the main eschatological metonym for Jesus in the Q group still is "Son of Man".

I only mention Q 11:25 in passing as it uses ἄρχων for Beelzebul, ruler of demons: monarchic categories or at least categories of defined power apply also for demons and their empire.

So far the passages calling Jesus "Lord" do not provide any special need to look for sources of *kyrios* imagery other than the social world of slavery and the polite secular and religious modes of address in everyday speech. How-

---

[30] For slaves having more than one master (combined ownership) see Cicero, pro Q. Roscio comoedo and also the plural in Act 16:16.

[31] For a history of interpretation in the Old Church see H.C. BRENNECKE, "Niemand kann zwei Herren dienen".

ever, we already encountered some instances where God's and Jesus' Lordship fluctuate in allegorical imagery into each other without any connection with Old Testament *kyrios* passages. There is no question as yet of Jesus taking over God's Lordship as in Phil 2:11. We are still strictly in the field of metonyms and metaphors, not titles.

I now proceed in more detail to Q 6:46 – the one text which most clearly expresses a *kyrios*-christology in Q, and which I believe has to be seen in connection with the term *maranatha*.

III. *Maranatha* and Q 6:46

All texts discussed so far are only on the threshold of a clear-cut christology. As a general characteristic of the Sayings Source we recognized that it contains many fragmentary pieces of information and only rarely exhibits a systematic whole. If we did not have the late addition Q 4:1–13 and a short "Aerolith, aus dem johanneischen Himmel gefallen"[32] (Q 10:22), who would have guessed that Son, Son of God was a major topic of christological reflection and meditation in the group that left us Q? The same mental reservation pertains to *kyrios*-christology: we have only a few hints, but these have to be seen in a much wider context. The text most telling in this regard is Q 6:46 which as a logion forms a part of the most intenselystructured piece of all Q, the inaugural sermon Q 6:20–49.

Q 6:46 refers to addressing Jesus as "Lord, Lord": τί με καλεῖτε κύριε κύριε, καὶ οὐ ποιεῖτε ἃ λέγω; (CE 94–95). Though this is mainly Luke's version, we rightly have an almost universal scholarly agreement that Matthew's different parallel Matt 7:21 is mainly a product of Matthean redaction. I take this for granted and will not discuss any details of reconstruction. "Lord, Lord" is not just a way of referring to Jesus: the double exclamation shows that a formal acclamation is in view. It is out of question that *kyrie* might here just be a reminiscence of how the disciples referred to Jesus during his earthly ministry: καλεῖτε is strictly present tense. Further, Q shows no historical awareness: the sayings are collected without any kind of scholarly concern, but as community rules and prophetic and apocalyptic words for the living Q group. Calling Jesus "Lord" in the situation of the Q community is what is intended: only this interpretation really explains of the logion. Jesus was not just "Lord" in former times: he is now, in the situation of the Q collection and composition. This does not mean that there is no chance 6:46 might go back to the historical Jesus, but it seems more probable it was spoken by early Christian prophets. However, our only concern here is to identify its meaning in the theological and historical world of Q.

---

[32] So called by the church historian K. VON HASE, Geschichte Jesu, 422.

Kyrie, kyrie simply cannot be "nur die Anrede an den Lehrer",[33] and cannot be just a mode of addressing the wisdom teacher who spoke and speaks in Q 6:20–49. No dead Rabbi or teacher is ever called "Lord, Lord!". The historical Jesus might have been *addressed* as "Lord" in the sense of "master" (teacher) in his days: but this is not what Q 6:46 is concerned with: τί με καλεῖτε κύριε κύριε. Already Dieter Zeller saw that 6:46 clearly exhibits "hoheitliche Züge".[34] The "Lord" of the inaugural sermon is not just a teacher like others: doing or not doing his words is decisive for eschatological salvation. Siegfried Schulz many years ago – contradicting Bultmann's view – gave an apocalyptic interpretation to the saying: "Im Hintergrund dieser eschatologischen Herr-Bezeichnung wie -Anrede in Q steht ohne Zweifel die apokalyptische Menschensohn-Anschauung und -Erwartung".[35] But this cannot be proven from passages where *kyrios* is part of the "Bildhälfte" in parables, and would not have come to mind in an obvious way to the addressees of Q (as is the case with the metonym "Son of Man", which has a Danielic background).

No sufficient attention has so far been given to the doubling of the acclamation. This is not just "typisch semitisierend".[36] All instances we have show that something special is intended, an intensification or enhancement of address, an emphatic exclamation having a special reason behind it. It is never just polite speech. This is already true of the Old Testament and later instances of the doubling of names: Gen 46:2 (cf. Jos Ant 2:172); Exod 3:4; 1 Sam 3:4₆; Jub. 18:1–2:10 (but cf. Gen 22:1–2, 11); 44:5; 4 Ezra 14:2; 2 Bar. 22:2; Apoc. Ab. 8:1; 9:1; Apc Ad et Ev 41; Ladder of Jacob 1:8; JosAs 14:4,6; TestIob 3:1; armen. Paenitentia Adami 48 (41)[37]; TestSol prol 1:5; also in the Samaritan Memar Marqah 1:1 (at the starting point of the revelation to Moses); Philo Abr 176. In Q we have a good example in Q 13:34: "O Jerusalem, Jerusalem, who kills the prophets and stones those sent to her!" (CE 420–421).

It is almost a conjuration, when Cicero three times repeats his brother's name (Quint Fr I 3:1–10). In the New Testament we immediately think of Luke 22:31; Acts 9:4; 22:7; 26:14. This collection of instances is certainly not complete, but reasonably comprehensive. We clearly see that the doubling of names most often is part of a revelation[38] or sometimes it has an imploring character. According to later rabbinic legend, king Joshaphat addresses every rabbi as *abbi abbi mari mari rabbi rabbi* "my father, my father, my Lord, my Lord, my teacher, my teacher" (bMak 24a; also bKet 103b without *abbi abbi* – for which cf. also 2 Kgs 2:12). This is of course anachronistic hyperbole and

---

[33] R. BULTMANN, Geschichte, 122 n. 1. So also e.g. A.D. JACOBSON, First Gospel, 107 and many others.
[34] D. ZELLER, Grundschrift, 400.
[35] S. SCHULZ, Q, 429.
[36] S. SCHULZ, Q, 428 n. 189, making reference of passages collected Bill. I 943 (cf. also II 258 ad Luke 22:31).
[37] Ed. M. STONE, CSCO 430, Leuven 1981, 20.
[38] In some cases we may have examples of hallucinatory echo phenomena. This cannot be discussed here more fully.

also quite obviously wishful thinking: roles have changed. As we will see, the king here addresses the rabbi as usually the rabbi would have to speak before the king. It is certainly not a "normal" way of address.

In pagan ritual doubling the epiclesis to the deity is a very common phenomenon. We may think of Il 5,31 (Ares); Archilochos frg. 88 (Zeus); Soph Ai 695 (Pan); Eur Ion 125f (Paian). Eduard Norden, who has collected many more examples,[39] distinguishes this usage from cultic calls in a more general sense ("sakrale Rufe") and examples from ancient magic. Examples abound, as Aristoph Thesm 295; Eur Ba 83, 152; Callimach 1:91ff; Apoll Rhod 2,704; Horat Carm II 19:7–8 for the cultic calls, and Sen Oed Rex 567. 622; Marcellus Med 36:70; Plin Nat Hist 27,131 for doubling of spells (Norden compares this magical use with Paul's very formal doubling of his curse Gal 1:8f). I abstain from giving examples from the PGM, which are also very common. See also Ovid, who begins the second book of his Ars Amatoria with *Dicite 'io Paean!' et 'io' bis dicite 'Paean'* (II 1).

In a strange episode in bHullin 139b we have the Greek *kyrie, kyrie* quoted as an acclamation of king Herod, presumably Herodes Magnus. This is of course not everyday secular usage either, but may indicate some knowledge of the Greek term in earlier times. We have no way, however, to discern how old the small legendary notice actually is.

We have seen the hieratic and formal κύριε κύριε cannot be explained as an address to the living teacher Jesus (which would make no sense in the situation of Q looking not backwards to the historical person Jesus, but forward to the coming Son of Man). It certainly is not just a polite metonym like *kyrios* in the social world of the parables. No slave-owner is formally acclaimed κύριε κύριε. We also have not the slightest hint the call might have any kind of traditio-historical connection with the Septuagint rendering of YHWH.[40] It is self-evident for Q that God is Lord, but that does not make Jesus Lord. So in what sense and based on what background can the heavenly Jesus, who is the future judge of the world, be addressed as κύριε κύριε?

I propose a new solution to this problem here that combines what we know about the early history of Aramaic Christianity with the linguistic and historical background of addressing people. The king in all oriental languages (not just Aramaic) is called "lord", as in Nabataean inscriptions *maran* ("our lord") always means simply the king.

Therefore it is obvious that the Messiah can be addressed *rabbi mari* (bSanh 98a).[41] Bultmann many years ago claimed: "Das Judentum hat jedenfalls den Messias nie als 'Herrn' bezeichnet. Im jüdischen Sprachgebrauch ist überhaupt das absolute 'der Herr' nicht denkbar. 'Herr' in der Anwendung auf

---

[39] E. NORDEN, Aeneis Buch VI, 136–137, 463. See also S. EITREM, Papyri Osloenses I, 58–59.
[40] For which see M. RÖSEL, op. cit., and also the short discussion in M. FRENSCHKOWSKI, Kyrios.
[41] With a slight correction of the traditional reading. See G. DALMAN, Worte Jesu, 268.

Gott erhält immer eine nähere Bestimmung."[42] This as a rule is still valid, but Joseph Fitzmyer has provided instances of absolute *mare*' for God (11QTgJob 24:6–7; 4QEn^{b}ar = 4Q 202, 1 IV, 5 a. o.),[43] as *adon* in Biblical Hebrew can very rarely refer to God (Ps 114:7; Sir 10:7), though usually *adonay* is used. So the strictness of language Bultmann took for granted is obsolete.

What Bultmann did not see clearly is how very often *maran* "our lord" is used for the king in Aramaic dialects. This has an immediate impact on messianic symbolism. Even the Herodian kings were called "our lord". A Nabataean temple inscription which we can date to 29/30 AD (from Si'a near Qanatha) has MRN' PLPS "our lord Philip".[44] In 38 AD some Alexandrians rather cruelly abused a lunatic named Carabas, setting him up high in the gymnasium, clothing him with rugs looking like a royal robe and putting on his head a diadem made from papyrus. They derided him, calling him μαριν, which παρὰ Σύροις according to Philo – who tells the episode – should mean κύριος (Flacc 36–39). This was meant as a mock coronation of Agrippa I. whose ambitions were well known. OGIS 418:1 may provide a more official example from Agrippa's reign, though some have dated this to the reign of Agrippa II.[45] From this latter one, who was destined to be the last Herodian king, we have a small number of instances (OGIS 423:2; 425:3; 426:3), though these inscriptions may have been set up by non-Jews. Even Herod the Great may have used the epithet (OGIS 415, from Batanaea, undated), but the attribution is not quite proven. We have already mentioned how very common *maran* is on Nabataean inscriptions, where it regularly refers to the king. We have an especially large number of examples from the reign of Aretas IV known also from 2 Cor 11:32. It is also common in Palmyrene Aramaic and older Imperial Aramaic.

It immediately springs to mind that we have one trace of archaic Palestinian christology in the original language of the Jesus movement. This of course of the μαράναθα as quoted by Paul 1 Cor 16:22 (and Did 10:6). The translation "Our Lord, come" is generally accepted because of Rev 22:20,[46] though the Church Fathers mostly understood the formula very differently. I am more concerned with what exactly is the religious context in which the Aramaic-speaking community called Jesus μαράν.

Maran is not simply "lord". As an acclamation it means "our royal lord", or as we should say: "messianic king". Only this makes sense in the post-easter situation of Jerusalem and Corinthian Christianity. *Maran* is the proper and traditional way of addressing the king, here: the messianic king. *Mare', mara'*

---

[42] R. BULTMANN, Theologie, 54.
[43] See J. FITZMYER, Semitic Background; also M. FRENSCHKOWSKI, Kyrios, for some minor new details.
[44] RÉS 1919 no. 2117 = E. LITTMANN (ed.), Syria: Publications of the Princeton University Archeological Expedition to Syria in 1904–1905 and 1909, vol. IV. A.-D. Semitic Inscriptions, Leyden 1914/49, 78 no. 101. On this text see also M. HENGEL/A.M. SCHWEMER, Paulus zwischen Damaskus und Antiochien, 198–199 n. 799.
[45] See N. KOKKINOS, Herodian Dynasty, 290 n. 92.
[46] For linguistic details see K. BEYER, Texte 124, 525.

can of course be used describing many different relations, but *maran* "our Lord" as an address used by a community is strictly royal language, language of the secular kingdom. It has nothing whatsoever to do with divine predicates for Jesus: indeed God is called Lord only as the heavenly *King*. *Maran* has exactly the same meaning as messiah, which is: king. It is not just a honorific term, in which case it would have a name with it, it is not just one Lord, it is *the one Lord*. So in the context of a messianic movement *maranatha* has to be translated as: "may the messianic king come back". The coming one is "Lord" also in 1 Thess 5:15ff; 1 Cor 4:5; 11:26; Phil 4:5 etc. Although in Did 10:6 the context is hortatory, the original meaning of μαράναθα seems to have been quite positive: the congregation prays for the parusia of its messianic Lord. In this context we are reminded of other early Palestinian instances of using "Lord" for Jesus in a special and singular way: we have the "Lord's brothers" (1 Cor 9:5; Gal 1:19; later we have the δεσπόσυνοι, Julius Africanus in Euseb h.e. I 7:14), also the "Lord's sayings" (1 Thess 4:15; 1 Cor 7:10,12 cf. 11:23). This seems to be pre-Pauline. We find "(our) Lord Jesus" (without "Christ") 27 times in the Corpus Paulinum, of which 10 instances are in 1/2 Thess (2 Thess probably imitates) – which indicates older language. Even for pre-Pauline Christianity Jesus was "Lord" in a special sense; no connection whatsoever is to be seen with *kyrios* as metonym for God. Could it be possible that the metonym for Jesus stems from a royal – which means messianic – interpretation of Jesus, as "Our Lord" had long become standard offical language in monarchies and empires, becoming once more very prominent during Nero's reign? Messianism is about eschatological monarchy: it takes its symbolism and imagery from its political, non-eschatological counterparts.

What does this mean for Q 6:46? Especially in present English language exegesis – whether it sees Jesus as a Jewish cynic and agent of counter-cultural wisdom or still adheres to the more traditional image of Jesus as a messianic prophet of the eschatological kingdom – this saying has regularly been played down as an expression of early christology. Often it is seen to address Jesus as a sage, who gives rules for new moral conduct or a radically different life-style to his disciples. Even Christopher Tuckett whose book on Q is a marvel of careful analysis and sound judgment, can interpret *kyrios* here as the "authoritative teacher".[47] But this is certainly not enough. Jesus is here seen as a living person that can be addressed. "*Kyrie, kyrie*" is an acclamation, and it is the usual acclamation for kings in Aramaic tradition. There is no need to repeat the examples given above.[48] All other explanations do not quite fit in (Jesus is no slave-owner, and Q 6:46 is certainly not about saying "Mister Jesus, Mister Jesus!"). The interpretation proposed here has the advantage of concurring

---

[47] C.M. TUCKETT, Q, 214.
[48] C.M. TUCKETT, Q, 214. Tuckett is wrong when complaining that not too much should be read into the "word κύριος itself" (op. cit. 215 n. 17). We do not have just the word: we have a formal acclamatory address to a living (though "exalted") person, spoken in ritual doubling of the epiclesis in the situation of the Q community – which is something very different.

both with what we know about Palestinian Christianity and the history of *maranatha*. That we have no more traces of messianic metonyms in Q need not trouble us, because the same applies to the Son of God christology that we also encounter in only two passages.

So what we have is a *messianic kyrios-christology* as part of a messianic interpretation of Jesus in a very broad sense. Messiah means king: as future king of Israel and the world, even as king of kings who can make a present of sitting on thrones to his disciples (Q 22:8,30, probably the climactic and apocalyptic last word of Jesus in Q) Jesus may justly be called κύριε κύριε. For all speakers of oriental languages (not just Aramaic) this is the normal, appropriate and to be expected way of addressing a king, by formal doubling of κύριε even hightened and becoming an acclamation. Parallels as we have seen are clear and revealing. The eschatological Son of Man is also the Son of God and the messianic *kyrios:* this needs no elaboration in Q, which after all is a sayings collection and not a christological tract. It remains now to combine this evidence with what was said about the explosion of *kyrios* as an epithet and metonym (not a title!) in the imperial ideology of the Neronic age (Acts 25:26) and *kyrios* in Q. For this we sketch the general political background of Q.

IV. The political background of Q

Calling Jesus Lord, calling the Son of Man the one *kyrios* to be obeyed, exactly at the same time when this term becomes a center piece of imperial piety cannot be just a coincidence. We know the epithet *kyrios* some years later to have formed a focus of conflict between church and state, precisely because it was an expression of imperial piety. Well-known examples are M. Polyc 8:2; Act. S. Maximi (final sentence); Act. Cypriani 6; Mart. Irenaei 6; Act. Carpi et Papylae 7 Lat. text; cf. already 1 Cor 8:5–6; Eph 4:5. Tertullian discusses the question Apol. 34:1–2, clearly seeing that *dominus* even when used for the emperor does not simply mean *deus*. What these texts share is an awareness of some rivalry here: calling Jesus "lord" and calling the emperor "lord" leads to conflicts, though there are many other "lords" as well who do not get in the way of the "one lord".

Q is strangely ambivalent about the world empire. The temptation narrative is strictly critical of worldly power and sees it as a demonic gift. But Q is not entirely anti-Roman. Two examples have to suffice. In Q 7:1–10 (the pericope of the centurion) the faithful foreigner is called a ἑκατονάρχος, which is a military officer. In John 4:46–53 he is called βασιλικός, a royal clerk. This is certainly the original version.[49] In Jesus' time and even later there were no Roman soldiers in Capernaum. But a βασιλικός here makes perfect sense, as Herodes Antipas was popularly seen as king. If this was the original tradition,

---

[49] A full discussion will be found in M. FRENSCHKOWSKI, Q-Studien.

changing the example of faith into a ἑκατονάρχος in the 60's can have only one meaning: there are good Romans as well. A ἑκατονάρχος in itself is not necessarily a Roman centurio. My argument is not about the word, but about the change of words.[50] And ἑκατονάρχος cannot be original, since nearer to Jesus' lifetime the anachronism of a centurio in Capernaum must have been strongly felt. Making a βασιλικός, against all historical probability, into an ἑκατονάρχος, when Roman military presence is more heavily felt than before, and envisioning this centurio as an exemplary man of faith, has a clear political implication. In fact, it is a pro-Roman statement. Paul Hoffmann has suggested that the "Love your enemies"-saying may contradict the political philosophy of the uprising,[51] and that the temptation narrative is critical of political messianism.[52] This is difficult to prove. But we have one other saying that is definitely about the Roman army, though only Matthew has it: I speak of course of Matt 5:41, that now almost universally is seen as derived from Q: "if anyone presses you into service for one mile, go with him two miles" (cf. CE 62–63). This is about the institution of *angaria*, the right of the Roman soldier to get his things carried by non-military persons. By law he would have to pay for this, but we have many letters of complaint from Egypt that show that they often in fact did not, and simply misused their right. *Angaria* is a well documented institution that later became part of the Roman postal system, but here it is an expression of the power of the Army. And, as once again Fergus Millar put it, in the Near East the Roman empire *is* the Roman army and simply nothing else, though not too many Roman soldiers were to be seen in Palestine. If Christians are called to comply with *Angaria*, they would have been seen by the Zealots and other rebel groups as decidedly pro-Roman. On the other side Christians saw Jesus as their *kyrios*, not Nero. The short-lived Palestinian vacuum of power in the 60's prior to the uprising may have prevented any more serious conflict, and perhaps also any need for a strict theological solution of the questions arising from two kyrioi claiming to become ultimate concern for men.

I come to a preliminary conclusion. In the area of tension between the Roman imperial presence and the strong national feelings that gave power to the revolt of 66 AD, the Q community was trying to remain faithful to its heritage that did not allow it either to join the rebellion or to comply with imperial piety. Like those who formulated the *maranatha*, it saw Jesus as messianic Lord. That the text of Q, as far as we can see, did not use the term messiah may simply be a coincidence. Calling Jesus *maran* is exactly what messiahship is about, and calling him *kyrie, kyrie* is the same in Greek. Perhaps they were reluctant to use the term messiah, but they were not reluctant to describe their relation to the exalted Jesus in the same terms that Aramaic culture uses to describe the monarchy. As said before, no dead sage is ever called *kyrie, kyrie* in Jewish literature, but the Roman emperor is and the Jewish king is. The

---

[50] My argument is here much abridged. The issue is of course a bit more complicated than can be indicated here. Cf. the discussion in Q-Studien.
[51] See e.g. P. HOFFMANN, Tradition, 3–61.
[52] Cf. P. HOFFMANN, Tradition, 193–207.

Jesus of Q as *kyrios* is not just more than Solomon, more than Jonah, he is also more than the *kyrioi* of political independence and of imperial piety and propaganda.

Bibliography

1. Text of Q: Basis, Reconstruction and Documention

KLOPPENBORG, John S. (ed.), Q Parallels. Synopsis, Critical Notes & Concordance, Sonoma, California 1988.
ROBINSON, James M./HOFFMANN, Paul/KLOPPENBORG, John S. (eds.), The Critical Edition of Q. Synopsis Including the Gospels of Matthew and Luke, Mark and Thomas with English, German, and French Translations of Q and Thomas, Leuven 2000.
ROBINSON, James M./HOFFMANN, Paul/KLOPPENBORG, John S. (eds.), Documenta Q: Reconstructions of Q through Two Centuries of Research, Louvain 1996ff. (5 vols. till Mai 2001).

2. Literature on Q (and general works)

ALLISON, Dale C., The Jesus Tradition in Q, Harrisburg, Pennsylvania 1997.
ID., The Intertextual Jesus. Scripture in Q, Harrisburg, Pennsylvania 2000.
BOWMAN, Alan K./THOMAS, J. David (ed.), The Vindolanda Writing Tablets, Tabulae Vindolandenses II, London 1994.
BULTMANN, Rudolf, Geschichte der synoptischen Tradition, FRLANT 29, Göttingen ^{9}1979 (= ^{2}1931).
CATCHPOLE, David R., The Quest for Q, Edinburgh 1997.
COTTON, Hannah M. /YARDENI, Ada, Aramaic, Hebrew and Greek Texts from Naḥal Ḥever and Other Sites with an Appendix Containing Alleged Qumran Texts (The Seiyâl Collection II), DJD 27, Oxford 1997.
FLEDDERMANN, Harry T., Mark and Q. A Study of the Overlap Texts, BEThL 122, Leuven 1995.
FRENSCHKOWSKI, Marco, Art. Nero, in: BBKL 6 (1993), 611–619.
ID., Welche biographischen Kenntnisse von Jesus setzt die Logienquelle voraus? Beobachtungen zur Gattung von Q im Kontext antiker Spruchsammlungen, in: From Quest to Q. FS James M. Robinson, ed. by Jon Ma. ASGEIRSSON/Kristin DE TROYER/Marvin W. MEYER, BEThL 146, Leuven 2000, 3–42.
ID., Q-Studien (forthcoming).
ID., Art. Kyrios, in: RAC (forthcoming)
HASE, Karl von, Die Geschichte Jesu, Leipzig ^{2}1876.
HOFFMANN, Paul, Studien zur Theologie der Logienquelle, NTA.NF 8, Münster ^{3}1982.
ID., Tradition und Situation. Studien zur Jesusüberlieferung in der Logienquelle und den synoptischen Evangelien, NTA.NF 28, Münster 1995.
HOPPE, Rudolf/BUSSE, Ulrich (eds.), Von Jesus zum Christus. Christologische Studien. Festgabe für Paul Hoffmann zum 65. Geburtstag, BZNW 93, Berlin – New York 1998.
HORSLEY, Richard A./DRAPER, Jonathan A., Whoever Hears You Hears Me. Prophets, Performance and Tradition in Q, Harrisburg, Pennsylvania 1999.
JACOBSON, Arland D., The First Gospel. An Introduction to Q, Sonoma, California 1992.

KIRK, Alan, The Composition of the Sayings Source. Genre, Synchrony, and Wisdom Redaction in Q, NT.S 91, Leiden et al. 1998.
KLOPPENBORG, John S., The Formation of Q. Trajectories in Ancient Wisdom Collections, Studies in Antiquity and Christianity, Philadelphia 1987.
KLOPPENBORG, John S., 'Easter Faith' and the Sayings Gospel Q, in: Semeia 49 (1990), 71–99.
ID., Excavating Q. The History and Setting of the Sayings Gospel, Minneapolis 2000.
LEWIS, Naphtali (ed.), The Documents from the Bar Kokhba Period in the Caves of Letters. Greek Papyri, Judean Desert Studies, Jerusalem 1989.
MACK, Burton L., The Lost Gospel. The Book of Q and Christian Origins, San Francisco 1993.
MANSON, Thomas W., The Sayings of Jesus, London [2]1949.
POLAG, Athanasius, Die Christologie der Logienquelle, WMANT 45, Neukirchen-Vluyn 1977.
SATO, Migaku, Q und Prophetie. Studien zur Gattungs- und Traditionsgeschichte der Quelle Q, WUNT II/29, Tübingen 1988.
SCHRÖTER, Jens, Erinnerung an Jesu Worte. Studien zur Rezeption der Logienüberlieferung in Markus, Q und Thomas, WMANT 76, Neukirchen-Vluyn 1997.
SCHULZ, Siegfried, Q. Die Spruchquelle der Evangelisten, Zürich 1972.
TOTTI, Maria, Ausgewählte Texte der Isis- und Sarapisreligion, Subsidia Epigraphica 12, Hildesheim et al. 1985.
TUCKETT, Christopher M., Q and the History of Early Christianity, Edinburgh 1996.
URO, Risto (ed.), Symbols and Strata. Essays on the Sayings Gospel Q, Publications of the Finnish Exegetical Society 65, Helsinki – Göttingen 1996.
WEGNER, Uwe, Der Hauptmann von Kapernaum, WUNT II/14, Tübingen 1985.
WELLHAUSEN, Julius, Evangelienkommentare, Berlin – New York 1987.
ZELLER, Dieter, Redaktionsprozesse und wechselnder "Sitz im Leben" beim Q-Material, in: DELOBEL, Noël (ed.), Logia. Les paroles de Jésus – The Sayings of Jesus. Mémorial Joseph Coppens, BETL 59, Leuven 1982, 395–409
ID., Eine weisheitliche Grundschrift in der Logienquelle?, in: F. VAN SEGBROECK/ Christopher M. TUCKETT, Gilbert VAN BELLE, J. VERHEYDEN (eds.), The Four Gospels 1992. FS Frans Neirynck, vol. 1, BETL 100, Leuven 1992, 389–401.

3. Literature on *kyrios*

BAUDISSIN, Wolf Wilhelm Graf von, Kyrios als Gottesname im Judentum und seine Stellung in der Religionsgeschichte, 4 vols., Gießen 1929.
BERLINGER, Leo, Beiträge zur inoffiziellen Titulatur der römischen Kaiser, Diss. Breslau 1935.
BEYER, Klaus, Die aramäischen Texte vom Toten Meer, Göttingen 1984.
BRENNECKE, Hanns Christof, "Niemand kann zwei Herren dienen". Bemerkungen zur Auslegung von Mt 6,24/Lk 16,13 in der Alten Kirche, in: ZNW 88 (1997), 157–169.
BRICAULT, Laurent, Myrionymi. Les épiclèses Grecques et Latines d'Isis, de Sarapis e d'Anubis, Beiträge zur Altertumskunde 82, Stuttgart – Leipzig 1996.
BULTMANN, Rudolf, Theologie des Neuen Testaments, Tübingen [7]1977.
BURETH, Paul, Les titulatures impériales dans les papyrus, les ostraca et les inscriptions d'Égypte (30 a. C. – 284 p. C.), Bruxelles 1964.
CERFAUX, Lucien, Kurios, in: DBS 5 (1957), 200–228.

CLAUSS, Manfred, Kaiser und Gott. Herrscherkult im römischen Reich, Stuttgart – Leipzig 1999.

DALMAN, Gustav, Die Worte Jesu mit Berücksichtigung des nachkanonischen jüdischen Schrifttums und der aramäischen Sprache I. Einleitung und wichtige Begriffe, Leipzig ²1930 = reprint Darmstadt 1965.

DREXLER, Hans, Art. Kyria and Kyrios, in: ALGM 2, 1 (1890/94 = 1965), 1755–1769.

DUNN, James D.G., ΚΥΡΙΟΣ in Acts, in: LANDMESSER, Christof/ECKSTEIN, Hans J./LICHTENBERGER, Hermann (eds.), Jesus Christus als die Mitte der Schrift. FS Otfried Hofius, BZNW 86, Berlin – New York 1997, 363–378.

EITREM, Sam, Papyri Osloenses 1, Oslo 1925

FAUTH, Wolfgang, Art. Kyrios/Kyria, in: KP 3 (1969), 413–417.

FITZMYER, Joseph A., Der semitische Hintergrund des ntl. Kyriostitels, in: Jesus Christus in Historie und Theologie. FS Hans Conzelmann, ed. by Georg STRECKER, Tübingen 1975, 267–298. Revised as: The Semitic Background of the New Testament Kyrios-Title, in: Joseph A. FITZMYER, A Wandering Aramean. Collected Aramaic Essays, SBL. MS 25, Chico, California 1979, 115–142.

ID., Art. Kyrios, in: EWNT 2 (1981), 811–820.

FOERSTER, Werner/QUELL, Gottfried/BEHM, Johannes, Art. κύριος κτλ, in: ThWNT 3 (1938), 1038–1100.

HAHN, Ferdinand, Christologische Hoheitstitel. Ihre Geschichte im frühen Christentum (1963), UTB 1873, ⁵1995.

HENGEL, Martin, "Setze dich zu meiner Rechten!" Die Inthronisation Christi zur Rechten Gottes und Ps. 110, 1, in: PHILONENKO, Marc (ed.), Le Trône de Dieu, Tübingen 1993 (WUNT 69), 108–194; engl. version in: HENGEL, Martin, Studies in Early Christology, Edinburgh 1995, 119–225.

ID./SCHWEMER, Anna Maria, Paulus zwischen Damaskus und Antiochien, WUNT 108, Tübingen 1998.

HURTADO, Larry W., One God, One Lord. Early Christian Devotion and Ancient Jewish Montheism, 1988.

HOWARD, George, The Tetragramm and the New Testament, in: JBL 96 (1977), 63–83.

JEREMIAS, Joachim, Die Sprache des Lukasevangeliums, KEK-Sb, Göttingen 1980.

JONES, D.L., The Title ΚΥΡΙΟΣ in Luke-Acts, in: SBL.SP 110,2 (1974), 85–101.

KARRER, Martin, Jesus Christus im Neuen Testament, GNT 11, Göttingen 1998.

KINGSBURY, Jack Dean, The Title "Kyrios" in Matthew's Gospel, in: JBL 94 (1975), 246–255.

KOKKINOS, Nikos, The Herodian Dynasty. Origins, Role in Society and Eclipse, JSP.SS 30, Sheffield 1998.

MARCUS, Ralph, Divine Names and Attributes in Hellenistic Jewish Literature, in: Proceedings of the American Academy of Jewish Research 2 (1932), 43–120.

MARTIN, Alain, La titulature épigraphique de Domitien, BKP 181, Frankfurt a.M., 1987.

MAYER, Günter, Die herrscherliche Titulatur Gottes bei Philo von Alexandrien, in: KOCH, Dietrich-Alex/LICHTENBERGER, Hermann (eds.), Begegnungen zwischen Christentum und Judentum in Antike und Mittelalter. FS Heinz SCHRECKENBERG, Schriften des Institutum Judaicum Delitzschianum 1, Göttingen 1993, 293–302.

MERKLEIN, Helmut, Maranā ("unser Herr") als Bezeichnung des nabatäischen Königs. Eine Analogie zur neutestamentlichen Kyrios-Bezeichnung?, in: HOPPE, Rudolf/ BUSSE, Ulrich, Von Jesus zum Christus (see above), 25–41.

MILLAR, Fergus, The Emperor in the Roman World (31 BC – AD 337), London ²1992.

ID., The Roman Near East 31 BC – AD 337, Cambridge, MA – London 1993.

MOMMSEN, Theodor, Römisches Staatsrecht 2,2, Reprint Darmstadt 1963 = ³1887.
NORDEN, Eduard, P. Vergilius Maro Aeneis Buch VI, Darmstadt ⁷1981.
O'NEILL, John C., The Use of ΚΥΡΙΟΣ in the Book of Acts, in: SJTh 8 (1955), 155–174.
PIETERSMA, Albert, Kyrios or Tetragram: A Renewed Quest for the Original Septuaginta, in: ID./COX, Claude E. (eds.), De Septuaginta. Studies in Honor of John W. Wevers, Mississanga, Ontario 1984, 85–101.
DE LA POTTERIE, Ignace, Le titre κύριος appliqué à Jesus dans l'Évangile de Luc, in: DESCAMPS, Albert (ed.), Mélanges Bibliques en hommage au B. Rigaux, Gembloux 1970, 117–146.
RÖSEL, Martin, Die Übersetzung der Gottesnamen in der Genesis-Septuaginta, in: Ernten, was man sät. FS Klaus Koch zu seinem 65. Geburtstag, ed. Daniels, D. R.; Gleßmer, U. and Rösel, Martin, Neukirchen-Vluyn 1991, 357–377.
ID., Adonaj – Warum Gott 'Herr' genannt wird, FAT 29, Tübingen 2000.
RONCHI, Giulia, Lexicon theonymum rerumque sacrarum et divinarum ad Aegyptum pertinentium quae in papyris ostracis titulis graecis latinisque in Aegypto repertis laudantur 3, Milano 1975.
SCHENK, Wolfgang, Die Sprache des Matthäus, Göttingen 1987.
SCHNEIDER, Gerhard, Gott und Christus als ΚΥΡΙΟΣ nach der Apostelgeschichte (1980), in: ID., Lukas. Theologe der Heilsgeschichte, BBB 59, Bonn 1985, 213–226.
SKEHAN, P.W., The Divine Name at Qumran, in the Masada Scroll, and in the Septuagint, in: Bulletin of the International Organization for Septuagint and Cognate Studies 13 (1980), 14–44.
SPICQ, Ceslas, Theological Lexicon of the New Testament 2, Peabody, Mass. 1994, 341–354.
SPRONK, Klaas, Art. Lord, in: DDD² (1999), 531–533.
STRECKER, Georg, Theologie des Neuen Testaments, ed. by HORN, Friedrich Wilhelm, Berlin – New York 1996.
THOMA, Clemens/LAUER, Simon, Die Gleichnisse der Rabbinen. Zweiter Teil. Von der Erschaffung der Welt bis zum Tod Abrahams: Bereschit Rabba 1–63, JCh 13, Bern et al. 1991.
VERMES, Geza, Jesus the Jew, London ²1983.
WILLIGER, Eduard, Art. Kyrios, in: PRE 12/1 (1924), 176–183.
ZELLER, Dieter, Art. Kyrios, in: DDD² (1999) 492–497.

Gudrun Guttenberger

Why Caesarea Philippi of all Sites?
Some Reflections on the Political Background and Implications of Mark 8:27–30 for the Christology of Mark

Peter's declaration at Caesarea Philippi is especially important to Mark's Gospel. Along with the transfiguration story and the discussion about Eliah it forms a christological section connecting the first and the second part of Mark's Gospel. Thus it also links up the traditions of miracle-stories and emphasis on Jesus' preaching to the Passion motif. Two direct references show this very clearly. First, the question concerning people's opinion towards Jesus reminds one of Mark 6:15 where this topic appears for the first time, subsequent to a summary about Jesus as a miracle worker and preacher. Second, the declaration of Jesus as Christ – and several sentences later as Son of God – points to Mark 14:61 where Jesus is asked if he claims to be "the Messiah, the son of the Blessed One." Peter's confession proves to be pivotal for Mark's Gospel – this central scene takes place at the outmost outskirts of Palestine, namely in the area of Caesarea Philippi. Jesus never travels further north in Mark's Gospel; the distance to Jerusalem is never greater than at this point.

There are only few proposals to explain the location of these events. Usually, Caesarea Philippi is interpreted as a symbolical place marking the turning point of the Gospel: from now on Jesus turns to Jerusalem and faces his Passion.[1] Only Stauffer in his popular book '*Christus und die Caesaren*'[2] (1951) pointed briefly to the political implications of locating Peter's declaration in Caesarea Philippi.

In this short essay a new approach is put forward: *By locating Peter's declaration at Caesarea Philippi, Jesus is introduced by Mark as the lawful king of Israel in competition with the Herodian kings and as the true emperor of the whole oikumene in competition with the Roman ruler.*

First will be suggested that Mark's choice of Caesarea Philippi as the setting for Peter's declaration was deliberate. Second the connection between Caesarea Philippi and Roman rule will be shown. Afterwards the relations between the Herodians and the Flavians beginning in the sixties are summed up. Finally the significance of all this for the understanding of Mark's Christology will be disclosed.

---

[1] E. BEST, Mark, 44f; W.H. KELBER, Kingdom, 69f; E.P. GOULD, Mark, 151; H. ANDERSON, Mark, 207.
[2] E. STAUFFER, Christus, 114. Cf. W.M. LANE, Mark, 289, who points to political consequences without naming any. W. SCHMITHALS, Markus, 381, is doubtful about political implications.

The Provenance of the Localization

In Mark's Gospel spatial settings are of great importance.³ Besides Capernaum as the centre of Jesus' activity in Galilee and Jerusalem as the capital of the Passion, there are only few other locations as prominent as Caesarea Philippi.⁴ Whether Mark himself is the author of the location or not, in any case a theological meaning is probably connected to it. Yet Mark is the author of Mark 8:27, as I will argue. Verse 27a opens the following scene by naming the place and introducing the question of Jesus. There are two introductory clauses: Καὶ ἐξῆλθεν ὁ Ἰησοῦς καὶ οἱ μαθηταὶ αὐτοῦ εἰς τὰς κώμας Καισαρείας τῆς Φιλίππου· (8:27a) and καὶ ἐν τῇ ὁδῷ ἐπηρώτα τοὺς μαθητὰς αὐτοῦ λέγων αὐτοῖς· (8:27ba). In the following sentence the question of Jesus is formulated.

There are some discrepancies: In V 27a a plural subject is followed by a singular predicate. By means of 'the villages of Caesarea Philippi' and 'on the way' localizations are duplicated. Three models are proposed to explain that: (1) Mark 8:27a is the end of the previous passage (Mark 8:22–26).⁵ However, the passage shows characteristics typical of the beginning of a passage: Jesus is called by name and a place is mentioned.⁶ (2) The duplication of the introductory clauses indicates two older units combined by Mark. Hahn's famous proposal⁷ reconstructs a newer tradition consisting of V 27b.28.29 and an older one composed of V 27a, a sentence similar to V 29 and V 33. To be sure, this theory is hypothetical. In my opinion the evidence for two different traditions is not sufficient. Besides one has to assume that the redactor on the one hand did not efface the duplication of the introduction in V 27 but on the other hand erased the equivalent of V 29 in the older tradition entirely. This does not seem credible. (3) Whereas V 27b belongs to tradition, Mark is considered the author of V 27a.⁸ In this reading the motif of 'the way' which is typical of

---

³ E.S. MALBON, Space; S.H. SMITH, Lion, 150–164; D. RHOADS/D. MICHIE, Mark, 65–72; E. LOHMEYER, Markus, 162.
⁴ Only Bethania near Jerusalem is important in a similar way. Bethania is the place of dwelling while Jesus stays in Jerusalem (Mark 11:1.11); here he is anointed by an anonymous woman (Mark 14:3). Mark 11:1 and 14:3 are significant for the Gospel's structure: Jesus enters Jerusalem (Mark 11:1) and the Passion begins (Mark 14:1f). In both passages there are allusions to Jesus as Messiah. Bethsaida is mentioned twice, once as the disciple's destination (Mark 6:45) and once as the place of a healing story (Mark 8:22–26) right before Peter's declaration. Mark refers once to Tyros, to Gerasa and to Jericho (Mark 7:24; 5:1; 10:46).
⁵ R. BULTMANN, Geschichte, 276.
⁶ It is true that Jesus can be called by name in the end of a passage as in Mark 2:17 and Mark 10:52. In these passages, however, a new and important logion is introduced which is the cause for calling Jesus by name. It is also true that a location can be mentioned in the end of a passage as in Mark 6:6 and Mark 8:13. In both passages the location is not specific. Mark 8:27 does not add a concluding logion to the healing of the blind man; its localization is very specific, and therefore it is to be interpreted as the beginning and not as the end of a passage.
⁷ F. HAHN, Hoheitstitel, 226–230.
⁸ For instance E. DINKLER, Petrusbekenntnis, 133.

Mark is interpreted as belonging to pre-marcan tradition. This is possible but not very probable.

In my opinion Mark is the author of all of verse 27. Three arguments are decisive: (1) the localizations of V 27a and V 27b are not in discrepancy but supplement each other. The expression 'the villages' does not point to an appointed place but to a whole region that needs the idea of being connected by something like a road. Corresponding to Mark 10:52 one may think of a specific road, namely the one leading from Bethsaida to Caesarea Philippi. The discrepancy concerning the numerus of subject and predicate may originate in the fact that Jesus is indeed the only actor in the previous passage. Because of this, Jesus is mentioned first; for the story beginning in V 27, however, the disciples are of great importance. They are mentioned in a supplementary appendix. (2) The localization 'in the villages of Caesarea Philippi' most probably is not traditional. A local tradition needs a group of people passing on their local stories and living together in one specific place, not just in a region. Besides in a local tradition one would expect the compositum εἰσέρχομαι instead of ἐξέρχομαι. (3) The reference to Caesarea Philippi forms part of a series of localizations beginning in Mark 7:24. Unfortunately it is difficult to reconstruct the idea of Mark in regard to geography; nevertheless it is obvious that he considers it of great consequence.

Mark being the author of V 27 requires us to ask for the significance of Caesarea Philippi in the late sixties and early seventies that induced Mark to single out the town as the backdrop of one of the most important stories of his Gospel.

Ancient Caesarea Philippi

Ancient Caesarea Philippi[9] is located at the foot of the southwestern extremity of Mount Hermon. One of the Jordan's sources rises there. There is a great cavern at the site, where Pan was worshipped. Therefore the ancient name of the site was Panias. The site is mentioned for the first time by Polybios (Hist 16.18.2): here – very close to the cave – the battle between Seleucids and Ptolemies was fought by Antiochus III and Scopas, Egypt's general in 200 B.C. Either the Paneion was founded by the Seleucids out of gratitude to the gods for helping them to victory, or it was an Egyptian foundation built prior to 200 B.C.[10] In this context Panias became popular among the Greco-Roman

---

[9] Cf. NEAEHL I, 136–142; G. SCHMITT, Siedlungen, 198f; Y. TSAFRIR/L. DI SEGNI/J. GREEN (eds.), Tabula Imperii Romani, 199; V. TZAFERIS, Cults, 190–201; ID./J.E. WILSON, Banias.

[10] Cf. V. TZAFERIS, God, 132f; in the second case a connection to emperor veneration may originate in Ptolemaic times: Alexander claimed to embody Dionysos; his adherents represented the thriambos in which Pan was prominent. The emperors of the succession states namely the Ptolemaic kings demanded to represent Pan. Ptolemy II e.g. built a temple dedicated to Pan in Alexandria. Cf. A. LICHTENBERGER, Baupolitik, 152.

world. The site is mentioned also by Pliny (Nat Hist 5.15.71; 5.16.18) and Ptolemy (Geogr 5.15.21; 8.20.12).[11]

Towards the end of the first century B.C. Panias was connected to the emperor cult. In 19 B.C. Herod the Great founded a temple and dedicated it to Augustus shortly after the emperor had visited Palestine.[12] The temple is depicted on many of Philip's coins.[13]

Bronze coin minted by Philip in AD 33/34. Obverse: Tiberius; reverse: Augusteum.[14]

---

[11] In Hellenistic times the sanctuary was mostly visited by people living in the region who travelled to the site to partake in „ritual dining" (A. BERLIN, Archaeology, 31); the pottery points to private cult by people who were not wealthy. In early Roman times fewer cooking vessels and many more lamps were found; the pottery is often imported and a few vessels are of great value; for A. BERLIN, Archaeology, 31f.42, this indicates a change in ritual. More people visited the sanctuary but stayed there only for a short time. Some of the worshippers were in contact with regions and cities far away.

[12] By this act the region became a local religious centre, that provides the Roman cult of the emperor, the Greek cult of Pan and not far away in Dan, the cult of the god of Dan who was venerated there for many centuries by Aramaic speaking people. Cf. V. TZAFERIS, God, 134. For Herod's building program connected to the three temples for emperor veneration, cf. D.W. ROLLER, Herod, 88f.

[13] Cf. Y. MESHORER, Coins, plates X–XI, no. 76–84. The coins show a tetrastyle temple. One has to consider, however, if the depiction is realistic or reduced; in any case the temple was probably smaller than the temple in Samaria. Cf. D.W. ROLLER, Herod, 191. A. LICHTENBERGER, Baupolitik, 151, argues that the temple imitates sanctuaries in Syria like the Temple for Bacchus in Baalbek; D.W. ROLLER, Herod, 92, states that it is a copy of Roman models and differs from Hellenistic style.

[14] From Staatliche Münzsammlung, Land, S. 64, Nr. 147.

There is a discussion whether the temple dedicated to Augustus was situated at the entrance of the cave as Ma'oz argues[15] or a little west on the ridge of a mountain as Netzer[16] proposes. There is strong evidence that in both places Herodian buildings were found. In my opinion it is more likely that Netzer is right and that Herod renovated the old sanctuary of Pan as well; in this case there is a satisfying explanation for the second Herodian building. If Ma'oz is right, one has to assume a large and obviously splendid additional building that is neither mentioned by Josephus nor anyone else. This seems less probable.

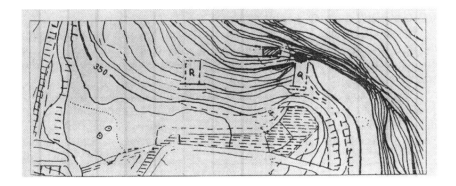

The letter "Q" signifies the place of discovery of opus quadratum in front of the Cave of Pan. The letter "R" marks the place where opus reticulatum was discovered.[17]

Why did Herod build a temple dedicated to Augustus in Panias?[18] One may assume that – provided Panias was founded by the Ptolemies – Herod seized the opportunity to demonstrate his loyalty to Augustus by selecting a place where Pan, the leading member in Dionysos' thriambos, was worshipped. This can be considered an act of loyalty because the former rival of Augustus, Anthony, claimed to represent Neos Dionysos. Herod had been Anthony's client – a person one may compare to Pan – till the battle of Actium. Now becoming client of Augustus, he built a new temple surpassing the older one at the very

---

[15] A. LICHTENBERGER, Baupolitik, 151, and D.W. ROLLER, Herod, 191, agree with Z.U. MA'OZ.
[16] The debate between Z.U. MA'OZ and E. NETZER is published in Qadmoniot 115–118 (1998/99).
[17] From Z.U. MA'OZ, Reply, 52.
[18] P. RICHARDSON, Herod, 184, argues that it was Herod's choice of place that induces Jewish people to face the facts. Panias was as well as Samaria and Straton's Tower of no significance for Jewish history and belief.

place that symbolizes the former relations.[19] Another reason is more evident: Panias is situated at the intersection of the roads leading from Damascus to Tyre and from south (Bethsaida) to the Beqaa-Valley in the north. In respect to the prominence of the location, one may compare the temple in Caesarea Philippi to the one in Caesarea Maritima. Both temples were situated at the land's borders in order to demonstrate to each traveller – whether he arrives by ship in Caesarea Maritima or travelled the road – to whom Herod's Palestine is indebted. The gates to Palestine were deeply colored by emperor veneration.

This bold character of Panias was further emphasized by Philip, one of the successors of Herod, who founded a city here, calling it – to honour Augustus – Caesarea and choosing it as his residence.[20]

The significance of Caesarea Philippi for the emperor cult continued during the next decades. Agrippa II renamed the city Neronias in 61 or 67 A.D. in honour of Nero.[21] Thereby the temple was dedicated to the living emperor who was venerated as well as or instead of Augustus.[22]

Having reconquered Galilee, Vespasian and Titus spent three weeks in the Jewish king's residence in September 67 (Jos Bell 3.444f) giving offerings to the god (ἀποδιδοὺς τῷ θεῷ χαριστήρια τῶν κατωρθωμένων, Jos Bell 3.445). For two reasons 'the god' appears to be the emperor: (1) in September the birthday of Augustus was celebrated as a religious feast.[23] The sojourn of Vespasian and Titus was contemporary to this event; Vespasian the victorious general as well as Agrippa, client king of a rebelling nation would most probably have seized the opportunity to demonstrate their loyalty to Rome. (2) The singular also indicates that it was the divine emperor the offerings were given to. Otherwise the name of the god would have been mentioned.[24] To be sure,

---

[19] If the new temple was situated at the entrance of the cave, the cult of Pan was reinterpreted; if the new temple was built on the ridge of the mountain, the cult of Pan was submitted to the new emperor.

[20] Philip calls himself κτίστης on one of his coins; Cf. Y. MESHORER, Coins, plate XI, no. 83.

[21] Although Panias was renamed Neronias by Agrippa II, the popular name of the town was Kaisareia till the end of the first century, as can be seen from Josephus' writings (e.g. Vit 52). Moreover, it appears probable that after the death of Nero the town was no longer called Neronias; the fact that Josephus prefers Kaisareia instead of Panias indicates that this was the popular name of the town at least for Jewish people. Mark applies the current name.

[22] In the second century the importance and splendidness of the sanctuary increased; fragments of 28 statues were discovered, the oldest ones dating to the late first and early second century. Cf. E.A. FRIEDLAND, Sculptures, 9, and A. BERLIN, Archaeology, 34.

[23] Celebrating the feasts connected to the emperor's venerations was required from the army; cf. M. CLAUSS, Kaiser, 317f; thank offerings (*supplicationes*) were the usual kind of offerings to the emperor. Cf. ibid., 321.

[24] Roland Deines proposed in his lecture during the meeting of the 'Deutsche Palästina-Verein' in December 2000 in Rauischholzhausen that Josephus indicates that it was the Jewish God who was in fact venerated in the temple dedicated to Augustus. Actually, Josephus sometimes means the Jewish God when he uses the words ὁ θεός, for example when he prophesies the emperorship to Vespasian only a few paragraphs before (Bell

the festivities on this occasion were more splendid than in other years and may have made them famous in the whole region. During the next stay of Titus in Caesarea Philippi in winter 70 there were festivities celebrating the Roman victory; a great number of captured Jews was put to death. Certainly this stay became also famous among the regional population. There are reasons to assume that the actions of Titus in this winter aroused the interest of people outside of Palestine as well. Titus participated in the rituals for Apis in Egypt in spring 71 wearing a diadem. The rumor sprung up that Titus planned to depose Vespasian. Titus had to travel to Rome in order to dispel the suspicions.[25] One may suppose that Titus was watched very carefully by his enemies in the whole span of time. *Caesarea Philippi is most suitable of all places in northern Palestine to demonstrate the significance of the emperor cult. In particular the city indicates the high grade of dependency of the Jewish kings on Roman rule since – unlike Caesarea Maritima – Panias was the residence of a Jewish king.*

The Relationship between Herodians and Flavians

During the years of the Jewish War a strong relationship developed between Vespasian and Titus on the one side and Agrippa and Berenice on the other. Agrippa II was entrusted by Claudius and Nero with the territories of Gaulanitis, Batanea, Trachonitis, Auranitis, Julias, Tiberias and Tarichaea. Agrippa, who had been educated in Rome was a very loyal client king. That he also was successful, can be seen from the long duration of his rule. Vespasian met Agrippa for the first time when the Roman general arrived at Antioch in March 67. At that time the position of Agrippa as Rome's client king was endangered since he had not been able to put down the riots himself. This was true although there was no doubt Agrippa would fight side by side with the Romans against the Jewish rebels. In Rome one major argument for the rule of client kings was the supposition that a native king would deal with his people and in particular with banditry more easily than a Roman procurator.[26] In this respect Agrippa had failed. Hence it is noteworthy to see how Vespasian put down revolts, for instance in Tiberias, presumably to act respectfully towards Agrippa II and to strengthen the client king's authority. Josephus stresses this

---

3.350f). Nonetheless there is an important difference between Josephus quoting his own sayings, reporting the actions of pagan characters and annotating them. In his own sayings ὁ θεός refers to the Jewish God, in his annotations Josephus sometimes suggests that the Jewish God as the true God is God of the whole universe and of the Romans as well (cf. Jos Bell 6.310). In Bell 3.444f, however, Josephus reports what the Roman general did in September 67; he gave offerings to a pagan god; besides it does not seem credible that Josephus the former priest would attribute an offering given to a pagan god in a pagan temple to the Jewish God.

[25] Suet Tit 5; cf. B. LEVICK, Vespasian, 69.
[26] Cf. D.C. BRAUND, King, 66; Accordingly there were rumours that Agrippa would be deposed in the beginning of the war; cf. Jos Vit 52.

factor when describing the events in the late summer of 67 (Bell 3.443–461). Since Agrippa was increasingly indebted to Vespasian, he owed loyalty as a client towards his patron not only to the Roman empire, the Senate and the emperor Nero but also to the person of Vespasian. The emergence of this patron-client relationship is connected to Caesarea Philippi since Agrippa welcomed Vespasian as a guest in his residence in the late summer of 67. This visit may be interpreted as a signal for a successfully arranged patron-client relationship. The association between the Flavians and the Herodians gained a new quality as soon as Titus and Berenice, the king's sister, became lovers. This happened at the latest after the end of the war but probably as early as autumn 67. Berenice traveled to Rome after Vespasian's death;[27] both planned to marry. Because of the opposition of the Roman urban population Titus had to renounce the marriage. Of course, one may consider their intentions of marriage as the climax of the Roman Jewish aristocratic relations.

This strong alliance between the Roman centre and the Jewish kings becomes all the more complex if one bears in mind that the Roman population dreaded the possibility of Rome's fall caused by a great campaign of revenge coming from Asia, commanded by the king of the East. In Rome many people interpreted the Jewish Rebellion as the beginning of this great war. Their fear increased when civil war broke out in 68/69. Tacitus reports: *pluribus persuasio inerat antiquis sacerdotum litteris contineri eo ipso tempore fore, ut valesceret Oriens profectique Iudaea rerum potirentur* (Hist 5.13.2). The same is written by Suetonius: *percrebuerat Oriente toto vetus et constans opinio, esse in fatis ut eo tempore Iudaea profecti rerum potirentur* (Vesp 4.5). In the year of crisis after Nero's death, the idea of the king of the East was amalgamated with the hopes and fears concerning *Nero redivivus* (Tac Hist 2.8.1; Suet Nero 57.2).[28] Jewish People likewise interpreted their war of liberation in terms of the Great War connecting it with messianic ideas. Josephus gives an account of the hopes from a Jewish perspective: Τὸ δ' ἐπᾶραν αὐτοὺς μάλιστα πρὸς τὸν πόλεμον ἦν χρησμὸς ἀμφίβολος ὁμοίως ἐν τοῖς ἱεροῖς εὑρημένος γράμμασιν, ὡς κατὰ τὸν καιρὸν ἐκεῖνον ἀπὸ τῆς χώρας αὐτῶν τις ἄρξει τῆς οἰκουμένης (Jos Bell 6.312f). These ideas originate from a hope popular in the whole Orient that world domination should pass from Rome to the East.[29] In the time of

---

[27] The coins Agrippa minted in the end of the seventies picture a ship on their reverse. Cf. Y. MESHORER, Coins, plate XVI, no. 118. From this one may see the hopes being connected to the visit of Berenice in Rome. Cf. B. OVERBECK, Land, 76.

[28] Someone – either a slave from Pontus or a 'libertus' from Italy – claimed to be Nero, concentrated his forces on the isle of Kynthos and was defeated and captured by Roman troops. In the late seventies someone pretending to be Nero appeared in the Parthian Empire and was supported by them (Suet Nero 57; Dio Cass 64.93).

[29] Cf. H.G. KIPPENBERG, Orient, 41–44; H. SCHWIER, Tempel, 241–250. This model was first applied to interpret the battle of Magnesia; in later times the war between Rome and Mithridates of Pontus, who claimed to represent Dionysos, was dominated by the hopes and by the fears related to the idea of the king from the East. In the Roman civil war following the death of Julius Caesar Anthony posed as Neos Dionysos side by side with

crisis Vespasian succeeded in reinterpreting those dreads and hopes by claiming to be the announced king from the East. Tacitus continues his report: *quae ambages Vespasanius ac Titum praedixerat, sed vulgus more humanae cupidinis sibi tantam fatorum magnitudinem interpretati ne adversis quidem ad vera mutabantur* (Hist V 13). Likewise did Suetonius: *id de imperatore Romano, quantum postea eventu parvit, praedictum Iudaei ad se trahentes, rebellarunt* ... (Vesp 4:5). Josephus himself participated in the reinterpretation of messianic ideas by prophesying that Vespasian would soon be emperor. He carries on: τοῦθ' οἱ μὲν ὡς οἰκεῖον ἐξέβαλον καὶ πολλοὶ τῶν σοφῶν ἐπλανήθησαν περὶ τὴν κρίσιν, ἐδήλου δ' ἄρα τὴν Οὐεσπασιανοῦ τὸ λόγιον ἡγεμονίαν ἀποδειχθέντος ἐπὶ Ἰουδαίας αὐτοκράτορος (Bell 6.312f). By doing so he tied the Jewish messianic hope with Roman triumph. For Vespasian this demand was a central part of his strategy to prove himself as the lawful emperor notwithstanding his 'common' origin.[30] The Jews played an important role not only in proving him to be the lawful emperor but also in establishing his power as the new Roman emperor. Vespasian made sure the 'East', the Parthians and the client kings at the border as well as the Jewish king, the emperors from Commagene and Emesa and the prefects of Egypt and Syria, would support his plans.[31] Because of Parthian power Agrippa and the Jews were important for Vespasian.[32]

In my opinion Titus tried to go on with Vespasian's strategy to amalgamate West and East. Marriage with the Jewish queen Berenice and perhaps the beginning of a new dynasty would have accomplished melting western and eastern traditions and ideals. From a Jewish aristocratic point of view the future marriage of the forthcoming Roman emperor with the Jewish princess may have disclosed the actual meaning of the prophecy of Num 24:17 and unveiled *how* this could become reality. The Roman urban population, however, was not willing to accept an empress from the East. The plans of Titus and Ber-

---

Cleopatra appearing as Nea Isis. To them the interpretation of the king coming from the East was applied also.

[30] Cf. Suet Vesp 1. His father made his money as a customs officer in Asia and as a banker in Switzerland; in the Roman Senate's view this was rather obscure. Vespasian refers to religious ideas, especially the Cult of Sarapis to legitimate himself. Cf. Tac Hist 4.81–82; Suet Vesp 7; Dio Cass 64.8.1; B. LEVICK, Vespasian, 67ff ; H. SCHWIER, Tempel, 295, M. CLAUSS, Kaiserkult, 113ff.

[31] Cf. B. LEVICK, Vespasian, 47f.

[32] In the first century Jewish kings were suspected of negotiating with the Parthians on their own terms on several occasions; Herod Antipas was accused of being in alliance with the Parthians by Agrippa I; Herod was banished to Gaul. Jos Ant 18.250. Some years later Agrippa I organised a meeting of five eastern client kings in Tiberias; when the Roman legate Marsus got aware of this he was very alarmed. Cf. Jos Ant 19.338. In the Jewish War the Jews may have hoped for support by the kingdom of Adiabene being under Parthian rule in the first century. Cf. Jos Bell 2.389. Cf. E. SCHÜRER, History I, 351–352 and 448. For the hopes of the kings of Adiabene connected to their conversion to Judaism cf. J. NEUSNER, Conversion, 60–63; ID., History, 61–67; ID., Note, 144–150.

enice failed and consequently the vision of uniting Roman and Jewish interests, hopes and beliefs was wrecked.

To sum up: Caesarea Philippi is characteristic of the veneration of Roman emperors as divine and of the dependency of Jewish kings on Roman rulers. *Contemporary to the making of Mark's Gospel, messianic hopes and Roman dreads related to the Jewish War were as vigorous as the attempts to overcome the conflicts by identifying the Roman Emperor with the Messiah and creating a new Roman-Jewish dynasty.*

The Significance of the Location for Mark's Christology

By locating Peter's declaration in the area of Caesarea Philippi,[33] the stage on which Mark had Jesus act was that of an explosive political background. He brings him in direct contact with the political dimension of Jewish messianic hope. In contrast to previous research that understands Peter's declaration as a rejection of the Jewish political implications of messianic hopes, it is my opinion that to locate Peter's declaration near Caesarea Philippi means to emphasise the political importance of Jesus. Nevertheless, the messianic idea still needs to be modified by the Passion tradition, as it is obvious from the following foretelling of the Passion.

Mark depicts Jesus against the background of the Jewish king's residence as the true king of the Jews in contrast to Agrippa II. In Mark this refers to the enmity of the Herodians towards God. Herod's adherents try to put Jesus to death (Mark 3:6); Herod himself is responsible for the death of God's eschatological messenger, John the Baptist (Mark 6:27). Corresponding to their enmity towards God the Herodians are friends and clients of the Romans. Herod's following attemps to lure Jesus into the trap by asking whether one should pay taxes to the Romans or not (Mark 12:13–17). By establishing a parallel of John and Jesus (Mark 9:13) the Herodians are interpreted as the minor counterpart of the Romans: they are putting John to death while the Romans had Jesus executed.

Against the background of the temple dedicated to *divi filius* Augustus Mark depicts Jesus as the true emperor arising from Judah, as the king coming from the East in contrast to Vespasian and perhaps in contrast to the hopes linked up to the marriage of Titus and Berenice associated with the hopes for a new Roman-Jewish dynasty. This interpretation reminds one of some other texts in Mark: Jesus heals a blind man in Bethsaida (Mark 8:22–26) just before

---

[33] One may wonder why Mark does not locate the scene within Caesarea Philippi; most probably this is the result of another interest of Mark; Jesus is not willing to enter cities; usually he stays in villages or in desert places. Further one might compare the scene with Mark 13; Jesus talks about Jerusalem and his fate sitting on the Mount of Olives facing temple and city. Apart from that, the temple dedicated to Augustus could be seen not only in the city but also from a distance because it was built on a platform higher than the surroundings (if Z.U. MA'OZ is right) or on the ridge of a hill in a rather prominent position (if E. NETZER is right).

he is called Messiah by Peter; this healing story is very similar to the one that is reported by Tacitus and Suetonius about Vespasian.[34] Jesus is called Son of God by God himself in the following scene (Mark 9:7)[35] and by a Roman *centurio* at the end of the Gospel (Mark 15:39)[36]. In chapter 13 Mark insists that the Jewish War is not the eschatological war and that the Messiah has not yet come (again) – neither in the person of someone like Simon Bar Giora nor in the Roman emperor Vespasian. If this is true, Vespasian is not the lawful emperor of the oikumene and future will reveal the human one entrusted by God with dominion (Mark 14:62).

---

[34] Cf. Tac Hist 4.81–82; Suet Vesp 7.

[35] In Mark's geography this most probably happens on Mount Hermon; Panias is situated at its foot. The true Son of God is as high above the Roman emperor as Mount Hermon is above Panias!

[36] Of all humans it is a Roman officer who for the first time calls Jesus Son of God. The fact that the confessor is a soldier, adds to my argument; in the army emperor veneration was very important; Vespasian established his authority with the help of the army and its loyalty. Declaring the crucified Jesus as Son of God (note the absence of an article and the past tense) the officer deserts the emperor's side and joins the opposition.

Bibliography

ANDERSON, Hugh, The Gospel of Mark, NCBC, Grand Rapids 1981.
BERLIN, Andrea M., The Archaeology of Ritual. The Sanctuary of Pan at Banias/Caesarea Philippi, in: BASOR 315 (1999), 27–45.
BEST, Ernest, Mark. The Gospel as Story. Edinburgh 1983.
BRAUND, David C., Rome and the Friendly King. New York 1984.
BULTMANN, Rudolf, Die Geschichte der Synoptischen Tradition. Mit einem Nachwort von Gerd THEISSEN, FRLANT 29, Göttingen [10]1995.
CLAUSS, Manfred, Kaiser und Gott. Herrscherkult im Römischen Reich. Stuttgart – Leipzig 1999.
DINKLER, Erich, Petrusbekenntnis und Satanswort. Das Problem der Messianität Jesu, in: Zeit und Geschichte. Rudolf Bultmann zum 80. Geburtstag hg.v. Erich DINKLER, Tübingen 1964, 127–153.
FRIEDLAND, Elizabeth A., Greco-Roman Sculptures in the Levant. The Marbles from the Sanctuary of Pan at Caesarea Philippi, in: John H. HUMPHREY (ed.), The Roman and Byzantine Near East 2, JRA.SS 31, Portsmouth 1999, 7–22.
GOULD, Ezra P., A Critical and Exegetical Commentary on the Gospel according to St. Mark, ICC, Edinburgh [10]1961.
GUNDRY, Robert H., Mark. A Commentary on His Apology for the Cross. Grand Rapids 1993.
HAHN, Ferdinand, Christologische Hoheitstitel. Ihre Geschichte im frühen Christentum, UTB 1873, [5]1995.
KELBER, Werner H.: The Kingdom in Mark. A New Place and a New Time. Philadelphia 1974.
KIPPENBERG, Hans G., "Dann wird der Orient herrschen und der Okzident dienen." Zur Begründung eines gesamtvorderorientalischen Standpunktes im Kampf gegen Rom, In: Spiegel und Gleichnis. FS für Jacob Taubes. Ed.: Norbert W. BOLZ/Wolfgang HÜBENER, Würzburg 1983, 40–48.
LANE, William L., The Gospel According to Mark, NIC, Grand Rapids 1974.
LEVICK, Barbara, Vespasian. London 1999.
LICHTENBERGER, Achim, Die Baupolitik Herodes des Großen, ADPV 26, Wiesbanden 1999.
LOHMEYER, Ernst, Galiläa und Jerusalem, FRLANT 34, Göttingen 1936.
ID., Das Evangelium des Matthäus. Für d. Druck erarb. u. hrsg. von Werner SCHMAUCH, KEK-Sb, Göttingen [4]1967.
MALBON, Elisabeth S., Narrative Space and Mythic Meaning in Mark, The Biblical Seminar 13, Sheffield 1991.
MESHORER, Ya'akov, Jewish Coins of the Second Temple Period. Translated from the Hebrew by I.H. Levine. Tel-Aviv 1967.
MA'OZ, Zvi U., The Sanctuary of Pan in Baniyas, in: Qadm. 115 (1998), 18–25.
ID., Where did Herod Really build the Temple in Honor of Augustus in Banias? Reply to remarks by E. Netzer, in: Qadm 117 (1999), 52f.
NETZER, Ehud, Where Did Herod Build the Temple Dedicated to Augustus at Banias, in: Qadm. 116 (1998), 134f.
NEUSNER, Jacob, History of the Jews in Babylonia. Vol I. Leiden [2]1969.
ID., Shorter Note, in: Numen 13 (1966), 144–150.
ID., The Conversion of Adiabene to Judaism, in: JBL 83 (1964), 60–63.

OVERBECK, Bernhard: Das heilige Land. Antike Münzen und Siegel aus einem Jahrtausend jüdischer Geschichte. Staatliche Münzsammlung München in Zusammenarbeit mit The Israel Museum Jerusalem. Katalog der Sonderausstellung 1993/94. München 1993.

RHOADS, David/MICHIE, Donald, Mark a Story. An Introduction to the Narrative of a Gospel. Philadelphia 1982.

RICHARDSON, Peter, Herod. King of the Jews and Friend of the Romans, Studies on Personalities of the New Testament, Columbia 1996.

ROLLER, Duane W., The Building Program of Herod the Great, Berkeley 1998.

SCHMITHALS, Walter, Das Evangelium nach Markus. Kapitel 1–9,1, ÖTbK 2/1, Würzburg/Gütersloh 1979.

SCHMITT, Götz, Siedlungen Palästinas in griechisch-römischer Zeit. Ostjordanland, Negeb und (in Auswahl) Westjordanland. Beihefte zum Tübinger Atlas zum Vorderen Orient. Reihe B 53. Wiesbaden 1995.

SCHÜRER, Emil, The History of the Jewish people in den age of Jesus Christ. Rev. and ed. by Geza VERMES, Fergus MILLAR and Matthew BLACK. Vol. I. Edinburgh 1993.

SCHWIER, Helmut, Tempel und Tempelzerstörung. Untersuchungen zu den theologischen und ideologischen Faktoren im ersten jüdisch-römischen Krieg (66–74 n. Chr.), NTOA 11, Fribourg/Göttingen 1989.

SMITH, Stephen H., A Lion with Wings. A Narrative-Critical Approach to Mark's Gospel, The Biblical Seminar 38, Sheffield 1996.

STAATLICHE MÜNZSAMMLUNG MÜNCHEN IN ZUSAMMENARBEIT MIT THE ISRAEL MUSEUM JERUSALEM (ed.): Das Heilige Land. Antike Münzen und Siegel aus einem Jahrhundert jüdischer Geschichte. Texte von Bernhard Overbeck unter Zugrundelegung der wissenschaftlichen Bestimmungen durch Yaakov Meshorer. Katalog der Sonderausstellung 1993/94 der staatlichen Münzsammlung München 1993.

STAUFFER, Ethelbert, Christus und die Caesaren. Hamburg 1952.

STERN, Ephraim (ed.), New Encyclopaedia of Archaeological Excavations in the Holy Land. The Israel Exploration Society. Vol I. New York 1993 (NEAEHL I).

TSAFRIR, Yoram/DI SEGNI, Leah/GREEN, Judith (eds.): Tabula Imperii Romani: Judaea Palaestina. Eretz Israel in the Hellenistic, Roman and Byzantinic Periods. Maps and Gazetteer. Jerusalem 1994.

TZAFERIS, Vassilios, Cults and Deities worshipped at Caesarea Philippi-Banias, in: Priests, Prophets and Scribes. Essays on the Formation and Heritage of Second Temple Judaism in Honour of Joseph Blenkinsopp. Ed.: ULRICH, Eugene/WRIGHT, John W./CARROLL, Robert P./DAVIES, Philip R., JSOTS 149. Sheffield 1992, 190–201.

ID., The "God who is in Dan" and the Cult of Pan in Banias in the Hellenistic and Roman Period. in: EI 23 (1992), 128–135.

ID., Ten Years of Archaeological Research at Baniyas, in: Qadm. 115 (1998), 2–17.

ID./WILSON, John E., Banias, in: BAR 24 (1998), 54–61.85.

Outi Lehtipuu

The Imagery of the Lukan Afterworld in the Light of Some Roman and Greek Parallels

The ideas of reward and retribution in the life hereafter, bliss for the pious and punishments for the wicked, occur frequently in the writings of the New Testament,[1] but there are very few more precise descriptions of the conditions of the afterworld. Most references to life after death are flickering images, such as weeping and gnashing of teeth (e.g. Matt 8:12; 13:42; 24:51; 25:30) or eating in the kingdom of God (Matt 8:11). Both these images occur also in the gospel of Luke, in the Q-saying of 13:28–29: 'There you will weep and gnash your teeth, when you see Abraham and Isaac and Jacob and all the prophets in the kingdom of God and you yourselves thrust out. And men will come from east and west, and from north and south, and sit at table in the kingdom of God.'

This saying is in the core of the Lukan imagery of the afterworld, but there is also a more elaborate picture of the conditions in the hereafter, namely in the story of the rich man and Lazarus (Luke 16:19–31). The rich man is not depicted actually as weeping, but as suffering great pain and begging for mercy, while Lazarus is consoled in Abraham's bosom – an image most probably referring to a heavenly banquet.[2] This short account and its description of the afterworld contain many details that do not occur frequently or at all in the rest of the gospel – or the New Testament. These include immediate reward or retribution after the death of an individual, angels carrying the dead, the fiery torments of the rich man with the burning tongue, the absence of water from the place of punishment and, obviously, fresh water in the place of consolation, the figure of Abraham in the hereafter, the idea of the dead recognizing each other, and a great chasm between them. This scene of the afterlife is so unusual in the New Testament that many commentators have had considerable difficulties trying to interpret it.

The difficulties are usually overcome by remarking that the story is not intended to be 'a guide to the hereafter.'[3] This observation is, of course, absolutely correct. The point of the story is in the reversal of the fates of the rich man and the poor man and in calling the brothers of the rich man to repentance. It is not a revelation of the conditions of the hereafter. The scene of life after death serves as a setting for the actual message. But the fact that the point

---

[1] E.g. Matt 13:40–42; 25:31–46; 2 Cor 5:10; Gal 6:7–10; Rev 20:11–21:4.
[2] D. SMITH, Table Fellowship, 625f.
[3] 'Die Erzählung ist kein Reiseführer für das Jenseits'; E. SCHWEIZER, Evangelium, 173. Similarly, e.g., N. GELDENHUYS, Commentary, 427; M. GILMOUR, Gospel , 290; E.E. ELLIS, Gospel, 201; E. WEHRLI, Luke, 277.

of the story is not in imagining the conditions of the afterworld does not mean that the way Luke depicts them is insignificant. It is a vital part of the message of repentance and thus central to the story. Moreover, there is no hint in the story that Luke intended the description not to be taken literally. Besides, whether it corresponded to Luke's own thinking or not, it became a part of scripture and has had a strong influence on later Christian thinking.[4]

Egyptian Origin?

But where does Luke's vision of the afterlife come from? The classical, almost unanimous answer points to Egypt. As early as in 1918, Hugo GRESSMANN introduced a Demotic folktale that told about the reversal of fate of a rich man and a poor man after death.[5] In addition, GRESSMANN cited seven Rabbinic versions that he considered as deriving from the Egyptian story. GRESSMANN's hypothesis completely dominates the scholarship on this story.[6] It is characteristic that in the *Religionsgeschichtliches Textbuch zum Neuen Testament* by Klaus BERGER and Carsten COLPE, published in 1987, the only parallels given to the story are those first introduced by GRESSMANN.[7]

Nevertheless, recent critics have shown that the Demotic story is not as illuminating a parallel as is usually maintained.[8] It is true that the Demotic folktale and the Lukan story share a common *topos* of the reversal of fates of a rich man and a poor man after death.[9] This *topos*, however, is typical of an-

---

[4] See, e.g., *Apocalypse of Peter* and its description of hell. Different punishments await different kinds of sinners, such as fornicators, murderers, those who have committed abortion, persecutors and betrayers of the righteous, slanderers, those who have trusted in their riches, worshippers of idols, those who have not honored their parents, those who did not retain their virginity until marriage, and slaves who were not obedient to their masters (7–12 in the Ethiopic version). After such a detailed description of hell, the text has much less to say about the bliss of the righteous in heaven. Other early Christian depictions are found in, e.g., Acts of Thomas 6.55–57; Christian Sibyllines 2.252–310; Apocalypse of Paul 31–42.

[5] H. GRESSMANN, Vom reichen Mann und armen Lazarus. Eine literargeschichtliche Studie.

[6] Ronald HOCK gives a list of scholars who accept the Demotic folktale as lying behind the story; R. HOCK, Lazarus, 449, n. 7. Others, some more recent than HOCK's article, can be added. These include, e.g., T.W. MANSON, Sayings, 297; H.J. CADBURY, Proper Name, 401; O. GLOMBITZA, Mann, 166f; G. SCHNEIDER, Evangelium, 340; R. OBERMÜLLER, Miseria, 64; M. GILMOUR, Luke, 289; R. MADDOX, Purpose, 49; J. DRURY, Stories, 150f; J. KREMER, Lukasevangelium, 166; W. WIEFEL, Evangelium, 298; E. REINMUTH, Ps.-Philo, 28; B.B. SCOTT, Hear Then, 145f; N.T. WRIGHT, Jesus, 255.

[7] K. BERGER/C. COLPE, Textbuch, 141ff.

[8] Besides HOCK, these include C.H. CAVE, Lazarus, 323; M.D. GOULDER, Luke, 634ff and R. BAUCKHAM, Rich Man, 227ff (reprinted in R. BAUCKHAM, Fate, 99ff).

[9] The folktale is published in an English translation in, e.g., M. LICHTHEIM, Literature, 138–51.

cient literature and occurs also in other narratives known to us.[10] There is absolutely no reason to maintain that this particular folktale lies behind the story.[11] In addition, the folktale does not clarify the Lukan depiction of the hereafter. The two stories share some common features, such as the honorary position of the poor man and the sufferings of the rich man.[12] But the details of Luke's description, angels carrying the dead, fire and absence of water in the place of torment, the great chasm between the bliss and the torments etc., are absent in the Egyptian folktale.

Greco-Roman Parallels

What other possibilities are there for relevant parallels? Obviously, the Jewish background for the story should not be underestimated. A clear reference to Jewish thinking is the figure of Abraham in the afterworld. I would like to take a look in another direction, however: to the Greco-Roman culture and some of its depictions of life after death. This I do for several reasons.

First of all, the abode of the rich man in the afterworld is called Hades (ᾅδης) which, of course, is a thoroughly Greek word. In the Septuagint, ᾅδης was used to translate Sheol (שְׁאוֹל), the underworld. As the language changed, many features of Greek thought found their way into Jewish thinking. Thus, the Jewish notions of the afterlife were hellenized, and there are numerous examples in Jewish writings how Greek ideas appear in perfect harmony with their Jewish counterparts.[13]

Secondly, Luke clearly intended his two-volume work for readers who were well acquainted with Greco-Roman society. Above all, the book of Acts shares many features in common with Greek historiography.[14] Luke seems to be sensitive to variations of style, a feature common to all ancient Greek literature where different dialects were even artificially preserved in different

---

[10] A good example is the story of *Cataplus* by Lucian of Samosata, introduced in detail by R. HOCK, Lazarus, 457–61. Also the last chapters of *1 Enoch* contain a sharp contrast between the rich and the poor combined with the idea that the earthly life will be compensated in the hereafter. See G. NICKELSBURG, Riches, especially 326–32.

[11] The reversal of status of rich and poor is a prominent feature also elsewhere in Luke's gospel. The fate of the rich man and Lazarus corresponds exactly to the beatitudes and woes in the sixth chapter. The rich man in the story parallels those against whom Jesus declares his woes: he has received his share, he is satiated, he rejoices. In like manner, the poor man in the story is fed in the afterworld (Luke 6:21) and ends up rejoicing. A similar contrast and reversal is depicted in the Magnificat (Luke 1:53). This may well be a sufficient background for the reversal in Luke's story.

[12] In the Demotic tale, the rich man is told to suffer from the bolt of the door that is fixed in his right eye. Other torments are also described. These include endless work and unsatisfied hunger and thirst. Both motives are well known punishments in the afterworld in Greek mythology. See Od 11.582–92; Paus 10.29.1.

[13] See some examples below. For more on Greek influences on Jewish conceptions of the afterlife, see T.F. GLASSON, Influence, esp. 1–38; M. HENGEL, Judaism, 180–210.

[14] For more, see E. PLÜMACHER, Lukas.

genres.[15] Lukan variations range from the Semitic style of the birth narratives (Luke 1–2), imitating the language of the Septuagint, to the high style, e.g., of Paul's speech in the Areopagus in Athens (Acts 17:22–31). Luke is well aware that in this context Paul cannot have referred to Jewish scriptures. Instead, he uses Greek poets as his authorities.[16]

Thirdly, it is oftentimes pointless to make a sharp distinction between 'Jewish' and 'Greek' influences. Luke, his readers, and even Jesus himself lived in a traditional society that prevailed all around the Mediterranean basin (and even further). Many features of this traditional society, including the world view, were broadly held in common.[17]

In what follows, I will examine some well known Greco-Roman depictions of the afterlife. I am not claiming any dependence on the part of Luke on any of these writings.[18] What I am suggesting is that the overall picture of the Lukan afterworld, reflected in the story of the rich man and Lazarus, fits well into the general world view, or mentality, of the ancient Mediterranean world.

The primary text I would like to discuss is the sixth book of Virgil's *Aeneid*. This great Roman epic, written during the last decades BCE, was published posthumously in 18/17 BCE. The sixth book gives an extensive account (6.236–901; a total of 666 verses) of Aeneas' *katabasis* to the netherworld. The reason for Aeneas' journey is to see the spirit of his deceased father Anchises and hear his prophecies of the future. These prophecies are the real culmination of the story: through them Virgil is able to make a strongly patriotic survey of Roman history from the earliest times down to his own day. But the journey through Hades in search of Anchises contains several details of the conditions and geography of the Underworld.

It is well-known that in his account of Hades, Virgil is also strongly dependent on Homer. Virgil's imitation of the great Homeric epics was a well known fact even to his contemporaries. Virgil was both criticized for his dependence on Homer and esteemed as a greater poet than his predecessor.[19] The relation between the *Aeneid* and the *Iliad* and the *Odyssey* has been defined differently at different times. In recent years, scholars have emphasized both Virgil's indebtedness to Homer in his intention to combine both the Greek epics into a single Roman epic and his originality in making considerable in-

---

[15] H.J. CADBURY, Making, 123.
[16] E. HAENCHEN, Apostelgeschichte, 504; E. PLÜMACHER, Lukas, 97f.
[17] R. HOCK, Lazarus, 456.
[18] On the other hand, I am not denying any dependence by Luke, either. It seems highly probable that Luke, an educated man, had known at least Homer and Plato. I am arguing, however, that there is no need to try to prove any literal dependence.
[19] The famous lines by Propertius have accompanied the *Aeneid* from the very beginning: 'cedite Romani scriptores, cedite Grai, nescio quid maius nascitur Iliade.' (In Ezra Pound's translation: 'Make way, ye Roman authors, clear the streets, O ye Greeks, For a much larger Iliad is in the course of construction.') See G.N. KNAUER, Virgil, 871.

novations in the theme.[20] Both these features are clearly visible in the sixth book of the *Aeneid*, which is based on the eleventh song of the *Odyssey*.[21]

The Afterworld in Homer

Odysseus journeys to Hades to learn the secrets of his future from the Theban seer Teiresias. Most of the eleventh book, however, tells about the inhabitants and conditions of Hades itself. Hades is described not as an underworld but as situated along the river Oceanus, at the limits of the world. The abode of the dead is 'shrouded in mist and cloud, and never does the shining sun look down on them with his rays, neither when he climbs up the starry heavens, nor when again he turns earthward from the firmament, but deadly night is outspread over miserable mortals' (Od 11.14–19).[22] Odysseus gets in touch with the dead by animal sacrifices. Thereupon, spirits of the dead appear, 'brides and youths unwed, and old men of many and evil days, and tender maidens with grief yet fresh at heart; and many there were, wounded with bronze-shod spears, men slain in fight with their bloody mail about them' and Odysseus is seized with 'pale fear' (38–41). The dead are flittering shades who cannot be touched (204–208; cf. Il 23.99–101). Fire has consumed their bodies (sinews, flesh and bones) and their spirit has flown to Hades (218–22).

The first spirit with whom Odysseus speaks to is that of his companion Elpenor who is unburied on earth and who begs Odysseus to do him this favor (51–83). After this, Odysseus meets the soul of Teiresias and hears what is to happen to him in the future. Along comes Odysseus' mother, some women who are well known in Greek mythology (225–332), and a group of heroes of the Trojan war (385–566). Odysseus learns that the lowest possible position on earth is preferable to the highest position in the underworld (489–91).[23]

The fate of all the dead is equal, regardless of their earthly life or, e.g., their social status. The dead are not happy but they are not suffering, either. To this equal fate, however, there are three exceptions (576–600).[24] Odysseus sees three mythical figures who suffer from eternal punishments. Tityos lies on the

---

[20] See T. GREENE, Style, 38ff; G.N. KNAUER, Virgil, 874ff.
[21] Even the journey to Hades is motivated in a similar fashion in both epics. In the tenth book of the Odyssey, Circe reveals to Odysseus, who has stayed with her for one year, that he must take the trip to Hades in order to seek the spirit of Teiresias (Od 10.491). In Virgil, the ghost of Anchises appears to Aeneas one year after his death. Also the following events are identical: both heroes pay the homage of burial to their dead comrade (Aen 7.1–20, Od 12.1–15). This means that Virgil has not only imitated Odyssey 11 in his sixth book, but has transformed the frame of the journey into his own account as well. G.N. KNAUER, Virgil, 878.
[22] All translations of Homer are by BUTCHER and LANG in: Odyssey by Homer.
[23] For more details, see R. SCHMIEL, Achilles, 35ff.
[24] These lines are often regarded as a later addition, see H. ATTRIDGE, Apocalypsis, 165. An opposite view is held by C. SOURVINOU-INWOOD, Crime, 51. Be that as it may, the eleventh book was known in its present form quite early, centuries before the Roman era.

ground, covering nine roods, and two vultures gnaw at his liver. Tantalus stands by the water, thirsty, but without being able to drink of it. Whenever he stoops down to drink, the water is swallowed up and vanishes. Similarly, tall trees shed their fruit above him, but whenever he reaches out his hands to clutch them, the wind tosses them away. The third punished figure is Sisyphus, whom Odysseus sees grasping a monstrous stone with both hands and trying to roll it upward toward the top of a hill. But as often as he is about to hurl it over the top, its weight drives him back and he has to start his toil over again.[25] The difference between these mythical figures and the other dead is that Odysseus sees the former from a distance and they do not come to discuss with him, as the other dead do.

In the *Odyssey* all the dead seem to be in Hades. In the *Iliad*, however, Homer describes another place of the dead, Tartarus. This is a prison of the enemies of Zeus, a deep gulf beneath the earth with iron doors and a bronze threshold (Il 8.13–15). A more elaborate picture of Tartarus is depicted by Hesiod (Theog 713–35), whose depiction differs slightly from that of Homer. According to Hesiod, in the beginning of times, when Zeus had conquered his father Chronos in the struggle for supremacy over the world, the Titans, who opposed Zeus, were locked up in Tartarus, in the lowest regions of the earth. It is a dark place, surrounded by a bronze wall and encircled by a threefold darkness, where sun never shines. According to Hesiod, Tartarus is situated beside (πρόσθεν) the abode of the ordinary dead, Hades, as far beneath the earth as the sky is above it. In Homer's description, however, Tartarus is beneath (ἐνερθ'[ε]) Hades, as far beneath as heaven is above the earth (!). Despite these geographical differences, it is clear that according to the archaic Greek notion, there was one abode for the ordinary dead, Hades, and a separate prison with terrible punishments for mythical figures and demigods, Tartarus.[26]

The Virgilian Netherworld

Turning back to the *Aeneid*, we can see plenty of similarities between its description of the afterworld and that in the *Odyssey*. Before entering the netherworld, Aeneas makes an offering of animals. Along his journey, he first encounters a throng of dead people, 'matrons and men ... and great-heart heroes, finished with earthly life, boys and unmarried maidens, young men laid on the

---

[25] For details, see C. SOURVINOU-INWOOD, Crime.
[26] A. BERNSTEIN, Formation, 32ff, tries to harmonize the different views. According to him, the mythical figures of *Odyssey* 11 are actually in Tartarus, which Odysseus can see from Hades – even though the name of Tartarus is not mentioned in the context. This kind of harmonization is, however, not necessary. The Homeric epics consist of material from various ages, which makes it natural to assume that they express different, even contradictory conceptions.

pyre before their parents' eyes.'[27] Aeneas is trembling by terror (6.273–312; cf. Od 11.38–41).

The first spirit he talks to is his helmsman Palinurus whose death is described at the end of book five: he had been overcome by sleep, fallen overboard and drowned, and now he begs Aeneas to bury him (337–83; cf. Od 11.51–83). Next Aeneas sees souls of women, unhappy in love, well known from Greek mythology (440–76; cf. Od 11.225–332). Among them is the soul of the Phoenician queen Dido, who committed suicide after Aeneas deserted her. Aeneas desires to talk with her but she does not utter a word as she turns herself away, full of wrath.[28] Still further on, Aeneas meets the souls of Trojan warriors and other heroes (477–534; cf. Od 11.385–566).

From there Aeneas sees a broad citadel 'girdled too by swift-running stream, a flaming torrent'. This is Tartarus, the prison of the sinners where Furies punish them (548–627). The sinners include Titans and other giants, as well as other legendary criminals, such as Tityos (cf. Od 11.576–81). Other punishments include those suffered by Tantalus and Sisyphus (cf. Od 11.582–600), even that their names are not mentioned. Tartarus, however, contains not only legendary figures, but all 'those who in life hated their own brothers, or struck their parents; those who entangled their dependants in fraudulent dealing; and those who sat tight on the wealth they had won, setting none aside for their own kin – most numerous of all are these; then such as were killed for adultery, took part in military treason, men who were bold to break faith with their masters: – all such await punishment' (608–14).[29]

Finally, Aeneas finds his father, and it is his speech that forms the climax of the sixth book, if not the whole epic (679–892). The encounter of father and son resembles Odysseus' meeting with his mother (cf. Od 11.152–224). Just as Odysseus tries three times in vain to embrace the soul of his dead mother, Aeneas also strives three times to throw his arms around his father, whose soul flees from his hands like 'a wisp of wind or the wings of a fleeting dream' (700–2).

---

[27] '*Matres atque viri, defunctaque corpora vita magnanimum heroum, pueri innuptaeque puellae impositique rogis iuvenes ante ora parentum.*' All translations of Virgil are by C.D. LEWIS.

[28] In his portrait of Dido, Virgil has made use of Homer's depiction of Aias (Od 11.541–66), who likewise does not want to speak with Odysseus as he still is filled with anger towards him in consequence of things that happened between the two on earth.

[29] '*hic quibus invisi fratres, dum vita manebat, pulsatusve parens, et fraus innexa clienti, aut qui divitiis soli incubuere repertis nec partem posuere suis (quae maxima turba est), quique ob adulterium caesi, quique arma secuti impia nec veriti dominorum fallere dextras, inclusi poenam exspectant.*' For more on Virgil's Tartarus, see J.W. ZARKER, Aeneas, 220ff.

From Neutrality to Rewards and Punishments

Despite all these similarities, there are remarkable differences between Virgil's and Homer's accounts. First of all, Virgil has transformed the journey to the underworld from Odysseus' first-person narrative into a book of action narrated in the third person. Moreover, the Virgilian abode of the dead is situated literally in the netherworld. The entrance is situated in Cumae, in a deep cave by the Lake Avernus.[30] In order to get there, Aeneas needs to have a golden bough as a gift to the Queen of the Underworld.[31] Unlike Odysseus, Aeneas has a guide with him all along, the Sibyl of Apollo.

The biggest differences, however, are related to the actual conditions of the afterworld. Firstly, Virgil has a much more developed and systematic picture of how the geography of the netherworld is arranged. The underworld is approached through an entrance court, at the side of which there is a threshold with doors that admit to the interior. There flow several rivers with familiar names from mythology, such as Acheron, Cocytos, Styx, and Phlegethon, but the arrangement of these is more or less confused – perhaps due to the fact that the poet never got the chance to revise his work.[32] A grim warden, the ferryman Charon, guards the river Acheron, across which all the dead must be carried. But Charon allows in his boat only those who have been buried. Those who have not must roam about the river shores for a hundred years.

On the other bank, at the portal of Hades, are placed all those who have suffered an untimely death: first infants, next those who have been condemned to die on a false charge, and in the region beyond are those who have committed suicide. All these souls remain there until they have fulfilled what would have been their normal lifetime, after which their judge, Minos, admits them into the inner parts of Hades.[33] Further away dwell those who have been re-

---

[30] The name 'Avernus' is also used as a synonym for the place of the dead. The meaning of the name is derived from the Greek word ἄορνος (without birds), as Avernus is described as a dark lake, above which 'no winged creatures could ever wing their way' [*quam super haud ullae poterant impune volantes tendere iter pinnis*]. This etymology, however, is usually considered as an interpolation.

[31] When Aeneas tells the Sibyl his wish to visit the underworld, the prophetess warns him that it is easy to descend there but hard to ascend from there. (The famous words: '*hoc opus, hic labor est*' refer to this difficulty.) However, in the narrative it is much harder for Aeneas to get to the abode of the dead, for the boatman Charon at first refuses to take him over. Coming back, on the other hand, seems fairly easy as Anchises just dismisses Aeneas and the Sibyl by an ivory gate for false dreams.

[32] Virgil died before the completion of the *Aeneid*. When realizing that his end was near, he gave instructions that his work should be destroyed. This instruction, however, was disregarded. Another explanation for the confusion between different names of rivers could be metric. The names might be used synonymously and each variant chosen for metric reasons.

[33] In Greek mythology, e.g. in Homer, Minos is usually described as the judge of all the dead, not just one group of the dead as in Virgil's account. According to the Aeneid, Rhadamanthys is the one who judges in Tartarus. In Plato's writings, both of these are named, along with a third judge, Aeacus; Gorg 524a.

nowned in war. Still further on, the road parts in two: the right path leads to Elysium, the land of joy, where the pious souls are, the left one to Tartarus.

Here is the second big difference between Virgil's and Homer's accounts. Homer's netherworld is neutral, Virgil's is moral.[34] The dead are rewarded or punished according to their deeds on earth. Those who have met an untimely death stay on a neutral ground, but others are either blessed or tortured in Tartarus, which is no longer reserved only for mythical figures. Elysium is described as 'the Happy Place, the green and genial glades where the fortunate live.' Elysium, or Greek Elysion ('Ελύσιον) is a place known also in the Homeric epic. In Homer, however, it is not a place for the dead but a region on the western edge of the earth where some few favorites of the gods are carried to continue their life ever after, without facing death (Od 4.561–69). Hesiod shares a similar view of Elysion, which he calls the Island of the Blessed. According to him, it is reserved for the heroes of the past (Op 167–73). In the *Aeneid*, however, all pious souls are taken to Elysium.[35] They spend their time there wrestling, dancing, chanting, and feasting while Orpheus plays his lyre. Only a few souls, however, as a reward for their virtues, are allowed to stay in the happy fields until the wheel of time is complete. After this period, these chosen few become the pure flame of air which they were before they entered into the wheel of birth. As for the vast majority of the souls, they spend a thousand years in the underworld, then drink from the river Lethe, the river of Oblivion, and undergo a rebirth on earth.

In other words, in Virgil's account all the dead face either punishment in Tartarus or reward in Elysium. Both these places derive from Greek mythology, but in Homer, they were reserved not for ordinary mortals, but for heroes, titans and demigods. Virgil's netherworld can thus be described as more 'democratic' than Homer's.

Other Greek Accounts

The description of the netherworld in Virgil is so much more developed that it is obvious that he is drawing from other sources besides Homer. These other sources are commonly labeled as Orphic and Pythagorean. Unfortunately, our knowledge of these religious movements is scant.[36] Some light on Orphic ideas of life after death is shed by the so-called golden plates found in southern Italy and dated to approximately 400 BCE. These Petelia tablets describe the soul's journey in Hades in the following manner:

> You will find in the realms of Hades on the left hand a spring. And by it a white cypress standing. Do not go near this spring. But you will find another, running with cool water from the lake of Memory. There are guardians before it. You must say: 'I am a child of earth and the starry heaven; I come from a heavenly race. You

---

[34] A. BERNSTEIN, Formation, 72f.
[35] See F. SULLIVAN, Virgil, 17ff.
[36] For details see, e.g. W. BURKERT, Greek Religion, 296ff.

yourselves know this. I am perishing with thirst; but give me quickly the cool water which runs from the lake of Memory.' And they will give you to drink of the divine spring.[37]

Orphic ideas occur also, e.g., in the descriptions of the afterworld in Plato's dialogues. In several of his writings, Plato depicts what happens to the souls after death (Gorg 523a–527e; Phaed 112a–114c; Phaedr 248e–249b; Resp 614b–621d), but the depictions are somewhat varied. Different, contradictory details seem to show that Plato himself did not take them literally. Plato's motive to describe the hereafter was not so much to satisfy human curiosity as to justify the philosophical way of life and the immortality of the soul.[38]

The common features of Plato's accounts resemble Virgil's description. Everybody will answer for his or her own deeds done on earth. The virtuous will be rewarded, the wicked punished. In the *Gorgias* (523a–b), for instance, the road running from the world to the hereafter meets with two other roads: the one leading to the Isle of the Blessed, the other to Tartarus. Virtuous souls are sent to the former, to be forever happy, the wicked to the latter to be punished. When their earthly life is thus atoned, their souls will be reincarnated. The only exceptions are those who have done extreme injustice, and as a result, have become incurable.[39] They will be locked up in the torments of Tartarus forever, as warning examples to others (Gorg 525b–526b; Phaed 113d–114c; Resp 615e–616b). In *Phaedo* (114b–c), Plato distinguishes yet another group, namely those who have spent their life in an especially virtuous way. They will ascend to earth, and some of them, namely those who have purified themselves through philosophy, will ascend even higher. A rather similar view is shared also by Plutarch (De gen 21–22, De sera 22–33), a rough contemporary to Luke.

As noted above, many of these features of the Greek concepts of the hereafter found their way into Jewish thinking. For instance, in the books of Enoch an Old Testament hero makes a journey to the realm of the dead similar to that made by Odysseus. In the First book of Enoch (17–19), rivers of fire are depicted as part of the place of punishment, resembling the Pyriphlegethon (cf. Phaed 113a–114a).[40] The name Tartarus became a common equivalent of Hell (4 Ezra 4–5; Ps-Phoc 60.3; T. Sol 6.3; SibOr 1.10,101; 2.303), and so on.

***

I have wandered far from Luke and the story of the rich man and Lazarus. I hope that this odyssey of mine has shown that the mentality of the Lukan description of the hereafter is not far from its Greco-Roman counterparts. The idea of fiery punishments on the one hand, and that of happiness by refreshing

---

[37] T.F. GLASSON, Greek Influence, 34f; W. BURKERT, Greek Religion, 293ff.
[38] Thus W. BURKERT, Greek Religion, 325; R.E. ALLEN, Comment, 229f.
[39] Such as Tityos, Tantalos and Sisyphos.
[40] In later writings, other rivers of the Greek Hades are also named. To give just one example, according to The Life of Adam and Eve, angels carry the dead Adam to the Lake of Acheron and wash him there (Vita 37.3). Cf. SibOr 2.337–8; 5.485.

waters on the other, is well rooted in Greco-Roman and other ancient thinking. As the Lukan story is much shorter than the other depictions under discussion, it is clear that it lacks their detailed descriptions. In addition, it goes without saying that some Greek beliefs, such as the rebirth of the souls, are absent in mainstream Christian (and Jewish) accounts.

Besides fire and water, also many other details of the Lukan story have their counterparts in the Greco-Roman accounts. For example, Luke mentions angels who carry the dead Lazarus. In Greek stories, Hermes is often depicted as an escort to Hades.[41] Hermes' role as ψυχοπόμπος has probably had an influence on Jewish belief of angel(s) escorting the dead souls, a feature that occurs in many intertestamental writings. Also the word χάσμα appears in several Greek accounts of the hereafter, albeit with slightly different meanings.[42]

The Appearance of the Dead

There is yet another detail in the Lukan description with counterparts in the Greco-Roman accounts, namely the presumed corporeality of the rich man and Lazarus in the hereafter. The rich man obviously has eyes (Luke 16:23) and a tongue (v. 24), and Lazarus likewise a finger (or at least the tip of a finger!). In all ancient – as well as modern – accounts that I know of, the souls of the dead are depicted in bodily terms. Even though Plato, for example, emphasizes that it is only souls who are judged, the souls bear marks of their earthly bodies (Gorg 524c–525a). This notion also occurs clearly in Homer. Despite the fact that the bodies of the dead are consumed by fire on a burial pyre and that the souls are explicitly depicted as shades who cannot be touched, the souls can drink blood. Likewise, the punishments of the legendary figures are real: even as a shade, Tityos has a liver and Tantalos suffers from real thirst and hunger.

The same can be seen in the *Aeneid*, where the real people are sharply distinguished from the shade people, the dead.[43] Somehow Aeneas is capable of recognizing who is who in the abode of the dead – just as the rich man immediately realizes who is the one in Abraham's bosom. It is necessary to be able to recognize one another in the hereafter – and this is the very reason why bodily terms are used to depict souls. The dead must resemble their earthly appearance also in the hereafter. (Even though Lazarus probably did not have any sores left!)

---

[41] The most ancient occurrence of this is probably the last song of the Odyssey (Od 24.1–10), even if it is usually considered as a later addition. Other early examples include an Orphic theogony (as reconstructed by M.L. WEST, Orphic Poems, 75) and some versions of Sisyphos' escape from Hades; see C. SOURVINOU-INWOOD, Crime, 47f.

[42] These include a variety of different writers, e.g., Hesiod (Theog 740), Plato (Resp 614c–d), Parmenides (1.18), Euripides (Phoen 1604ff), Plutarch (De sera 27–8) and Lucian (Philops 25).

[43] The weight of Aeneas and the Sibyl almost sink Charon's boat that is intended to carry a much lighter load (6.413); see N. REED, Gates, 311ff.

The notion of the 'corporeality' of the dead souls was widespread in popular belief. Even without a body the dead were able to eat and drink and communicate with the living. This becomes evident from a quotation from Cicero:

> 'Though they knew that the bodies of the dead were consumed with fire, yet they imagined that events took place in the lower world which cannot take place and are not intelligible without bodies; the reason was that they were unable to grasp the conception of souls living an independent life and tried to find for them some sort of appearance and shape.'[44]

All in all, the conditions in the hereafter seem to be imagined in a quite similar way among all who believed in life after death in the ancient Mediterranean world. This is supported also by archeological findings of coins in sculls in some Jewish graves, the coins being considered as payment for Charon's ferry service across the river in Hades.[45] The Lukan description does not differ fundamentally from its Greek and Roman counterparts.

On the other hand, the pagan hero Aeneas was soon interpreted as a forerunner of Christianity. His chief virtue, that of *pietas*, was easily assimilated into the Christian ideas of righteousness and charity.[46] In the light of this, it is small wonder that in his *Divina Commedia* Dante has Virgil as his guide in the hereafter.[47] Who could be a better guide? But Dante was also sensitive to the fact that Virgil lived in a pre-Christian era. That is why the poet can only serve as a guide in Hell, as not even the most virtuous pagans were allowed elsewhere.[48]

---

[44] '*Ut, corpora cremata cum scirent, tamen ea fieri apud inferos fingerent, quae sine corporibus nec fieri possunt nec intelligi; animos enim per se ipsos viventes non poterant mente complecti, formam aliquam figuramque quaerebant*' (Tusc 1.16). Translation by J.E. KING in: Tusculan Disputations.

[45] See R. HACHLILI/A. KILLEBREW, Customs, 118.128, on the excavations performed at the Jericho necropolis. Cf. the findings near Jerusalem in E. PUECH, Tombeau, 42.46f.

[46] See R.D. WILLIAMS, Intention, 25ff; V. PÖSCHL, Aeneas, 24.

[47] For more on Virgil and Dante, see, e.g. P. ARMOUR, Dante's Virgil.

[48] In Dante's work, Elysium is the first circle of Hell where the souls of those virtuous pagans reside, including Virgil himself, who did not know Christ; P. ARMOUR, Dante's Virgil, 71.

Bibliography

ALLEN, Reginal E., Comment on Gorgias, in: Plato, Euthyphro, Apology, Crito, Meno, Gorgias, Menexenus. Transl. with Comment by Reginal E. ALLEN, New Haven – London 1986.
ARMOUR, Peter, Dante's Virgil, in: Virgil in a Cultural Tradition. Essays to Celebrate the Bimillenium. Ed. by Richard A. CARDWELL/Janet HAMILTON, University of Nottingham Monographs in the Humanities 4, Nottingham 1986, 65–76.
ATTRIDGE, Harold W., Greek and Latin Apocalypsis, in: Semeia 14 (1979), 159–86.
BAUCKHAM, Richard, The Rich Man and Lazarus. The Story and the Parallels, in: NTS 37 (1991), 225–46.
ID., The Fate of the Dead. Studies on the Jewish and Christian Apocalypses, NT.S 93, Leiden et al. 1998.
BERGER, Klaus/COLPE, Carsten, Religionsgeschichtiches Textbuch zum Neuen Testament, Texte zum Neuen Testament. Das Neue Testament Deutsch Textreihe 1. Göttingen 1987.
BERNSTEIN, Alan E., The Formation of Hell. Death and Retribution in the Ancient and Early Christian Worlds, Ithaca 1993.
BURKERT, Walter, Greek Religion. Archaic and Classic. Transl. by J. Raffan. Oxford 1985.
CADBURY, Henry J., The Making of Luke-Acts, Peabody 1999 (First Edition 1927).
ID., A Proper Name for Dives, in: JBL 81 (1962), 399–402 .
CAVE, C.H., Lazarus and the Lukan Deuteronomy, in: NTS 15 (1968), 319–25.
CICERO, Tusculan Disputations, Loeb Classical Library, Cambridge, MA 1960.
DRURY, John. The Parables in the Gospels. History and Allegory, Cambridge 1985.
ELLIS, Edward Earle, The Gospel of Luke, NCeB, London ³1977.
GELDENHUYS, Norval, Commentary on the Gospel of Luke, NIC, Grand Rapids ⁶1966.
GILMOUR, S. MacLean, The Gospel According to Luke, IntB 8, Nashville ²⁴1982.
GLASSON, T. Francis, Greek Influence in Jewish Eschatology With Special Reference to the Apocalypses and Pseudepigraphs, London 1961.
GLOMBITZA, Otto, Der reiche Mann und der arme Lazarus Luk 16,19–31. Zur Frage nach der Botschaft des Textes, in: NT 12 (1970), 166–80.
GOULDER, Michael D., Luke. A New Paradigm, JSNTS 20, Sheffield 1989.
GREENE, Thomas, Virgil's Style, in: Virgil's Aeneid. Modern Critical Interpretations. Ed. by Harold BLOOM, New York 1987, 31–55.
GRESSMANN, Hugo, Vom reichen Mann und armen Lazarus. Eine literargeschichtliche Studie, Abhandlungen der königlich preussischen Akademie der Wissenschaften. Philosophisch-historische Klasse, 1918 no. 7. Berlin 1918.
HACHLILI, Rachel/KILLEBREW, Anne, Jewish Funerary Customs during the Second Temple Period, in the Light of the Excavations at the Jericho Necropolis, in: PEQ 115 (1983), 109–39.
HAENCHEN, Ernst, Die Apostelgeschichte. KEK 3, Göttingen ⁷⁽¹⁶⁾1977.
HENGEL, Martin, Judaism and Hellenism. Studies in their Encounter in Palestine during the Early Hellenistic Period. 2vols, Transl. by J. BOWDEN, Philadelphia 1974.
HOCK, Ronald F., Lazarus and Micyllus. Greco-Roman Backgrounds to Luke 16:19–31, in: JBL 106 (1987), 447–63.
KNAUER, Georg N., Virgil and Homer, in: ANRW II.31.2 (1981), 870–918.
KREMER, Jacob, Lukasevangelium, NEB.NT 3, Würzburg 1988.

LEWIS, C. Day, The Eclogues, Georgics and Aeneid of Virgil, London 1966.
LICHTHEIM, Miriam, Ancient Egyptian Literature. A Book of Readings. 3: The Late Period, Berkeley 1980.
MADDOX, Robert, The Purpose of Luke-Acts, FRLANT 126. Göttingen 1982.
MANSON, Thomas W. The Sayings of Jesus As Recorded in the Gospels According to St. Matthew and St. Luke Arranged with Introduction and Commentary, London ^{5}1957.
NICKELSBURG, George W.E., Riches, the Rich and God's Judgement in 1 Enoch 92–105 and the Gospel According to Luke, in: NTS 25 (1979), 324–44.
OBERMÜLLER, Rodolfo, La miseria de un rico: Un juicio neotestamentario – Lucas 16,19–31, in: Les pobres. Encuentro y compromiso. (Ed.) J. Severino CROATTO/Hans-Hartmut SCHROEDER et al., Buenos Aires 1978, 45–66.
THE ODYSSEY. The Odyssey by Homer. With Introduction by John A. SCOTT. New York 1941 (first edition 1930).
PLÜMACHER, Eckhard, Lukas als hellenistischer Schriftsteller. Studien zur Apostelgeschichte, StUNT 9. Göttingen 1972.
PÖSCHL, Victor, Aeneas, in: Virgil's Aeneid. Modern Critical Interpretations. Ed. by Harold BLOOM; New York 1987, 9–30.
PUECH, Emile, A-t-on redécouvert le tombeau du grand-prêtre Caïphe?, in: Le monde de la Bible 80 (1993), 42–47.
REED, Nicholas, The Gates of Sleep in *Aeneid* 6, in: CQ 23 (1973), 311–15.
REINMUTH, Eckart, Ps.-Philo, *Liber Antiquitatum Biblicarum* 33,1–5 und die Auslegung der Parabel Lk 16:19–31, in: NT 31 (1989), 16–38.
SCHMIEL, Robert, Achilles in Hades, in: CP 82 (1987), 35–37.
SCHNEIDER, Gerhard, Das Evangelium nach Lukas, ÖTK 3/2, Gütersloh 1977.
SCHWEIZER, Eduard, Das Evangelium nach Lukas, NTD 3, Göttingen ^{18}1982.
SCOTT, Bernard Brandon, Hear Then the Parable. A Commentary on the Stories of Jesus, Minneapolis 1989.
SMITH, Dennis E., Table Fellowship as a Literary Motif in the Gospel of Luke, in: JBL 106 (1987), 613–38.
SULLIVAN, Francis A., Virgil and the Latin Epitaphs, in: CJ 51 (1955/56), 17–20.
SOURVINOU-INWOOD, Christiane, Crime and Punishment. Tityos, Tantalos, and Sisyphos in Odyssey 11, in: BICS 33 (1986), 37–58.
WEHRLI, Eugene S., Luke 16,19–31, in: Interp 31 (1977), 276–80.
WEST, Martin Litchfield, The Orphic Poems, Oxford 1983.
WIEFEL, Wolfgang, Das Evangelium nach Lukas, ThHK 3, Berlin 1988.
WILLIAMS, R.D., The Poetic Intention of Virgil's *Aeneid*, in: Virgil and his Influence. Bimillenial Studies. Ed. by Charles MARTINDALE, Bristol 1984, 25–35.
WRIGHT, Nicholas Thomas, Jesus and the Victory of God. Christian Origins and the Question of God 2, Minneapolis 1996.
ZARKER, John W., Aeneas and Theseus in Aeneid 6, in: CJ 62 (1966/67), 220–26.

Michael Labahn

‚Heiland der Welt'*
Der gesandte Gottessohn und der römische Kaiser – ein Thema johanneischer Christologie?

0. Einleitung

Wie andere Sprachformen bedient sich religiöse Sprache in ihrer Mitwelt bereits vorhandener Ausdrucksweisen und Bilder auch dann, wenn sie gewandelte oder andere bzw. neuartige religiöse Erfahrungen explizieren will. Leser und Leserinnen eines Textes partizipieren wie sein Autor an den kulturellen – religiösen wie politischen – Konventionen und Voraussetzungen ihrer Zeit.[1] Der Rückgriff auf gemeinsame Konvention ist notwendig, um einen gelungenen Sprechakt zu ermöglichen.[2] Dies gilt wie für das gesamte neutestamentliche Schrifttum[3] auch für das vierte Evangelium, das in eigenständiger Weise den präexistenten und Fleisch gewordenen Logos als den universellen Heilsbringer vorstellt, durch den Gott allein der Welt sein Leben vermittelt (vgl. z.B. Joh 5,26; 6,32ff.57[4]).

Texte wie das vierte Evangelium sind daher vor dem Hintergrund ihres zeitgenössischen *Repertoires* zu lesen.[5] Allerdings kommen der *implied author* und sein *real reader* nicht immer mit ihren Vorstellungen und Bildern zur

---

* Eine erste Version dieses Beitrages wurde vor dem 16th *International Meeting* der *Society of Biblical Literature* in Krakau 1998 und eine gekürzte Fassung vor der *Arbeitsgemeinschaft neutestamentlicher Assistenten und Assistentinnen an evangelisch-theologischen Fakultäten* in München 2001 vorgetragen.
[1] Der *kulturelle Code* (BARTHES spricht etwas eng von „Wissen und Weisheit") gehört zum „Gewebe der Stimmen", die einen Text wie „eine Art Netz" durchziehen: R. BARTHES, S/Z, 24.25. Zum kulturellen Code vgl. z.B. auch M. TITZMANN, Textanalyse, 263–330 (Abschn. 3.2; zu den Präsuppositionen bzw. der Enzyklopädie des Textes s.a. den folgenden Absatz), der die Bedeutung des kulturellen Wissens für die Textinterpretation reflektiert und eingrenzt.
[2] D. ZELLER, Königsideologie, 543, plädiert beim religionsgeschichtlichen Vergleich für die „Konzentration auf die Situation des Verfassers, der sich verständlich machen möchte".
[3] So rechnet A.Y. COLLINS, Worship, 242, mit *bewußten* Aufnahmen nicht-jüdischer religiöser Traditionen schon in der Frühphase der nachösterlichen Jesusbewegung.
[4] In einem späteren Zusatz, der aber in der johanneischen Christologie fundiert ist; zum literarkritischen Problem vgl. M. LABAHN, Offenbarung, 68–78; zur Interpretation s.a. J. FREY, Eschatologie II, 141f.
[5] Vgl. zur Repertoire-Theorie U. ECO, Lector, *passim*, bes. 15ff. 94ff, und die Aufnahme dieser Konzeption durch S. ALKIER, Wunder, 72–74.

Deckung.⁶ Unterschieden werden kann daher zwischen *faktisch* relevanten und *potentiell* relevanten Voraussetzungen, also solchen, die „für die Interpretation nicht zwingend notwendig sind".⁷ Es ist weiter zu prüfen, wo der kulturelle *Code* des *implied author* mit dem seiner Leser und Leserinnen zur Deckung kommt oder wo wir mit einem kulturellen Überschuß bei der Leserschaft gegenüber dem kulturellen *Code* des Textes zu rechnen haben, der neue Sinnpotentiale entwickelt.

Im zeitgenössischen kulturellen Kontext lässt sich der römische Kaiser als Wohltäter, Wundertäter, Lebensbringer und Friedensstifter verehren. Der römische Herrscherkult⁸ verwendet damit Titel, Sprache, Motive und Bilder, die auch für die johanneische Christologie charakteristisch sind. Implizieren die sprachlichen Beobachtungen einen Konflikt zwischen johanneischem Kreis und dem Herrscherkult? Sehr pointiert sucht Richard J. CASSIDY in „John's Gospel in New Perspective" das gesamte Johannesevangelium im Gegenüber zum römischen Staat zu verstehen, wie er im repressiven Vorgehen eines Plinius gegen die Christen auftritt.⁹ Dieser These möchte ich im folgenden nachgehen und zwar anhand einer Textauswahl, die m.E. signifikante Ergebnisse verspricht, die für das gesamte Johannesevangelium Gültigkeit beanspruchen: dem Titel ‚Heiland der Welt' (Joh 4,42), dem Bekenntnis ‚mein Herr und mein Gott' (20,28) sowie dem Portrait Jesu in den johanneischen Wundergeschichten. Die Fragestellung lautet: *Lässt die Darstellung des johanneischen Jesus erkennen, dass sich der Verfasser des vierten Evangeliums mit Ansprüchen des römischen Staates, repräsentiert durch die Kaiserpropaganda und die Kaiserverehrung, polemisch auseinandersetzt?*

1. Joh 4,42: Jesus, der *Heiland der Welt*

In der Ringkomposition Joh 2,1–4,54 führt der Verfasser Jesus von Kana in Galiläa über Jerusalem zurück nach Kana, um auf dem Weg eine Begegnung zwischen Jesus und einem um Hilfe für seinen in Todesgefahr befindlichen Sohn bittenden *Königlichen* herbeizuführen (4,46ff).¹⁰ Diese Komposition zeichnet sich dadurch aus, dass der sich im folgenden steigernde Konflikt zwischen Jesus und seinen jüdischen Opponenten fast völlig fehlt; demgegenüber finden sich, wie Francis J. Moloney in verschiedenen Beiträgen herausge-

---

⁶ Vgl. D. ZELLER, Königsideologie, 546, in Aufnahme von K. BERGER, Exegese, 198, im Blick auf die Rezeption neutestamentlicher Texte; s.a. S. ALKIER, Wunder, 73.

⁷ Vgl. D. ZELLER, Königsideologie, 543, in Aufnahme von M. TITZMANN, Analyse, 274–297.

⁸ Vgl. jetzt die Darstellung von M. CLAUSS, Kaiser, *passim*. Clauss vertritt gegen starke Tendenzen in der Forschung (vgl. z.B. P. HERZ, Kaiser, 137–139) die These, dass sich der römische Kaiser bereits zu Lebzeiten als Gott verehren lies und zwar nicht allein im Osten, sondern auch im Westen des römischen Reiches; vgl. DERS., *Deus praesens, passim*. – Zur Literatur zum Kaiserkult vgl. HERZ, Bibliographie, *passim*.

⁹ Vgl. R.J. CASSIDY, Gospel, ix.

¹⁰ Vgl. M. LABAHN, Tradition, 192–195.

stellt hat, Beispiele exemplarischen Glaubens.[11] Nach der Feststellung des Jüngerglaubens (2,11) und dem verdeckt sympathisierenden Nikodemus (3,1ff)[12] missioniert Jesus in Samarien;[13] die Samaritaner akklamieren Jesus aufgrund seiner Lehre als *Heiland der Welt*.[14] Findet Jesus bei den Samaritanern Glauben und vermittelt er in diesem Sinne Leben, so illustriert die Samaritanerepisode, wie der Strom des Lebenswassers (4,10.13f) die Grenzen jüdischer (aber auch samaritanischer; vgl. 4,21.23) Gottesverehrung überströmt. Das samaritanische Schlussbekenntnis weitet den Blick noch stärker: Selbstoffenbarung und Predigt zeichnen Jesus als den aus, der für die ganze Welt und ihr Leben grundlegende Bedeutung hat. Mit der Überschreitung religiöser Grenzen ist die kosmologische Bedeutung des Offenbarers, die bereits in 3,16f (s.a. 1,12.29) deutlich expliziert wird, erzählerisch eingeholt. Die Begegnung mit dem *Königlichen* (4,46–54) realisiert narrativ die kosmologische Weite des Sotertitels, indem sich ein heidnischer Beamter mit seinem Haus zu Jesus bekennt.[15] Damit möchte ich den Titel *Heiland der Welt* nicht allein als Schlusspunkt von Joh 4,4ff lesen, sondern im Gesamtzusammenhang von 2,1–4,54.[16]

Das einfache σωτήρ ist als Epitheton einer Gottheit in der griechisch-römischen Umwelt des vierten Evangeliums zahlreich belegt (z.b. für Zeus, Athena, Apollon, Asklepios, die Dioskuren, Poseidon, Isis und Sarapis).[17] Sodann ist der Titel aber auch auf heroisierte Menschen (vor allem Herakles[18]), bedeutende Einzelpersönlichkeiten[19] und schließlich auch in der griechischen Herrscherverehrung bis hin zum römischen Kaiserkult verwendet. Er ist nicht auf göttliche Wesen eingeschränkt und orientiert sich, wie auch als Götterbeiname, nicht primär an religiösen Gehalten, sondern hat auch das materielle Wohlergehen einzelner oder von Gemeinschaften im Blick (z.B. Kriegsgefah-

---

[11] F.J. MOLONEY, Cana, *passim*; DERS., Mary, 422f; DERS., Belief, 198 (u.ö.); DERS., Gospel of John, 65.
[12] Zur mehrschichtigen Darstellung des Nikodemus vgl. P. DSCHULNIGG, Jesus, 106–121.
[13] Zu Joh 4,1–42 vgl. zuletzt J. ZANGENBERG, Christentum, 87–196. Das antike Quellenmaterial zu den Samaritanern bietet DERS., ΣΑΜΑΡΕΙΑ, *passim*.
[14] Joh 4,41f: ἐπίστευσαν διὰ τὸν λόγον αὐτοῦ, οὐκέτι διὰ τὴν σὴν λαλιὰν πιστεύομεν, αὐτοὶ γὰρ ἀκηκόαμεν· οὗτός ἐστιν ἀληθῶς ὁ σωτὴρ τοῦ κόσμου.
[15] Obwohl umstritten, nehme ich aufgrund des johanneischen Erzählgefälles an, dass der *Basilikos* ein Heide und kein Jude ist; vgl. M. LABAHN, Jesus, 176f.
[16] Anders z.B. R.J. CASSIDY, Gospel, 34f; C.R. KOESTER, Savior, *passim*.
[17] Belege in Auswahl: Xen An 1,8,16; Pind Olymp 5,17; Ael Arist Or 43,1.30 (Zeus); Diog L 5,16 (Zeus und Athena); Syll³ 408,6f (Zeus und Apollon); Ael Arist Or 47,66 u.ö. (Asklepios); Luc Alex 4; Paus 2,1,9 (Dioskuren); Hom Hymn 22,5 (Poseidon); Artemid 2,39 (Sarapis, Isis Anubis und Harpokrates); Ael Arist Or 45,20.25 (Sarapis). S.a. P. WENDLAND, Σωτήρ, 336f; W. FOERSTER, Art. σωτήρ, 1006.
[18] Vgl. z.B. Dio Chrys Or 1,84: „Und deswegen ... ist er der Retter der Welt und der Menschheit (τῆς γῆς καὶ τῶν ἀνθρώπων σωτῆρα), nicht weil er sie vor den wilden Tieren schützte ..., sondern weil er die rohen und schlechten Menschen bestrafte und die Macht überheblicher Tyrannen brach und vernichtete" (Übers.: W. ELLIGER, Reden, 20).
[19] Z.B. Philipp (Demost Or 18,43), bei den Diadochen: vgl. Ptolemaios IV (Paus 1,8,5; Diod S 20,100,3) oder Mithridates (Diod S 37,26,1).

ren, politische Rechte, Hungersnot, Krankheit).[20] Die politische Verwendung des σωτήρ-Titels ist also eine verbreitete Vorstellung,[21] die den Zusammenhang von Herrscherkult und σωτήρ-Titel zum gemeinsamen *kulturellen Code* des Johannesevangeliums und seiner Leserschaft rechnen läßt. Daneben wird in unterschiedlichen Texten das politisch förderliche Wirken des Herrschers für die *Oikumene* ausgesagt.

Antike philosophische Schulen orientierten sich als Kosmopoliten auf den *Kosmos* hin; dass dies nicht allein für die Stoa,[22] sondern auch für die Schule der Kyniker gelten kann, hat John L. MOLES zu zeigen gesucht.[23] Plutarch stellt Alexander d.Gr. ausdrücklich in der stoischen Linie als Philosophen dar. Er ist es, der die Staatsverfassung des Xenon in praktische Politik umsetzt: „Er trug vielmehr das Bewußtsein in sich, von den Göttern gekommen zu sein als Ordner und Friedensstifter für die Welt (ἀλλὰ κοινὸς ἥκειν θεόθεν ἁρμοστὴς καὶ διαλλακτὴς τῶν ὅλων νομίζων). Führte er sie nicht durch sein Wort zur Einheit, so zwang er sie zusammen und versuchte, die Völker aus aller Welt in einem einzigen Staat zu vereinigen ...".[24]

Der universelle römische Herrschaftsanspruch[25] findet sich bei Nero titular expliziert: So belegt SIG³ 814 seinen weltweiten Anspruch für den Osten des Reiches; er ist ‚Herr *der ganzen Welt*' (ὁ τοῦ παντὸς κόσμου κύριος).[26] Auch wenn die Orientierung auf die gesamte antike Oikoumene im Kaiserkult seltener als der Titel σωτήρ selbst begegnet, findet sich die Verbindung des σωτήρ-Titels und des universellen Anspruchs seit Julius Caesar in inschriftlichen Belegen:

---

[20] S.a. D. CUSS, Imperial Cult, 64ff, mit verschiedenen Beispielen (der *Neue Wettstein* wird eine Reihe von Belegen zu Lk 2,11 bieten). Die Hoffnungen auf eine Rettergestalt angesichts der römischen Herrschaft bei den Griechen beleuchtet P. HERZ, Osten, *passim*. Das Retten des Staates und der Menschen sowie ihr Heil als Aufgabe des Kaisers stellt Plinius d.J. in seinem Panegyrikus heraus: z.B. 5,6; 6,1.2; 8,1; 30,5; 42,3; 67,6; s.a. 22,3 (hierzu s.u. Anm. 72). Die *salus* des Kaisers ihrerseits verbirgt das Heil des Staates und seiner Bewohner; vgl. A. SCHEITHAUER, Studien, *passim*. – Nach Dion Hal Ant Rom 4,32,1 gehört der σωτήρ-Titel neben εὐεργέτης und πατέρ zu den „ehrenvollsten Namen, welche Menschen nur immer schönen Handlungen geben" (Übers.: G.J. SCHALLER, Werke 4, 452); vgl. Plut Camill 10,6; Dion 46,1; dort steht σωτήρ jeweils neben der Bezeichnung Vater und Gott.

[21] S.a. D. CUSS, Imperial Cult, 67f. Nach L. WINKLER, Salus, 32f, wäre der titulare Gebrauch in Rom (*servator* oder *conservator*) erst seit dem 1.Jh. v.Chr. möglich und seine Verbreitung durch Ciceros Reden entscheidend gefördert.

[22] Kurz M. POHLENZ, Stoa, 133.

[23] J.L MOLES, Cynic Cosmopolitanism, *passim*.

[24] Plut De Fortuna Alexandri 329b–c (Übers.: W. AX, Moralia, 268f); vgl. E. LOHMEYER, Christuskult, 12.

[25] Vgl. z.B. Dion Hal Ant Rom 1,3,3.

[26] Übersetzung bei H. FREIS, Inschriften, 14f. Nero wird hier als befreiender Zeus (Ζεὺς Ἐλευθέριος Νέρων) dem Gott Zeus, dem Erretter (Ζεὺς Σωτήρ), angeglichen (zur Bezeichnung von Nero als Zeus Eleutheros vgl. die Belege bei C. BREYTENBACH, Zeus, 378 Anm. 75). Nero gilt nach P.Ox 1021 auch als Ἀγαθὸς Δαίμων τῆς οἰκουμένης ὤν τε πάντων ἀγαθῶν.

Caesar (ermordet 44 v.Chr.): IG XII/5 557 (σωτὴρ τῆς οἰκουμένης; s.a. die ebenfalls universell formulierte Inschrift aus Ephesus: SIG³ 760, sowie IGR IV 305 [τῶν Ἑλλήνων ἁπάντων σωτὴρ καὶ εὐεργέτης]), *Augustus* (31v.–14n.Chr.): IBM IV/1 894; IGR III 718.719 (σωτῆρα τοῦ σύνπαντος κόσμου; s.a. OGIS 458,35); *Tiberius* (14–37 n.Chr.): IGR III 721; *Claudius* (41–54 n.Chr.): IG² III/1, 3273 (σωτῆρα τοῦ κόσμου); *Nero* (54–68 n.Chr.): I.Smyr 519; *Vespasian* (69–79 n. Chr.): IGR III 609. 610; *Domitian* (81–96 n.Chr.): IGR III 729 (σωτῆρι τοῦ κόσμου; in dieser Inschrift wurde der Name des Kaisers entfernt);[27] *Trajan* (98–117 n.Chr.): IG² II 3284 (σωτῆρα τῆς οἰκουμένης); IG VIII 1840; IG V/1 380; IG² III/1 3384; XII/1 978; *Hadrian* (117–138 n.Chr.): CIG 4335 (σωτῆρι τῆς οἰκουμένης).4336.4337.4339; Le Bas III 1342; IG² III/1 3293.3385; CIG 2349m; I.Eph 271F).[28]

Auch wenn die Zahl der inschriftlichen Belege für die Verbindung von σωτήρ-Titel und universeller Orientierung zwischen den Anfängen der Kaiserzeit und dem zweiten Jahrhundert (vor allem wieder bei Trajan und Hadrian) zurückgeht, so wird in der vorliegenden Interpretation die durchgängige Präsenz der universellen Orientierung des Sotertitels stärker gewichtet als ihre relative Verteilung. Diese Ausrichtung der mit dem römischen Kaiser verbundenen Heilshoffnungen ist auch in anderen Texten bezeugt.[29] Außerdem bleiben die frühen Inschriften ihren Lesern und Leserinnen präsent; zudem ist schwer zu entscheiden, ob die Fundsituation auch die Verwendung unter den verschiedenen Kaisern adäquat abbildet.

Auch der hellenistisch-jüdische Traditionsbereich hält instruktive religionsgeschichtliche Parallelen bereit, wenngleich die bei Craig R. KOESTER genannten Josephus-Texte[30] nur zum Teil die ihnen aufgebürdete Beweislast tragen können; sie belegen nicht die universelle Verwendung des Titels und entsprechen römischer Diktion.

In Jos Bell 3,479 wird der spätere Kaiser Vespasian als σωτὴρ καὶ εὐεργέτης akklamiert; den spezifisch universalen Gebrauch, wie wir ihn im vierten Evangelium

---

[27] Vgl. Mart 2,91,1 (*rerum certa salus, terrarum gloria, Caesar*); 5,1,7 (*o rerum felix tutela salusque*); 8,66,6 (*rerum prima salus et una Caesar*).
[28] Zu den bisher gefundenen kaiserlichen Soter-Titulaturen in Ephesus vgl. S. VAN TILBORG, John, 47f (mit weiteren Belegen). Zu Inschriften, die als Parallelen zu Joh 4,42 gelten können, s.a. die Auflistung von C.R. KOESTER, Savior, 667, sowie die Belege im NEUEN WETTSTEIN I/2 ad Joh 4,42.
A. DEISSMANN, Licht, 311, meint, „daß der volle Ehrentitel *Weltheiland*, mit dem Johannes den Meister schmückt, in mannigfacher Variation des griechischen Ausdruckes in Inschriften des hellenistischen Ostens dem Julius Cäsar, Augustus, Claudius, Vespasianus, Titus Traianus, Hadrianus und anderen Kaisern beigelegt wird. Zudem hebt DEISSMANN die Bedeutung für Nero hervor. Ein Einzelnachweis von Quellentexten wird hier nicht geboten; DEISSMANNs wichtigster Zeuge ist D. MAGIE, De romanorum iuris publici sacrique vocabulis. Auch verzichtet DEISSMANN auf eine Interpretation des interessanten Sachverhaltes. S.a. für die ältere Forschung E. LOHMEYER, Christuskult, 36, ebenfalls ohne Einzelnachweis.
[29] Vgl. z.B. Ps-Ovid Nux 145f: „Doch jener Gott (sc. Augustus) beschränkt den Frieden nicht auf die Stadtmauern: / Seine Hilfe verteilt er auf die ganze Welt (*auxilium toto spargit in orbe suum*)" (B.W. HÄUPTLI, Ibis, S. 151. 153); OGIS 458,32ff.
[30] C.R. KÖSTER, Savior, 666.

finden, belegt dieser Text nicht. Diese Verwendung dokumentiert auch Bell 7,70f nicht, wo das Volk Vespasian als τὸν εὐεργέτην καὶ σωτῆρα καὶ μόνον ἄξιον ἡγεμόνα τῆς ῾Ρώμης akklamiert. Der spezifisch universale Charakter der Huldigung läßt sich bei Josephus eben so wenig für Titus belegen: weder in Bell 4,112f noch bei den Huldigungen der Antiochener mit dem Ziel, die unbeliebten Juden aus der Stadt zu vertreiben (Bell 7,100–115), wird Titus der Titel σωτήρ angetragen.

Die LXX bietet Textmaterial, das sich als sprachlicher und religionsgeschichtlicher Hintergrund der johanneischen Aussagen anbietet: vgl. bes. Sap 16,7 (ὁ γὰρ ἐπιστραφείς ... διὰ σὲ τὸν πάντων σωτῆρα); Ester D2 (ad 5,1) (ἐπικαλεσαμένη τὸν πάντων ἐπόπτην θεὸν καὶ σωτῆρα);[31] s.a. 2Mac 7,9 (König der Welt).[32] Die schwierig zu datierende Predigt *Pseud-Philo De Jona* bietet eine Reihe von Gottes-Epitheta, die eine sprachliche Nähe zu Joh 4,42 aufweisen: so ist Gott der Herr der Welt (Jona 39,155) sowie der „wahre" (Jona 52,214) und „alleinige Retter" (Jona 2,7).[33] Auch der alexandrinisch-jüdische Philosoph Philo hält Parallelen zum universellen Gebrauch des Titels ‚Retter' bereit: Philo Spec Leg II 198;[34] Fug 162; Deus Imm 156; s.a. Sobr 53.[35] Sprachlich sind Joh 4,42 und 1Joh 4,14 somit im hellenistischen Judentum vorbereitet.

Wichtig für die Frage nach der Beeinflussung der johanneischen Aussagen durch hellenistische Religionspraxis und mehr noch durch den Kaiserkult selbst ist die Beurteilung des auf σωτήρ bezogenen Genitivs τοῦ κόσμου. Ist die Ergänzung der Soter-Titulatur durch den Kosmosbezug Ausdruck der johanneischen Theologie – dies unterstützt auch das Vorkommen des Titels σωτήρ τοῦ κόσμου im NT ausschließlich im johanneischen Schrifttum[36] – und damit allein gruppen- und schriftenimmanent zu interpretieren?[37] Dafür spre-

---

[31] Im LXX-Zusatz zu Est 8,12 (E 13) wird ein Mensch, Mardochai, von Artaxerxes als τόν τε ἡμέτερον σωτῆρα καὶ διὰ παντὸς εὐεργέτην bezeichnet, was sich auf konkrete Rettungen des Königs vor Mordanschlägen des Hofpersonals bezieht (vgl. I. KOTTSIEPER, Zusätze, 192f).

[32] Die Belege, in denen Jahwe in der LXX als σωτήρ eines einzelnen (z.B. PsLXX 24,5; 26,1.9; 61,2.6) oder Israels (Jes 45,15; 1Mac 4,30; 3Mac 6,32; 7,16; sowie die Bezeichnung ‚Gott unser Retter': z.B. PsLXX 64,5; Bar 4,22) angesprochen wird, lassen sich vermehren. Auch einzelne Gottesmänner können dieses Epitheton erhalten: Ri 3,9.15; Neh 9,27.

[33] F. SIEGERT, Predigten 2, 105f, betont, dass es sich hierbei um „ein konkretes und kontingentes Eingreifen Gottes" und nicht nur um „ein Erhalten in einer gewissen Ordnung" handelt. Solches Retten und Rettungen sind ein wichtiges Thema dieser ‚Predigt'.

[34] „Die Gnadengaben der Natur haben wir freudig empfangen und bewahren sie auf; aber nie bezeichnen wir Vergängliches als die Ursache unserer Erhaltung, sondern den Erzeuger, Vater und Erhalter der Welt (τὸν γεννητὴν καὶ πατέρα καὶ σωτῆρα τοῦ τε κόσμου) und dessen, was sie füllt, Gott, der uns sowohl mit als auch ohne jene zu ernähren und zu erhalten vermag"; Übers.: I. HEINEMANN, in: COHN U.A., Werke II, S. 162f.

[35] Die Texte sind zitiert bei NEUER WETTSTEIN I/2 z. Joh 4,42.

[36] D.h. nicht, dass die neutestamentlichen Belege für σωτήρ außerhalb des *Corpus Iohanneum* übersehen werden sollen; vgl. die Aufstellung bei J. BEUTLER, Johannesbriefe, 112.

[37] Besonders betont wird die gruppeninterne Erklärung z.B. durch J. ZANGENBERG, Christentum, 177f: „Da sich der Titel σωτήρ in 4,42 aus dem Sprachgebrauch der joh. Ge-

chen Äußerungen, die das Auftreten des inkarnierten Logos in seiner Heilsfunktion für die ganze Welt ansprechen: Joh 1,29 par V.36 und 3,16.[38] Auch Joh 11,52 macht deutlich, obgleich ohne den Kosmosbegriff, dass der Tod Jesu eine universelle Heilsbedeutung hat. Er geschieht für τὰ τέκνα τοῦ θεοῦ τὰ διεσκορπισμένα. Wenn die überraschende Aussage 4,22 (ἡ σωτηρία ἐκ τῶν Ἰουδαίων ἐστίν)[39] zum ursprünglichen Textbestand des Evangeliums gehört,[40] so liegt hierin ein wichtiger *Co-Text*[41] für den Titel in 4,42 vor. Bestätigt das vierte Evangelium die Abkunft des Heils von den Juden, möglicherweise in Unterstreichung der inkarnatorischen Aussage, da V.22 den präexistenten Logos, eingegangen in Zeit und Welt, als Glied des jüdischen Volkes vorstellt,[42] so ist dies Heil jedoch nicht national gebunden. Der heilsrelevante Streit um den richtigen Ort der Anbetung wird nicht nur spiritualisiert, als Anbetung in Geist und Wahrheit, sondern durch die Lösung von einem Kultort universalisiert;[43] dies unterstreicht der durch 1,29; 3,16f vorbereitete Titel deutlich. Wie die Verehrung Gottes vom Garizim und Jerusalemer Tempel entschränkt ist, so ist das in Jesus nahe gekommene Heil eine universelle Gabe.[44] Dann ist die offensichtlich als zutreffende christologische Aussage festgehaltene Bezeichnung Jesu als König der Juden auch im Lichte dieser Universalität zu lesen.

Was aber bedeutet die Feststellung der Samaritaner, dass Jesus *wahrhaftig* der Heiland der Welt ist (ἀληθῶς ὁ σωτὴρ τοῦ κόσμου) in der Erzählwelt? Ist hier eine polemische Absicht greifbar? In Kombination mit dem bestimmten

---

meinde ableiten läßt, entfällt jegliche Notwendigkeit, externen Einfluß, etwa aus dem heidnischen Herrscherkult, oder gar eine Anspielung auf den Augustuskult in Sebaste anzunehmen." Anders J. BEUTLER, Johannesbriefe, 112: „an hellenistischem Verständnis orientiert".

[38] S.a. R.J. CASSIDY, Gospel, 34.
[39] Dieser Text selbst hat einen wichtigen *Co-Text* in dem *titulus crucis* (Joh 19,19). Gerade wenn dort Jesus als Ἰησοῦς ὁ Ναζωραῖος ὁ βασιλεὺς τῶν Ἰουδαίων bezeichnet wird, so ist dies im Kontext der johanneischen Königschristologie (vgl. zu diesem Aspekt der johanneischen Christologie J. KÜGLER, König, 37ff [s.a. meine Rez. in SNTU 25 sowie die kritischen Bemerkungen zu Küglers religionsgeschichtlichem Ansatz von D. ZELLER, Königsideologie, 547ff] sowie die bei M. LABAHN, Revelation, 151 Anm. 8, genannte Lit.; vgl. jetzt S. SCHREIBER, König, *passim*; DERS., Gesalbter, 483ff) eine durchaus zutreffende Wertung, die die jüdische Abkunft Jesu unterstreicht.
[40] Dies ist vor allem in der älteren Forschung umstritten (R. BULTMANN, Evangelium, 139 Anm. 6, auch J. BECKER, Evangelium, 167.175f; s.a. W. BAUER, Johannesevangelium, 70). Gegenwärtig scheint mir die Zustimmung für die literarische Ursprünglichkeit ein deutliches Übergewicht zu gewinnen: z.B. J. BLANK, Evangelium, 297; L. SCHENKE, Johannes, 87; U. SCHNELLE, Evangelium, 90; K. SCHOLTISSEK, Antijudaismus, 165, J. ZANGENBERG, Christentum, 150f.
[41] Zur linguistischen Theorie des *Co-Textes* vgl. E.R. WENDLAND, Tale, 115.
[42] Vgl. hierzu U. SCHNELLE, Juden, 221f; s.a. K. SCHOLTISSEK, Antijudaismus, 180; J. BLANK, Evangelium, 297: „Der johanneische Kreis bekennt sich ... zu dem grundlegenden, heilsgeschichtlich bedeutsamen Faktum der Herkunft des Heils, konkret der Person Jesu, aus dem Judentum."
[43] Anders z.B. J. ZANGENBERG, Christentum, 151.
[44] S.a. C.R. KOESTER, Savior, 668.

Artikel des Titels schließt Charles H. TALBERT auf eine deutlich exkludierende Tendenz.[45] Das Adverb ἀληθῶς in Joh 4,42 ist jedoch zunächst vor allem im Zusammenhang mit dem semantischen Feld ἀληθ- im vierten Evangelium zu lesen.

Nathanel, der wahrhaftig ein Israelit ist (1,47), erkennt in Jesus den König Israels (1,49). Die gespeiste Volksmenge begreift, dass Jesus *wahrhaft* der Prophet ist (6,14), zieht aber falsche Schlüsse daraus, indem sie seine göttliche Dignität hin zu einem irdisch-materiellen Königtum missdeutet (6,15).[46] Auch 7,25.40 kreisen um die Anerkennung Jesu hinsichtlich seines Ursprungs. Wer zum Glauben kommt und darin bleibt, ist wahrhaftig ein Glied der Heilsgemeinschaft mit Jesus (8,31). Es geht in diesen Belegen also durchaus um das „Sich-Erschließen dieser W(ahrheit; Vf.) im glaubenden Erfassen".[47] Wer die Selbstvorstellung des in die Welt Gekommenen als Gottes Wahrheit für sich annimmt als jemand, der auf Gottes wahr machendes Handeln in Jesus angewiesen ist, hat in Wahrheit Leben.

So erschließt sich Jesus in 2,1–4,54 als Wahrheit zum Leben und ist denen, die zum Glauben gelangen, wahrhaftig der Retter; der einzige, durch den Gott der Welt bindend Rettung verschaffen will. Damit ist eine affirmative Funktion des Adverbs wahrscheinlich,[48] der ein gewisses Maß an Exklusivität eigen ist. Eine polemische Interpretation gehört hingegen eher zur Rezeption.

---

[45] C.H. TALBERT, John, 118 „they seem to exclude others from the function of savior. It is possible the Fourth Gospel's audience would have taken it to exclude Caesar" (mit Hinweis auf Sebaste [Jos Bell 1,403]); Talbert greift auf C.R. KOESTER, Savior, 680, zurück: „The title 'Savior of the world' was used by Caesar, but the Samaritans recognized that it truely belonged to Jesus, whom they received in a manner appropriate for a king"; s.a. R.J. CASSIDY, Gospel, 35.

[46] Vgl. M. LABAHN, Offenbarung, 100–114. Zu meiner Analyse von Joh 6,15 als abgelehnte Akklamation wies mich Prof. Dr. Klaus Berger, Heidelberg, freundlicherweise brieflich auf seine formkritischen Analysen hin: K. BERGER, Formgeschichte, 354: demzufolge geht es um „Jesu wiederholten Wunsch, verborgen zu bleiben", da er „als *Gottes Gesandter* ... auf Legitimation allein durch *Gott* angewiesen" ist. Auf der inhaltlichen Ebene liegen zwischen beiden Deutungen beachtenswerte Konvergenzen vor.

[47] H. HÜBNER, Art. ἀλήθεια, 144.

[48] Neben den bereits genannten Inschriften ist die inschriftliche Kopie eines Schreibens des Statthalters Pomponius Pius an die Stadt der Histrier (51 n.Chr.) beachtenswert (SEG I 329,29–39 = ISM 68,28–38). Zwar weist der Text nicht die universelle Orientierung von Joh 4,42 auf, aber in dem von Adolf WILHELM unterbreiteten Rekonstruktionsvorschlag, der bis in gegenwärtige Publikationen der Inschrift massgeblich geblieben ist (A. WILHELM, Nr. XV–XVIII, 79; vgl. jetzt D.M. PIPPIDI, Inscriptiones, 192), findet sich das Adverb ἀληθῶς zur Charakterisierung des Soter-Titels: „Pomponius Pius [grüßt] Beamten, [Rat und Volk der Histrier]: Aus den Schreiben des Fl(avius) [Sabinus und des Ailijanus, ausgezeichneter Männer und die von mir [sehr gesch|ätzt werden] an Euch [konnte man] erkennen, daß der Schwäche Eurer [Stadt | Fürsorge zuteil wurde. Da also] der gottgleiche [Caesar? und gleichsam] unser [*wahrhaftiger Retter*] ([καὶ ὡς ἀληθῶς σωτὴρ ἡμῶν)] vor allem Fürsorge trifft, damit die Rechte der Städte nicht nur bewahrt, sondern auch [vermehrt werden,] habe ich entschieden, daß die Einkünfte aus dem Fischfang [längst der Peuke] Euch gehören [gemäß dem Recht, nach dem] Eure Vorfahren und Väter diese Zölle dank [der Güte der Kaiser] ohne Unterbrechung hatten" (Übers.: H. FREIS, Inschriften, 66 [Hervorhebung: M.L.]). Trifft dieser Rekonstuktionsvorschlag zu,

Die Bezeichnung Jesu als *Retter der Welt* hat folglich ihr Fundament in der johanneischen Christologie selbst; die auf den Kosmos hin orientierten Heilsaussagen des Evangeliums bereiten den Titel in 4,42 vor oder greifen auf ihn zurück. Sprachliche Vorbilder bietet die Septuaginta; auch die zeitgenössisch-jüdische Literatur stellt Gott in seiner Heilsbedeutung für die Welt insgesamt vor. Die Grenze dieser Parallelen liegt jedoch darin, dass in den johanneischen Schriften nicht Gott, sondern der von Gott in die Welt gesandte Logos selbst als *Retter der Welt* und damit mit dem Gottesprädikat bezeichnet wird. Der Titel bleibt also hinsichtlich der christologischen Anwendung auffällig. Zu den bedenkenswerten werkexternen Faktoren für die Bildung des Titels gehört der Kaiserkult, auch wenn seine Ausformungen im einzelnen sich in unterschiedlichen Zeiten und an unterschiedlichen Orten anders artikuliert haben. Gehören die römischen Kaiser zu den σωτῆρες der religiösen Umwelt des johanneischen Christentums und wird ihre universelle Bedeutung als Rettergestalt gefeiert, wofür das inschriftliche Material in zeitlicher Nähe zur Abfassung des vierten Evangeliums spricht, so schließt der Titel im Johannesevangelium diese Ansprüche für den zeitgenössischen Leser aus.[49] Es ist schwer vorstellbar, dass die Akklamation in Joh 4,42 völlig vom genannten zeitgenössischen Sprachgebrauch absieht. Möglicherweise ist der Kaiserkult sogar ein Katalysator, der zur titularen Verdichtung der Vorstellungen der johanneischen Christologie geführt hat. Die *faktische Relevanz* des Herrscherkultes als Voraussetzung gelungenen Verstehens ist allerdings nicht zwingend nachweisbar, da die johanneische Semantik hinreichend Sinnbildungspotentiale bereithält. Dennoch ist die überraschende Verdichtung dieser Sinnstrukturen zum Titel beachtlich.

In der johanneischen Semantik bezeichnet der Titel σωτὴρ τοῦ κόσμου Jesus als den Retter, der Gottes Heilswillen mit dem Kosmos in der Einheit mit diesem in letztgültiger Weise zum Ziel bringt. Dies schließt nicht nur implizit, sondern auch explizit jeden anderen religiösen Anspruch aus. Hat *Polemik* ihren *Sitz im Leben* in einer direkten Auseinandersetzung zwischen unterschiedlichen Systemen, seien es religiöse, philosophische, ideologische oder politische, so wird der johanneische Gebrauch des Titels mit dem Adverb ἀληθῶς allerdings nicht hinreichend gekennzeichnet. Eher ist der Gebrauch als *affirmativ* zu bezeichnen: Der Titel entfaltet die johanneische Christologie, die in Jesus Gottes eschatologische Krisis in die Welt gekommen weiß, die trotz seiner Ablehnung in der Welt deren Rettung im Blick hat. Die diese Erzähleinheit abschließende Wundergeschichte, Joh 4,46–54, bestätigt diese Christologie narrativ nicht allein dadurch, dass in der Fernheilung Jesu eschatologische

---

so würde die Inschrift belegen, dass das Adverb ἀληθῶς in der Herrscherpropaganda verwendet wird und einen *bekräftigenden* Sinn hat. Damit ist nicht notwendig eine polemische Konnotation verbunden. – Ich danke meinem Hallenser Kollegen Dr. Manfred LANG und Herrn stud. theol. Fabian GROH für die Unterstützung bei der Klärung offener Fragen.

[49] Nach D. CUSS, Imperial Cult, 71, liegt hierin das eigentliche Problem der Verwendung des universellen σωτήρ-Titels: „It was enough that it *was* used, and this aggravated the dispute between the authorities and the Christian community".

Lebensgabe antizipiert wird, sondern auch darin, dass die Begegnung mit dem Lebensspender zum Glauben des Königlichen und seines ganzen Hauses führt (4,53). Sollte der Königliche als Repräsentant des kaiserlichen Verwaltungsapparates fungieren, so wäre auch damit noch keineswegs der polemische Aspekt vorherrschend. Vielmehr zeigt sich auch an ihm, dass das Heil durch den von Gott gesandten Retter erfolgt, auch für die, die als Repräsentanten der Welt außerhalb des Kreises auftreten. Selbst sie suchen ihr Heil beim *Heiland der Welt*, der ihnen dies nicht aufgrund menschlicher Bitten, sondern aufgrund seiner Übereinstimmung mit der Sendung seines Vaters gewährt (4,47–49).[50]

Begegnet dieser Titel auch in 1Joh 4,14, ohne dass Joh 4,42 und 1Joh 4,14 in direkter literarischer Abhängigkeit zu sehen sind, so gehört die Akklamation Jesu als Heiland der Welt zum Gut der johanneischen Gemeinde, dessen *Sitz im Leben* ähnlich den Kyrios-Akklamationen im Gottesdienst gefunden werden kann.[51]

2. Joh 20,28: Jesus, *mein Herr und mein Gott*

Für die Fragestellung dieses Beitrages ist die Kombination von Herr und Gott im Thomas-Bekenntnis von erheblichem Gewicht. Der als ‚König der Juden' Gekreuzigte tritt nach seiner Auferstehung zum zweiten Mal vor die versammelten Jünger und bietet dem bisher zweifelnden Thomas die Kreuzigungsmale zum Begreifen dar. Thomas antwortet mit einem Bekenntnis, das die existentielle Bedeutung Jesu für den Anrufenden formuliert: Du bist *mein* Herr und *mein* Gott.

> Kreuzigung und Auferstehung möchte ich als textliche Einheit fassen; dies ist durch den Hinweis auf die Wunden, die die Identität des Gekreuzigten mit dem Auferstandenen betonen, festzuhalten. Der zur Kreuzigung führende Proceß vor Pilatus kreist insbesondere um die Bezeichnung Jesu als *König der Juden* (Joh 18,33.37.39; 19,3.19.21). Damit ist eine soteriologische Linie berührt, die zurück zu den Aussagen von Joh 4,22.42 führt. Gottes Logos kommt in die Welt zu ihrer eschatologischen Rettung als geschichtliche Wirklichkeit. Dieses Geschehen anerkennen die Samaritaner im Wissen darum, dass Gottes Rettungshandeln an Israel in diesem Jesus den Retter der Welt bringt. So ist Jesus König der Juden. Findet der Prozess im wesentlichen vor den römischen Instanzen statt, was auch historisch plausibel ist, so läuft er damit vor der entscheidenden politischen Herrschaftsmacht der damaligen Welt, den Römern, ab und hat damit, wie Thomas SÖDING zu Recht herausstellt, eine *universelle Bedeutung*.[52]

---

[50] Vgl. M. LABAHN, Jesus, 209–211.
[51] Dass die ‚gottesdienstliche' Verehrung des Kyrios Jesus ein Feld von Berührungen und Auseinandersetzungen mit der kultischen Verehrung des römischen Kaisers (Elemente kultischer Kaiserverehrung benennt P. HERZ, Kaiser, 118–120) war, hat A.Y. COLLINS, Worship, 249, für die hymnische Verehrung Jesu (Phil 2,6–11) wahrscheinlich zu machen gesucht. Ähnliches wäre m.E. für die Anrede ‚Heiland der Welt' und ‚mein Herr und mein Gott' denkbar.
[52] T. SÖDING, Macht, 37.

Tatsächlich ruft die Darstellung des Prozesses auch den Leser zu einer Entscheidung auf. Auf der einen Seite lässt der vierten Evangelist ‚die Juden' stehen, die ihrem Heilskönig nicht akklamieren (vgl. 19,14), sondern in seiner von bitterer Ironie inspirierten Darstellung sich – vertreten durch die Hohenpriester – zum Kaiser als ihrem König bekennen: Οὐκ ἔχομεν βασιλέα εἰ μὴ Καίσαρα (19,15); ein Bekenntnis, das nach jüdischem Selbstverständnis eine ungeheuerliche Blasphemie darstellt.[53] Die so Bekennenden suchen in irdischer Macht ihr Heil (vgl. 6,15). Die textpragmatische *Alternative* bietet das *große Bekenntnis des Thomas* gegenüber dem Auferstandenen: *mein Herr und mein Gott* (20,28).

Das Bekenntnis des Thomas spricht in der Begegnung mit dem Auferstandenen das *pro me* von Gottes Heilshandeln stellvertretend für die Leser und Leserinnen aus. Damit wird der Retter der Welt als Retter *für die Leser* vorgestellt, wenn sie sich dem Bekenntnis des Thomas anschließen[54] – mehr noch sie werden selig gepriesen, wenn sie in dies Bekenntnis einstimmen als die, die nicht unmittelbare Augen- und ‚Tast'-Zeugen des Auferstandenen sind (20,29).[55] Die Entscheidung findet also statt zwischen irdisch-immanenten Heilsofferten und Gottes eschatologischem Heilsangebot in dem Mensch gewordenen Logos. Joh 20,30f zeigt, dass keine wirkliche Alternative zu diesem eschatologischen Geschehen besteht, da der menschliche Wille zum Leben allein im Glauben an Jesus, den Christus, zum Ziel kommt. Verweigerung ist Gericht und verfehlt das Leben.

Über Kaiser Domitian berichtet *Sueton* in seinen Kaiserviten von dessen Überheblichkeit, die darin besteht, dass er sich in der zweiten Hälfte seiner Regierungszeit selbst in seinen amtlichen Briefen als *dominus et deus noster* einführt.[56] Danach sei er nie mehr anders angeschrieben oder angesprochen

---

[53] Vgl. P.D. DUKE, Irony, 134–136. Zur Verwendung der Ironie im Johannesevangelium s.a. K. SCHOLTISSEK, Ironie, *passim*.

[54] Das Perfekt πεπίστευκας wird von J. FREY, Eschatologie II, 105, als auf eine die Gegenwärtigkeit des Glaubens gehende Intensivierung gedeutet, das das „im Partizip des ingressiven Aorist ausgedrückte(.) Zum-Glauben-Kommen anderer kontrastiert".

[55] S.a. U. WILCKENS, Evangelium, 318.

[56] Das Material stellt R.A. MASTIN, Cult, 355ff, zusammen: Mart 5,8,1; 7,34,8; 8,2.6; 9,66,3; 10,72,1–3 (zur Relation von Dichter und Kaiser, die Martial nicht wie häufig behauptet als devoten Parteigänger Domitians erkennen läßt; vgl. N. HOLZBERG, Martial, 74–85); Dio Cass 67,13,4 (67,4,75); Dio Chrys Or 45,1 (Dion referiert in seiner Rechenschaft an seine Heimatstadt zunächst kurz über seine Verbannung: „Wie ich meine Verbannung durchgestanden habe, ohne dem Mangel an Freunden, der materiellen Not und körperlichen Hinfälligkeit zu erliegen; wie ich zu dem allen ausgeharrt habe unter einem Feind [sc. Domitian], der nicht der erste beste von Leuten meines Standes oder, wie sie manchmal genannt werden, von Gleichberechtigten war, sondern der mächtigste und grimmigste, von allen Griechen und Nichtgriechen Herr und Gott genannt, in Wirklichkeit aber ein böser Dämon; ..."; Übers.: W. ELLIGER, Reden, 594); spätere Belege bei römischen Historikern listet B.W. JONES, Emperor, 108, auf (z.B. Aurelius Victor Caes 11,2). S.a. Philostrat, VitAp 8,4. Der Ankläger fordert Apollonius auf, der den Kaiser keines Blickes würdigt, zu ihm als den *Gott aller Menschen* (τὸν ἁπάντων ἀνθρώπων θεόν) aufzublicken. Auch Plinius, Paneg 2,3 (*Nusquam ut deo, nusquam ut numini blandiamur*: ...) wird als Polemik gegen die postulierte Selbstbezeichnung Domitians herangezogen: z.B. W. KÜHN, Lobrede, 185 (Erläuterungen zu 2,3); s.a. Paneg 52,2; hier redet

worden (Suet Dom 13,2).⁵⁷ Diese Beschreibung des Kaisers ist schon angesichts der Überlieferungssituation mit einer Reihe von Fragen behaftet und somit historisch unsicher.⁵⁸ Domitian ist der *damnatio memoriae* anheim gefallen und so Gegenstand von Polemik geworden. Daran schließt auch die christliche Überlieferung an, die ihn als einen der bedeutendsten Verfolger der Kirche anprangert (Lact. mort. pers. 3).⁵⁹

Der von Sueton berichtete Anspruch kann durch Münz- und Inschriftenfunde nicht untermauert werden.⁶⁰ Hier kann der zeitgenössische Dichter Martial etwas Licht ins Dunkel bringen. Im zehnten Buch seiner Epigramme beschreibt er die Veränderung, die sich mit der Herrschaft des neuen Herrschers Trajan vollzieht:

> Schmeicheleien, ihr naht euch mir vergeblich, / ihr elenden, mit euren abgefeimten Lippen. / Von einem „Herrn und Gott" habe ich nicht vor zu sprechen (*dicturus dominum deumque non sum*), / Ihr habt keinen Platz mehr in dieser Stadt; / geht weit fort zu den Parthern mit ihren Filzhüten / und küßt schmachvoll, erniedrigend und fußfällig / bunt gewandeter Könige Sandalen. / Hier gibt es keinen Herrn, einen Imperator nur, / nur den Gerechtesten von allen Senatoren; / durch ihn wurde aus dem stygischen Haus zurückgeführt / mit unparfümiertem Haar die schlichte Wahrheit. / Hüte dich, Rom, wenn du klug bist, unter diesem Fürsten / mit Worten zu sprechen aus früherer Zeit (*hoc sub principe, si sapis, caveto / verbis, Roma, prioribus loquaris*)!⁶¹

Martial spricht in seinem Epigramm speziell die Stadt Rom an und warnt sie, den neuen Princeps weiter als „Herr und Gott" zu bezeichnen. Dies kann bedeuten, dass die Verwendung der Anrede auf Rom und hier vor allem auf den Kaiserhof beschränkt war.⁶² Martial rechnet sie zu den „Schmeicheleien". Dann wird die Bezeichnung nicht, wie es Sueton behauptet, ein offizieller Titel gewesen sein. Der literarisch recht breite Nachweis der Anrede erzeugt trotz fehlender inschriftlicher und numismatischer Zeugnisse hinreichend Wahrscheinlichkeit, dass die Anrede tatsächlich genutzt und geduldet, vielleicht auch vom Hof gefördert wurde. Die Anrede fehlt auf Münzen und in Inschrif-

---

Plinius den neuen Princeps gerade als den an, der nicht (wie Domitian; vgl. 52,3) einen „Platz unter den Götter" erstrebt: *deorum ipse non adpetas* (Übers.: W. KÜHN, Lobrede, 103).

⁵⁷ Dies steht im Kontrast zum vorbildlichen Verhalten des Augustus, dem die Anrede *dominus* noch „Abscheu wie vor einem Schimpf oder einer Schmähung" verursachte (Suet Aug 53,1; s.a. Suet Tib 27; Übers.: O. WITTSTOCK, Kaiserbiographie, 139).

⁵⁸ Zum Problem s.a. B.J. LIETAERT PEERBOLTE in diesem Band, S. 252ff. Grundsätzliche historische Zweifel an der Darstellung bei Sueton formuliert B.W. JONES, Emperor, 108f.

⁵⁹ Vgl. kurz W. ECK, Domitianus, 747f.

⁶⁰ Vgl. H.-J. KLAUCK, Umwelt, 60. Zum Fehlen des Titels in Inschriften vgl. A. MARTIN, Titulature, *passim*.

⁶¹ Mart 10,72. Übers.: P. BARIÉ/W. SCHINDLER, Epigramme, 739.

⁶² W. ECK, Domitianus, 749, hält es beispielsweise für möglich, dass es sich um eine „falsche Verallgemeinerung einer vielleicht beim kaiserlichen Gesinde üblichen Anrede" handelt. Gänzlich als historisch wertet H. BENGTSON, Flavier, 185f, den Selbstanspruch, um ihn psychologisierend als Ausdruck eines „übersteigerten Selbstbewußtseins" (aaO., 187) zu verstehen.

ten, da ihre Verwendung auf den Hof konzentriert und zeitlich begrenzt war; sie wurde unter dem Nachfolger nicht mehr verwendet. Dass sie dennoch auch außerhalb Roms bekannt war, ist angesichts des Austausches zwischen dem Hof und den Provinzen wahrscheinlich, so dass sie durchaus für die *kulturelle Enzyklopädie* des vierten Evangeliums und seiner Leserschaft beansprucht werden kann.

Diese recht starken Parallelen zu Joh 20,28 sind jedoch nicht das einzige Material, was zu einem Vergleich herangezogen werden kann. Schon Adolf DEISSMANN hatte den Zusammenhang zwischen Joh 20,28 und der Titulatur des Domitian hergestellt, allerdings unter der Betonung der direkten Anregung durch die LXX.[63] Besonders nahe steht dem Thomas-Bekenntnis PsLXX 34(35),23: ὁ θεός μου καὶ ὁ κύριός μου.[64] Daneben sind die Kombination κύριος und θεός in PsLXX 35(36),15; 87(88),2 zu beachten.

Manfred LANG zeigt in seiner *Hallenser Dissertation* das Dilemma auf. Er weist auf die formalen Parallelen in der Septuaginta, bestimmt eine antidoketische Zielrichtung des Bekenntnisses, das zugleich „Material, um auf das dominus et deus noster hoc fieri iubet (Suet Dom 13,2) reagieren zu können", bereitstelle.[65] Dennoch handele es sich um keine Polemik gegen den Herrscherkult.[66] Das Bild klingt widersprüchlich, trifft aber doch wohl den Kern des Problems. Die Verwendung des paganen Titels wird dadurch gefördert, dass er sich in sprachlich analoger Form in den als religiös anerkannten Schriften der johanneischen Gemeinschaft findet. Auch hier darf angenommen werden, dass der christliche Titel aus dem Gottesdienst der Gemeinde stammt. Das Verständnis der Thomas-Anrede ist nicht vom Bezug auf den Herrscherkult abhängig, so dass keine *faktische Relevanz* beansprucht werden muss, um zu einer gelungenen Kommunikation zu gelangen – die Bekanntschaft mit dem Titel ist aber wahrscheinlich, weil eine politische Konnotation durch den Königstitel und die in der vorausgehenden Gerichtsverhandlung angesprochene Machtfrage (s.u. Abschn. 4) explizit angesprochen werden. So ist ein apologetischer Nebensinn auch beim *implied author* im Rückgriff auf den gemeinsamen kulturellen *Code* nicht ausgeschlossen: Das *dominus et deus* exkludiert andere Herrschaftsansprüche.

3. Jesu Wunder – Polemik gegen die Kaiserideologie?

Die Wundergeschichten des vierten Evangeliums sind ein wichtiges Mittel, theologische, christologische und anthropologische Einsichten literarisch-

---

[63] A. DEISSMANN, Licht 309f
[64] M. KARRER, Jesus Christus, 320.
[65] M. LANG, Johannes, 292.
[66] M. LANG, Johannes, 258 Anm. 909. Ähnlich M. DALY-DENTON, David, 267, die einerseits konzediert, dass Joh 20,28 „may reflect a Christian reaction against the imperial cult under Domitian", aber zugleich zu bedenken gibt: „It is unlikely ... that this address to Jesus is merely a parody of the pagan title".

narrativ zu präsentieren und Hörer wie Leser zum Glauben zu rufen (Joh 20,30f). Wenn mit dem Auftreten der flavischen Kaiserdynastie (69–96: Vespasian – Titus – Domitian) das Erzählen von Wundergeschichten in der römischen Geschichtsschreibung die Aufgabe erhält, die Verbundenheit der Kaiser mit dem Göttlichen zu illustrieren,[67] so verspricht der Vergleich zwischen Herrscherpropaganda und johanneischen Wundererzählungen weitere Einsichten in die Fragestellung dieser Untersuchung. Methodisch geht es nicht um die Konstruktion literarischer oder traditionsgeschichtlicher Abhängigkeit zwischen den dargestellten Texten; es geht vielmehr darum, wie die Wundererzählungen vor dem Hintergrund der zeitgenössischen Herrscherpropaganda gelesen werden können und ob es Hinweise gibt, dass solche Lektüre durch Signale im Text des Evangeliums nahegelegt ist – es geht also um die Aktualisierung der *potentiellen* Relevanz der vorgestellten religionsgeschichtlichen Parallelen, wie sie angesichts der Enzyklopädie zeitgenössischer Leser und Leserinnen möglich ist.

Das vierte Evangelium teilt mit den Synoptikern die Erzählfolge von der Speisung der 5000 und dem Seewandel Jesu: Joh 6,1–25a. Von Interesse ist für unsere Fragestellung besonders der Seewandel Jesu, für den Adela Yarbro COLLINS den Zusammenhang der Seewandelgeschichten mit der antiken Herrscherpropaganda herausgestellt hat. Folgende Aspekte sind mir von Bedeutung. In der Tat spielen Seewandelmotive eine beachtenswerte Rolle in der hellenistischen Herrscherpropaganda, so dass dieser Hintergrund auch im Blick auf die neutestamentlichen Texte ein möglicher Interpretationszusammenhang ist: vor allem sind Dio Chrys Or 3,31; Menand Fr 924K; Suet Cal 19,3; 2Mac 5,21 zu nennen; s.a. Hdt 7,35.65; Lysias Or 2,29; Isoc Panegyricus 88f; Sib 4,76–78; Jos Ant 19,6.[68] Die Herrscherpropaganda stellt den Herrscher in eine qualifizierte Relation zu den Göttern. Die Geschichten verfolgen also die textpragmatische Ansicht, den Herrscher als Günstling der Götter bzw. als den Göttern ähnlich oder gleich darzustellen. Jesu Seewandel schreibt diesem vor allem göttliche Machtfülle zu, indem er als der vorgestellt wird, der

---

[67] Vgl. H.C. KEE, Miracle, 180: „Beginning with the rise of the Flavians, and mounting in importance in the Antonine period, another dimension of miracle is apparent in the writings of Roman historians: by performing miracles and by personal revelations, the rulers display a personal relationship with the divine."

[68] Zur Interpretation vgl. M. LABAHN, Offenbarung, 207ff, wo die wichtige Arbeit von A.Y. COLLINS, Rulers, *passim*, sowie die Überlegungen von P.J. MADDEN, Walking, 54ff, aufgenommen worden sind; vgl. kurz M. LABAHN, Revelation, 169f mit Anm. 58.
R. STRELAN, Storm Stories, *passim*, bietet in seiner Analyse von Lucan 5 verschiedene Belege für die Bewältigung stürmischer See (vgl. den Sturm Joh 6,18); vgl. bes. Arr An 1,26,2; Plut Alex 17; App Bell Civ 2,21,149f. Interessant ist bes. Plut Caes 37,7, wo angesichts Caesars Plan, trotz Winter und Sturm nach Italien überzusetzen, festgestellt wird: ὥραν δὲ χειμῶνος καὶ πνεύματος ἐν θαλάττῃ καιρὸν οὐδὲ θεῷ βιάζεσθαι δυνατόν. Doch Caesar legt ab und ermutigt den Schiffsführer τόλμα καὶ δέδιθι μηδέν· Καίσαρα φέρεις καὶ τὴν Καίσαρος Τύχην συμπλέουσαν (38,5). Letztlich scheitert Caesars Unternehmen – anders die neutestamentlichen Sturmstillungs- (Mk 4,35ffparr) und Seewandelerzählungen (Mk 6,45ff par Mt 14,22ff; Joh 6,16–21); vgl. STRELAN, aaO., 178f.

die chaotischen Mächte beherrscht. Mehr noch, er wendet sich in dieser Machtfülle den Seinen rettend zu, was ihn als Vermittler von göttlichem Leben und Heil zu erkennen gibt. Der solchermaßen Handelnde ist aber im Erzählgefälle des Johannes der, der zuvor als der Prophet bekannt wurde (6,14) und sich der Ausrufung zum Königtum entzog (6,15). Das vierte Evangelium selbst stellt den Bezug zur Herrscherverehrung her! Jesus entzieht sich irdisch-politischen Fehldeutungen aufgrund seines Speisungswunders, um sich sogleich wie hellenistische Herrscher in der Macht Gottes zu zeigen. Diese Dialektik bedient sich der Argumentationsfigur der Herrscherpropaganda aber im Horizont biblischer Texte, die Gott als Beherrscher der Chaosmächte preisen (eine Reihe alttestamentlicher Belege feiern Jahwe, der in seinem Schöpfungshandeln das Meer als Chaosmacht in die Schranken gewiesen hat: z.B. Ps 74,12ff; 89,10; 93,3; 104,6f; Jer 5,22; Hi 26,12f; 38,4–11; Spr 8,28f).[69] Jesu Herrschaft ist nicht eine am Materiellen orientierte, sondern hat ihren Ursprung in Gott mit dem Ziel, der Welt das Heil zu vermitteln, wenn sich die Welt im Zeugnis Jesu Handelns als die erkennt, die seiner Rettung bedarf.

Nicht allein der Seewandel Jesu lässt sich vor dem Hintergrund antiker Herrscherpropaganda lesen. Auch für andere johanneische Wundergeschichten sind beachtenswerte Berührungen namhaft zu machen. Auffallend ist die Blindenheilung in Joh 9,1ff, die durch eine mit Erde und Speichel zubereitete Masse geschieht. Die Berührung durch Speichel findet sich auch in der antiken Herrscherpropaganda in der Blindenheilung durch Kaiser Vespasian.[70] Sie wird berichtet bei Suet Vesp 7,2 (*restituturum oculos, si inspuisset*); Dio Cass 66,8,1[71] und Tac Hist 4,81,1–3.[72] Umstritten ist, welche Verbreitung und wel-

---

[69] Weitere Texte bei M. LABAHN, Offenbarung, 213f.
[70] Zur Wundertradition vom heilenden *Vespasian* vgl. auch M. CLAUSS, Kaiser, 113–116 (weiteres zu Heilungen und Wunder der römischen Kaiser: aaO. 346–352); H.C. KEE, Miracle, 130f.180f; B. KOLLMANN, Jesus, 106–109; G. ZIETHEN, Heilung, 182–185, sowie ausführlich S. MORENZ, Vespasian, *passim*.
[71] Über die Heilung heißt es hier: τοῦ μὲν τὴν χεῖρα πατήσας τοῦ δὲ τοῖν ὀφθαλμοῖν πηλὸν προσπτύσας, ὑγιεῖς ἀπέφηνε. Ist der Ablauf der Handlung auch im einzelnen von Joh 9,6f zu unterscheiden, so fallen sprachliche Überschneidungen auf; dies spricht nicht für eine Abhängigkeit, möglicherweise aber für bekannte Erzählformen und/oder einen Rückgriff auf volkstümliche und magische Heilungsversuche.
[72] So z.B. A. JACOBY, Heilung, 186f.192, der die Nähe feststellt, selbst aber keine Abhängigkeit, sondern eine rationalisierende und historisierende Deutung vertritt: 192ff. Die Texte sind in Übersetzung leicht zugänglich in NEUER WETTSTEIN I/2 *ad* Joh 9,1ff. – Auch die Lebensbeschreibung *Hadrians* weiß von zwei Blindenheilungen zu berichten (Historia Augusta, Hadrianus 25 [die Quelle ist Marius Maximus, demzufolge diese Vorgänge auf Täuschung zurückgingen]), die kurz vor seinem Tode stattgefunden haben sollen. Obgleich diese Heilungen in einem späteren Text stehen, ist auf ihren altertümlichen Charakter hingewiesen worden (vgl. F. TAEGER, Charisma 2, 371f) und belegen sie die Zugehörigkeit dieses Erzählmotivs zur Herrscherpropaganda. Plinius d.J. scheint ähnliche Traditionen zu kennen, wenn er angesichts der Traian bei seinem Einzug in Rom entgegengebrachten Heilserwartungen formuliert: „auch die Kranken, sie schlugen die Vorschriften ihrer Ärzte in den Wind und schleppten sich herbei, als ob dein Anblick Heil und Gesundheit verbürge (*ad salutem sanitatemque prorepere*)" (Paneg 22,3; Übers.: W. KÜHN, Lobrede, 49). – Zur therapeutischen Sprache im Kaiserportrait vgl. G. ZIETHEN,

che Bedeutung diese Geschichten in der römischen Herrscherpropaganda haben. Beides wird von Manfred CLAUSS sehr hoch eingeschätzt:

> „Während des Aufenthaltes in Alexandria fanden auch jene Krankenheilungen statt, die Vespasian durchführte und *als erste Regierungshandlungen im Sinne öffentlicher Selbstdarstellung reichsweit propagieren ließ.*"[73]

Die Überlieferungsbasis ist für derart weitreichende Urteile etwas schmal; dennoch ist mit der Möglichkeit der Kenntnis dieser Geschichten durch den Verfasser wie den Leser des Johannesevangeliums zu rechnen. Der religionsgeschichtliche Primärhintergrund der johanneischen Blindenheilung liegt jedoch nicht in diesem Überlieferungsbereich; Blindenheilungen vermittels Speichel sind kein Spezifikum der römischen Herrscherpropaganda;[74] zudem sind sie auch außerhalb dieses Überlieferungskontextes bekannt. Die neutestamentlichen Blindenheilungen knüpfen wie die Kaiserpropaganda an antike Erzählpotentiale an. Eine direkte überlieferungsgeschichtliche Linie zwischen Joh 9,1.6–7 und der Kaiserpropaganda ist damit nicht zu ziehen.

Dennoch ist beachtenswert, dass das vierte Evangelium die Heilung eines Lahmen (Joh 5,1ff) und die Blindenheilung auffällig parallel aufbaut und so auf einander bezieht.[75] Dabei handelt es sich um Heilungen von zwei Behinderungen, die nach antikem Verständnis nahezu unheilbar sind, Paralyse und Blindheit.[76] In schweren Fällen kann lediglich das Eingreifen der Götter (insbesondere das Eingreifen der bekannten Heilgötter Asklepios, Isis, Sarapis) Abhilfe schaffen.[77] Dort, wo diese Grunderkenntnis durchbrochen wird, schreiben diese Heilungsgeschichten dem Wundertäter eine außergewöhnliche Macht zu, die diesen glorifiziert und deifiziert.[78] Heilungen von Lahmen (Mk

---

Heilung, *passim*. Die *salus* des Kaiser ihrerseits verbirgt das Heil des Staates und seiner Bewohner; vgl. A. SCHEITHAUER, Studien, *passim*.

[73] M. CLAUSS, Kaiser, 113 (Hervorhebungen: M.L.); s.a. G. ZIETHEN, Heilung, 182. H. BENGTSON, Flavier, 62, meint, dass das alexandrinische Doppel-Wunder Vespasians „im Ganzen Reich die Runde gemacht hat"; immerhin sind diese Geschichten mehrfach überliefert, was man wahrscheinlich nicht für die Mehrzahl solcher Legenden beanspruchen kann. Natürlich droht hier eine schwierige *argumentatio e silentio*, so dass die Warnung von E. KOSKENNIEMI, Apollonius von Tyana, 223f, nicht zu überhören ist, die auf den schmalen Überlieferungsbestand für unsere Überlegungen hinweist. P. HERZ, Kaiser, 132, sieht in diesen Wundergeschichten eine Ausnahme, die zur Legitimierung eines Dynastiewechsels dienen.

[74] Vgl. die Belege bei M. LABAHN, Jesus, 328ff.

[75] Vgl. M. LABAHN, Jesus, 374ff.

[76] Vgl. W. SCHRAGE, Art. τυφλός, 273. So erwähnt Suet Vesp 7,2, dass das Ansinnen, einen Blinden und einen Lahmen zu heilen, kaum möglich schien. Ähnliches beobachtet W.D. HAND, Curing, 81, in Volkssagen: „the cure of blindness itself being almost always regarded as one of the miracles of medicine, and often as miracles wrought by God himself, or by the Virgin Mary".

[77] Vgl. W. SCHRAGE, Art. τυφλός, 274 mit Belegen.

[78] Ist es bei dieser Begebenheit der ägyptische Gott *Sarapis*, der die Kranken durch eine Weissagung zum Kaiser *Vespasian* schickt, so könnte die Realisierung der angesagten Heilung durchaus als ein Ausdruck dafür gewertet werden, dass in der vorliegenden Erzählung der römischen Herrscherpropaganda *Vespasian* als irdische Verkörperung dieses

2,1ffparr) und Blinden (Mk 8,22–26; Mk 10,46–52parr; Mt 9,27–31) finden sich auch in der synoptischen Tradition. Dies entspricht der gleichermaßen alttestamentlich-jüdischen wie auch frühchristlichen Erwartung solcher Wunder in der Endzeit (zum Sehend-Werden Blinder: Jes 35,5; 42,7; 61,1; 4Q 521 Frgm. 2 col. II 8;[79] in der christlichen Rezeption wurzeln solche Hoffnungen in Jesu Verkündigung und spiegeln seine Wahrnehmung der Gegenwart angesichts der im Kommen begriffenen Gottesbasileia: vgl. bes. Q 7,22[80]).

Die Parallelität im Aufbau der johanneischen Kapitel über die Lahmenheilung und die Blindenheilung schreibt dem Wundertäter Jesus eine besondere *qualitas* zu, die bei Kenntnis der Wunder Vespasians zu deren kritischer Bewertung herausfordern.[81] Dass herrscherliche Züge im Blick sein können, legt die der Blindenheilung folgende Hirtenrede in Joh 10 nahe. Der alttestamentliche Hintergrund der Hirtenmotivik setzt bei einem Verständnis der Führer Israels als Hirten des Volkes ein, die ihrem Auftrag nicht gerecht geworden sind. So tritt Jahwe selbst als Hirte seines Volkes ein; erhofft wird auch, dass Jahwe einen zuverlässigen Hirten senden wird, der der ‚gute Hirte‘ ist. Auch in der hellenistisch-griechischen Welt ist die Metapher vom Hirten, auf Herrscher oder militärische Führer angewendet, nicht fremd;[82] bei Homer begegnet der Hirte als Begriff für den König (ποιμὴν λαῶν) und ist seit Platon (Pol 267e; 275b–c; Resp I 345b–e) als Bild für den Staatsmann in der griechischen Staatsphilosophie belegt.[83] Vor solchem Hintergrund entfaltet Joh 10,1ff in Abgrenzung gegen innerweltliche Macht- und Führungsansprüche die Bedeutung von Jesu Gekommensein und von Jesu Handeln. Erinnert man sich zudem daran, dass Blindenheilungen auch im Zusammenhang der Kaiserviten überliefert werden und damit wohl auch in der Herrscherpropaganda eine Rolle spielten, dann ist das kritische Potential der Hirtenrede in der Tat weitaus umfassender. Der sich in parabolischer Redeweise als der wahre Hirte vor-

---

Gottes auftritt (vgl. H. BENGTSON, Flavier, 62; Vespasian werde als das „lebende Abbild des Gottes Sarapis" und als „der Auserwählte des Allerhöchsten" dargestellt).

[79] Vgl. z.B. J. BECKER, Jesus, 220. Anders aber H. KVALBEIN, Wunder, 121f, der die Erwartung individueller Heilungswunder für die Endzeit negiert: es gibt „*überhaupt keine klaren Belege für Heilungswunder an einzelnen Israeliten in der Heilszeit*". Die diskutierten Belege seien vielmehr als „bildhafte Ausdrücke für die Restitution des Volkes in seiner Ganzheit zu verstehen" (Zitate: aaO. 122). Entsprechend deutet KVALBEIN auch den Qumrantext: „Die Heilsverheißungen dürfen ... nicht auf körperliche Heilungswunder bezogen werden. Es geht um eine bildlich-poetische Darstellung der Erneuerung des Gottesvolkes in der Endzeit".

[80] Vgl. M. LABAHN, Significance.

[81] Diese Interpretation bestreitet nicht, dass auch die beiden möglichen Reaktionen auf diese Persönlichkeit in ihren Konsequenzen bedacht werden (vgl. z.B. R. METZNER, Verständnis, 55), so dass sie in ihrer Pragmatik auf die angemessene Reaktion der Leserschaft, den Glauben, vor einer bedrohlichen Welt zielen. Deren Repräsentanten suchen Jesus zu töten (Joh 5,18; 7,1; 11,53; s.a. 7,19ff; 8,37ff) und gefährden auch den Zum-Glauben-Gekommenen – ist hier der Text offen für eine als Bedrohung verstandene Umwelt; eine Umwelt, deren religiös-politische Propaganda narrative Parallelen bereit hält?

[82] Vgl. kurz J.D. TURNER, History, 35f.

[83] Vgl. J. ENGEMANN, Art. Hirt, 587f.

stellende johanneische Jesus distanziert sich von den irdischen religiösen (dafür mögen die Pharisäer eingesetzt werden, von denen unmittelbar zuvor die Rede war: Joh 9,39–41) wie auch den politischen Führern. Dieses kritische Potential wird jedoch nicht in sozialer, sondern in soteriologischer Hinsicht entfaltet, ohne dass beide Aspekte völlig auseinander gingen. Der hellenistische politische Führer lässt sich als Retter (σωτήρ) feiern und mißt sich damit zugleich soteriologische Qualität zu.

Ist Jesus der durch den Einsatz des eigenen Lebens lebensgewährende Hirte und kann das Wunder als eine antizipierende Sichtbarwerdung dieser lebensgewährenden Macht verstanden werden, so erscheint dies vor dem alttestamentlichen, aber auch vor dem hellenistisch-griechischen Hintergrund als Überbietung jeglicher realer irdischer Herrschermacht.[84] Wer diesen Hintergrund vor Augen hat, kann in der Heilung des Blindgeborenen die Opposition zur vorgenannten Herrscherpropaganda präsent finden.[85]

---

[84] Auch U. BUSSE, Metaphorik, 128, setzt den Zusammenhang von 9,1–10,21 voraus und interpretiert vor diesem Hintergrund das Hirtenthema: „Die dramatische Zuspitzung ... bis hin zum Synagogenbann ist erzählerisch geboten, um die Fragen nach dem für Gott allein legitimen Hirten und nach den Eigenschaften der Mitglieder des eschatologischen Gottesvolkes für die Leser beantworten zu können." Die Frage nach einem möglichen Bezug zum antiken Herrscherkult wird nicht reflektiert, da bei dieser Interpretation die Opposition zum Aposynagogos von erheblichem Gewicht ist.

[85] Nur am Rande ist auf einen weiteren möglichen Bezugspunkt zum Kaiserkult zu verweisen, der zu Joh 2,1–11 gezogen werden kann. Wird akzeptiert, dass Joh 2,1ff Motive aus dionysischen Erzählparallelen aufnimmt (vgl. M. LABAHN, Jesus, 148ff; I. BROER, Weinwunder, *passim*), dann kann man darauf verweisen, dass römische Kaiser in Kleinasien als ‚neuer Dionysos' (νέος Διόνυσος) verehrt werden: *Antonius* (vgl. L.R. TAYLOR, Divinty, 107–110.121f.269), *Caligula* (vgl. F. TAEGER, Charisma 2, 285 mit Belegen), *Hadrian* (z.B. in Ancyra: IGR III 209. 210; vgl. D. MAGIE, Rule I, 617f. II 1477f Anm. 24 [Quellen und Lit.]; s.a. R.E. OSTER, Ephesus, 1676), *Commodus* (vgl. z.B. R. MERKELBACH, Dionysosmysten, 155f [Referat von GIBM 600; OSTER, aaO., 1675]). Auch *Marc Aurel* ließ sich mit diesem Titel benennen (Plut Ant 24,4; Dio Cass 48,39,2; vgl. TAEGER, aaO., 90ff; OSTER, aaO., 1674); vgl. allgemein R. SCHLESIER, Art. Dionysos, 659. Es ist ein verlockender Gedanke, dass in der Zeichnung der Epiphanie Jesu in seinem Weinwandel wie Dionysos jener auch in eine implizite Konkurrenz mit oder besser vor den römischen Kaiser tritt; vgl. S. VAN TILBORG, John, 98. Anders als bei den zuvor genannten Parallelen wird hier jedoch kein *ausdrücklicher* Zusammenhang mit herrscherlichen Ansprüchen hergestellt, es sei denn Joh 2,1ff wird in engen Zusammenhang mit Joh 1,19ff gerückt; hier wird Jesus aber als König Israels (1,49) bekannt. M.E. ist jedoch die Wandlung von Wasser in Wein in Joh 2,1ff erzählerisch mit der Tempelreinigung, 2,13ff, als *Co-Text* verbunden (vgl. M. LABAHN, Jesus, 125–127). Doch kann der Sorge um das Heiligtum auch ein Ausdruck herrscherlicher Pflichterfüllung entnommen werden und das im Blick auf die Lesersteuerung wichtige Zitat aus Ps 69,10 (Joh 2,17) geht auf einen Davidspsalm zurück (hierzu jetzt M. DALY-DENTON, David, 118ff). Solche Sorge käme in Passion und Auferstehung zum Ziel (vgl. zuletzt J. FREY, Eschatologie II, 69–71, im Rekurs auf die Tempusänderung im LXX-Zitat vom Aorist zum Futur).

4. Johanneisches Christusbekenntnis und der römische Staat: Zusammenfassung und Ausblick

Die Einzelanalyse hat gezeigt, dass sich sprachlich und motivlich neben den Analogien zum Kaiserkult jüdisch-alttestamentliche oder christliche, vor allem johanneische Parallelen nicht übersehen lassen, aus denen der Erzähler des vierten Evangeliums schöpft. Eine *direkte* Polemik gegen einen Anspruch, wie er im Kaiserkult vertreten wird, die auf einen unmittelbaren Konflikt zwischen johanneischen Gemeinden und dem Kaiserkult schließen lässt, kann aus den christologischen Aussagen nicht erhoben werden. Es gehört vielmehr zum Wesen johanneischer Christologie, die universelle Geltung des Heilsangebotes Gottes, wie es in der eschatologischen Sendung Jesu in die Welt kommt, zu betonen. Doch damit steht diese Christologie *de facto* in einem scharfen Konkurrenzverhältnis zu allen anderen religiösen, politischen wie auch philosophischen Heilsofferten. Wie auch immer sich der Exeget/die Exegetin zu diesem Ausschließlichkeitsanspruch stellt, *das vierte Evangelium selbst formuliert eine exklusiv an dem gesandten Logos orientierte Soteriologie.*

Auch wenn der *affirmative Charakter dieser christologischen Aussagen* festgehalten werden muss, so sind m.E. sprachliche und motivliche Parallelen dennoch nicht zu ignorieren, da die Parallelen zur römischen Herrscherpropaganda dem antiken Leser kaum verborgen waren. Die umstrittene, aber m.E. noch immer historisch wahrscheinlichste Annahme der Abfassung dieses Evangeliums im kleinasiatischen Raum – möglicherweise in Ephesus –[86] weist in ein geographisches Gebiet mit hoher Präsenz solcher Motive, aber auch die syrisch-palästinische Umwelt ist keineswegs für eine Begegnung mit Leitgedanken des Kaiserkultes ungeeignet.[87] Mag der Einfluss des Herrscherkultes eher beiläufig dazu beigetragen haben, biblische Formulierungen und johanneische Semantik zu konzentrieren, so schließt das christologische Bekenntnis jegliche Heilsansprüche antiker Götter wie auch des Kaiserkultes aus. Der wahre und damit in Einheit mit dem göttlichen Willen als Rettung zum Leben für den gesamten Kosmos gesandte Retter ist allein der johanneische Jesus; für die Rettung in universeller Hinsicht ist allein der von Gott gesandte und Mensch gewordene Logos zuständig. Dies kann und wird realen Lesern und Leserinnen des Evangeliums nicht entgangen sein.

Der exklusive Anspruch der johanneischen Christologie konkurriert somit mit der universellen Herrschaft Roms. Versagt sich der johanneische Jesus jeglichem innerweltlich-politischen Machtanspruch (Joh 18,36), der in Konkurrenz zum weltimmanenten römischen Machtanspruch gesehen werden könnte, so bedeutet dies keineswegs den Verzicht des Anspruchs auf die Menschheit und die Fürsorge für ihr Leben. Die überraschende Aussage, dass Jesu Reich nicht von dieser Welt ist, obgleich das durch ihn vermittelte *Heil*

---

[86] Vgl. mit Diskussion M. LABAHN, Jesus, 28–30; s.a. U. SCHNELLE, Einleitung, 485f.
[87] Vgl. die interessanten Überlegungen von G. GUTTENBERGER zu Caesarea Philippi in diesem Band.

schon im *Jetzt* den Christen zugesprochen werden kann,[88] zeigt aber deutlich einen unterschiedlichen Machtbereich gegenüber dem Römischen Reich. Dies ist keine Unterscheidung hinsichtlich Ort und Zeit, die für ein allein vergeistigtes Verständnis der Macht in Anspruch genommen werden könnte. Vielmehr geht es um eine Unterscheidung hinsichtlich des *Ursprungs*: aus Gott oder aus der Finsternis. Es geht um die existentielle Entscheidung, ob der Ursprung zum eigenen Heil in diesem Jesus anerkannt oder verweigert wird. So entzieht sich Jesus der Akklamation des Volkes zum König (6,15), obgleich er sich als der wahre göttliche Machthaber sogleich im Seewandel ausweist (6,16ff). Jesu Königtum stellt die irdisch-immanente Herrschaft des Kaisers nicht in Frage, weil seine Herrschaft durch die des Kaisers und seiner Vasallen nicht tangiert wird. Jesus tritt den jüdischen und römischen Häschern entgegen und lässt sich verhaften, weil es seiner (und seines Vaters) Entscheidung entspricht (18,4–12; mit 12,23–28). Der johanneische Jesus lässt sich vom Stellvertreter der römischen Macht, Pilatus, verhören, weil Gott ihm diese Macht zuerkennt (19,10f). So gesehen ist die Macht des Kaisers im Vergleich zu der Jesu als König eine *zugebilligte Macht*. Dies wird auch darin deutlich, dass Jesus und sein Richter, Pilatus, den Verlauf des Prozesses bestimmen. Es geht also auch um eine Entscheidung über wirkliche oder unwirkliche Macht. Der Herrscher dieser Welt ist besiegt worden (12,31: νῦν ὁ ἄρχων τοῦ κόσμου τούτου ἐκβληθήσεται ἔξω), so dass die Finsternis ihr Reich als uneigentliche, aber doch noch verderbende Wirklichkeit bei denen führt, die sich der göttlichen Herrschaft verweigern.

Gehört der Kaiser mit seinem Herrschaftsbereich zum Kosmos als der sich Gott verweigernden Größe (vgl. 1,9f; 3,19)? Jedenfalls ist es kaum hilfreich, hinter der Aussage 18,36 eine Rücksichtnahme der johanneischen Gruppe auf die irdischen Machtansprüche des Kaiserkultes zu sehen, wie es B.A. Mastin behauptete:

„the Fourth Gospel insists that Christ does exercise genuine kingship, it is *sui generis* and need cause earthly rulers no alarm – unless they wish to claim more for themselves than an earthly ruler should".[89]

Eine solche apologetische Tendenz zerbricht, da der religiöse Anspruch der Herrscherpropaganda, der zugleich dem Zusammenhalt des Reiches dient,[90] an seinen Wurzeln hinterfragt wird. So wird im vierten Evangelium auch keine

---

[88] Zu beachten bleibt, dass in Joh 3 der Zentralbegriff des synoptischen und auch des historischen Jesus, die βασιλεία τοῦ θεοῦ, in der ζωὴ αἰώνιος überführt wird; vgl. hierzu J. FREY, Eschatologie III, 248–282. Für Frey ergibt sich aus dem Begriff der βασιλεία zudem eine Klammer; sie „umrahmt somit das Wirken und Reden des johanneischen Jesus, doch während am Anfang in Aufnahme der älteren Tradition von der Königsherrschaft *Gottes* die Rede ist, ist dieses Motiv am Ende durch die Rede von der Königswürde *Jesu* ersetzt" (aaO., 271). Im Kreuz verwirklicht sich nach Johannes die Gottesherrschaft als „*Herrschaft des Gekreuzigten*" (aaO., 276).
[89] B.A. MASTIN, Cult, 363.
[90] Vgl. z.B. S.R.F. PRICE, Rituals, 239–248: „The imperial cult, along with politics and diplomacy, constructed the reality of the Roman empire" (aaO., 248).

positive Rolle des Staates entfaltet. Sind die Frauen und Männer in der Nachfolge Jesu dem Hass der Welt ausgesetzt (15,18f), dem sie in Liebe untereinander begegnen sollen (15,17; s.a. 13,34; 15,12), so gehören sie mit Jesus in einen anderen Herrschaftsbereich, in dem sie trotz der physischen Bedrohung als die Geretteten das Leben haben. Entscheidend ist das Bleiben an Jesus (Joh 15,4), das sich in liebender Zuwendung zueinander (13,34f; 15,12f) und in der Sendung an die Welt vollzieht (15,16f). Der Fürbitte für die Obrigkeit wird anders als etwa in den Pastoralbriefen kein Raum zugemessen, was dort gerade ein Zeichen für Loyalität in der christologisch begründeten Distanz zum Kaiserkult darstellt (1Tim 2,1f; Tit 2,12).[91]

Natürlich kann gefragt werden, ob die fehlende Reflexion der staatlichen Macht im Selbstverständnis des johanneischen Kreises begründet ist. Als mögliche Antwort sollte nicht von sektiererischer Weltabgewandtheit gesprochen werden.[92] Dem widerspricht die universelle Orientierung des im Sohn Fleisch gewordenen Heils. Auch der Verzicht auf materielle ethische Aussagen bzw. die christologische Orientierung können dieses Schweigen nicht erklären. Vielmehr zielt der Verfasser des vierten Evangeliums auf das rechte Verhalten des Auditoriums bzw. der Leserschaft seines Evangeliums angesichts des verkündigten Jesus (Joh 20,30f). Jede Größe, die mit diesem Ziel konkurriert, wird zur Welt als der sich Gottes Wahrheit verweigernden Finsternis gerechnet. Daran werden aber nicht nur der Kaiser und seine Herrschaft gemessen. In seinem Repräsentanten Pilatus, der konfrontiert mit dem Heilskönig die unverständige Frage nach der Wahrheit stellt (18,38), verweigern sich römische Herrschaft und Gesellschaft der Wahrheit und dem Leben[93] wie ‚die Juden', die sich in der Erzählwelt auf die Seite dieses irdisch-politischen Reiches stellen (19,15).[94] Hierzu sind auch die kleinasiatischen Städte und ihre Bevölkerung zu rechnen, soweit sie ihre gesellschaftliche und machtpolitische Struktur über den Kaiserkult zu definieren suchen. So geht die Ausgrenzung nicht auf den fernen Kaiser in Rom, sondern auf die Welt, in der sich die johanneische Gemeinde mit der Ablehnung des Retters durch die Welt konfrontiert findet. Indem sich Jesus in seinem Reden und Handeln als Heiland der Welt, „als *Beherrscher der chaotischen Wassermächte und auch als Herr der lebensbedrohenden Naturmächte und damit in der Machtfülle Jahwes*",[95] als Täter kaiserlicher Wunder und als König, als Herr und Gott vorstellt, bestreitet dies jeden legitimen Anspruch göttlicher *auctoritas*, wie er in der Herrscherpropaganda entfaltet wird. Handelt Jesus in der Einheit mit Gott, weil er aus der Einheit mit Gott stammt (programmatisch in der generellen Leseinstruktion des

---

[91] So M. REISER, Christentum, 35f.
[92] Vgl. dagegen z.B. K. SCHOLTISSEK, Johannes, 42–51.
[93] Im Gegensatz zur markinischen Kreuzigungsszene, wo der römische Hauptmann über Jesus ausruft: Ἀληθῶς οὗτος ὁ ἄνθρωπος υἱὸς θεοῦ ἦν (Mk 15,39); eine Szene, die eine beachtliche Nähe zum samaritanischen Bekenntnis in Joh 4,42 aufweist.
[94] Hierzu s.o. S. 157.
[95] M. LABAHN, Offenbarung, 214.

Evangeliums, dem Prolog, vorangestellt:[96] 1,1; s.a. 1,18) und in sie zurückkehrt und somit Gott ist, so trifft ihn nicht der Vorwurf, dass er sich Gott gleich mache (5,18).[97] Ganz anders aber ist in dieser Perspektive der Anspruch des Kaisers zu sehen, dessen Ambition neben Jesus durch nichts legitimiert ist. Mit dem Kaiser ist wiederum der *Kosmos* betroffen, der die Auslegung Gottes durch seinen Logos als das wahre göttliche Heil nicht anerkennt und damit anderen Institutionen religiöser Verehrung des Kaiserreichs heilbringende Funktionen zuschreibt.[98]

Trotz dieser Bewertung des römischen Kaisers und damit auch der durch seine Verehrung sich selbst definierenden Gesellschaft kann auch das Phänomen des Kaiserkultes nicht als *der* hermeneutische Schlüssel des vierten Evangeliums betrachtet werden. Wie die Spuren der Auseinandersetzung mit der jüdischen Synagoge verweisen auch die Parallelen zum Kaiserkult darauf, dass die zeitgeschichtlichen politischen Entwicklungen, religiösen Ansprüche und gesellschaftlichen Veränderungen ein beachtenswerter Hintergrund der neutestamentlichen Schriften sind; diese weithin anerkannte Aussage gilt auch für die Interpretation des von *Clemens Alexandrinus* als ‚pneumatisches Evangelium' der Wirklichkeit entrückten Johannesevangeliums (bei Euseb, h.e. 6,14,7). Es gehört zur Fleischwerdung des Logos, dass die Konflikte der sich zu ihm bekennenden Gemeinde und ihr Ringen darum, die christologischen Erfahrungen in angemessene Sprache und Bilder zu fassen, Gegenstand der Auslegung dieses Evangeliums sind.

---

[96] Zur leserleitenden Funktion des Prologs vgl. z.B. F.J. MOLONEY, Belief, 12: „He (sc. the author) is interested in the reader's being called to decision in the light of what has been told in the prologue". S.a. J. ZUMSTEIN, Prozess, 21f; DERS., Prolog, *passim*, U. SCHNELLE, Johannes, 18.

[97] Übersehen werden darf nicht, wem jeweils vorgeworfen wird, sich selbst Gott gleich zu machen; vgl. 2Mac 9,11f (Antiochus IV. Epiphanes); PsSal 2,25–29 (Pompeius); Philo Leg Gai 114.118.162; Jos Ant 19,4 (Gaius Caligula).

[98] In seiner Auslegung von Joh 19,11 findet R. METZNER, Verständnis, 260, in diesem Vers „das letzte und grundsätzliche Urteil Jesu über die Schuld der ‚Juden'" als „*theologische(s) Grundsatzurteil* über die gottfeindliche Welt" gesprochen; die gesellschaftspolitischen Konnotationen dieses Urteils sollten m.E. angesichts der Machtfrage und des zur Diskussion stehenden Königstitels nicht übersehen werden.

Literatur

ALKIER, Stefan, Wunder und Wirklichkeit in den Briefen des Apostels Paulus. Ein Beitrag zu einem Wunderverständnis jenseits von Entmythologisierung und Rehistorisierung, WUNT 134, Tübingen 2001.
AX, Wilhelm, Plutarch. Moralia, Sammlung Dieterichs 47, Leipzig 1950.
BARIÉ, Paul/SCHINDLER, Winfried, Martial. Epigramme. Lateinisch und deutsch, TuscBü, Darmstadt 1999.
BARTHES, Roland, S/Z, stw 687, Frankfurt a.M. 1987.
BAUER, Walter, Das Johannesevangelium, HNT 6, Tübingen ³1933.
BECKER, Jürgen, Das Evangelium des Johannes. Kapitel 1–10, ÖTbK 4/1, Gütersloh / Würzburg ³1991.
DERS., Jesus von Nazareth, GLB, Berlin – New York 1996.
BENGTSON, Hermann, Die Flavier. Vespasian, Titus, Domitian. Geschichte eines römischen Kaiserhauses, München 1979.
BERGER, Klaus, Exegese des Neuen Testaments. Neue Wege vom Text zur Auslegung, UTB 658, Heidelberg 1977.
DERS., Formgeschichte des Neuen Testaments, Heidelberg 1984.
BEUTLER, Johannes, Die Johannesbriefe, RNT, Regensburg 2000.
BLANK, Josef, Das Evangelium nach Johannes. 1. Teil a, GSL 4/1a, Düsseldorf 1981.
BREYTENBACH, Clilliers, Zeus und Jupiter auf dem Zion und dem Berg Garizim. Die Hellenisierung und Romanisierung der Kultstätten des Höchsten, in: JSJ 28 (1997), 369–380.
BROER, Ingo, Das Weinwunder zu Kana (Joh 2,1–11) und die Weinwunder der Antike, in: Das Urchristentum in seiner literarischen Geschichte. Festschrift für Jürgen Becker zum 65. Geburtstag. Hg.v. Ulrich MELL u. Ulrich B. MÜLLER, BZNW 100, Berlin – New York 1999, 291–308.
BULTMANN, Rudolf, Das Evangelium des Johannes, KEK 2, Göttingen ²⁰1985.
BUSSE, Ulrich, Metaphorik in neutestamentlichen Wundergeschichten? Mk 1,21–28; Joh 9,1–41, in: Metaphorik und Mythos im Neuen Testament, hg. v. Karl KERTELGE, QD 126, Freiburg u.a. 1990, 110–134.
CASSIDY, Richard J., John's Gospel in New Perspective. Christology and the Realities of Roman Power, Maryknoll, NY, 1992.
CLAUSS, Manfred, *Deus praesens*. Der römische Kaiser als Gott, in: Klio 78 (1996), 400–433.
DERS., Kaiser und Gott. Herrscherkult im römischen Reich, Stuttgart – Leipzig 1999.
COLLINS, Adela Yarbro, Rulers, Divine Men, and Walking on the Water (Mark 6:45–52), in: Religious Propaganda and Missionary Competition in the New Testament World. Essays Honoring Dieter Georgi. Ed. by Lukas BORMANN, Kelly DEL TREDICI, Angela STANDHARTINGER, NT.S 74, Leiden u.a. 1994, 207–227.
DIES., The Worship of Jesus and the Imperial Cult, in: The Jewish Roots of Christological Monotheism. Papers from St. Andrews Conference on the Historical Origins of the Worship of Jesus, ed. by Carley C. NEWMAN, James R. DAVILA, Gladys S. LEWIS, JSJ.S 63, Leiden u.a. 1999, 234–257.
CUSS, Dominique, Imperial Cult and Honorary Terms in the New Testament, Paradosis XXIII, Freiburg, CH, 1974.
DALY-DENTON, Margaret, David in the Fourth Gospel. The Johannine Reception of the Psalms, AGJU 47, Leiden, Boston, Köln 2000.

DEISSMANN, Adolf, Licht vom Osten. Das Neue Testament und die neuentdeckten Texte der hellenistisch-römischen Welt, Tübingen [4]1923.

DSCHULNIGG, Peter, Jesus begegnen. Personen und ihre Bedeutung im Johannesevangelium, Theologie 30, Münster 2000.

DUKE, Paul D., Irony in the Fourth Gospel, Atlanta 1985.

ECK, Werner, Art. Domitianus [1], in: KP 3 (1993), 746–750.

ECO, Umberto, Lector in fabula. Die Mitarbeit der Interpretation in erzählenden Texten, dtv 30141, München [3]1998.

ELLIGER, Winfried, Dion Chrysostomos. Sämtliche Reden, BAW.GR, Zürich – Stuttgart 1967.

ENGEMANN, Josef, Art. Hirt, in: RAC 15 (1991), 577–607.

FOERSTER, Werner, Art. σωτήρ A. σωτήρ im Griechentum, in ThWNT 7 (1964), 1004–1012.

FREY, Jörg, Die johanneische Eschatologie. Band II. Das johanneische Zeitverständnis, WUNT 110, Tübingen 1998.

DERS., Die johanneische Eschatologie. Bd. III: Die eschatologische Verkündigung in den johanneischen Texten, WUNT 117, Tübingen 2000.

FREIS, Helmut, Historische Inschriften zur römischen Kaiserzeit von Augustus bis Konstantin, TzF 49, Darmstadt [2]1994.

HÄUPTLI, Bruno W., Publius Ovidius Naso. Ibis. Fragmente. Ovidiana, TuscBü, Zürich – Düsseldorf 1996.

HAND, Wayland D., The Curing Of Blindness In Folk Tales, in: Volksüberlieferung. Festschrift für Kurt RANKE zur Vollendung des 60. Lebensjahres. Hg. v. Fritz HARKORT, Karel C. PETERS u. Robert WILDHABER, Göttingen 1968, 81–87.

HERZ, Peter, Bibliographie zum römischen Kaiserkult (1955–1975), in: ANRW II 16,2 (1978), 833–910.

DERS., Der römische Kaiser und der Kaiserkult. Gott oder primus inter pares?, in: Dieter ZELLER (Hrsg.), Menschwerdung Gottes – Vergöttlichung von Menschen, NTOA 7, Freiburg (Schweiz)/Göttingen 1988, 115–140.

DERS., „Aus dem Osten wird ein Retter kommen ..." Der Widerstand der Griechen gegen die römische Herrschaft, in: Hans WISSMANN (Hrsg.), Zur Erschließung von Zukunft in den Religionen. Zukunftserwartung und Gegenwartsbewältigung in der Religionsgeschichte, Würzburg 1991, 67–88.

HOLZBERG, Niklas, Martial, Heidelberger Studienhefte zur Altertumswissenschaft, Heidelberg 1988.

HÜBNER, Hans, Art. ἀλήθεια κτλ., in: EWNT 1 ([2]1992), 138–145.

JACOBY, Adolf, Zur Heilung des Blinden von Bethsaida, in: ZNW 10 (1909), 185–194.

JONES, Brian W., The Emperor Domitian, London – New York [2]1993.

KARRER, Martin, Jesus Christus im Neuen Testament, GNT 11, Göttingen 1998.

KEE, Howard Clark, Miracle in the Early Christian World. A Study in Sociohistorical Method, New Haven – London 1983

KLAUCK, Hans-Josef, Die religiöse Umwelt des Urchristentums II. Herrscher- und Kaiserkult, Philosophie, Gnosis, Studienbücher Theologie 9,2, Stuttgart u.a. 1996.

KOESTER, Craig R., 'The Savior of the World' (John 4:42), in: JBL 109 (1990), 665–680.

KOLLMANN, Bernd, Jesus und die Christen als Wundertäter. Studien zu Magie, Medizin und Schamanismus in Antike und Christentum, FRLANT 170, Göttingen 1996.

KOSKENNIEMI, Erkki, Apollonius von Tyana in der neutestamentlichen Exegese. Forschungsbericht und Weiterführung der Diskussion, WUNT 61, Tübingen 1994.

KOTTSIEPER, Ingo, Zusätze zu Ester, in: Odil Hannes STECK/Reinhard G. KRATZ/Ingo KOTTSIEPER, Das Buch Baruch, Der Brief des Jeremia, Zusätze zu Ester und Daniel, ATD. Apokryphen 5, Göttingen 1998, 109–207.

KÜGLER, Joachim, Der andere König. Religionsgeschichtliche Perspektiven auf die Christologie des Johannesevangeliums, SBS 178, Stuttgart 1999.

KÜHN, Werner, Plinius der Jüngere. Panegyricus. Lobrede auf den Kaiser Trajan, TzF 51, Darmstadt 1985.

KVALBEIN, Hans, Die Wunder der Endzeit. Beobachtungen zu 4Q521 und Matth 11,5p, in: ZNW 88 (1997), 111–125.

LABAHN, Michael, Jesus als Lebensspender. Untersuchungen zu einer Geschichte der johanneischen Tradition anhand ihrer Wundergeschichten, BZNW 98, Berlin – New York 1999.

DERS., Between Tradition and Literary Art. The Miracle Tradition in the Fourth Gospel, in: Bib 80 (1999), 178–203.

DERS., Offenbarung in Zeichen und Wort. Untersuchungen zur Vorgeschichte von Joh 6,1–25a und seiner Rezeption in der Brotrede, WUNT II/117, Tübingen 2000.

DERS., Rez. J. Kügler, Der andere König (s.o.), in: SNTU.A 25 (2000), 259f.

DERS., Controversial Revelation in Deed and Word. The Feeding of the Five Thousand and Jesus' Crossing of the Sea as a 'Prelude' to the Johannine Bread of Life Discourse, in: IBS 22 (2000), 146–181.

DERS., The Significance of Eschatological Signs in Luke 7:22–23, in Comparison with Isaiah 61 and Qumran's 4Q521, in: From Prophecy to Testament: The Function of the Old Testament in the New, ed. by Craig A. EVANS, Peabody (erscheint voraussichtlich 2002).

LANG, Manfred, Johannes und die Synoptiker. Eine redaktionskritische Analyse von Joh 18–20 vor dem markinischen und lukanischen Hintergrund, FRLANT 182, Göttingen 1999.

LOHMEYER, Ernst, Christuskult und Kaiserkult, Tübingen 1919.

MADDEN, Patrick J., Jesus' Walking on the Sea. An Investigation of the Origin of the Narrative Account, BZNW 81, Berlin – New York 1997.

MAGIE, David, De romanorum iuris publici sacrique vocabulis sollemnibus in graecum sermonen conversis, Leipzig 1905.

DERS., Roman Rule in Asia Minor to the End of the Third Century after Christ, 2Bde., Princeton 1950.

MARTIN, Alain, La titulature épigraphique de Domitien, BKP 181, Frankfurt a.M., 1987.

MASTIN, B.A., The Imperial Cult and the Ascription of the Title Θεός to Jesus (John XX.28), in: Studia Evangelica VI. Ed. by Elizabeth A. LIVINGSTONE, TU 112, Berlin 1973, 352–365.

MERKELBACH, Reinhold, Die ephesinischen Dionysosmysten vor der Stadt, in: ZPE 36 (1979), 151–156.

METZNER, Rainer, Das Verständnis der Sünde im Johannesevangelium, WUNT 122, Tübingen 2000.

MOLES, John L., Cynic Cosmopolitanism, in: The Cynics. The Cynic Movement in Antiquity and Its Legacy, ed. by R. Bracht BRANHAM and Marie-Dile GOULET-CAZÉ, Hellenistic Culture and Society 23, Berkeley u.a. 1996, 105–120.

MOLONEY, Francis J., From Cana to Cana (John 2:1–4:54) and the Fourth Evangelist's Concept of Correct (and Incorrect) Faith, in: Studia Biblica 1978 II, ed. by Elizabeth A. LIVINGSTONE, JSNT.S 2, Sheffield 1980, 185–213.

DERS., Mary in the Fourth Gospel: Woman and Mother, in: Sal. 51 (1989), 421–440.

DERS., Belief in the Word. Reading John 1–4, Minneapolis, MN, 1993.
DERS., The Gospel of John, Sacra Pagina 4, Collegeville 1998.
MORENZ, Siegfried, Vespasian, Heiland der Kranken. Persönliche Frömmigkeit im antiken Herrscherkult?, in: Würzburger Jahrbücher für die Altertumswissenschaft 4 (1949/50), 370–378.
NEUER WETTSTEIN. Texte zum Neuen Testament aus Griechentum und Hellenismus. Band I/2. Texte zum Johannesevangelium. Hg.v. Udo SCHNELLE u. Mitarb. v. Michael LABAHN u. Manfred LANG, Berlin – New York 2001.
OSTER, Richard A., Ephesus as a Religious Center under the Principate, I. Paganism before Constantine, in: ANRW II 18.2 (1990), 1661–1728.
DERS., Art. Ephesus, in: Anchor Bible Dictionary 2 (1992), 542–549.
PIPPIDI, Dionisie M., Inscriptiones Scythiae Minoris Graecae et Latinae I, Inscriptiones Daciae et Scythiae Minoris Antiquae II, Academia Scientiarum Socialum et Politicarum Dacoromana, Bukarest 1983.
POHLENZ, Max, Die Stoa. Geschichte einer geistigen Bewegung, Göttingen ^{4}1970.
PRICE, S.R.F., Rituals and Power. The Roman Imperial Cult in Asia Minor, ND Cambridge 1985.
REISER, Marius, Bürgerliches Christentum in den Pastoralbriefen, in: Bib 74 (1993), 27–44.
SAUTER, Franz, Der römische Kaiserkult bei Martial und Statius, TBAW 21, Stuttgart – Berlin 1934.
SCHALLER, Gottfried Jakob, Dionysius von Halikarnaß Werke. Viertes Bändchen, Stuttgart 1832.
SCHEITHAUER, Andrea, Epigraphische Studien zur Herrscherideologie I. salvis Augustis felix... Enstehung und Geschichte eines Formulars, in: ZPE 114 (1996), 213–226.
SCHENKE, Ludger, Johannes. Kommentar, Kommentare zu den Evangelien, Düsseldorf 1998.
SCHLESIER, Renate, Art. Dionysos (Διονύσος). I. Religion, in: DNP 3 (1997), 651–662.
SCHNELLE, Udo, Johannes als Geisttheologe, in: NT 40 (1998), 17–31.
DERS., Die Juden im Johannesevangelium, in: Gedenkt an das Wort. Festschrift für Werner VOGLER zum 65. Geburtstag, hg.v. Christoph KÄHLER, Martina BÖHM, Christfried BÖTTRICH, Leipzig 1999, 217–230.
DERS., Einleitung in das Neue Testament, UTB 1830, Göttingen ^{3}1999.
DERS., Das Evangelium nach Johannes, ThHK 4, Leipzig ^{2}2000.
SCHOLTISSEK, Klaus, Ironie und Rollenwechsel im Johannesevangelium, in: ZNW 89 (1998), 235–255.
DERS., Antijudaismus im Johannesevangelium. Ein Gesprächsbeitrag, in: Rainer KAMPLING (Hg.), „Nun steht aber diese Sache im Evangelium ..." Zur Frage nach den Anfängen des christlichen Antijudaismus, Paderborn 1999, 151–181.
DERS., Johannes auslegen I. Forschungsgeschichtliche und methodische Reflexionen, in: SNTU.A 24 (1999), 35–84.
SCHRAGE, Wolfgang, Art. τυφλός κτλ., in: ThWNT 8 (1969), 270–294.
SCHREIBER, Stefan, Gesalbter und König. Titel und Konzeptionen der königlichen Gesalbtenerwartung in frühjüdischen und urchristlichen Schriften, BZNW 105, Berlin – New York 2000.
DERS., Rätsel um den König. Zur religionsgeschichtlichen Herkunft des König-Titels im Johannesevangelium, in: Stefan SCHREIBER/Alois STIMPFLE (Hg.), Johannes aenigmaticus. Studien zum Johannesevangelium für Herbert LEROY, BU 29, Regensburg 2000, 45–70.

SIEGERT, Folker, Drei hellenistisch-jüdische Predigten. Ps.-Philon, „Über Jona", „Über Simson" und „Über die Gottesbezeichnung ‚wohltätig verzehrendes Feuer'": I. Übersetzung aus dem Armenischen und sprachliche Erläuterungen, WUNT 20, Tübingen 1980, II. Kommentar nebst Beobachtungen zur hellenistischen Vorgeschichte der Bibelhermeneutik, WUNT 61, Tübingen 1992.

SÖDING, Thomas, Die Macht der Wahrheit und das Reich der Freiheit. Zur johanneischen Deutung des Pilatus-Prozesses (Joh 18,28–19,16), in: ZThK 93 (1996), 35–58.

STRELAN, Rick, A Greater Than Caesar: Storm Stories in Lucan and Mark, in: ZNW 91 (2000), 166–179.

TAEGER, Fritz, Charisma. Studien zur Geschichte des antiken Herrscherkultes, 2 Bde., Stuttgart 1957. 1960.

TALBERT, Charles H., Reading John. A Literary and Theological Commentary on the Fourth Gospel and the Johannine Epistles, New York, NY, 1992.

TAYLOR, Lily Ross, The Divinity of the Roman Emperor, Philological Monographs published by the American Philological Association, Middletown 1931.

TITZMANN, Michael, Strukturale Textanalyse. Theorie und Praxis der Interpretation, UTB 582, München ³1993.

TURNER, John D., The History of Religions Background of John 10, in: Johannes BEUTLER/Robert T. FORTNA (eds.), The Shepherd Discourse of John 10 and its Context, SNTSMS 67, Cambridge 1991, 33–52. 147–150.

WENDLAND, Ernst A., A Tale of Two Debtors: On the Interaction of Text, Cotext, and Context in a New Testament Dramatic Narrative (Luke 7:36–50), in: Linguistics and New Testament Interpretation, ed. by D.A. BLACK with K. BARNWELL and S. LEVINSOHN, Nashville 1992, 101–143.

WENDLAND, Paul, Σωτήρ. Eine religionsgeschichtliche Untersuchung, in: ZNW 5 (1904), 335–353.

WILHELM, Adolf, Nr. XV–XVIII, in: AAWW.PH, Wien 1922, 43–84.

WILCKENS, Ulrich, Das Evangelium nach Johannes, NTD 4, Göttingen 1998.

WINKLER, Lorenz, Salus. Vom Staatskult zur politischen Idee. Eine Archäologische Untersuchung, Archäologie und Geschichte 4, Heidelberg 1995.

WITTSTOCK, Otto, Sueton. Kaiserbiographien, Schriften und Quellen der Alten Welt 39, Berlin 1993.

ZANGENBERG, Jürgen, ΣAMAPEIA. Antike Quellen zur Geschichte und Kultur der Samaritaner in deutscher Übersetzung, TANZ 15, Tübingen – Basel 1994.

DERS., Frühes Christentum in Samarien. Topographische und traditionsgeschichtliche Studien zu den Samariatexten im Johannesevangelium, TANZ 27, Tübingen – Basel 1998.

ZELLER, Dieter, Ägyptische Königsideologie im Neuen Testament? Fug und Unfug religionsgeschichtlichen Vergleichens, in: Axel VON DOBBELER, Kurt ERLEMANN, Roman HEILIGENTHAL (Hg.), Religionsgeschichte des Neuen Testaments. Festschrift für Klaus BERGER zum 60. Geburtstag, Tübingen – Basel 2000, 541–552.

ZIETHEN, Gabriele, Heilung und römischer Kaiserkult, in: Sudhoffs Archiv 78 (1994), 171–190.

ZUMSTEIN, Jean, Der Prozess der Relecture in der johanneischen Literatur, in: DERS., Kreative Erinnerung. Relecture und Auslegung im Johannesevangelium, Zürich 1999, 15–30.

DERS., Der Prolog, Schwelle zum Evangelium, in: aaO., 78–98.

Martin Meiser

Lukas und die römische Staatsmacht

In einer Zeit längst fortgeschrittener Säkularisierung unserer Gesellschaft ist auch eine Neubesinnung des Verhältnisses zwischen Kirche und Staatsgewalt durchaus angezeigt. Es kann zwar nicht darum gehen, im unmittelbaren Rückgriff auf neutestamentliche Aussagen unser heutiges Verhältnis als Christengemeinde gegenüber dem legitimieren zu wollen, was sich bei uns als moderner Staat entwickelt hat. Christliche Gemeinde steht heute nicht am Anfang ihrer eigenen Geschichte, sondern erfährt diese auch noch in einer nachchristlichen Zeit als Chance und auch als Problem; der moderne weltanschaulich neutrale Staat ist nicht mit dem Staat des römischen Prinzipates zu verwechseln. Dennoch oder vielleicht gerade deswegen kann uns das Nachdenken vom Neuen Testament her wenigstens unsere eigene christliche Gegenwart als geschichtlich bedingt und als nicht selbstverständlich wahrnehmen lassen.

Freilich scheint unter den biblischen Zeugnissen zum Verhältnis zwischen Christentum und Staat der Beitrag des lukanischen Doppelwerkes der am wenigsten Weiterführende zu sein. An Einseitigkeit der Darstellung der Römer steht Lukas den Worten des Paulus in Röm 13,1–7 kaum nach. Zusätzlich belastet uns heute die lukanische Darstellung der Juden, soweit sie nicht an Jesus glauben. Unverkennbar ist der Gedanke leitend, den der lukanische Paulus in Apg 28,17–19 in der Rückschau auf seinen Prozeß formuliert: „Die Römer" hätten ihn freigelassen, wenn nicht „die Juden" widersprochen hätten, ein mit Apg 26,32 kaum in Einklang zu bringender Satz.[1]

Eine einprägsame Aufstellung der Akte römischen Wohlwollens hat Ernst Haenchen gegeben: „Der Prokurator Sergius Paulus hat sich bekehren lassen, der Prokurator Gallio hat eine jüdische Klage gegen Paulus abgewiesen, die mit der Förderung des Kaiserkults betrauten Asiarchen[2] sind teilweise mit Paulus befreundet (Apg 19,31), der Kanzler in Ephesus verteidigt die Christen gegen den Vorwurf der Asebie (Apg 19,37), der Kommandeur von Jerusalem, Claudius Lysias, und die Statthalter Felix und Festus lehnen eine Verurteilung des Paulus ab (Apg 23,29; 24,22; 25,4.16.25; vgl. Apg 26,32), und Paulus darf

---

[1] Vgl. T. MOMMSEN, Rechtsverhältnisse, 93 Anm 1. Selbst wenn Mommsens Hinweis auf das lukanische Nichtverstehen der juristischen Materie in diesem Text zeitbedingt verkennt, daß der Bemerkung Apg 28,17–19 vornehmlich leserlenkende Funktion zukommt, kann dies umso deutlicher die problematische (von B. WANDER, Apologien, 466 Anm 2 m.E. zu Unrecht bestrittene) Tendenz des Lukas unterstreichen, die Juden zu belasten.

[2] Die Freundschaft der Asiarchen mit Paulus wäre weniger anrüchig, wenn man sie nicht als Beamte zur Förderung des Kaiserkultes, sondern nur als Mitglieder des Landtages zu Ephesus ohne kultische Aufgaben ansehen dürfte. Doch ist nach A. MEHL, Asiarchie, 80, aufgrund der literarischen und epigraphischen Belege die „Gleichsetzung von Oberpriester und Asiarches ... zu bevorzugen".

ungehindert als Gefangener in Rom missionieren".[3] Bekannt ist auch die Menschenfreundlichkeit des römischen Offiziers Apg 27[4] sowie vor allem das positive Bild römischer Soldaten in Lk 3,14; 7,1–10; Apg 10. Ergänzend kann man auf Widersprüche zwischen Paulus und Lukas, die das Ende des Aufenthaltes in Philippi betreffen,[5] verweisen wie auch auf die Widersprüche zwischen historischer Wirklichkeit und lukanischer Darstellung. Diese geht stets zu Lasten der Juden, die als Feinde Jesu und als Verfolger des Apostels Paulus dargestellt werden.[6] Daß christliche Gemeinde *auf Kosten des Judentums* vor den heidnischen Römern ihre Unschuld erweist, ist heute gewiß am allerwenigsten nachzuvollziehen.

Nun gibt es bei Lukas auch Texte, die ein rein positives Bild des Imperium Romanum in Frage stellen: das Zusammenwirken des Herodes und Pilatus zur Vernichtung Jesu Apg 4,27, die nach Apg 2,10 erstmalige Erwähnung der „Römer" in Apg 16,21 in einem negativen Zusammenhang, die panegyrische Verherrlichung der Qualitäten des Antonius Felix ausgerechnet im Munde des Christengegners Tertullus Apg 24,2–4,[7] der Hinweis auf die Habsucht des Antonius Felix in Apg 24,22–27[8] und dessen wie seines Nachfolgers Ansinnen, den Juden eine Gunst zu erweisen in Apg 24,27; 25,9. Und für den lukanischen Christen gilt das an Sokrates erinnernde Wort „Man soll Gott mehr gehorchen denn den Menschen" (Apg 5,29). Aber sind diese wenigen kritischen Bemerkungen bei Lukas nicht lediglich der Tribut an das Unvermeidliche, das angesichts des gewaltsamen Lebensendes bei Jesus und Paulus auszusagen war? Kann eine solche beschönigende Darstellung römischer Staatsmacht uns heute hilfreich sein?

1. Forschungsgeschichtlicher Überblick und methodische Überlegungen

Ein Blick auf die Forschungsgeschichte zeigt, daß keineswegs ein Konsens besteht hinsichtlich der lukanischen Intention. Wollte Lukas die Christen sei-

---

[3] E. HAENCHEN, Apostelgeschichte, 113.
[4] Vgl. dazu M. LABAHN, Paulus.
[5] Nach Apg 16,39 gehen die Prediger nach ihrer Entlassung aus dem Gefängnis in voller Freiheit. „Diese Rehabilitierung ist durch I Th nicht gedeckt" (H. CONZELMANN, Apostelgeschichte, 103).
[6] K. WENGST, Pax Romana, 121.124f., verweist auf Lk 23,1–25 sowie auf Apg 9,23f diff. 2 Kor 11,32f; Apg 17,5 diff. 1Thess 2,14.
[7] S. LÖSCH, Tertullus, stellt zu Recht heraus, daß der Abschnitt von einem „Kenner redetechnischer Formen herrühren muß" (317), der die „Einzelheiten der Regeln der Lobrede auf eine neuere bessere Zeit zum Ruhme eines provinzialen Vertreters der kaiserlichen Regierung, wie sie in jenem Jahrzehnt mit besonderer Vorliebe gehandhabt wurden", beherrsche, faßt den Text jedoch als unverändert aufgenommenes vorlukanisches „Aktenmaterial" (319) auf.
[8] Die Darstellung von Apg 24,22–27 ist nach T. MOMMSEN, Rechtsverhältnisse, 88, „alles andere als römerfreundlich".

ner Zeit bei ihrer Verteidigung beraten?[9] Will er die Duldung des Christentums als des wahren Judentums seitens der römischen Obrigkeit erwirken?[10] Will er, im Bewußtsein kommender Bedrängnisse, das Unrecht der gegenüber den Christen vorgebrachten Beschuldigungen erweisen?[11] Hofft Lukas „auf eine wohlwollende Neutralität Roms auch für seine eigene Zeit, ja eine Garantie für den Freiraum einer ungehinderten Entfaltung der Kirche",[12] hofft er, daß die römischen Behörden zu seiner Zeit die Sache Jesu genauso beurteilen wie die Statthalter den Prozeß des Paulus?[13] Appelliert Lukas „an die Traditionen römischen Rechts und römischer Politik, keinen Zwang in Glaubensdingen auszuüben, sondern nur kriminelle Vergehen gerichtlich zu ahnden"?[14] Hofft er, mit seiner politischen Apologetik „einzelne heidnische Leser zu erreichen und für die Sache der Christen zu gewinnen"?[15] Ist es sein Ziel, „Christentum und Staat dauerhaft auszusöhnen",[16] erstrebt er eine Synthese zwischen beiden?[17] Ist er der Überzeugung, „daß die Einheit der Welt unter dem Zepter des römischen Kaisers dem vom Weltenlenker gefaßten Plan für die Ausbreitung seiner Heilsbotschaft dient"?[18] Oder wollte er umgekehrt eine apologia pro imperio präsentieren?[19]

In zwei neueren Beiträgen wird das Phänomen der Dreieckskonstellation zwischen Paulus, den Juden und den Römern als Element des „parting of the ways" zwischen Judentum und Christentum bedacht. Friedrich Wilhelm HORN formuliert als Erkenntnisgewinn der lukanischen Darstellung für den christlichen Leser: Das von Rom gezeigte Verhalten ist durch Druck seitens der religiösen Führung Israels veranlaßt. Der römische Leser, der vielleicht um die Urteile gegen Jesus und Paulus weiß, erfährt unter anderem: Mit der Herodesfamilie sind zuverlässige und ideale Zeugen aufgetreten, ideal wegen ihrer Romtreue, ihrer Kenntnis des Judentums und ihres Interesses am Christentum.[20] Nach Michael WOLTER thematisieren vor allem die in Apg 21–26 gesammelten Episoden nicht eigentlich das Verhältnis zwischen Christengemeinde und römischer Staatsmacht, sondern den Prozeß der Auseinanderentwicklung von Judentum und Christentum: Die Juden versuchen, die Verkündi-

---

[9] M. DIBELIUS, Paulus, 180.
[10] E. HAENCHEN, Apostelgeschichte, 663f.
[11] M. HENGEL, Geschichtsschreibung, 55; B. WANDER, Apologien, 474.
[12] W. SCHRAGE, Ethik, 163; vgl. schon E. HAENCHEN, Apostelgeschichte, 113, ferner J. ECKERT, Imperium Romanum, 266. Daß allerdings speziell um dieser Tendenz willen die Martyrien des Petrus und Paulus verschwiegen würden, halte ich nicht für zwingend.
[13] G. SCHNEIDER, Verleugnung, 194.
[14] J. MOLTHAGEN, Rom, 141. Nach Molthagen muß man „eine kaiserliche Initiative annehmen, die in rechtlich wirksamer Weise das Christstein im römischen Reich strafbar machte", in Form einer „an die Statthalter gerichtete(n) Verwaltungsanordnung Domitians" (138). Ist ein solches Postulat methodisch zulässig?
[15] W.G. KÜMMEL, Einleitung, 131.
[16] S. SCHULZ, Ethik, 480; vgl. schon H. CONZELMANN, Mitte, 129.
[17] V.K. ROBBINS, Luke-Acts, *passim*.
[18] A. DIHLE, Literatur, 223.
[19] P. WALASKAY, Rome, 64; J. ROLOFF, Kirche, 211.
[20] F.W. HORN, Haltung, 221.

gung des Evangeliums zu verhindern, die römische Staatsmacht wird unwissend zu ihrer Schutzmacht.[21] Ist dann die Themenstellung unseres Beitrages falsch gewählt?

Angesichts der Breite und der Brisanz des στάσις-Motives im lukanischen Doppelwerk scheint mir die adäquate Wahrnehmung der lukanischen politischen Apologetik immer noch der Mühe wert. Freilich gilt es, das Verhältnis zwischen positiven und gemäßigt kritischen Aussagen bei Lukas unter Voraussetzung christlicher Leserschaft des Doppelwerkes[22] nochmals zu überdenken. Denn die Funktion der wenigen kritischen Stellen ist häufig nicht wirklich geklärt.

Methodisch wird die Spannung zwischen den vielen positiven und den wenigen kritischen Äußerungen zur römischen Staatsmacht zumeist in der Weise gelöst, daß man letztere entweder der Tradition zuweist[23] oder ebenfalls positiv uminterpretiert.[24] Beides ist jedoch unbefriedigend: Die Zuweisung kritischer Aussagen an vorlukanische Traditionen ist angesichts der häufig gegebenen Schwierigkeit, solche Traditionen wortwörtlich zu rekonstruieren, zu sehr mit der Gefahr des Zirkelschlusses belastet. Überdies sieht sich dieser Ansatz angesichts des bekannten lukanischen Umgangs mit heikler, das Christentum inkriminierender Überlieferung der Frage ausgesetzt, warum Lukas eine kritische Tradition überhaupt in seinem Werk aufnimmt. Die positive Uminterpretation will nur bei einigen, aber nicht bei allen Aussagen gelingen. Weiterzuführen scheint mir das Ansinnen, unsere exegetischen Lesegewohnheiten des lukanischen Doppelwerkes kritisch zu hinterfragen, die zu sehr von der eigenen Erfahrung einer westlichen freiheitlichen Demokratie geprägt sind. Zwar wird durch solche Hinterfragung Lukas nun keineswegs zum Widerstandskämpfer par excellence, und doch wird man seine Leistung auf diesem Hintergrund gerechter beurteilen können.

Martin DIBELIUS hat aus dem Mißverhältnis zwischen der aufwendigen Darstellung des Paulusprozesses und dem Umstand, daß sein Ende dann gar nicht erzählt wird, die Intention des Lukas dahingehend erschlossen, den Christen seiner eigenen Zeit den Rat zu geben, die in Apg 21–26 ausgeführten Gedanken „zu ihrer Verteidigung zu gebrauchen. Sie sollen betonen, daß sie sich weder gegen den Kaiser noch gegen den Tempel noch gegen das Gesetz erhoben haben, und daß der wesentliche Streitpunkt zwischen ihnen und den Juden die Frage der Auferstehung ist"[25]. Anknüpfend daran sei die eigene These formuliert: Lukas will in seinem Doppelwerk angesichts zunehmender Repressalien in einer der politischen Situation angemessenen Weise seine christlichen Adressaten dazu befähigen, die Harmlosigkeit der eigenen Bewegung für das Imperium Romanum offensiv zu vertreten. Mit dieser These ist

---

[21] M. WOLTER, Juden, 277–290.
[22] Vgl. die implizite Warnung von F.W. HORN, Ethik, 56, den „Einfluß der Evangelienliteratur auf staatliche Instanzen" zu überschätzen.
[23] P. WALASKAY, Rome, 64.
[24] K. WENGST, Pax Romana, 122, zu Lk 22,25.
[25] M. DIBELIUS, Paulus, 180.

auch die Gliederung der folgenden Ausführungen gesetzt: Nach einem kurzen Blick auf die Situation der Christen im ausgehenden 1. Jh. n.Chr. ist die Erzählstrategie des Lukas darzustellen, von der aus die gegenseitige Zuordnung der einzelnen Aussagen vorgenommen werden kann.

2. Die Situation der Christen innerhalb des Imperium Romanum

Nach Wolfgang STEGEMANN[26] hat es eine regelrechte „Verfolgung" von Staats wegen nicht gegeben; Staatsorgane sind nicht initiierende Subjekte antichristlicher Maßnahmen, sondern Adressaten von Delationen von Diasporajuden (Apg 17,6f; 18,12) wie von Heiden (Apg 16,19; 19,23–27); Martyrien von Christen der eigenen Zeit scheint Lukas, so STEGEMANN, nicht zu kennen. Wohl aber kann von einer Gefährdung von Christen gesprochen werden: Sie werden von den Heiden noch als Juden angesehen, in allgemeiner antijüdischer Aggressivität mit Vorwürfen „typisch jüdischer" Handlungsweise belastet und möglicherweise wegen des *fiscus Iudaicus* belangt, während sich die Juden ihrerseits von den Christen distanzieren, um nicht selbst der Gefahr von Repressionen ausgesetzt zu sein. Das *nomen ipsum*[27] ist zur Zeit des Lukas noch kein Grund für Repressalien.

Die Vorwürfe an die Christen lauten auf unrömische ἔθη (Apg 16,21),[28] Lehre einer fremden βασιλεία (Apg 17,7), Lehre einer Gottesverehrung παρὰ τὸν νόμον (Apg 18,13),[29] βλασφημία und ἱεροσυλία gegenüber heidnischen Gottheiten (Apg 19,37),[30] στάσεις für alle Juden (Apg 24,5), Entheiligung des Tempels (Apg 24,6). Die Verteidigung des Paulus in Apg 25,8 faßt zusammen: Paulus hat weder gegen das Gesetz gelehrt, ihm darf also seine jüdische Identität nicht abgesprochen werden; er hat nichts gegen den Tempel gelehrt, d.h. er hat die Heiligkeit des Tempels ebenso gewahrt und sich damit nicht außerhalb des den Juden römischerseits zugestandenen Rahmens der Selbstverwaltung bewegt, und er hat nichts Unrechtes gegen den Kaiser gesagt, d.h. keine staatsgefährdenden Lehren vorgetragen.

Lukas weiß explizit von einem Martyrium unter römischer Staatsgewalt, von dem des Paulus. Man kann aber fragen, ob er nicht bereits um mehr Mar-

---

[26] W. STEGEMANN, Synagoge, *passim*.
[27] Arist Apol 15,8; Just 1 Apol. 4; Athenag Leg. 2.
[28] W.C. VAN UNNIK, Anklage, 383, erinnert an die mit dem Vorwurf der Untergrabung römischer Sitten begründete Vertreibung der Juden aus Rom 139 v. Chr. durch den Praetor Peregrinus Hispalus als *exemplum* für das Vorgehen der Behörden in Philippi.
[29] Lukas läßt bewußt doppeldeutig, ob das römische oder das jüdische Gesetz gemeint sein soll.
[30] Im Gegensatz zur βλασφημία fiele die ἱεροσυλία unter römisches Strafrecht (T. MOMMSEN, Religionsfrevel, 406). Inwieweit allerdings MOMMSENs strikte Trennung zwischen *iurisdictio* und *coercitio* für die Praxis der Provinzialmagistrate in der Prinzipatszeit haltbar ist, ist in rechtshistorischer Forschung umstritten, vgl. A. HEUSS, Entwicklung, 92; J. BLEICKEN, Rez. KUNKEL, 697.

tyrien weiß. Aufschlußreich ist, wie in Lk 21,12, anders als in Mk 13,9, die Reihenfolge von „Königen" und „Statthaltern" gewählt ist, um an den Geschehensablauf in Apg 12; 21–26 anzugleichen. Damit ist im lukanischen Sinn die Zuverlässigkeit der Worte Jesu bezeugt, die aber nicht einfach mit dem in Apg 12; 21–26 Berichteten abgegolten, sondern auch für die Gegenwart aktuell sind. Ferner kann man fragen, ob nicht der ausführliche Rückverweis auf Apg 25,5 in Apg 25,16 bereits das Problem der anonymen Delationen reflektiert.

3. Lukas als Schriftsteller innerhalb des Imperium Romanum

Wie ist die schriftstellerische Leistung des Lukas adäquat zu beschreiben? Unverkennbar sind der in Lk 1,1–4 und Apg 1,1f geäußerte literarische Anspruch und das gegenüber seinen Vorlagen verbesserte Griechisch, unverkennbar ist sein Bestreben nach sachgemäßem Ausdruck auch in den einschlägigen Amtsbezeichnungen: Herodes Antipas I. wird korrekt als Tetrarch bezeichnet, nicht als König,[31] während dieser Titel für Agrippa I. angemessen ist.[32] Philippi wird in Apg 16,12 zu Recht als römische Kolonie bezeichnet, was jedoch bei Thessaloniki und Korinth unterbleibt. In Thessaloniki ist die in Apg 17,6.8 genannte Amtsbezeichnung πολιτάρχαι auch archäologisch belegt.[33] Wenn allerdings Lukas mit dem Wortfeld ἡγεμών römische Statthalter wie Pontius Pilatus oder mit ἀνθύπατος die Prokonsuln Sergius Paulus und Iunius Annaeus Gallio benennt, dann entspricht dieser Sprachgebrauch zwar dem usus auch höherer griechischer Literatur,[34] doch sind die Titel nicht sehr präzise, ebensowenig wie der Titel στρατηγοί für die *duumviri* in Philippi.[35] Ἔπαρχος (*praefectus*) für Pilatus[36] und ἐπίτροπος (*procurator*) für Antonius Felix wären korrekt.[37]

---

[31] Lk 3,1.19; 9,7 diff. Mk 6,14.
[32] Vgl. Apg 12,20 und Philo Flacc 103.
[33] J. FINEGAN, Archeology, 108.
[34] Vgl. Philo Flacc 163: Flaccus ist ἡγεμών von Ägypten.
[35] H. CONZELMANN, Apostelgeschichte, z. St.: volkstümliche Bezeichnung. Hingegen gibt ῥαβδοῦχοι die Bezeichnung *lictores* angemessen wieder.
[36] Jos Ant 18,33.35.
[37] Vgl. Jos Bell 2,247. – Das Christentum ist nicht mehr nur Angelegenheit ‚kleiner Leute', vgl. E. PLÜMACHER, Apostelgeschichte, 517. Daß Lukas sich um Bildung bemüht, das Ziel aber nicht immer erreicht, ist auch anderweitig festzustellen: Der lukanische Paulus zitiert in Apg 17,28 bekanntlich aus den „Phainomena" des Aratos; der lukanische Jesus ist Hauptredner während mehrerer Gastmahlssituationen (Lk 11,37–52; 14,1–24), wie Sokrates in den Dialogen Platons; völlig unphilosophisch freilich erweist Jesus in Lk 14,1–6 die Berechtigung dazu anhand seiner Schlagfertigkeit im Kommentar zu einer vorausgegangenen Wunderhandlung. Die Dornen aus dem Sämannsgleichnis aktualisiert der lukanisch Jesus in Lk 8,14 u.a. durch die Verstrickungen in die ἡδοναὶ τοῦ βίου – philosophischer Schulterminologie gemäß hätte der einfache Singular ἡδονή völlig ausgereicht.

Besser weiß Lukas mit Einzelheiten aus römischem Recht umzugehen: Er weiß um den Sachverhalt der Lex Iulia und der Lex Porcia, er weiß um die Verlegung von Kapitalprozessen nach Rom, er weiß darum, daß man seit den Zeiten des Kaiser Claudius das Bürgerrecht[38] kaufen konnte,[39] und er spielt mit dem Topos der Überlegenheit des Altbürgers gegenüber dem gekauften Bürgerrecht.[40]

Lukas erstrebt eine Annäherung an die Werte der geistigen Elite, während er die wirtschaftlichen Eliten zum Besitzverzicht mahnt; auch kann er Lk 22,25 nur schreiben, weil er nicht selbst zur Oberschicht gehört.[41] So müssen wir davon ausgehen, daß er seine Informationen über die von ihm genannten römischen Autoritäten eher aus zweiter und dritter denn aus erster Hand bekam. Methodisch hat dies die Konsequenz, daß wir nicht ohne weiteres unser historisches Wissen um interne Zusammenhänge für ihn reklamieren dürfen. Das Bild, das Lukas von bestimmten Personen und Vorgängen hatte, dürfte sich eher nach dem richten, was eine interessierte, aber nur halbwegs informierte Öffentlichkeit zu sagen wußte, als nach den Fakten selbst, eher nach dem, was man auf der Straße hören konnte, als nach dem, was in der Kurie oder gar im Palast des Princeps bekannt war. Hinzu kommt, daß die Lokalisierung des lukanische Doppelwerkes in Rom möglich, aber nicht gesichert ist, und wir möglicherweise auch für Domitian damit rechnen müssen, daß er von Stadtrömern und von Provinzialen verschieden beurteilt wurde, ähnlich wie Christoph SCHUBERT auf Differenzen des Nerobildes in der lateinischen und in der griechischen Literatur verwiesen hat.[42] Das Beispiel zeigt aber auch die Notwendigkeit, die Bedingungen der Literaturproduktion zur Zeit des römischen Prinzipates, speziell zur Zeit Domitians, ein wenig näher ins Auge zu fassen.

Es ist an der Zeit, die von moderner althistorischer Forschung vorgenommene Revision des traditionellen, im wesentlichen aus Tacitus, der Johannesoffenbarung und einigen Kirchenvätern gespeisten Bildes Domitians auch für die Lukasexegese fruchtbar zu machen; zu relativieren ist das Ausmaß dessen, wie sich Domitian von seinen Vorgängern und Nachfolgern im Nega-

---

[38] Zur Diskussion um das römische Bürgerrecht des Paulus vgl. einerseits W. STEGEMANN, Apostel, *passim*; andererseits M. HENGEL, Paulus, 174–178; B. WANDER, Apologien, 474f. – Was hätte Lukas, hätte er Paulus fälschlich das römische Bürgerrecht zugesprochen, denjenigen unter den Christen genützt, die nicht das römische Bürgerrecht besitzen und somit gegen Maßnahmen der *coercitio*, wie sie in Apg 16,22–24; 17,9 u.ö. geschildert werden, nicht das Provokationsrecht hatten? Ob Theophilos römischer Bürger war und Lukas auf seinesgleichen seine Darstellung berechnet hätte, muß unsicher bleiben. Stadtrömische Juden mit römischem Bürgerrecht hat es gegeben (vgl. Philo Leg Gai 155.157), doch gab es bis zur Wende vom 2. zum 3.Jh. n.Chr. kaum Christen in vergleichbarer Rechtsstellung (vgl. P. LAMPE, Christen, 66.97–99 u.ö.).
[39] Dio Cass 60,17,5.
[40] Vgl. Ovid Trist 4,10,7f.
[41] Allerdings weiß er offensichtlich, wie man einen *homo honestus et iustus* beschreibt; vgl. dazu M. LABAHN, Paulus, *passim*.
[42] C. SCHUBERT, Nerobild, 245.

tiven abhebt. Einige politische Karrieren, die unter Domitian schon recht weit gediehen waren, gingen unter Trajan recht bald ebenso erfolgreich weiter, so bei Plinius d. J. und Cn. Octavius Titinius Capito.[43] Ferner unterschied sich die Stellung einzelner Autoren und Personengruppen gegenüber dem Princeps teilweise je nach Herkunft aus dem Senatoren- oder dem Ritterstand. Sah ersterer in der damaligen Erscheinungsform des Prinzipates alte republikanische Ideale verraten, so war für den Ritterstand die „Effektivität der Verwaltung als Vorbedingung wirtschaftlicher Prosperität" wichtiger als die Beziehungen des Princeps zum Senat.[44] Schließlich muß man damit rechnen, daß sich einige, z.B. Plinius[45] und Tacitus, erst im Nachhinein als standhafte Oppositionelle gegen Domitian stilisiert haben.[46] Ebensowenig muß es viel besagen, wenn die Dichter Statius und Martial Domitian zu dessen Lebzeiten, aber auch nur in dieser Zeit,[47] panegyrisch feiern.

Die Qualität der Reichsverwaltung Domitians ist nicht nur bei Sueton[48] vor allem hinsichtlich der Rechtspflege festgehalten, sondern ist nach Karl CHRIST auch literarisch und epigraphisch zu belegen.[49] Gerade Provinzstatthalter hat Domitian streng beaufsichtigt[50]. Die bei Martial bekannte[51] und bei Statius vorauszusetzende[52] Adresse *dominus ac deus noster* könnte ein Mißverständnis einer nur am Hof des *princeps* üblichen Anrede sein,[53] denn die Wendung *dominus ac deus* fehlt in den Dokumenten, die nachweislich von Domitian selbst ausgehen.[54] Die These einer umfassenden, von höchster Stelle veranlaßten Christenverfolgung unter Domitian und dessen Parallelisierung mit Nero ist eine apologetische Fiktion der Kirchenväter,[55] basierend auf der unzulässigen Verallgemeinerung einzelner teilweise mißverstandener Quellen. Trajan war vielleicht nicht weniger autokratisch, wenn auch in der Durchführung seines Prinzipates konzilianter als Domitian.[56] Er verstand es eher, dem

---

[43] S. FEIN, Beziehungen, 151–155.
[44] A. DIHLE, Literatur, 151. So zeichnet der aus der Perspektive des Ritterstandes schreibende Velleius Paterculus ein positives, der dem Senatsadel entstammende Tacitus hingegen ein düsteres Bild des Tiberius (DIHLE, ebd.).
[45] S. FEIN, Beziehungen, 147f.
[46] W. ECK, Traian, 114.
[47] Vgl. die Huldigung an Nerva bei Mart 12,6,3f: *recta fides, hilaris clementia ... iam redeunt*.
[48] Suet Dom 8,2.
[49] K. CHRIST, Geschichte, 278.
[50] P. SOUTHERN, Domitian, 55–58. P. SOUTHERN, aaO., 58, warnt aber auch „vor der Überschätzung dieses Umstands für unser Domitianbild".
[51] Für die Anrede „Gott" vgl. Mart 4,1,10; 5,5,2; 7,2,6; 7,8,2; für die Anrede „Herr und Gott" (erwähnt bei Suet Dom 13,2) vgl. Mart 5,8,1; 10,72,3.
[52] Statius feiert Domitian als *genitor deorum* (Stat Silv 1,61ff).
[53] W. ECK, Domitianus, 749.
[54] „Nichts weist in den Quellen auf eine Selbstvergötterung des Herrschers hin. Wohl aber schlugen über ihm die Wogen der Adulation zusammen" (U. SEIDEL, Christenverfolgung, 138).
[55] Vgl. J. ULRICH, Euseb, *passim*; P. GUYOT/R. KLEIN, Christentum, 319.
[56] J. BENNETT, Trajan, 208–213.

senatorischen Selbstwertgefühl zu schmeicheln[57]; immerhin mußte er keine Verschwörung gegen seine eigene Person erleben. Doch war die Bearbeitung der Zeitgeschichte gegebenenfalls auch zu Trajans Zeiten nicht ganz ungefährlich.[58] Daß Christen von Trajan wohl kaum anderes zu erwarten hatten als von Domitian, belegt der berühmte, juristische Unlogik offenbarende Briefwechsel zwischen Trajan und Plinius d.J.[59]

Von da aus ist auch ein gerechtes Urteil über Lukas zu formulieren: Angesichts der Realität der Provinzverwaltung Domitians muß der lukanische Hinweis auf das korrekte Vorgehen römischer Beamter nicht *pura blanditia* sein, selbst wenn man nicht wie Martin HENGEL so weit gehen will, daß das häufige Lob des korrekten Vorgehens römischer Behörden einen Reflex dessen darstellt.[60] Maßnahmen der *coercitio* standen ohnehin im freien Ermessen des dazu berechtigten Beamten. Lukas' Zeichnung der jüdischen Gegner ist bedenklicher als die der römischen Staatsmacht. Erkennt man ferner, daß die philosophische und die senatorische Opposition speziell gegen Domitian zweifellos vorhanden waren, aber durch Tacitus und Plinius teilweise in einseitiger und fragwürdiger Selbstrechtfertigung über-stilisiert sind, wird man auch von einem Nicht-Senator wie Lukas nicht ein stärkeres Maß an Opposition erwarten.

Freilich bestand generell im Prinzipat für alle im einzelnen unterschiedlich weit zugestandene Meinungsfreiheit ihre Grenze in der Wahrung der *maiestas principis*, „deren Verletzung in Majestätsprozessen geahndet wurde".[61] SCHUBERT hat 1998 eindringlich auf die Problematik der Deutung der unter solchen Bedingungen naturgemäß „komplexen, oft vagen und anspielungsreichen Aussagen"[62] verwiesen. So haben wir auch bei Lukas die romfreundlichen Aussagen auf ihre Funktion hin zu befragen, und wir haben negative Bewertungen in bestimmten Texten auch dann wahrzunehmen, wenn wir sie nicht als Hauptintention der Aussage betrachten, und mit einer Dislozierung von Aussagen über bestimmte Personen zu rechnen. Manches hatte der Leser aus seiner eigenen Kenntnis heraus zu ergänzen, vor allem zu Apg 28,30f (διετίαν ... ἀκολύτως) die Tatsache, daß Paulus als Märtyrer starb.

Diese Situation der eingeschränkten Meinungsfreiheit konnte eine bestimmte Strategie für Lukas veranlassen:

1. Kritik an *vergangenen* Autoritätspersonen war unter den Bedingungen des Prinzipates mit seinen *wechselnden* Herrschern und Herrscherhäusern nicht unbedingt gefährlich, sondern konnte sich durchaus mit der „offiziellen" Linie vereinbaren lassen, zumal dann wenn besagte Personen – wodurch und

---

[57] K. CHRIST, Geschichte, 291.
[58] S. FEIN, Beziehungen, 207f.
[59] Plinius Ep 10,96f. Zur juristischen Unlogik vgl. Just 2 Apol 2,15 sowie Tert Apol 2,8: (*Trajanus*) negat (scil. *Christianos*) inquirendos ut innocentes et mandat puniendos ut nocentes.
[60] M. HENGEL, Geschichtsschreibung, 55.
[61] S. FEIN, Beziehungen, 82.
[62] C. SCHUBERT, Studien, 11.

durch wen auch immer – in Ungnade gefallen waren. Allerdings hat Lukas nicht die vergangenen Autoritätspersonen als dunkle Folie für die Darstellung ihrer gegenwärtigen Nachfolger benutzt. Die Frage nach der Funktion dieser kritischen Anmerkungen muß dann eigens gestellt werden.

2. Konflikte mit jüdischen Autoritäten werden manchmal transparent auch für Konflikte mit römischen Autoritäten dargestellt; römische Autoritäten werden sowohl direkt als auch gelegentlich indirekt durch das Verhalten anderer Autoritäten beschrieben.

Beide Strategien sind im einzelnen kurz zu entfalten:

Lukas kritisiert vorzugsweise Personen, die auch anderweitig kritisiert werden, und Kritik an vergangenen Autoritäten muß nicht gefährlich sein, sondern kann der offiziellen Linie durchaus entsprechen, wie SCHUBERT an dem Anti-Neronismus der Flavier Vespasian und Titus zeigt.[63] Insofern ist die Kritik in Lk 3,19 an Herodes Antipas I. ungefährlich, obwohl dieser eigentlich ein Freund der Römer war: Bei dem Versuch, sich ähnlich wie der spätere Agrippa I. den Königstitel zu holen, wurde Herodes Antipas von Caligula aufgrund seiner Habgier mit der Verbannung bestraft und starb zwar eines natürlichen Todes, aber eben durch die offizielle römische Staatsmacht geächtet. Ungefährlich ist des weiteren in Lk 13,1–5; Apg 4,27 die kritische Erwähnung des Pontius Pilatus, der ja nicht freiwillig im Jahr 36 n.Chr. von Judäa abzog. Ungefährlich ist dann auch die Kritik an Gallios Desinteresse an den Vorgängen vor seinem βῆμα Apg 18,17,[64] die Kritik an einem Menschen, der in römischer Literatur reichlich unterschiedlich bedacht wird: Neben einem positiven Gallio-Bild bei dessen Bruder Seneca und bei Statius[65] stehen kritische Bemerkungen vor allem bei Dio Cassius: In dessen Geschichtswerk ist Gallio vor allem als Spötter über die Himmelfahrt des toten Claudius an einem Fleischerhaken und als Conferencié bei einem Kithara-Konzert Neros eingegangen.[66] Ungefährlich ist denn auch die lukanische Kritik an der widergesetzlichen Habsucht und der daraus resultierenden Verzögerungstaktik sowie der privaten Lebensführung des Antonius Felix. Daß Lukas hier plötzlich mit kritischen Äußerungen des Josephus und des Tacitus[67] konform geht, darf nicht als Ausdruck einer nunmehr auch lukanischen Opposition gewertet werden, denn angesichts der Abberufung des Antonius Felix fällt auch auf Nero ein ungünstiges Licht: Antonius Felix entgeht dank der Fürsprache seines

---

[63] C. SCHUBERT, Studien, 292.
[64] M.E. wird Gallios Verhalten innerhalb des Prozesses Apg 18,12–16 zu Unrecht als vorbildliches Verhalten bezeichnet (H. CONZELMANN, Mitte, 133 u.v.a.). Gallio ist nicht ein Freund der Christen, sondern ein Feind der Juden (W. STEGEMANN, Synagoge, 247). Daß Paulus den Vorfall lebend überstanden hat, ist für Lukas historisches Faktum. Die *jetzigen* christlichen Leser der Apg müssen u.U. damit rechnen, *Opfer* eines solchen Antisemitismus zu werden.
[65] Vgl. Sen Nat Quaest 4 praef 10f; Stat Silv. 2,7,32, und dazu W. ELLIGER, Paulus, 234f.
[66] Cass Dio 60,35,4; 61,20,1. Nicht sicher scheint mir, ob Tac Ann 15,73 wirklich in malam partem, Gallio betreffend, zu deuten ist (so aber W. ELLIGER, Paulus, 235).
[67] Tac Hist 5,9,3 und vor allem ders. Ann 12,54,1.

Bruders Pallas der gerechten Strafe.[68] Kritik an Nero und an seiner Administration mußte aber zur Zeit des Lukas nicht mehr als gefährlich gelten.

Doch sind wir mit der Interpretation der angeblichen lukanischen Kritiken noch nicht am Ende. Denn bei Lukas fehlt ein Verwendungszusammenhang völlig, der uns eher peinlich berühren würde: Diese Bemerkungen dienen nicht als dunkle Folie, um die gegenwärtigen Vertreter der jeweiligen Staatsmacht in ein um so helleres Licht zu rücken. Näher liegt dann gerade in Kombination mit den „römerfreundlichen Stellen" eine andere Interpretation für die christlichen Leserinnen und Leser im ausgehenden 1.Jh. n.Chr.: Es gibt das Neben- und Nacheinander von korrekten und korrupten Inhabern staatlicher Gewalt. So wenig Christen von sich aus das Recht zur Auflehnung gegen Obrigkeiten haben, so sehr müssen sie auch mit deren Fehlverhalten rechnen.

Transparent auch für Konflikte mit nichtjüdischen Autoritäten sind vor allem Apg 5 und Apg 12. In Apg 5 wird mit nicht typisch jüdischen Motiven argumentiert; der Konflikt erscheint gegenüber Apg 4 verschärft.[69] In Apg 4,27 werden Herodes und Pilatus als Gegner Jesu eingeführt. Man hat die Stelle ähnlich wie Lk 13,1–5 aufgrund des Widerspruches zu Lk 23,1–25 für traditionell gehalten, doch hätte Lukas, wollte er Pilatus schonen, besser völlig auf die Aussage verzichtet. Auf synchroner Ebene lädt Apg 4,27 dazu ein, auch in Apg 5 nach weiteren Signalen für eine mögliche Aktualisierung in Richtung auf Konflikte mit der römischen Obrigkeit zu suchen. Ferner erinnert die Weigerung des Petrus, von der ihm durch das Synhedrion verbotenen Verkündigung abzulassen (Apg 5,29), an die bekannten Worte des Sokrates (πείσομαι ...μᾶλλον τῷ θεῷ ἢ ὑμῖν)[70] und ist generell auf das Thema „Verleugnen oder Bekennen" anwendbar. Die Aussage in Apg 5,41, die Apostel seien gewürdigt worden, um seines Namens willen Schmach zu leiden, ist ebenfalls unabhängig von der Frage, ob jüdische oder heidnische Subjekte als Akteure von Repressionen anzusprechen sind. Vor allem aber: Der lukanische Gamaliel kontrastiert den nur menschlichen Zelotismus mit der christlichen Mission, die als mögliches ἔργον ἐκ θεοῦ gilt (Apg 5,38f), dem man sich darum nicht blindlings als θεομάχος widersetzen sollte. Θεομαχεῖν ist gemäß 2Mac 7,19 das Verhalten des Antiochus IV. Epiphanes, dem durch einen der Märtyrer Gottes Strafe vorausgesagt wird. Bedenkt man diesen auch dem Menschen der griechisch-römischen Kultur geläufigen[71] Zusammenhang zwischen Tun und Ergehen des θεομάχος für die Exegese von Apg 5,37 mit, dann impliziert der genannte intertextuelle Bezug auf 2Mac 7,19 nicht nur, daß damit die Juden mit ihren Feinden auf eine Ebene gestellt werden, sondern gewinnt für die christlichen Leserinnen und Leser auch Trostfunktion angesichts heidnischer Autoritäten, die den Unterschied zwischen Gott und Mensch vergessen und die Macht des Gottes der Christen unterschätzen. Wovor Gamaliel in Apg 5,38f

---

[68] Jos Ant 20,182f.
[69] Apg 5 könnte einen traditionellen Kern haben, weil die Gegnerangaben mit Apg 4 nicht übereinstimmen. Und doch ist die lukanische Überarbeitung nicht zu vernachlässigen.
[70] Plat Ap 29d.
[71] Vgl. Eur Ba 45–48 sowie allgemein W. NESTLE, Legenden, *passim*.

warnt, wird in dem Erzählzusammenhang Apg 12,20–24 (sic!) narrativ umgesetzt: Der Verfolger der Gemeinde endet mit vorzeitigem Tod, während das Wort Gottes sich weiter ausbreitet.

Der Tod des Agrippa I. wird in intertextueller Relation zu 2Kön 19,35 und 2Mac 9,9 erzählt: Sanherib und Antiochus IV. Epiphanes werden von Gott für ihre Lästerung bestraft, und so rettet Gott Israel. Auch in Apg 12 sichert die Fortsetzung Apg 12,24f das Verständnis der vorangegangenen Erzählung im Rahmen der ursprünglich jüdischen, christlich übernommenen Literatur *de mortibus persecutorum*. Nicht ausgeschlossen scheint mir, daß Lukas bei der Aufnahme der möglicherweise vorlukanische Erzählung Apg 12,20–23 auch an die ihm zu Ohren gekommene „Tatsache" der quasigöttlichen Huldigungen gegenüber Domitian gedacht hat – hier ist methodisch wiederum daran zu erinnern, daß nicht die geschichtliche Wirklichkeit über, sondern das damalige Bild des Außenstehenden von Domitian den Rahmen unserer Auslegung bilden muß. Zugegebenermaßen ist die in Apg 12 beschriebene Situation von der der Apotheose der römischen principes verschieden: Agrippa ist noch am Leben, und die Akklamation durch die Volksmenge ist etwas anderes als ein formeller Senatsbeschluß. Ferner ist der Kult der *divi* als Versuch der Verbindung der „neue(n) Form der Herrschaft mit dem vorhandene religiösen und politischen System"[72] aufzufassen, und in paganem Denken nicht als Verehrung eines Gottes im jüdisch-christlichen Sinne zu verstehen.[73] Auch steht nicht die Verweigerung gegenüber dem Herrscherkult, sondern die Abkehr vom Kult der Götter „an erster Stelle der heidnischen Vorwürfe gegen die Christen".[74] Doch ungeachtet dieser historischen Einwände haben wir Apg 12,20–23 als Produkt einer jüdisch-christlichen Polemik zu interpretieren, deren Hintergrund sich von dem der griechisch-römischen Polemik eines Seneca, Lukian[75] oder Dio Cassius[76] durchaus unterscheidet. Auch Lk 21,24fin ist nur dem *christlichen* Leser als Einschränkung der römischen Macht erkennbar.

Das Nebeneinander positiver und negativer Gestalten soll den christlichen Lesern den Eintrag ihrer divergierenden Erfahrungen ermöglichen. Auch im Prinzipat kommt es nicht nur auf den Willen des Princeps an, sondern auch darauf, wie energisch die lokalen Autoritäten gewisse Beschlüsse umzusetzen gewillt sind. Es gibt dabei auch das Phänomen einer positiven Verschleppung.[77] Bewältigung von Leidenserfahrungen soll damit ermöglicht werden.

---

[72] W. PÖHLMANN, Herrscherkult, 251.
[73] Daß Domitian seinen verstorbenen Vater und seinen Bruder in den Staatskult hat aufnehmen lassen, ist für Quint Inst 3,7,9, ein Akt der *pietas*.
[74] W. PÖHLMANN, Herrscherkult, 252.
[75] Vgl. Luc Dial Mort 12; 14; 16.
[76] Vgl. F. TAEGER, Kampf, *passim*.
[77] Vgl. das Verhalten des Petronius bei Jos Ant 18,261–288.

4. Die lukanische Zurüstung für ein offensives Vertreten des christlichen Standpunktes

Für die Frage, wie Lukas seine christlichen Leserinnen und Leser für das offensive Vertreten des christlichen Standpunktes zurüstet, ist auf die lukanische Konzeption der Erzählfiguren ebenso zu achten wie auf die als auktorialer Kommentar formulierten Textelemente.

Wie verhalten sich christliche Erzählfiguren? Trotz Bedrängnis missionieren sie weiter, gegebenenfalls woanders, so Jesus (Lk 4,31–44 nach Lk 4,28–30), Petrus (Apg 4,20), die Apostel (Apg 5,42) und Paulus (Apg 14,19f u.ö.). Ihre weitere Missionstätigkeit begründen sie mit ihrem Gehorsam gegenüber Gott (Apg 4,19; 5,29). Gegenüber staatlichen Autoritäten nutzen sie alle legalen Mittel aus, um sich selbst zu schützen.[78] Sie beteuern ihr gutes Gewissen (Apg 23,1; 24,16) und ihre Unschuld (Apg 25,8.10; vgl. 26,22); sie stellen die gegnerische Anklage als unbeweisbar hin (Apg 24,13); sie pochen auf ihr Recht (Apg 16,35–40; 22,25; 25,10f). Dies steht nicht im Widerspruch zu der gemeinde*intern* geäußerten Leidens- und Martyriumsbereitschaft (Apg 14,22; 21,13).

Als auktoriale Ergänzung ist das Bewußtsein zu benennen, daß Gott der Herr der Geschichte ist, auch in Zeiten der Unterdrückung (Apg 4,25–29), daß er widerständige Autoritäten bezwingen (Apg 9) oder strafen kann (Apg 12,21–23), und daß die Feinde des Christentums diesem nicht wirklich etwas anhaben können (Apg 12,21–24; sic!). Der Nachweis der Harmlosigkeit der christlichen Bewegung erfolgt durch *testimonia externa*: (Lk 20,20.26; 23,1–25; Apg 19,37–39 sowie in den behördlichen Stellungnahmen Apg 23,29 und Apg 25,25). Der lukanische Demetrius verweist auf die Wege des Rechtsstaates (Apg 19,38f).

Die Begriffe σωτήρ in Lk 2,11 und εἰρήνη in Lk 2,14 werden gelegentlich im Sinne einer impliziten Distanz gegenüber den Selbstansprüchen römischer Staatsmacht gedeutet. Doch erheben sich gegen diese Interpretation Bedenken: Das Wortfeld σωτήρ wird hier wie an allen übrigen theologisch relevanten Stellen auf Israel bezogen gebraucht, und auch der εἰρήνη-Begriff in Lk 2,14 dürfte eher, biblischer Tradition folgend, umfassend im Sinne von „Heil" zu verstehen sein. Ob Lk 4,6b lukanisch ist und eine implizite Kritik am römischen System der Klientelkönigtümer darstellt, ist aufgrund der ungeklärten literarkritischen Verhältnisse zu Lk 4,6 nicht zu entscheiden,[79] wenngleich man im Gegenzug wieder fragen könnte, warum Lukas nicht abgemildert hat. Schon eher in Richtung auf eine implizite Relativierung römischer Selbstansprüche kann es angesehen werden, wenn Lukas den einzigen wirklich sicher politischen, auf das Imperium Romanum bezogenen εἰρήνη-Beleg der *blanditia* des Christentumsgegners Tertullus in den Mund legt (Apg 24,2).

---

[78] R. O'TOOLE, Position, 8.
[79] Den Dissens der Auslegungen dokumentieren S. CARRUTH/J.M. ROBINSON/C. HEIL, Q 4:1–13,16, 306–316.

5. Die Nachgeschichte lukanischer Aussagen zum Thema

Die nicht sehr reichhaltige Nachgeschichte der lukanischen Aussagen zum Imperium Romanum ist nicht ohne den größeren Horizont des Themas „Der Christ und die antike Gesellschaft" zu beschreiben, so wenig beide Themen deckungsgleich sind. Nach Hanns Christoph BRENNECKE ist „das Verhältnis der Christen zur pluralistischen Gesellschaft des römischen Kaiserreiches der ersten drei Jahrhunderte ... geprägt von einem geradezu dialektischen Verhältnis von Distanz und Integration".[80] Diese Dialektik gilt allgemein für den christlichen βίος: Man gehorcht den staatlichen Gesetzen, lebt innerhalb der gesellschaftlichen Strukturen, selbst im römischen Militär,[81] als Christ und bewährt sich durch die Überlegenheit der eigenen Lebensführung als *Elite*;[82] und das Christentum beansprucht auch nach außen, eine für das römische Weltreich nützliche Bewegung zu sein.[83] Die Erfahrung der gesellschaftlichen Ausgrenzung, gipfelnd in den Vorwürfen des Inzestes, der Anthropophagie[84] und der angeblichen Propaganda für eine weltliche βασιλεία,[85] deutet man als Erfahrung der eben durch das Christsein bedingten *Fremde*.[86] So könnte man zusammenfassend das Selbstverständnis des Christentums inmitten seiner nichtchristlichen Umwelt auf die Formel „loyal fremde Elite" bringen. Das Wort des lukanischen Petrus „Man soll Gott mehr gehorchen als den Menschen" in Apg 5,29[87] konnte dabei den theonomen Bezug christlicher Moral bezeugen.

Die genannte Dialektik gilt aber auch für unser spezielleres Thema. Christen gehorchen den staatlichen Autoritäten im Wissen darum, daß sie von Gott eingesetzt sind, und beten für sie, unterscheiden jedoch zwischen der menschlichen und der göttlichen Autorität;[88] sie müssen aber seit der Regierungszeit Trajans wenigstens prinzipiell mit jederzeit möglicher Bedrohung aufgrund des *nomen ipsum* rechnen und haben keine Rechtssicherheit über das von Trajan Festgelegte hinaus, das zu Beginn des 3.Jh. n.Chr. allmählich für alle Provinzen unumstößlich verbindlich wird und eine Appellation an den Kaiser sinnlos macht. In diese Situation hinein ist aus dem lukanischen Doppelwerk

---

[80] H.C. BRENNECKE, Bekenntnis, 50.
[81] Nachweise bei H.C. BRENNECKE, Bekenntnis, *passim*.
[82] Diogn. 5,10. – Ein anderer Grund für das Selbstverständnis als Elite ist in dem Wissen um die sola gratia durch Offenbarung erschlossene Wahrheit gegeben (Polyc Ep. 2,3; Diogn. 7,1f).
[83] Just 1 Apol 12; Polyc Ep 12,3; Diogn. 5.
[84] Thph Ant Autol 3,8.
[85] Just 1 Apol. 11.
[86] Daß die Erfahrung der Fremde nach dem 1. Petrusbrief theo-logisch begründet ist, zeigt R. FELDMEIER, Christen, *passim*. – Die Terminologie der „Fremde" wurde gelegentlich schon von Israel auf seine Diasporaexistenz bezogen (vgl. Ex 18,3; Num 20,15 LXX).
[87] Zur Wirkungsgeschichte von Apg 5,29 insgesamt vgl. R. PESCH, Apostelgeschichte I, 222–224, der auch auf ihre Verwendung gegenüber christlichen Kaisern und Bischöfen verweist.
[88] Just 1 Apol 17,3; M Polyc 21,1; Thphl Ant Autol 1,11,1.

neben dem auch dort tradierten Jesuswort „Gebet dem Kaiser, was des Kaisers ist" vornehmlich wiederum Apg 5,29 wirksam geworden.

Der generelle Gehorsam gegenüber den staatlichen Autoritäten wird aus Röm 13,1–7; 1Tim 2,1f und 1Petr 2,17[89] gefolgert, während in der apologetischen Literatur zunächst das Erste Gebot,[90] dann, bei Irenäus und Tertullian, auch Jesu „Gebet dem Kaiser, was des Kaisers ist, und Gott, was Gottes ist" die Unterscheidung zwischen Gott und dem Kaiser begründet.[91] Das eben genannte Jesuswort begründet unter anderem bei Tertullian in seiner montanistischen Periode die Forderung nach der Bereitschaft zum Martyrium,[92] und auch Apg 5,29 galt für Origenes und Euseb[93] als *locus classicus* der Martyriumsparänese und wurde durch Dionysius von Alexandrien (Mitte 3.Jh. n.Chr.) und Felix von Carthago (303–305 n.Chr.)[94] *in actu* befolgt. Hingegen ist zumindest für die in der Biblia Patristica indizierten Autoren eine auch im Sinne des eben Gesagten *eingeschränkte* staatskritische Rezeption von Lk 13,1–5.31;[95] Apg 4,27; 18,12–17; 24,22–27[96] nicht nachzuweisen. Euseb rezipiert Apg 12,21–23 unter dem Aspekt des *de mortibus persecutorum*,[97] weniger unter dem der Deifizierung des Agrippa I.;[98] Epiphanius liest aus Lk 13,1–5 gar die Zustimmung Jesu zu der Handlungsweise des Pilatus heraus.[99] Die relative Wirkungslosigkeit der genannten kritischen Stellen zum Imperium Romanum resultiert aus dem Nebeneinander von Röm 13; 1Tim 2; 1Petr 2 einerseits, Mt 22,21; Apg 5,29 andererseits, das eine *politische* Kritik an der römischen Staatsmacht nicht zuließ.

---

[89] Für die Nachwirkung von Röm 13,1–7 vgl. M.Polyc 10,2; Iren Haer 5,24; für die Nachwirkung von 1Petr 2,17 vgl. M.Scill 9; M.Apollon 37; für die Nachwirkung von 1Tim 2,1f. vgl. Thphl Ant Autol. 3,14; Tert Apol 30,4; Athenag Leg 37 sowie faktisch das große Gebet in 1Clem 59–61.
[90] Thphl Ant Autol 1,11.
[91] Iren Haer 3,8,1; Tert Scorp 14,2f.
[92] Tert Fug 12,8.9.
[93] Orig Comm. in Rom. 9,27; Eus PE 13,10,13. Für Johannes Chrysostomus vgl. Cramer, Catena 93.
[94] Für Dionysios vgl. Eus., h.e. 7,11,5, sowie C.L. FELTOE, Dionysiou Leipsana, 29,7; für Felix vgl. M.Fel 15.
[95] Lk 13,1–5 wird als allgemeine Bußmahnung zitiert bei Ps.-Cyprian Ad Novat 15,4; Singul Cler 5, und bei Bas Moral 11,3.
[96] Zu Apg 18,12–17 ist in der Biblia Patristica, Bd. 1–6, kein einziger Verweis zu finden; Apg 24,22–26 ist von Tert., fug. 12,6 als Beispiel der vorbildlichen Haltung des Paulus rezipiert: Er nahm nicht die Möglichkeit wahr, sich durch Bestechung aus der Haft freikaufen zu lassen.
[97] Apg 12,21–23 fehlt erstaunlicherweise auch in der gleichnamigen Schrift des Laktanz. – Apg 12,21–23 wird erstmals bei Bas Moral 59,1 als allgemeine Warnung vor der Ehrsucht rezipiert.
[98] Eus HE 2,10,1.
[99] Epiph Haer 42,11,15.

6. Zusammenfassung

In einer Zeit zunehmender Repressalien für die Christen durch antichristliche und antijüdische Aggressionen einerseits, durch Distanzierungsversuche der Synagoge andererseits will Lukas unter den Bedingungen eingeschränkter Meinungsfreiheit den Christen dazu verhelfen, die Harmlosigkeit des Christentums für das Imperium Romanum offensiv zu vertreten, ihre Unschuld zu erweisen und auf ihr Recht zu pochen. Das Domitianbild moderner althistorischer Forschung ist auch für die Lukasexegese fruchtbar zu machen; es relativiert neuzeitliche Kritik an einer allzu opportunistischen Darstellung der römischen Staatsmacht bei Lukas. Kritische Bemerkungen über einzelne Angehörige der römischen Staatsmacht (z.B. Apg 24,22–27) zeigen den Christen, daß man mit dem Nebeneinander von korrektem und unkorrektem Verhalten bei den Vertretern der Staatsgewalt rechnen muß, ohne daß dadurch die Pflicht zur politischen Loyalität der Christen eingeschränkt würde. Doch hält Lukas daran fest, daß Gott der eigentliche Herr der Geschichte ist, der widerständige Autoritäten strafen kann, und daß die Feinde des Christentums diesem nicht wirklich etwas anhaben können.

Versteht sich das Christentum der spät- und nachneutestamentlichen Zeit als loyale fremde Elite, dann ist mit einer politisch motivierten Kritik an der römischen Staatsmacht kaum zu rechnen; dementsprechend ist eine staatskritische Rezeption von Lk 13,1–5; Apg 24,22–27 u.a. nicht nachzuweisen. Immerhin ist u.a. Apg 5,29 als *locus classicus* der Martyriumsparänese wirksam geworden.

Literatur

BENNETT, Julian, Trajan optimus princeps. A Life and Times, Bloomington 1997.
BLEICKEN, Joachim, Rez. Wolfgang KUNKEL, Untersuchungen zur Entwicklung des römischen Kriminalverfahrens in vorsullanischer Zeit, in: Gnomon 36 (1964), 696–710.
BRENNECKE, Hanns Christof, ‚An fidelis ad militiam converti possit'? [Tertullian, de idolatria 19,1]. Frühchristliches Bekenntnis und Militärdienst im Widerspruch?, in: Dietmar WYRWA (Hg.), Die Weltlichkeit des Glaubens in der Alten Kirche, Festschrift Ulrich Wickert, BZNW 85, Berlin, New York 1997, 45–100.
CARRUTH, Shawn/ROBINSON, James M./HEIL, Christoph, Q 4:1–13,16. The Temptations of Jesus – Nazara, Documenta Q, Reconstructions of Q Through Two Centuries of Gospel Research Excerpted, Sorted, and Evaluated, Leuven 1996.
CHRIST, Karl, Geschichte der römischen Kaiserzeit von Augustus bis zu Konstantin, München 1988.
CONZELMANN, Hans, Die Apostelgeschichte, HNT 7, Tübingen [2]1972.
ID., Die Mitte der Zeit. Studien zur Theologie des Lukas, BHTh 17, Tübingen [6]1977.
DIBELIUS, Martin, Paulus in der Apostelgeschichte, in: ID., Aufsätze zur Apostelgeschichte, hg. v. Heinrich GREEVEN, Göttingen [2]1953, 175–180.
DIHLE, Albrecht, Die griechische und lateinische Literatur der Kaiserzeit. Von Augustus bis Justinian, München 1989.
ECK, Werner, Domitianus I., in : DNP 3 (1997) 746–750.
ID., Traian, in: Manfred CLAUSS (Hg.), Die römischen Kaiser. 55 historische Portraits von Caesar bis Iustinian, München 1997, 110–124.
ECKERT, Jost, Das Imperium Romanum in Neuen Testament. Ein Beitrag zum Thema ‚Kirche und Gesellschaft', in: TThZ 96 (1987), 253–271.
ELLIGER, Winfried, Paulus in Griechenland. Philippi, Thessaloniki, Athen, Korinth, SBS 92/93, Stuttgart 1978.
FEIN, Sylvia, Die Beziehungen der Kaiser Trajan und Hadrian zu den Litterati, BzA 26, Stuttgart – Leipzig 1994.
FELDMEIER, Reinhard, Die Christen als Fremde. Die Metapher der Fremde in der antiken Welt, im Urchristentum und im 1. Petrusbrief, WUNT 64, Tübingen 1992.
FELTOE, Charles Lett, Dionysiou Leipsana. The Letters and other Remains of Dionysios of Alexandria, Cambridge 1904
FINEGAN, Jack, The Archeology of the New Testament, Boulder 1981.
GUYOT, Peter/KLEIN, Richard, Das frühe Christentum bis zum Ende der Verfolgungen. Eine Dokumentation. Bd. 1, TdF 60, Darmstadt 1993; Bd. 2, TdF 62, Darmstadt 1994; 2. Aufl. (unveränderter Nachdruck; in einem Band) Darmstadt 1997.
HAENCHEN, Ernst, Die Apostelgeschichte neu übersetzt und erklärt, KEK 3, Göttingen [7/16]1977.
HENGEL, Martin, Der vorchristliche Paulus, in: ThBeitr 21 (1990) 174–195.
DERS., Zur urchristlichen Geschichtsschreibung, Calwer Paperback, Stuttgart 1979.
HEUSS, Alfred, Zur Entwicklung des Imperiums der römischen Oberbeamten, in: ZSRG.R 64 (1944), 57–133.
HORN, Friedrich Wilhelm, Die Haltung des Lukas zum römischen Staat im Evangelium und in der Apostelgeschichte, in: Joseph VERHEYDEN (ed.), The Unity of Luke-Acts, BEThL 142, Leuven 1999, 203–224.
DERS., Ethik des Neuen Testaments 1982–1992, in: ThR 60 (1995) 32–86.

KÜMMEL, Werner Georg, Einleitung in das Neue Testament, Heidelberg²¹1983.

LABAHN, Michael, Paulus – ein *homo honestus et iustus*. Das lukanische Paulusportrait von Apg 27–28 im Lichte ausgewählter antiker Parallelen, in: Friedrich Wilhelm HORN (Hg.), Das Ende des Paulus. Historische, theologische und literaturgeschichtliche Aspekte, BZNW 106, Berlin – New York 2001, 75–106.

LAMPE, Peter, Die stadtrömischen Christen in den ersten beiden Jahrhunderten. Untersuchungen zur Sozialgeschichte, WUNT II/18, Tübingen ²1989.

LÖSCH, Stefan, Die Dankesrede des Tertullus: Apg 24,1–4, in: ThQ 112 (1931) 295–319.

MEHL, Andreas, Art. Asiarchie, in: DNP 2 (1997) 80.

MOLTHAGEN, Joachim, Rom als Garant des Rechts und als apokalyptisches Ungeheuer, in: Edwin BRANDT, Paul S. FIDDES, Joachim MOLTHAGEN (Hg.), Gemeinschaft am Evangelium, Festschrift Wiard POPKES, Leipzig 1996, 127–142.

MOMMSEN, Theodor, Die Rechtsverhältnisse des Apostels Paulus, in: ZNW 2 (1901) 81–96.

DERS., Der Religionsfrevel nach römischen Recht, in: DERS., Juristische Schriften 3, Berlin 1907, 389–422.

MUSURILLO, Herbert, The Acts of the Christian Martyrs, Oxford 1972.

NESTLE, Wilhelm, Legenden vom Tod der Gottesverächter, in: ARW 33 (1936), 246–269.

O'TOOLE, Robert, Luke's Position on Politics and Society, in: Richard J. CASSIDY/Philip J. SCHARPER (ed.), Political Issues in Luke-Acts, New York 1983, 1–17.

PESCH, Rudolf, Die Apostelgeschichte, 1. Teilband, Apg 1–12, EKK 5/1, Zürich u.a. 1986.

PLÜMACHER, Eckhart, Art. Apostelgeschichte, in: TRE 3 (1978), 483–528.

PÖHLMANN, Wolfgang, Art. Herrscherkult II. Neues Testament und Alte Kirche bis Konstantin, in: TRE 15 (1986), 248–253.

ROBBINS, Vernon K., Luke-Acts: A Mixed Population Seeks a Home in the Roman Empire, in: Loveday ALEXANDER (ed.), Images of Empire, JSOTS 122, Sheffield 1991, 202–221.

ROLOFF, Jürgen, Die Kirche im Neuen Testament, GNT 10, Göttingen 1993.

SCHNEIDER, Gerhard, Verleugnung, Verspottung und Verhör Jesu nach Lukas 22,54–71. Studien zur lukanischen Darstellung der Passion, StANT 22, München 1969.

SCHRAGE, Wolfgang, Ethik des Neuen Testaments, GNT 4, Göttingen ²1989.

SCHUBERT, Christoph, Studien zum Nerobild in der lateinischen Dichtung der Antike, BzA 116, Stuttgart – Leipzig 1998.

SCHULZ, Siegfried, Neutestamentliche Ethik, ZGB, Zürich 1987.

SEIDEL, Ulrich, Die Christenverfolgung zur Zeit Domitians, Diss. Theol. A. Leipzig 1983.

SOUTHERN, Pat, Domitian. Tragic Tyrant, London, New York 1997.

STEGEMANN, Wolfgang, War der Apostel Paulus ein römischer Bürger?, in ZNW 78 (1987), 200–229.

ID., Zwischen Synagoge und Obrigkeit. Zur historischen Situation der lukanischen Christen, FRLANT 152, Göttingen 1991.

TAEGER, Fritz, Zum Kampf gegen den antiken Herrscherkult, in: ARW 32 (1935), 282–292.

ULRICH, Jörg, Euseb, HistEccl III,14–20 und die Frage nach der Christenverfolgung unter Domitian, in: ZNW 89 (1996), 269–289.

URNER, Christiana, Kaiser Domitian im Urteil antiker literarischer Quellen und moderner Forschung, Diss. Augsburg 1993.

VAN UNNIK, W.C., Die Anklage gegen die Apostel in Philippi, in: ID., Sparsa Collecta I, NT.S 29, Leiden 1973, 374–385.

WALASKAY, Paul W., 'And so We Came to Rome'. The Political Perspective of St. Luke, MSSNTS 49, Cambridge 1983.

WANDER, Bernd, Apologien und Unschuldsbeteuerungen als besonderes Mittel des Lukas, in: Axel von DOBBELER, Kurt ERLEMANN, Roman HEILIGENTHAL (Hg.), Religionsgeschichte des Neuen Testaments. Festschrift Klaus Berger, Tübingen 2000, 465–476.

WENGST, Klaus, Pax Romana, Anspruch und Wirklichkeit. Erfahrungen und Wahrnehmungen des Friedens bei Jesus und im Urchristentum, München 1986.

WOLTER, Michael, Die Juden und die Obrigkeit bei Lukas, in: Klaus WENGST/Gerhard SASS (Hg.), Ja und nein. Christliche Theologie im Angesicht Israels, Festschrift Wolfgang SCHRAGE, Neukirchen 1998, 277–290.

Francois P. Viljoen

Song and Music in the Early Christian Communities.
Paul's Utilisation of Jewish, Roman and Greek Musical Traditions to Encourage the Early Christian Communities to Praise God and to Explain his Arguments

1 Introduction

In *Romans 15:9–12* Paul encourages the Christian congregation to praise God with song and music.
- He quotes from the *Jewish* Scriptures;
- He quotes in *Greek*; and
- He addresses a congregation in the centre of the *Roman* world.

These three cultures each had a long musical tradition. The question arises as to what extent Paul utilises Jewish, Greek and Roman musical traditions to encourage the congregation.

In *1 Corinthians 13–15* Paul several times refers to objects and practices of singing and music of the congregation in his explanation of the function of the gifts of the Spirit in the church.

Again we find his exhortations to sing in *Colossians 3:16* and *Ephesians 5:19*[1].

It is therefore a question whether and to what extent Jewish, Greek and Roman musical traditions are reflected in these three passages.

---

[1] Up till the beginning of the nineteenth century the authorship of Paul of the letters of Colossians and Ephesians was commonly accepted. There is no evidence that the Pauline authorship of these epistles was ever disputed until that time. However, since 1820 many scholars became skeptical that Paul was genuinely the author of Colossians and Ephesians. Questions were raised with regard to the so-called unusual language and style which are found in these letters, the theology of these letters that differs from the other letters of Paul and the strong correlation between Colossians and Ephesians (L. FLOOR, Efeziërs, 11; D. GUTHRIE, Introduction, 507, 554). While all these objections are considered, it remains difficult to overthrow the overwhelming external attestation to Pauline authorship, and the Epistle's own claims. To maintain that a Paulinist through his own self-effacement composed the letter, attributed it to Paul and immediate readiness from the Church to recognize it as such, is considerably less credible than the simple alternative of regarding it as Paul's own work.

2 The Context of Jewish, Greek and Roman Musical Traditions

During the expansion of the Roman world in the Western Mediterranean, the influence of hellenization and a strong inter cultural exchange developed between peoples of all countries. With regard to music, it was also the case.[2] It is not possible for us to know exactly what and how much of each tradition respectively was implied in Paul's admonitions. It is clear, however, that strong influence from the Jewish, Greek and Roman traditions were implied in Paul's writings.[3]

In order to understand some musical features and practices Paul describes, it is important to be knowledgeable of the musical traditions to which he might have referred.

2.1 Jewish Musical Traditions

Because of its inescapable cultural environment, early Christianity had a specific heritage in the music and ritual of the Jewish temple and synagogues. Early Christian writings testify that the first Christian congregations adopted the Jewish organisation of daily prayer hours as well as the custom of singing psalms in their services.[4]

The Jewish people had a *strong musical tradition*.[5] The origin of their music is ascribed to Jubal "the father of all those who play the lyre and pipe" (Gen 4:21). From archaeology we know that Jewish music is very old. Music was already relatively developed as early as the third millennium BC.[6] Reading the ancient history of Israel in the Pentateuch (e.g. Exod 15), it is evident that Israel was accustomed to singing during religious and national feasts.[7] At times of celebration and in times of lamentation Israel sang.

Before the monarchy a more simple type of music existed in which emotion and free effusion shaped the patterns of melody and rhythm. In the time of King David, singing was professionally organised, as is evident from the fact that he appointed professional musicians from the house of Levi for that purpose (1 Chr 6:31; 16:5–7; 23:5). Solomon continued this development (2 Chr 5:11–13). More complex forms of music developed as a result of more complex forms of political and cultic institutions.[8] In Jerusalem guilds of professional musicians (e.g. sons of Korah) were established. At the time of the es-

---

[2] G. ABRAHAM, History, 37.
[3] D.J. GROUT, History, 19–20.
[4] J.A. LAMB, Psalms, 9; W.D.E. OESTERLEY, Background, 99,149; F.P. VILJOEN, Betekenis 61.
[5] G. ABRAHAM, History, 39.
[6] C. SACHS, Rise, 57.
[7] G.N. BLOEM, Skrif, 48.
[8] P.J. VAN DYK, Music, 374.

tablishment of the monarchy and the building of the temple of Solomon, the music of Israel was raised to a higher level.[9]

After the Babylonian exile, music played an even more important part in Temple worship than before. Some scholars note that many of the developments, which happened after the Babylonian exile, were projected back into the past. Many of these later developments were ascribed to David and Solomon.[10] The temple singers were highly organised; some played instruments, others sang. According to Abraham[11] something like a liturgical calendar even emerged: Ps 24 the first day of the week, 48 on the second, 82 on the third, 94 on the fourth, 81 on the fifth, 93 on the sixth, 92 on the sabbath, and 30 annually on the anniversary of the "dedication of the House of David".[12] It is in this situation that the form of the book Psalms came into existence. Although many of the Psalms were much older and had been transmitted for a long time, as well as being incorporated into smaller collections earlier, they were combined into one book. The book of Psalms can therefore be described as the songbook of the congregation of the second temple.[13]

After the fall of the temple in 70 CE, many of its practices, including its musical traditions, were *continued* in the *synagogues*.[14] Also for many Jews in the diaspora the synagogue was regarded as some kind of a substitute for the temple. The liturgy of the synagogues in different places deviated, however, in different ways and intensity from that of the temple. In some places the liturgy was even influenced by Greek religious practices.[15] However, it is certain that the synagogal liturgy was based on that of the temple.[16]

There is ample evidence as to the central elements in the synagogal liturgy being based on the temple ceremonies (Philo Vit Mos 3.216; Jos Ant 16.43, Ap 3.216). The most important was *teaching* (it centred on the reading of the Law and the Prophets). Scripture reading was followed by the *discourse*. *Prayer* was also an essential element. The *priestly blessing* also was a crucial element. The congregational *amen* was uttered after each of the three sentences of which the priestly blessing was composed. Singing, or saying as the case may be, of Psalms, was another element in the synagogal service.

Paul was accustomed to Jewish religious rituals. He introduced himself: "I am a true born Jew ... a native of Tarsus in Cilicia. I was brought up in this city, and as a pupil of Gamaliel I was thoroughly trained in every point of our ancestral law" (Acts 22:3). As Paul proclaimed Christianity as the fulfilment of expectations of the Jewish religion, unmistakably he therefore would have had

---

[9] C. SACHS, Rise, 59.
[10] P.J. VAN DYK, Music, 375.
[11] G. ABRAHAM, History, 39.
[12] Also consult J.A. LAMB, Psalms, 12–16.
[13] P.J. VAN DYK, Music, 376.
[14] G. ABRAHAM, History, 39; J.P. LOUW, Fasette, 68.
[15] C. HÖWELER, Inleiding, 14.
[16] W.O.E. OESTERLEY, Jews, 214–215.

the rich Jewish musical traditions in mind when writing to the early Christian communities about song and music in the church.

The most important musical traditions that he most probably had in mind are the following.

Among the Hebrews, songs were sung in different forms of *alteration*.[17] Among these was *responsorial* psalmody by which the leader sang the first line(s) and the congregation responded by singing the following line(s). In such a way, parallel phrases were sung. A thought was restated, continued or amplified by the responding participant (eg. Ps 103; 118; 136). Alteration was also done by *antiphonical* psalmody in which two parts of a verse, or alternate verses, were sung in turn by two choruses.[18]

Another familiar way of "singing" was the *reciting of passages* from Scripture by a soloist, using melodic formulas.[19] In many cases the recitation was answered with outcries like "Hallelujah," "Amen," or "Hosanna".[20]

Paul should have been accustomed to the musical instruments of the Jews. To identify all the *musical instruments* in the Old Testament is a mammoth task.[21] From pictures and archaeological finds we can summarise the different musical instruments as follows:

- idiophones (these are clapping, banging and shaking instruments: e.g. shakers, rattles, cymbals, sistrums and castanets);
- membranophones (these are different types of drumming devices: e.g. the hand-drum, tambourine and kettledrum);
- aerophones (these are blowing instruments: e.g. flutes, trumpets and the horn); and
- cordophones (these are string instruments: e.g. the lyre, harp and lute).

Music had different functions in the Old Testament. With the help of music, the ancient prophet delivered his *oracle*. For example in 2 Kgs 3:15 it is said that the hand of God came upon Elisha while music was played and that he prophesied. From 1 Sam 16:14–23 and 18:10 it is clear that the Israelites attributed *powers* to music. David was commanded to play for Saul, and consequently calmed the evil spirit within him.

A wide *variety* of Jewish songs are known from the Old Testament, too many to mention them all. Apart from the compiled book of the Psalms, one should also take note of the songs like that of Moses (Exod 15:1–19 and Deut 32:1–42), the Prayer of Hannah (1 Sam 2:1–10), the Prayer of Habakkuk (Hab 3), the Prayer of Isaiah (Isa 26:9–20), the Prayer of Jonah (Jonah 2:3–10) and the songs of the three young men (Dan 3:26–83). It is evident that religious music did not belong to the temple alone. Religious songs existed for every occasion: personal prayers, love songs, funeral songs, war songs, working songs, drinking songs, songs praising God, songs to be sung during sacrifice

---

[17] W.O.E. OESTERLEY, Background, 75ff.
[18] G. FOHRER, Introduction, 263.
[19] D.J. GROUT, History, 20; M. KEUCHENIUS, Muziek, 9–10.
[20] H. SCHLIER, Halleluja, 264.
[21] See I.H. JONES, Instruments, 101–115, for a complete treatment.

and songs for specific festivals. Music and singing were part of the formal institutionalised cult as well as the informal religion of everyday life. Music covered every sphere of life in ancient Israel and could be described as humankind's response to the world and to God. Not only was it sung by the priests or levites, it was the "voice" of the people.

It is therefore necessary to take into consideration the Jewish musical traditions when investigating the meaning of Rom 15:9–12, 1 Cor 13–15, Col 3:16 and Eph 5:19 where Paul refers to song, music and musical instruments and elements.

2.2 Greek Musical Traditions

Paul grew up in a cosmopolitan city, Tarsus. Many scholars regard that city as a centre of Greek religion and culture in Paul's days.[22] Surely he was acquainted with Greek civilisation. As Greeks and Hellenistic people were converted to the Christian faith, it is most probable that Paul, in his argumentation on music, also accumulated musical elements from their Greek traditions.

Greek mythology ascribed to music a *divine origin* and named as its inventors and earliest practitioners gods and demigods, such as Apollo, Amphion and Orpheus. The Greeks were the only people to lay stress on the musical abilities of some of their divinities. Gods and men alike made music, finding in it a noble form of expression.[23] The word *music* had a much *wider meaning* to the Greeks than it has for us.[24] It was the adjectival form of *Muse*. In classical mythology the Muse were the nine daughters of Zeus and Mnemosyne who presided over arts and sciences. They sang and danced during feasts of gods under guidance of Apollo.[25] The verbal relation between *Muse* and *music* suggests that among Greeks music was thought of as something common or basic to activities that were concerned with the pursuit of truth and beauty.[26] From earliest times music was an inseparable part of religious ceremonies and had a strong ethical character.[27] These ceremonies were held to honour the gods and to celebrate their truth, beauty and influence on the cosmos and humans.

In the cult of *Apollo* the lyre was the characteristic instrument. This instrument was used to create calmness and harmony, which was associated with the Apollo cult. Very much in contrast to the cult of *Dionysos,* the aulos was the characteristic instrument.[28] This instrument tended to produce excitement and enthusiasm associated with the Dionysos cult. Both these instruments were used for solo playing and accompanying singing and reciting of epic poems.[29]

---

[22] Cf. L. FLOOR, Persone, 4.
[23] K.H. WÖRNER, History, 50
[24] G. ABRAHAM, History, 27.
[25] M. KEUCHENIUS, Muziek, 16.
[26] D.J. GROUT, History, 7.
[27] C. HÖWELER, Inleiding, 17; F. SOKOLOWSKI, History, 215ff.
[28] G. ABRAHAM, History, 25; W.C.M. KLOPPENBURG, Muziek, 2–33.
[29] D.J. GROUT, History, 8–11.

The myth of the competition between Apollo with his lyre and Marsyas with his aulos reflects the clash between the two different musical attitudes. Apollo was victorious. The lyre (and other cordophones) and the aulos were distinctive of two essentially different forms of musical activity. These two were not used together until the rise of tragedy in the 5th century.[30]

Friedrich Nietzsche in *The Birth of Tragedy* (1871) recognised in the Apollonian and the Dionysian two attitudes toward art that were separate in both origin and aim. He assigned the Apollonian principle the realm of dream, of the beautiful light of the inner imaginative world, of higher truth, of measure, of simple transparent beauty, and of the individual. To the Dionysian he attributed intoxication, forgetfulness of self, magic transformation, excess, mystic feeling of identification, titanic and barbaric lust for life, and universality.[31] The Apollonian concept is regarded as that of supra personal, quiet, and reserved type of artistic attitude. The Dionysian is regarded as subjective, uninhibited and orgiastic.

There was a close unity between *melody and poetry*.[32] Greek *music* was almost always associated with *words* or dancing or both. This ruled out a purely contemplative or passive aesthetic enjoyment of music. Song unequivocally possessed pre-eminence. The really sonorous aspect of music was called *melos*. According to Plato, *melos* was composed of *logos* (word), *harmonia* (modulation) that is the relation in terms of tension between successive tones), and *rhythmos* (movement). Tone and *rhythmos* had to subordinate themselves to the word.[33]

The melody and rhythm of music were most intimately bound with the melody and rhythm of poetry. A poet was a composer and vice versa. As a matter of fact, poetry and music were practically synonymous. Lyric poetry was poetry sung to the lyre. Tragedy incorporates the verb ἄδειν (to sing). Many Greek words that designate different kinds of poetry, such as ᾠδή, are in fact musical terms. Forms that lacked music were not designated at all. In the beginning of his *Poetics,* Aristotle, after setting forth melody, rhythm and language as the elements of poetry, continues to say: "There is further an art which imitates by language alone, without harmony, in prose or in verse ... This form of imitation is to this day without name" (I 1447.28). Therefore Greeks were in search for *perfect union of words and music*. Music and words were seen in a complementary relationship. Words are rational while sounds are emotional. When used correctly in union, it could have an immense influence. The composition and performance of this kind of music (Greek amusement) was regarded as a highly developed science rather than a mere form of amusement (in the modern sense of the word).

Greeks attributed *strong power* to music. People thought "amusement" (by music) could heal sickness, purify the body and mind, and work miracles in the

---

[30] K.H. WÖRNER, History, 42.
[31] K.H. WÖRNER, History, 43.
[32] M. KEUCHENIUS, Muziek, 16.
[33] K.H. WÖRNER, History, 42.

realm of nature. Music created a *katharsis* (cleansing) of the *ethos*.[34] They believed there was a *power in music* akin to the power of words that could influence human thought and action. An artist is under obligation to exercise this power with due regard for its effect on others. This probably was the most important aspect of Greek thought about music. The sound combination of music plus words was seen to have a strong ethical effect. Music was not to be used alone or merely to create an emotional effect.

Music had a dominant role as the moral pillar of the political and educational structure. According to the Greek view of music, depending on its particular kind, music had a positive or negative effect on the human will. *Pythagoras,* for instance, argued strongly that humans should take cognisance of the *ethos* or the moral qualities and effects created by music. Music is a force that could affect the universe. Accordingly Pythagoras was supposed to have charged aulos playing with being undisciplined, ignoble and harmful.[35] Hence the attribution of miracles to legendary musicians of mythology. Music has ethical and therapeutic effects on the will and thus the character and conduct of human beings, for music was conceived as a system of musical sounds and rhythms that exemplified the harmony of cosmos and humans corresponding to it.

According to *Aristotle* music imitates (represents) the passions of the soul, i.e. gentleness, anger, courage, temperance, and their opposites. Hence, when one listens to music that imitates a certain passion, he becomes imbued with the same passion. If over a long time he habitually listens to the kind of music that imitates noble or ignoble passions, his character will be shaped accordingly. Thus, if one listens to the wrong kind of music, he will become the wrong kind of person, and vice versa.

Different kinds of music affect character in different ways. Some music tends towards calmness and upliftment. This was typical in the worship of Apollo, where the lyre was used as instrument along with ode- and epic-poetry. Other music tended to produce excitement and enthusiasm. This was typical in the worship of Dionysos, where the aulos was used along with dithyramb and the drama.

Plato and Aristotle were quite clear as to what they meant by a *"right"* person. It is a person who is able to practice self-discipline (ἐγκράτεια). The way to produce such a "right" person was through the system of public education in which the two principle elements were *gymnastic* and *music*. One was suitable for discipline of the body and the other for that of the mind. It was important to balance these two elements. "Mousike" was good for the soul and gymnastic for the body.[36]

Plato wrote: *"Let me make the songs of a nation and I care not who makes the laws"* (Resp III 398ff; Leg VII 812e) while Aristotle argued that the music used for education the young should be regulated by law (Pol 5–7).

---

[34] C. HÖWELER, Inleiding, 24.
[35] K.H. WÖRNER, History, 52.
[36] G. ABRAHAM, History, 32–33; W.C.M. KLOPPENBURG, Muziek, 28.

Musical performances, however, were mostly *improvised*. The skilled performer was, to a certain extent, also the composer. For specific circumstances and needs, the musician could improvise accordingly. This music was composed according to one of the many individual artistic forms. The *hymnos*, for example, was a lofty art song for the gods or late heroes, usually accompanied by a stringed instrument. Also the living heroes were entertained with song at their banquets with *aoidoi*, which were heroic songs to be believed to arise directly from divine inspiration – an idea that went back to the conception of the magical force of music.[37]

In the closer examination of the musical references in Rom 15:9–12, 1 Cor 13–15, Col 3:16 and Eph 5:19 it is therefore also important to take these Greek musical traditions into consideration.

2.3 Roman Musical Traditions

We have no authentic remains of Roman music, but only second hand information from accounts of performances and theoretical treatises. From these accounts it is uncertain whether Romans made any significant contributions to the theory and practice of music. They seemingly took most of their art music from Greece, especially after that country became a Roman province in 146 BC.[38] During the Hellenistic period the Roman culture was suffused with the Greek cultural heritage. This imported culture replaced much of indigenous Etruscan and Italian music. The result is that Rome did not make much of an independent contribution to the history of music.

From the writings of Cicero and Quintilian it is clear that *familiarity with music* was considered a part of the education of a cultivated person.[39] There are reports of the popularity of virtuosos, prevalence of large choruses and orchestras, and grandiose musical festivals and competitions. Singing in every sphere of social activity, such as at work, recreations, and worship are described, along with festive songs, satirical songs, love-songs and drinking songs. Many emperors were patrons of music. Nero even aspired to personal fame as a musician.

Romans invented or developed music *chiefly for military* purposes. For this purpose some *brass instruments* of trumpet and horn types were developed. Their innovations were limited to the trumpet family. These instruments were used in the first place for military signals but also in religious ceremonies.[40]

To a lesser extent than with the Jewish and Greek musical traditions, Roman traditions should be taken into consideration in an investigation of possible influences in passages in which Paul refers to musical elements. It should not be neglected, however.

---

[37] F.P. VILJOEN, Betekenis, 219–220; K.H. WÖRNER, History, 50.
[38] W.C.M. KLOPPENBURG, Muziek, 34; K.H. WÖRNER, History, 55, 58.
[39] D.J. GROUT, History, 18.
[40] G. ABRAHAM, History, 42.

3 Influences in Christian Music?

Within the context of the Jewish, Greek and Roman musical traditions, passages in which Paul refers to musical elements are now investigated. Thus it is determined to what extent these traditions had influenced his consideration on these kind of issues. Some light from the musical traditions is also given to the understanding of these passages.

3.1 Romans 15:9–12

In *Romans 15:6* Paul encourages the congregation to praise the God and Father of our Lord Jesus Christ with one mind and voice:

ἵνα ὁμοθυμαδὸν ἐν ἑνὶ στόματι δοξάζητε
τὸν θεὸν καὶ πατέρα τοῦ κυρίου ἡμῶν Ἰησοῦ Χριστοῦ.

His readers were Christians in Rome (1:7,15). It seems that most of the church consisted of non-Jews. However, there must have been a considerable amount of Jews in the church of Rome as well.[41]

The encouragement in Romans 15:6 occurs within the larger context of Rom 15:1–13, which forms an *antithetical correlation* with Rom 1:1–17.[42] In Rom 1:1–17 the nations are described as denying God his glory. In Rom 15:1–13, in contrast, people are described who glorify Him. In Rom 1:18–21 the essence of the iniquity of the heathen nations is identified as their refusal to glorify and thank God as God. In Rom 15:1–13 the church, however, is depicted as a doxological community. This doxological function is the church's reaction to the mercy of God (Rom 12:1).

It is significant how strongly Paul places the emphasis on unity within the doxological community.[43] Rom 15:5–6 describes a *prayer for unity* of mind in the congregation by following the example of Christ's self-denial, it calls for pleasing others for their good, to build up their faith, so that with one heart and mouth the congregation may praise the God and Father of our Lord Jesus Christ. The prayer aims at and implies singing in unison of strong and weak believers, of Jews and Gentiles, united in their praise of God and in making one another happy, instead of despising or condemning one another (15:1–3, 8–9, 14:3,10).[44]

The influence of *Jewish traditions* is remarkable in Paul's encouragement of the community to praise God in unison. In Romans 15:9–12 he quotes four passages from Jewish Scriptures, viz. the Law (*Torah*) (Deut 32:43), the Prophets (*Nebiim*) (Isa 11:20, 2 Sam 22:50) and Writings (*Ketubim*) (Ps 18:50; 117:1). Paul's acquaintance with these passages and songs *testifies to their influence* in his thinking and religious practice.

---

[41] G.M.M. PELSER, Brief, 44–45.
[42] A.B. DU TOIT, Kirche, 69–77.
[43] C.E.B. CRANFIELD, Romans. A Shorter Commentary, 396.
[44] G. SASS, Röm 15,7–13, 510ff.

- Romans 15:9

διὰ τοῦτο ἐξομολογήσομαί σοι ἐν ἔθνεσιν
καὶ τῷ ὀνόματί σου ψαλῶ. (Ps 18:50 [17:49, LXX[45]])

The first of the four supporting Old Testament quotations is from the Writings. The phrase is structured according to typical Jewish parallelism. Paul cites David's song of royal thanksgiving as proof of God's saving will to join Jew and Gentile in praise. According to this quotation it was David's desire that the nations become acquainted with his Lord who delivered and enthroned him. Therefore he tells them about the Lord by singing with accompaniment. Paul may have seen in the psalmist's words a foreshadowing of his own mission as the Jewish apostle of the Gentiles.[46]

- Romans 15:10

εὐφράνθητε, ἔθνη, μετὰ τοῦ λαοῦ αὐτοῦ. (Deut 32:43, LXX).

Paul takes his second supporting quotation from the Law. In this song of Moses the gentiles are summoned to join Israel, rejoicing in God's salvation of his people. Paul quotes this song to substantiate his admonition that Jews and Gentiles should accept one another and so glorify God in unison, thereby implying joyful singing together in the congregation.

- Romans 15:11

αἰνεῖτε, πάντα τὰ ἔθνη, τὸν κύριον
καὶ ἐπαινεσάτωσαν αὐτὸν πάντες οἱ λαοί. (Ps 117:1 [116:1 LXX]).

This song is a post-exilic psalm from the Writings which calls on the aid of all the nations of the world to sing the praise of the graceful and faithful covenant Lord. Paul utilises this post-exilic psalm, with its repetition of "all" in two parallel phrases, to call on Jews and Gentiles to sing the praise of the Father of our Lord Jesus Christ with one heart.

- Romans 15:12

ἔσται ἡ ῥίζα τοῦ Ἰεσσαὶ
   καὶ ὁ ἀνιστάμενος ἄρχειν ἐθνῶν,
ἐπ' αὐτῷ ἔθνη ἐλπιοῦσιν. (Isa 11:10, LXX).

The last quotation refers to the scion from Jesse, probably referring to Hezekiah in whom people, seeking after God, would put their hope. Paul applies this prophetic chorus to the humble Christ as ruler and hope of Jews and Gentiles in their united praise of God. In his mission Christ fulfils the universal

---

[45] The psalm also occurs in 2Sam 22:50.
[46] C.E.B. CRANFIELD, Romans II, 745.

salvation of the nations. This quotation from the Prophets completes the Old Testament validation of Paul's declaration in verse 8–9.

Writing in Greek, quoting from a Greek translation of the Jewish Bible (LXX) to a congregation in Rome, Paul seemingly expects them to sing together in the *lingua franca* to express their faith in the Father of their mutual Lord, Jesus Christ.[47] Singing was an essential and integral part of worship in Judaism, and Paul carries their practice of singing, as well as their songs as such, over to early Christian worship.[48] The Christians in Rome consisted of Gentiles (Romans and Greek) and Jews. Thus Paul presents a compelling vision of the church as community of redeemed Jews and Gentiles, praising God together for his faithfulness and mercy, made possible by Christ.[49]

3.2 1 Corinthians 13–15

Paul writes 1 Corinthians to a church with a cosmopolitan composition.[50] In 1 Cor 13–14 he makes several musical references in his discussion of the gifts of the Spirit. All these gifts ought to be used in worship to build up one another (1 Cor 14:3–9).[51] It is clear, however, that not all of the references to musical instruments and elements in these passages refer to real musical activity. In some cases he uses musical terminology to illustrate his point.

In *1 Corinthians 13:1* he refers negatively to the clank of a brass gong and the shrill clash of a cymbal:

Ἐὰν ταῖς γλώσσαις τῶν ἀνθρώπων λαλῶ καὶ τῶν ἀγγέλων, ἀγάπην δὲ μὴ ἔχω, γέγονα χαλκὸς ἠχῶν ἢ κύμβαλον ἀλαλάζον.

Although Paul does not refer to real music as such, he refers to these instruments to make his argument more precise and convincing. In the Greek and Hellenistic world, the brass gong and cymbal, which produced a loud and harsh sound, were associated with orgiastic cults of Cybele and Dionysos.[52] These instruments' enslaving rhythm overstimulates the nerves to captivate the mind on its way to ecstasy. Against this background, the meaning of Paul's words in this verse becomes clear. Speaking the best speech of earth or heaven without love is but a noise. Then these speeches are worthless like empty hollow noises associated of pagan worship. They only stir up peoples' nerves and stimulate them towards mindless ecstasy.[53]

In *1 Corinthians 14:7* Paul again illustrates his argument by referring to the sound of musical instruments.

ὅμως τὰ ἄψυχα φωνὴν διδόντα, εἴτε αὐλὸς εἴτε κιθάρα,

---

[47] F.S. MALAN, Church Singing, 511.
[48] Cf. G.D. FEE, First Corinthians, 671.
[49] J.R. WAGNER, Christ, 473ff.
[50] B.C. LATEGAN, 1 Korintiërs, 59.
[51] Cf. P.W. HOON, Liturgy, 482–497.
[52] L. MORRIS, First Corinthians, 182.
[53] G.D. FEE, First Corinthians, 313.

ἐὰν διαστολὴν τοῖς φθόγγοις μὴ δῷ,
πῶς γνωσθήσεται τὸ αὐλούμενον ἢ τὸ κιθαριζόμενον;

Once again he does not discuss real musical activity. However, he uses musical references to explain his argument. He rebukes the Corinthians' affinity to the spectacular character of ecstatic utterances. In doing this, he reminds them that neither the flute (αὐλός) or the harp (κιθάρα) makes sense unless there is a meaningful variation in sounds produced.

If one keeps in mind that the Corinthian people would immediately associate the flute (αὐλός) with the Dionysos cult and the harp (κιθάρα) with the Apollo cult, it seems that Paul is referring to an even more confusing sound. For the traditional Greeks these two instruments were used for opposite effects. The flute, as used in the Dionysos cult, was meant to stimulate its hearers towards ecstasy. In contrast to that, the harp, as used in the Apollo cult, was used to calm down its hearers. These two instruments were thus distinctive of two essentially different forms of musical activity. Being played simultaneously and without distinction, they would have been extremely confusing. Such, says Paul, is the meaningless and unintelligible ecstatic sounds of the Corinthians. It is an aimless jangle that means nothing.

Paul continues his argumentation in *1 Corinthians 14:8* by referring to the sound of a bugle or trumpet.

καὶ γὰρ ἐὰν ἄδηλον σάλπιγξ φωνὴν δῷ, τίς παρασκευάσεται εἰς πόλεμον;

With this references Paul places his first readers in the military realm known in the Roman Empire. Although not unknown by the Jews, it was the Romans who developed brass instruments chiefly for military purposes. The Corinthians were familiar with to the use of a σάλπιγξ (bugle) to summon soldiers to a battle. But the bugle call is confusing if the bugler blows the bugle without sounding the battle cry. In the same way, if one's ecstatic utterances yield no precise meaning, they are meaningless.

In *1 Corinthians 14:15–17* Paul once again uses musical references in his argumentation to explain the value of the gifts. In this case, however, he refers to real musical activity as well.

(14:15) τί οὖν ἐστιν; προσεύξομαι τῷ πνεύματι, προσεύξομαι δὲ καὶ τῷ νοΐ· ψαλῶ τῷ πνεύματι, ψαλῶ δὲ καὶ τῷ νοΐ.
(14:16) ἐπεὶ ἐὰν εὐλογῇς [ἐν] πνεύματι, ὁ ἀναπληρῶν τὸν τόπον τοῦ ἰδιώτου πῶς ἐρεῖ τὸ ἀμὴν ἐπὶ τῇ σῇ εὐχαριστίᾳ; ἐπειδὴ τί λέγεις οὐκ οἶδεν·
(14:17) σὺ μὲν γὰρ καλῶς εὐχαριστεῖς ἀλλ' ὁ ἕτερος οὐκ οἰκοδομεῖται.

Along with prayer, hymn singing (ψάλλειν) is inspired by God, but should be intelligible. One should enter into these practices with the mind and with the spirit.[54] The Corinthians had a shamanistic idea of prophecy accompanied by trance as in Greco-Roman religions. Paul argues that this should not be the case in the Christian religion.[55] People praying and singing praise to God

---
[54] G.T. EDDY, Understanding, 12–16.
[55] T. CALLAN, Prophecy, 125–140.

should do it with active minds to build up themselves and one another. Seen within the context of Greek theory of music as described by Plato and Aristotle, the correct use of song and music could be a powerful instrument to build up a person's character. According to Greek mythology, song and music were created by gods and are given to people through the inspiration of the Muse to be used in religious ceremonies and the edification of the humans. Over and against Greek mythology, Paul describes the inspiration to song and music as a gift from God. It is to be used for praise and thanksgiving to God (14:16). It also serves as instruction in the gathered community (14:17).

In *1 Corinthians 14:26* Paul takes up the theme again of song and music as one of a variety of gifts God gives to the church.

Τί οὖν ἐστιν, ἀδελφοί; ὅταν συνέρχησθε,
ἕκαστος ψαλμὸν ἔχει, διδαχὴν ἔχει, ἀποκάλυψιν ἔχει, γλῶσσαν ἔχει, ἑρμηνείαν ἔχει· πάντα πρὸς οἰκοδομὴν γινέσθω.

When the church come together for worship, individuals have something to contribute. One kind of contribution is that of singing a hymn. Here the meaning is that someone will have a song, presumably of his own composition or perhaps a spontaneous creation.[56] According to Greek traditions of music, performances were usually based on solo improvisation. While singing, music was created anew, using certain traditional musical formulas. Within this frame of mind, Paul probably refers to songs composed at the spur of the moment thanks to the Spirit's inspiration. In context of the different gifts of the Spirit, these songs of praise are to be seen as gifts for upbuilding of the congregation's faith in Jesus Christ (14:3). Paul is pleased with a contribution of each member to the liturgy on the condition that it edifies the church.

In 1 Corinthians 15 Paul discusses the issue of resurrection. Paul exults in the triumph won over death. In *15:52* Paul mentions the trumpet (bugle) that signals the resurrection of the dead in a figurative manner.

ἐν ἀτόμῳ, ἐν ῥιπῇ ὀφθαλμοῦ, ἐν τῇ ἐσχάτῃ σάλπιγγι· σαλπίσει γὰρ καὶ οἱ νεκροὶ ἐγερθήσονται ἄφθαρτοι καὶ ἡμεῖς ἀλλαγησόμεθα.

Within the Hellenistic world, especially among the Romans, the bugle was very much associated with battles and triumph over the enemy. Within the Jewish tradition the sound of the bugle was also associated with the triumph of God over his enemy at the end of time.[57] With this frame of reference, Paul describes the sounding of the bugle figuratively to be the signal for the dead to rise. The last enemy is conquered. Death is swallowed up. Victory is won! The end of time has come. It is time for festivity and triumph.

---

[56] G.D. FEE, First Corinthians, 671.
[57] L. MORRIS, First Corinthians, 233.

3.3 Ephessians 5:19

In Eph 5:19 Paul encourages his readers to praise God with song and music. This act distinguishes the behaviour of a believer from that of an unbeliever.

In 5:3–14 Paul refers to light and darkness to compare the behaviour of the believing community in contrast with unbelieving outsiders. He continues in 5:15–20 to describe wise living over against foolish and reckless living. A wise person is one with insight into the norm of life given by the Lord (5:15,17), and one having the insight to apply it to everyday life (5:21ff). The contrast between the two conditions also becomes evident from the way people are elevated. The foolish person is filled with wine, but the wise with the Holy Spirit.[58] The foolish person is excited as a result of drunkenness. The wise person is elevated because of the enlightenment and inspiration of the Holy Spirit.[59]

The bad influence of drunkenness leads a person to become unwise (5:15) and foolish (5:16). Drunkenness leads towards dissipation, recklessness and most probably to filthy drinking songs. Drunkenness in the Hellenistic world was quite common.[60] In contrast to drunkenness, Spirit-filled persons sing to one another psalms, hymns and spiritual songs in worship to God.

(5:18) καὶ μὴ μεθύσκεσθε οἴνῳ, ἐν ᾧ ἐστιν ἀσωτία,
ἀλλὰ πληροῦσθε ἐν πνεύματι,
(5:19) λαλοῦντες ἑαυτοῖς [ἐν] ψαλμοῖς καὶ ὕμνοις καὶ ᾠδαῖς πνευματικαῖς,
ᾄδοντες καὶ ψάλλοντες τῇ καρδίᾳ ὑμῶν τῷ κυρίῳ,
(5:20) εὐχαριστοῦντες πάντοτε ὑπὲρ πάντων ἐν ὀνόματι τοῦ κυρίου ἡμῶν
Ἰησοῦ Χριστοῦ τῷ θεῷ καὶ πατρί.

When reading Eph 5:18, knowing the way the Greeks and Romans worshipped their gods with song, an even further allusion of Paul's words seems probable. Their worship to the god of the vine, Bacchus (according to the Romans) or Dionysos (according to the Greeks) was known for its emotional and mass ecstasy.[61] Bacchus or Dionysos was the cheerful god of ecstasy. During their worship, people were filled with the fruit of the wine and became drunk, believing to be filled with the god and being "high" to their god. After a bemusing and outrageous dance the revelator fell into a trance and received a message from Dionysos.[62] Paul contrasts this behaviour at the Dionysos feasts to the worship of the Lord Jesus Christ and his Father. The Christian community should rather be filled with the Holy Spirit so as to sing in an elevated manner in honour of God.

The contrast is clear. A person, who is filled with the fruit of the vine and Dinonysos behaves foolish and reckless. With foolish songs that person has a bad influence on his or her community. Typical elements of the Dionysion

---

[58] Cf. P.W. GOSNELL, Ephesians 5:18–20, 363ff.
[59] S.D.F. SALMOND, Epistle of the Ephesians, 363.
[60] F.W. GROSHEIDE, Brief aan de Efeziërs, 83.
[61] H.L. DRUMWRIGHT, Dionysia, 127; A. VAN ROON, Lied, 135.
[62] E.M. BLAIKLOCK, Dionysos, 128–129.

intoxication were forgetfulness of self, excess and a barbaric lust of life. Such behaviour is not fitting for a believer. A believer should be filled with the Holy Spirit. A person who is filled with the Holy Spirit, is guided by the Spirit. Such a person celebrates the truth and influence of the Lord on the world. He or she receives insight into the will of the Lord, and has the insight to apply it to everyday life.

By singing he or she *finds out how the Lord wants* him or her to live. Through the songs in the congregation in which wholehearted praise is offered to God, the believers build up each other in their faith.[63] In Jewish and Greek musical tradition, song and music have the power and mandate to teach.[64] Song and music had a dominant role as a moral pillar of the political and educational structure to create moral qualities and effects. Paul most probably refers to that connotation of music in Eph 5:18ff.

Paul encourages the Christians to honour God with *psalms, hymns and spiritual songs* (ψαλμοῖς καὶ ὕμνοις καὶ ᾠδαῖς πνευματικαῖς). These terms refer to a wide *array and diversity of songs*.[65] These musical terms were known in the Greek, Roman and Jewish communities. In the Hellenistic world, *psalms* often testified to gladness and singing by the accompaniment of a string instrument. String instruments were used to create calmness and harmony in Jewish and Greek music. Jewish people might also have thought of the many Old Testament songs as a prototype of psalms here mentioned. With a wide variety of psalms the Israelites celebrated the Lord and his great deeds in relation with his people. *Hymns* in the Hellenistic world were lofty songs, which often testified and recounted a heroic act of a late person[66] or god. By these songs worshippers would express their respect for such a person or god. Paul uses this known term to encourage his readers to sing songs in which they express their trust in the Lord, his might and his salvation in numerous situations. Paul also refers to *spiritual songs*. The term "songs" is quite a neutral term for singing. In the Greek musical tradition, heroes were entertained with these songs during the banquets. These heroic songs were mostly sung in an improvised manner and were believed to arise directly form divine inspiration. Paul probably referred to this kind of songs, but in honour of the Lord. These songs should be inspired by the Holy Spirit.[67]

---

[63] F. GRIFFITH, Role, 37ff.
[64] Cf. L.R. PAYTON, Musician, 81–84.
[65] G.V. WIBERG, Looks, 35.
[66] Hymns were usually not dedicated to living humans. Only after death they would be honored with hymns.
[67] F.P. VILJOEN, Betekenis, 250.

3.4 Colossians 3:16

Colossians and Ephesians are closely related[68] and consequently we find a close link between Col 3:16 and Eph 5:18–19. Once again, in Col 3:16, Paul describes song and music in his discussion of the contrast between a people living the old life and the new life. With their psalms, hymns and spiritual songs the members admonish one another to put to death the earthly desires in them, and clothe themselves with the qualities of Christ (3:5–15).

(3:16) Ὁ λόγος τοῦ Χριστοῦ ἐνοικείτω ἐν ὑμῖν πλουσίως,
ἐν πάσῃ σοφίᾳ διδάσκοντες καὶ νουθετοῦντες ἑαυτούς,
ψαλμοῖς ὕμνοις ᾠδαῖς πνευματικαῖς
ἐν [τῇ] χάριτι ᾄδοντες ἐν ταῖς καρδίαις ὑμῶν τῷ θεῷ·
(3:17) καὶ πᾶν ὅ τι ἐὰν ποιῆτε ἐν λόγῳ ἢ ἐν ἔργῳ,
πάντα ἐν ὀνόματι κυρίου Ἰησοῦ,
εὐχαριστοῦντες τῷ θεῷ πατρὶ δι' αὐτοῦ.

Most remarkable is the *parallel between being filled with the Spirit* (πληροῦσθε ἐν πνεύματι) (Eph 5:18) and being filled with the *Word of Christ* (ὁ λόγος τοῦ Χριστοῦ ἐνοικείτω ἐν ὑμῖν πλουσίως) (Col 3:16). This indicates the close link between the work of the Spirit and the Word in believers' lives. Reading these verses with the reference to the Hellenistic Dionysos and Bacchus cult in mind, the meaning of Paul's admonition becomes more clear. In the Hellenistic religious ceremonies the worshipper would become full of their god by means of the wine and then in an outrageous trance would speak the word from their god. In contrast to the Hellenistic worship, believers being filled by the Holy Spirit will speak out words and insights given by the Holy Spirit. In such a way the Word of Christ would play a comprehensive role among them, forming the centre of their interest. The Word of Christ would form the source and substance of their singing while bowing to Christ's authority. While singing, Christians minister the word of Christ to each other so that the word indwells the corporate life of the church.[69]

This edifying role of song and music correlates with the Greek theory of music. Music was concerned with the pursuit of truth and beauty. According to Plato and Aristotle, this should be the most important use of song and music. Paul writes that members should teach and admonish *one another in their pursuit of truth, very much the way prescribed by the Greek theory of music*. The mutual edification of one another could probably happen by means of responsorial, antiphonical and/or solo singing of typical of Jewish music.

Thus Paul advises Spirit-prompted singing by which believers would instruct one another and glorify God by witnessing the rich dwelling of the word of Christ among them. Though psalms, hymns and spiritual songs are primarily the means of the congregation's worship of God, it is also a very effective

---

[68] Because of this close relation between Colossians an Ephesians, some scholars question the authorship of one or both of these letters. Consult my first footnote.
[69] C. BUCHANAN, Doctrine, 17–20.

teaching aid.[70] Christian psalms, hymns and spiritual songs should therefore contain both devotion and doctrine in content.

4 Conclusion

Knowledge of the Greek, Jewish and Roman musical traditions are necessary for a better understanding of passages in the writings of Paul in which he refers to musical terms. Apparently in these passages he assumes knowledge of these traditions among his first readers.

Paul encourages Christians in a Hellenised world, knowledgeable of Greek, Roman and Jewish musical traditions to praise God in unison. This is very much so in Rom 15:9–12, 1 Cor 14:15–17, 26, Eph 5:19 and Col 3:16. In the other passages from 1 Corinthians discussed above, Paul utilises musical elements and terminology to explain his argument. The modern exegete attains better insight into what Paul meant in each of these references to music when he also takes note of various musical traditions known in the Hellenistic world.

Thus even today this explanation and encouragement could be applicable to Christians in another time, environment, and with different cultural origins. In addition to a better understanding of Paul, Christians can also unite in praise and worship to the triune God.

---

[70] F.S. MALAN, Church Singing, 522.

Bibliography

ABRAHAM, Gerald, The Concise Oxford History of Music, Oxford 1985.
BLAIKLOCK, Edward Musgrave, Dionysos, in: TENNEY, Merrill C. (ed.), The Zondervan Pictorial Encyclopaedia of the Bible 5, Grand Rapids 1977, 128f.
BLOEM, G.N., Skrif en lied, in: SMUTS, Albertus Jesse (red.), Die Woord aan die werk. Oor die kerkliked, prediking, kategese. Referate van die SA Werkgemeenskap vir Praktiese Teologie 1983–1985. Pretoria 1985, 46–53.
BUCHANAN, Colin,. Doctrine and Worship. in: Evangel 16 (1998), 17–20.
CALLAN, Terrance, Prophecy and Ecstacy in Greco-Roman Religions and in 1 Corinthians, in: NT 27 (1985), 125–140.
CRANFIELD, Charles E.B., A Critical and Exegetical Commentary on the Epistle to the Romans 2. Commentary on Romans 9–16 and essays, ICC, Edinburgh 1979.
ID., Romans. A shorter commentary. Grand Rapids 1985.
DRUMWRIGHT, Huber L., Dionysia, in: Merrill C. TENNEY (ed.), The Zondervan Pictorial Encyclopaedia of the Bible 5, Grand Rapids 1977, 127.
DU TOIT, Andrie B, Die Kirche als doxologische Gemeinschaft im Romerbrief, in: Neot 27 (1993), 69–77.
EDDY, G.Thackray, "With the Understanding", in: ExpT 95 (1983/84), 12–16.
FEE, Gordon D., The First Epistle to the Corinthians, NICNT, Grand Rapids 1987.
FLOOR, Lambertus, Persone rondom Paulus. Pretoria 1978.
ID., Efeziërs – Eén in Christus. Commentaar op het Nieuwe Testament. Ser. 3. Afd. Brieven van Paulus 1, Kampen 1995.
FOHRER, Georg, Introduction to the Old Testament. London 1968.
GOSNELL, Peter.W., Ephesians 5:18–20 and Mealtime Propriety, in: Tyndale Bulletin 44 (1993), 363–371.
GRIFFITH, Frank, The Role of Singing in the Life and Worship of the Church, in: Reformation and Revival Journal 4 (1995), 37–60.
GROSHEIDE, Frederik W., De Brief van Paulus aan de Efeziërs, Kampen 1960.
GROUT, Donald Jay, A History of Western Music, New York 1960.
GUTHRIE, Donald, New Testament Introduction, Leicester 1970.
HOON, Paul W., Liturgy of Gamesmanship? in: Religion in Life 38 (1969), 482–497.
HÖWELER, Casper, Inleiding tot de Muziekgeschiedenis, Amsterdam 1951.
JONES, Ivor H., Musical instruments in the Bible (I), in: Bible Translator 37 (1986), 101–115.
KEUCHENIUS, Mieke (ed.), Muziek onder woorden. Utrecht 1977.
KLOPPENBURG, W.C.M., Muziek door de eeuwen. Amsterdam 1963.
LAMB, John. Alexander, The Psalms in Christian Worship, London 1962.
LATEGAN, Bernard C., 1 Korintiërs, in: Andrie B. DU TOIT (red.), Handleiding by die Nuwe Testament, Volume V, Pretoria 1984, 57–79.
LOUW, Jannie P., Fasette van die Hellenisme. Pretoria 1981.
MALAN, Francois S., Church Singing According to the Pauline Epistles, in: Neot 32 (1998), 509–524.
MORRIS, Leon, The First Epistle of Paul to the Corinthians, The Tyndale New Testament Commentaries. Leicester 1983.
OESTERLEY, William Oscar Emil, The Jews and Judaism during the Greek Period: Background of Christianity, London 1941.
ID., The Jewish Background of Christian Liturgy. London 1965.

PELSER, Gerhardus M.M., Die Brief aan die Romeine in: Andrie B. DU TOIT (red.), Handleiding by die Nuwe Testament, Volume V, Pretoria 1984, 41–56.
PAYTON, Leonard R., A Chief Musician is a Pastor-Teacher, in: Reformation and Revival Journal 3 (1994), 81–84.
SASS, Gerhard, Röm 15,7–13 – als Summe des Römerbriefs gelesen in: EvTh 53 (1993), 510–527.
SACHS, Curt, The Rise of Music in the Ancient World: East and West, New York 1943.
SALMOND, S.D.F., The Epistle of the Ephesians. The Expositor's Greek Testament. Grand Rapids 1951.
SCHLIER, Heinrich,. Halleluja, in: Gerhard KITTEL (ed.), Theological Dictionary of the New Testament I (Grand Rapids 1969), 264.
SOKOLOWSKI, F., From the History of the Worship of Apollo at Actium, in: HThR 52 (1959), 215–221.
VAN DYK, P.J., Music in Old Testament Times, in: Old Testament Essays 4 (1991), 373–380.
VAN ROON, A., De lied van Paulus aan de Epheziers, De prediking van het Nieuwe Testament 10, Callenbach 1976.
VILJOEN, Francois P., Die Betekenis van "Psalmois, Humnois" en "Odais Pneumatikais" in Kolossense 3:16 en Efesiërs 5:19, Th.D. Thesis Potchefstroomse Universiteit vir CHO, Potchefstroom 1990.
WAGNER, J. Ross, The Christ, Servant of Jew and Gentile: A Fresh Approach to Romans 15:8–9, in: JBL 116 (1997), 473–485.
WÖRNER, Karel Heinrich, History of Music, New York – London 1973.
WIBERG, Glen V., A Covenanter Looks at Praise Songs, in: Covenant Quarterly 56 (1998), 34–41.

Lauri Thurén

Jeremiah 27 and Civil Obedience in 1 Peter

1 Peter, like Romans 13, includes a rare explicit discussion of the relationship between the first Christians and Roman officials. The addressees are enjoined to be submissive to the Gentile authorities.[1] This seemingly simple thrust of the Epistle, however, involves several problems. Whence does it come? Is obedience to the officials a purposeful tactical move? Is it an innovation of early Christianity, or can it be traced back to older traditions? Further, can we speak of "ein hündisches Verhalten",[2] or is the proper attitude more critical? Finally, how can it be explained that 1 Peter simultaneously advocates a diametrically opposite view when speaking of other Gentile neighbors?

In this paper I shall focus on the ambivalence toward the Gentiles in 1 Peter, search for the roots of obedience toward the Roman officials, and study the function and limits of this attitude. Instead of modern connotations that could easily lead into anachronisms, the Old Testament, here especially Jeremiah 27, and the early Jewish background is of vital importance.

1. A Critical Attitude toward Society

1 Peter instructs its recipients to be submissive to "every human authority": king, governors, masters, and non-believing husbands (1 Pet 2–3). They ought to honor and show proper respect to all these people, who supposedly are mostly non-Christians.

This fits well the general style of 1 Peter, which can be described as friendly and civilized, and not only toward its recipients. The epistle differs from most New Testament writings, in which authors are frequently hostile to their enemies and use strong, vilifying language.[3] No direct antagonists are apparent, perhaps due to the nature of the text as letter to be circulated over a vast area. Unlike the Apocalypse, no sweeping statements about the authorities are presented.

However, in diametric contrast to the respectful, submissive attitude toward the Gentile officials, the rest of the surrounding society, viz. the Gentile neighbors, is frequently depicted negatively – although not directly attacked. How is this difference in attitude toward two types of Gentiles to be explained? Is it

---

[1] Also Tit 3:1, like in Romans and in 1 Peter, the recipients are commanded "to be subject (ὑποτάσσεσθαι) to rulers and authorities, to be obedient."
[2] N. BROX, Petrusbrief, 124, emphatically denies this interpretation.
[3] I have studied the polemical and vilifying language in Galatians, 2 Peter and Jude (L. THURÉN, Style; Jude; Paul). See also C. SCHLUETER, Filling up.

attributable to early Christian political opportunism or are other solutions available?

The first part of the letter (1:1–2:10) describes the addressees' former way of life. In 1:1 they are called "strangers". This is hardly done in order to provide sociological information about their own status in the society,[4] but rather to dissociate them from other people and to build their identity as members of Israel, viz. God's people.[5]

According to 1:3 the addressees have been born into a living hope, which presumably neither they nor their neighbors had in the past. This is stated more explicitly in 1:14, which reports that the addressees formerly lived "in ignorance" and had "evil desires". This way of life, inherited from their forefathers, was "futile" (1:18) and perishable (1:23). Such expressions not only emphasize the addressees' present glory as members of God's people, but simultaneously indirectly describe the attributes of the surrounding society. Although not yet stated clearly, it becomes obvious that people who do not belong to the addressees continue to lead a futile, perishable life filled with evil desires.

The second part of the letter is more explicit concerning the addressees' fellow citizens. 2:25 still speaks only of the addressees' past life ("you were like sheep going astray"). However, according to 3:16, in the present other people "speak maliciously against your good behavior", and will be put to shame. Finally, in 4:2–6 the true nature of the Gentiles is revealed: they live for evil desires, they have chosen to lead lives of "debauchery, lust, drunkenness, orgies, carousing and detestable idolatry." They are "plunging into the flood of dissipation", but will be judged by God. In other parts of the letter, the ideas of judgment and doom are reiterated (2:7–8; 4:17–18).

The antagonists are vilified with a stereotypical list of vices, which resemble Paul and standard Hellenistic language.[6] In fact, the author is doing exactly what he claims that the addressees' neighbors are doing – speaking maliciously of them. Vilification of others on the one hand highlights the addressees' current status – it typically occurs in an antithetical setting, where the two ways of life are compared. Simultaneously the addressees are warned against falling back to such vices, as this may jeopardize their new status. The objective, in other words, is to dissociate the addressees from the surrounding society.

This becomes especially clear in 3:18–22, where the example of Noah is utilized. The addressees and their baptism are identified with Noah and the other seven souls, who were saved "through water" (δι' ὕδατος). *Dia* cannot be understood locally (meaning "Noah walked to the Ark through water") or instrumentally, as if the Flood carried the Ark. The danger, from which the Flood saved Noah, was the unjust society. As the water separated Noah from

---

[4] Against J. ELLIOTT, Home, who imposes a modern sociological framework on the letter. His main hypothesis is that the recipients were not religious but sociological foreigners, and that the major advantage of Christian congregations was that they could provide these immigrants with security and self-esteem. For criticism see R. FELDMEIER, Christen.

[5] See L. THURÉN, Argument, 195–202.

[6] See E. KAMLAH, Form, 145–148.

his neighbors, so also the baptismal water separates the addressees from those around them.[7] Thus the whole society is labeled as wicked; the emperor is not excluded. This, however, remains implicit: the emphasis is on baptism, not on political criticism.

2. A Positive Portrayal of Roman Power

Contrary to everything said or hinted about the pagan neighbors, the statements concerning the Roman officials are very positive.

In 2:13–14 the addressees are told to be submissive to every human authority: to the king as the supreme authority and to the governors who are appointed by him. This is not just clever tactics: the author is speaking of a specific attitude. In 2:17 it is reiterated that the addressees ought to honor the king. Both the king and the governors are described as acting righteously, punishing criminals and rewarding those who do right: "[they are] sent by him to punish those who do wrong and to praise those who do right." In fact, the officials are compared to God, who follows exactly the same principle: "For the eyes of the Lord are on the righteous, and his ears are open to their prayer. But the face of the Lord is against those who do evil" (3:12).

The difference in the language as concerns the pagan neighbors and the pagan officials is obvious. Whereas the first group is vilified and dissociative language is used to establish a distance between them and the addressees, the latter are described almost as divine agents, or righteous servants of the divinity. Nowhere is it claimed or even hinted at that the officials would cause the addressees "all kinds of trials", which are more or less attributed to the pagan neighbors.

The judgment of God will fall on those who do evil (3:12; 4:5,18), but the officials are not included in this category. However, they are not described as devout either. As non-baptized they could be imagined to belong to the wrong group in the Flood story, but this may already be a far-fetched assumption.

3. The Origins of Obedience

How can the sharp difference between bad neighbors and good officials be explained if they both belong to the pagan community? Is it attributable to some strategic plot by the author? Despite what the Christians actually think of the officials, they may have decided that it is advantageous to appear as loyal citizens. If the officials cannot be resisted, it may be better just to try to cope with them and be humble.[8] But the author's exclusively positive way of de-

---

[7] For a more detailed discussion, see L. THURÉN, Argument, 161 n. 236, and Strategy, 116 n. 75.
[8] E.g. J.R. MICHAELS, 1Peter, 126–127, describes "Peter's strategy", according to which one should not "offend needlessly the civil authority".

scribing the authorities and comparing them to God does not easily fit such an understanding. Moreover, even if there was such a clever opportunistic strategy, it seems unlikely that the Christians invented it.

The first Christians are often credited with many theological innovations, but such thinking easily runs the risk of anachronism. Early Christianity was not yet a large independent religion, but merely a small Jewish sect. Thus it is more natural to seek the roots of the "strategy" in early Jewish thought than in the ideological and tactical creativity of the first Christians.

> When speaking of 'Christians' and 'Christianity' we tend to think of the great, well-defined religion which conquered the Roman Empire. It is easy to visualize first-century Christianity as its fourth century equivalent in miniature. However, at the time of writing 1 Peter,[9] the contours and content of 'Christianity' were still vague. The Christians' own ideology or theology was still in the making and correspondingly the relationship to the state officials was presumably not very fixed or original either. Thus we have in the New Testament traces of very different attitudes toward the Roman officials; beside the moderate Pauline and Petrine line, there are the more critical comments in the Apocalypse.[10]
>
> Historically, the first recipients of 1 Peter were small groups in Asia Minor, with little political, economic, or even religious influence.[11] Thus it is no wonder that we have no evidence of major official persecutions of the Christians. Not until several decades later does the correspondence between the younger Pliny and Trajan (about 110 AD) indicate official interest in these groups in Asia Minor.[12] Christians would attract little official attention before the second century.[13] Thus, in order to avoid anachronistic reasoning it must be emphasized that the qualities of later Christianity must not be imposed directly on the author or recipients of 1 Peter. However, as the Epistle gives the addressees explicit guidelines on how to live within the community, it can be seen as a "handbook" of Christian behavior, which has undoubtedly influenced the attitudes and life of later Christian generations. Thereby the letter can be seen as a source for second and third generation Christianity and its relationship to the state officials, since it was growing but not yet a "state religion".

Could the attitude toward civil authorities originate from the historical Jesus? Some scholars see the *chreia* in Mark 12:13–17 as a background to Christian civil obedience, since it ends with the poignant saying: "Jesus said to them: 'Give to the emperor the things that are the emperor's, and to God the things

---

[9] Although the suggestions vary from 40 to 110 AD, the 'window' for dating 1 Peter is actually narrow. It was written under the influence of the Apostle himself in the early 60's, or by his pupils a couple of decades later. For discussion see L. THURÉN, Strategy, 30–34; J.R. MICHAELS, 1Peter, lv–lxvii.

[10] Rev 17–18.

[11] J.H. ELLIOTT, Home, 59–100 discusses the social setting of the addressees. Although somewhat hypothetical, the description is the best available.

[12] Plinius Ep 10.96–97. Correspondingly, the labels given by Tacitus (Ann 15.44 "hatred toward mankind") and Suetonius (Nero 16 "new and mischievous superstition") do not prove that first-century Christianity was seen as a major factor which warranted official persecution.

[13] Thus also C. BIGG, St. Peter, 137.

that are God's.'"[14] However, the *chreia* was hardly intended to establish the Christians' relationship to Caesar; in Mark, the story is perhaps used in order to demonstrate Jesus' superiority towards his opponents.[15] Furthermore, in this episode Jesus criticizes the Pharisees for paying undue attention to the question of political obedience. The emphasis is on the second half of the saying: Jesus argues that the *status confessionis* is in the relationship to God, not to Caesar.[16] The Pharisees are apparently criticized for carrying the picture of Caesar. Perhaps the story later became politically important for early Christians during the Jewish War, when it was beneficial to be loyal to the state,[17] but – irrespective of the date of 1 Peter – it is difficult to see this development as a background of Rom 13, which was probably written earlier. Thus at least a literary dependence is ruled out.

It is reasonable to assume that the attitudes of the Christian groups toward the Roman Empire corresponded to those of ordinary Jewish diaspora congregations. It is typical of 1 Peter to use Jewish imagery freely with no traces of any tension between Christians and Jews.[18] If the Jewish diaspora terminology well suited the social situation of the Christians, it is feasible that also the attitudes toward the surrounding society closely resembled each other. Perhaps the author and his group did not even see Christianity as very different from Judaism. If this is the case, the origins of the first Christians' civil obedience are to be sought in diaspora Judaism.

In early Christianity, this obedient attitude can be found not only in 1 Peter and Rom 13, but also in Tit 3:1 ("Remind them to be subject to rulers and authorities, to be obedient, to be ready for every good work"). The Epistle to Diognetus (ch. 5) describes the Christians as following these rules. However, direct dependence between 1 Pet 2 and Rom 13 cannot be demonstrated; it is safer to say that they represent the same tradition.[19]

GOPPELT finds parallels to Christian civil obedience in Hellenistic Jewish political attitudes, e.g. in the Epistle of Aristeas,[20] and BROX speaks of the

---

[14] G. DELLING, ὑποτάσσεσθαι, 45,6–7, L. GOPPELT, Petrusbrief, 181; J.R. MICHAELS, 1Peter, 131. He sees Prov 24:21 ("My child, fear the Lord and the king, and do not disobey either of them") as an even more important source, but there it is not Gentile authorities that are meant.

[15] Thus it ends with a comment: "And they were utterly amazed at him." (Mark 12:17). See R. PESCH, Markusevangelium, 228.

[16] Cf. M. HENGEL, Christus, 19–20.

[17] R. PESCH, Markusevangelium, 228. See also W. SCHRAGE, Christen, 30–40.

[18] See J. R. MICHAELS, 1Peter, xlix–lv.

[19] One problem when reading 1Peter is the preoccupation of NT scholarship with Paul. Paul's massive presence in the NT has yielded an overemphasis on the Apostle (especially in Western churches) with respect to the history of first-century Christianity and the development of Christian theology. Thus even 1Peter is often seen as a pseudo-Pauline text reflecting ideas which originate in Paul. The assertion of Paul's missionary or theological supremacy in the first century church is, in my opinion, a misconception. Historically, Peter may have been a more powerful figure. Consequently, most scholars who study 1Peter emphasize its independence.

[20] Ep. Arist. § 187–300.

"jüdisch-konventionelle ethische Aufruf zur Unterordnung".[21] BALCH studies corresponding exhortations in Greek popular philosophy and also finds an equivalent solution in Hellenistic Judaism, e.g. Josephus, Against Apion.[22] However, in the end he sees exhortation to submissiveness as the author's innovative and sophisticated apologetic strategy.

The Jews living in the Diaspora, e.g. in Alexandria, enjoyed civil rights, and many were Roman citizens. In general, the Roman authorities protected them and their religious rights.[23] Thus their loyalty to the emperor and their trust in the central government are easy to understand.[24] For example, during the pogroms in Alexandria, two delegations were sent to Rome in 39/40 AD.[25] This positive attitude was, of course, also condemned among the Jews: Josephus tells how fellow Jews were rebuked for their submission to Romans.[26] However, it is more plausible that the Christians, who according to 1 Peter live in the Diaspora, inherited the idea of deference to the Roman authorities from Diaspora Jews, who had accepted the Hellenistic "Staatsethos", rather than that they invented the same attitude themselves.

4. Helpful Insights from the Old Testament

A theological problem still remains. How could both the Jews and the Christians not only be submissive to Gentile authorities, but even justify their submission with strong theological statements?

The LXX refers to submissiveness 31 times, but the master is always God or the king of Israel or Judah. Even Antiochus is said to be finally submissive to God and Judas Maccabeus (2 Macc 9:12; 13:23).[27] Prov 24:21, which is often suggested as a background for civil obedience, follows the same line.[28] But the solution of Hellenistic Judaism and early Christianity, to be apparently uncritically submissive to Roman officials, is *theologically* very different. How can it be motivated?

In the Old Testament, there is one passage where unconditional submissiveness to Gentile power is discussed and even theologically motivated. In Jeremiah 27 the prophet emphatically urges Judah to be submissive to Nebuchadnezzar, the King of Babylon.[29] Judah should not listen to the false prophets, who refuse to serve Nebuchadnezzar. This chapter together with Dan 2:21

---

[21] N. BROX, Petrusbrief, 120; E. KAMLAH, ὑποτάσσεσθαι, 239.
[22] D.L. BALCH, Wives, 108–109.
[23] E. SCHÜRER, History, 128–137.
[24] See also A. KASHER, Jews, 357.
[25] A. KASHER, Jews, 22–23.
[26] Jos Bell 2.433; 4.175–80.
[27] D.L. BALCH, Wives, 98.
[28] "My child, fear the Lord and the king, and do not disobey either of them." J.R. MICHAELS, 1Peter, 131–132, for instance, argues that 1Peter is directly influenced by this verse.
[29] Jer 27–29 is a separate collection within the book; see P.J. SCALISE, Jeremiah, 35–38.

raises the theological question: How can submission and surrender to a foreign power be a mark of faithfulness to God?[30]

Jeremiah 27 contains several important theological ideas. The submission to a Gentile ruler is religiously possible because it is God's own command. The exhortation is not justified by practical or tactical reasons, viz. that since Nebuchadnezzar will win anyway it is prudent to obey him. Instead, the submissiveness is motivated by a divine threat (Jer 27:8): "But if any nation or kingdom will not serve this king, Nebuchadnezzar of Babylon, and put its neck under the yoke of the king of Babylon, then I will punish that nation with the sword, with famine, and with pestilence, says the LORD, until I have completed its destruction by his hand." Anybody who does not obey the foreign king will be destroyed by God, who uses the king as his vassal; on the other hand God promises life to those who obey the King (Jer 27:12): "Bring your necks under the yoke of the king of Babylon, and serve him and his people, and live."

Historically this attitude may be due to political realism; from past experience it was clear that rebellion resulted in further suffering.[31] However, the motivation is theological in an astonishing way. It refers to the absolute power of God. For an unknown reason, he has given all nations into the power of Nebuchadnezzar, who is now regarded as God's servant.[32]

SCALISE argues that according to Jer 27, the actual danger for Judah was not the loss of political sovereignty, but "the decay of national and personal integrity of faith and service to the LORD".[33] God is thus said to use the Gentile king only in order to warn his people against their true peril. Correspondingly, disobedience to the King means revolt against God himself.

However, it is difficult to follow SCALISE's claim that Jer 27 refers to an exception, from which no general principle of "the divine right of emperors" can be inferred. First, she herself discusses the book of Daniel, and states that the theological questions raised by Jer 27 are addressed.[34] Second, the text in Jer 27 includes almost no limitations. The submissiveness to the king of Babylon is presented as unconditional. There are no qualifications such as "as far as the king follows the will of God." The only limit presented is temporal: "All the nations shall serve him and his son and his grandson, until the time of his own land comes; then many nations and great kings shall make him their slave" (Jer 27:7).

Although there are specific markers (name and date formulas), the chapter nonetheless serves as an example of how God's people can be told to be submissive to Gentile officials, and therefore must have had great theological

---

[30] P.J. SCALISE, Jeremiah, 59. "He changes times and seasons, deposes kings and sets up kings; he gives wisdom to the wise and knowledge to those who have understanding."
[31] R.E. CLEMENTS, Jeremiah, 160–165.
[32] R.E. CLEMENTS, Jeremiah, 162. For closer discussion, see W.E. LEMKE, Nebuchadnezzar.
[33] P.J. SCALISE, Jeremiah, 59.
[34] P.J. SCALISE, Jeremiah, 37.

importance. Thus Jer 27 may well have played an important role in the development of the positive relationship between different Jewish groups and the Gentile state. Its theological significance is indicated by the fact that already in Daniel "Babylon" had become a symbol for new Gentile rulers.

The alternative, a negative attitude toward the Gentiles, is far better attested in the Old Testament and early Judaism,[35] and is represented in the New Testament by the Apocalypse. In early Judaism and early Christianity, it was a commonplace to speak of Rome with the pejorative code word "Babylon",[36] although not until after the destruction of Jerusalem in 70 AD.[37]

How then is "Babylon" in 1 Pet 5:13 to be explained? Most scholars agree that it must mean Rome, but why? GOPPELT argues that the corresponding negative use of the word was not derived from Judaism but prompted by the Neronian persecution in the Sixties.[38] But BROX rightly states that the state is nowhere in 1 Peter referred to as a persecutor; on the contrary. He also remarks that a reference to the author living in the exile does not befit the epistle, since in the prescript all the recipients are said to live in the diaspora.[39] However, BROX is not entirely happy with his own solution, viz. Jewish apocalyptic language, because of the positive role of the state in the epistle. As MICHAELS rightly observes, "the only thing wrong with 'Babylon' is that it is not home." It signifies both the city and the exile.[40] This statement corresponds well with 1 Pet 5:9, which refers to the solidarity of the brethren, apparently in Rome.[41]

The frequent use of Babylon (14 times) in the theologically poignant Jer 27 makes it a cornerstone of Jewish Babylon-theology. CLEMENTS rightly argues that the chapter is "one of the most central theological assessments of [Jeremiah] and has wide political and theological implications for the development of Judaism."[42] In my view, its importance for the emerging Christianity can be hardly overestimated either. The open appeal to political submissiveness made Jer 27 very attractive for the author of 1 Peter: Babylon signifies the Gentile superpower which is utilized by God. God's people are told to submit to Babylon, neither because of any tactical plans (such can be read only between the lines) nor due to its own qualities, but because it is the will of God.

Summarizing, it can be argued that the unfortunate foreign politics of ancient Judah and the strong theological thrust of Jeremiah offered a good basis for a positive Jewish attitude toward Gentile authorities. It enabled acceptance

---

[35] In Mishnah and Tosefta the attitude toward Gentiles is generally described pejoratively. However, it was often practical to maintain good relations. See G. PORTON, Goyim.
[36] Repeatedly in Rev, esp. 17:18; 4 Ezra, 2 Bar.; Sib. Or. 5.143,159.
[37] L. GOPPELT, Petrusbrief, 352.
[38] L. GOPPELT, Petrusbrief, 352.
[39] N. BROX, Petrusbrief, 247.
[40] J.R. MICHAELS, 1Peter, 311.
[41] The positive use of Babylon and an optimistic attitude toward the state inevitably has some importance for the date of 1Peter. It fits well a direct Petrine authorship, viz. a date in the early sixties.
[42] R.E. CLEMENTS, Jeremiah, 162.

of the Hellenistic civil ethos, and alleviated severe theological problems inherent therein. Because submissiveness and an "optimistic" view of the Gentiles were theologically and not empirically motivated, and since this obedience was strictly limited to the king and his men, viz. the emperor and his governors, it by no means prohibited constant criticism of Gentile neighbors and their lifestyle in general. This same approach was then adapted by emerging Christianity.

5. Active, Critical Obedience?

But was submission to the state actually so unconditioned and uncritical? Especially for post-World War II scholars it has been important to emphasize that the *hypotassesthai*-thinking in the NT does not enjoin an uncritical attitude toward civil authorities. Instead, a more active and critical line is described. Even the word ὑποτασσόμενοι is translated "ordnet euch in die Stände ein!" instead of "be submissive."[43] BROX thereby rejects "ein hündisches Verhalten" in 1 Peter and argues that the Christians are told to be sovereign and free even toward the state. Submission is based on their free choice. There is no theory about the state, and no naive, dangerous loyalty is commended.[44] Likewise, MICHAELS emphasizes the Christians' free choice and rejects any "naively optimistic" attitude. The authorities just happen to be the addressees' first recourse, which dictates Peter's strategy "to view them in a positive light." But should the obligations to the state come into conflict with obligations to God, they must rely on the last judgment.[45] They are slaves of God, not of the emperor, and no human authority is their Lord. Thus there is a "tacit understanding that the religious commitment to God and the brotherhood inevitably limits and qualifies the civic commitment to the empire and its citizens." MICHAELS thereby argues that the optimistic view of the state as protecting its good citizens is only the surface level in 1 Peter.[46]

I suspect that these explanations are conditioned by our contemporary political thinking rather than a careful study of the text and its Old Testament background. Critical obedience and careful distinction between civil and religious obedience are well suited to modern post-war Western Christian thinking as well as in South Africa, where especially the official grave misuse

---

[43] L. GOPPELT, Petrusbrief, 176.177.
[44] N. BROX, Petrusbrief, 124.
[45] J.R. MICHAELS, 1Peter, 126–127.
[46] J.R. MICHAELS, 1Peter, 131–132. Correspondingly G. HERRICK, Apostle, 15 and n. 21, speaks of "willing, intelligent submission to the authorities" and argues that uncritical submission is ruled out in 1 Peter, since a) Mark 12:13–17 is critical of the state, b) Romans 13 has an underlying critical premise, c) according to Peter in Acts 5:29 we must obey God, not men; d) Paul accuses the governing authorities in Acts 16:37. However, none of these passages is within 1 Peter. HERRICK's argument presupposes that the NT presents an unanimous, fixed doctrine, which is hardly the case.

of Rom 13 challenged Biblical scholars.[47] However, for historical exegesis, finding critical obedience in 1 Peter appears somewhat anachronistic and overly optimistic.[48] I am afraid that the ancient recipients of First Peter were less democratic. As readers we may be tempted to describe too easily the attitudes recommended in 1 Peter so that they correspond to good Western postwar democratic ideals, as if the New Testament ought to represent those values which we hold as good and noble.[49]

MICHAELS mixes up the critical attitude toward fellow Gentile citizens and the unconditional obedience toward the officials. Being God's slaves is not presented as an alternative to obedience to the king. On the contrary, the latter is motivated by the former. Civil obedience is thereby not differentiated from religious duties, nor is any conflict between God and Caesar discussed. Just as in Jer 27, the king and his governors are performing a function typical of God, punishing the wicked and rewarding the good.

Moreover, 1 Peter discusses the case when the masters (he does not dare to talk about political rulers, but the resemblance is obvious) are "crooked" (1 Pet 2:18). Even in that case one should be obedient, not only insofar as they punish the wicked and reward the good. No distinction is made: one ought to be submissive to every (πάσῃ) human authority (1 Pet 2:13). Although a critical, intelligent and selective submission with several qualifications would well suit our contemporary democratic society, 1 Peter does not think in these terms. On the contrary, he presents Christ as the greatest example for the addressees; Christ did not retaliate or make threats against the obviously unjust authorities (1 Pet 2:21–24).

However, it is somewhat daring to speak of a "naive" or "hündisch" attitude. For Jeremiah hardly held any "naive" illusions about the qualities of Nebuchadnezzar – and yet he told Judah to be submissive. For him, as far as we can perceive it from the text, the call for obedience to the king was not motivated by a strategy to "view him in a positive light". And yet the king was to be obeyed – because it was the will of the Lord. Likewise, the ultimate reason why the addressees of 1 Peter are exhorted to submissiveness to the king (1 Pet 2:13) does not consist in their qualities or even their function, but simply the will of the Lord: διὰ τὸν κύριον.

---

[47] See J. BOTHA, Romans. V. RIEKKINEN, Römer, offers another critical study of Rom 13.
[48] Thus BROX repeatedly warns against anachronistic questions and attitudes, although making such himself (e.g. N. BROX, Petrusbrief, 120.124.).
[49] So also, for example, in feminist criticism, one school of scholars tends to read the Bible in an overly positive light, explaining all currently politically incorrect sections as later misunderstandings: Paul, for instance, can be presented almost as a modern feminist. The opposite, pessimistic view is also possible: the New Testament is seen as an oppressive and chauvinist document. See A.Y. COLLINS, Feminist.

6. Critical Views After All?

The varying attitude to different types of Gentiles still seems somewhat odd. As the author had hardly studied Augustinus' De Civitate Dei or LUTHER's Two Kingdoms Doctrine, could he have made such a distinction so clearly?

In fact, in 1 Pet 5:2–5 some indirect criticism of the officials can be traced. When giving guidelines for internal matters in chapter 5, the author presents a negative model, which the elders ought not to follow. They should not "lord" over the congregation (κατακυριεύοντες, 5:3), which is identified with being "forced" or "greedy for money" (5:2).[50] It is possible that this negative model indirectly describes also some officials in the society? But even if this is so, the criticism is carefully camouflaged, as the author appears to be speaking only of internal relations in the congregation.

Another type of indirect criticism could be found in 2:18–20. The epistle repeatedly tells its recipients on the one hand to be submissive in their social status, and on the other to be ready for unjust suffering. However, only in the case of slaves (2:18) is it explicitly stated that these two phenomena can be combined, viz. that the masters can be *skolioi*, crooked. In this case, the unjust suffering of Christ is presented as an example for the slaves.

However, it is hard to believe that the beautiful section describing Christ's example in 2:21–25 would apply only to the slaves. I have argued that the actual aim of the *paraenesis* for different groups (slaves, wives [2:18–3:7], younger [5:5]) is not just to guide their life. Instead, the position of these groups reflects the status of all recipients in the larger society.[51] The relationship between slaves and masters, or wives and husbands corresponds to the Christians' lower status under the Roman officials. Thus the text addresses everybody, not only regarding the christological motivation of Christian behavior, but also with the explicit command to be submissive. And indeed, the same exhortation to be submissive is directed to all recipients in 2:13. This, however, means that the criticism leveled against the masters of the slaves, and the reference to those who made Christ suffer, also applies to the officials in general. But it is important to note that such a "criticism" is never made even close to explicit.

However, the exhortation to submission in 1 Peter differs essentially from Jer 27 in one regard: the motivation. Whereas Jeremiah threatens with God's wrath (through Nebuchadnezzar) and promises life, 1 Peter goes further, stating that the officials punish and reward people according to their behavior. The long motivation after 2:13–17 is christological: Christ left the addressees an example that they should follow since they have been saved by him (1 Pet 2:21–25).[52]

---

[50] The meaning of "forced" (ἀναγκαστῶς) is not specified in the text (see L. THURÉN Origins, 179 n. 283).
[51] N. BROX, Petrusbrief, 139–140; L. THURÉN, Strategy, 146 n. 55.
[52] For the structure of motivation, see L. THURÉN, Origins, 142–145.

7. Conclusions

The study of how Christians related to Roman power in 1 Peter is complicated. First, there is a risk of double anachronism. We easily attribute the qualities of the later church to the small Christian groups of the first century and dismiss the Jewish background and surroundings. Likewise it is difficult to keep the study of the text free from modern religious and political interests, as the text continues to be important, even normative, for different religious communities with different attitudes toward the political authorities. The ethics of interpretation is an important issue. One cannot avoid asking about the relevance of 1 Peter in Germany in the 1930's, in South Africa in the 1980's or in the European Union today.

However, although it would be politically correct, 1 Peter does not recommend an active, critical and democratic attitude toward the state officials. The main message is unequivocal and resembles that of Jer 27; the addressees are to be unconditionally submissive. Yet we know that in both cases the authorities did not just punish the wicked and reward the good. Only indirect roots of a more critical attitude can be traced, but it would be an overinterpretation to emphasize these features. Thus, for example, Babylon bears almost no negative connotations. A politically far more critical, if not opposite, political attitude in early Christianity can be found in the Apocalypse. But the latter was born in another historical setting and has different theological roots.

Bibliography

BALCH, David L., 'Let Wives be Submissive': The Domestic Code in 1 Peter, SBLMS 26, Chico 1981.

BIGG, Charles, A Critical and Exegetical Commentary on the Epistles of St. Peter and St. Jude, ICC, Edinburgh 1901.

BOTHA, Jan, Reading Romans 13. Aspects of the ethics of interpretation in a controversial text, Stellenbosch 1991.

BROX, Norbert, Der erste Petrusbrief, EKK 21, Zürich/Einsiedeln/Köln/ Neukirchen-Vluyn 1979; ²1986.

CLEMENTS, Ronald Ernest, Jeremiah, Interpretation, Atlanta 1988.

COLLINS, Adela Yarbro (ed.), Feminist Perspectives on Biblical Scholarship, Chico 1985.

DELLING, Gerhard, ὑποτάσσω, in: ThWNT VIII (1969), 40–47.

ELLIOTT, John Hall, A Home for the Homeless: A Sociological Exegesis of 1 Peter, Its Situation and Strategy, Philadelphia 1981.

FELDMEIER, Reinhard, Die Christen als Fremde. Die Metapher der Fremde in der antiken Welt, im Urchristentum und im 1. Petrusbrief, WUNT 64, Tübingen 1992.

GOPPELT, Leonhard, Der Erste Petrusbrief, ed. by Ferdinand HAHN, KEK 12/1, Göttingen ⁸1978.

HENGEL, Martin, Christus und die Macht. Die Macht Christi und die Ohnmacht der Christen, Stuttgart 1974.

HERRICK, Greg, The Apostle Peter on Civil Obedience An Exegesis of 1 Peter 2:13–17 http//www.bible.org/docs/nt/books/1pe/1pe213.htm (1997)

KAMLAH, Ehrhard, Die Form der katalogischen Paränese in Neuen Testament, WUNT 7, Tübingen 1964.

ID., ὑποτάσσεσθαι in den neutestamentlichen "Haustafeln", in: Verborum Veritas, FS Gustav STÄHLIN, Wuppertal 1970, 237–43.

KASHER, Aryeh, The Jews in Hellenistic and Roman Egypt. The Struggle for Equal Rights, TSAJ 7, Tübingen 1985.

LEMKE, Werner E., Nebuchadnezzar, My Servant, in: CBQ 28 (1966), 45–50.

MICHAELS, J. Ramsey, 1 Peter, WBC 49, Waco 1988.

PESCH, Rudolf, Das Markusevangelium, HThK 2, Freiburg 1977.

PORTON, Gary G., Goyim: Gentiles and Israelites in Mishnah-Tosefta, Brown Judaic studies 155, Atlanta 1988.

RIEKKINEN, Vilho, Römer 13. Aufzeichnung und Weiterführung der exegetischen Diskussion, AASF.DHL 23, Helsinki 1980.

SCALISE, Pamela J., Jeremiah 26–52, WBC 27 by Gerald L. KEOWN/Pamela J. SCALISE/Thomas G. SMOTHERS, Dallas 1995.

SCHLUETER, Carol J., Filling Up the Measure. Polemical Hyperbole in 1 Thessalonians 2.14–16, JSNTS 98, Sheffield 1994.

SCHRAGE, Wolfgang, Die Christen und der Staat nach dem Neuen Testament, Gütersloh 1971.

SCHÜRER Emil, The History of the Jewish People in the Age of Jesus Christ (175 B.C. – A.D. 135). A New English Version, III/1. rev. and ed. Geza VERMES, Fergus MILLAR and Martin GOODMAN, Edinburgh 1986.

THURÉN, Lauri, The Rhetorical Strategy of 1 Peter, Åbo 1990.

ID., Argument and Theology in 1 Peter. The Origins of Christian Paraenesis, JSNTS 114, Sheffield 1995.

ID., Style Never Goes out of Fashion – 2 Peter Re-evaluated, Rhetoric, in: PORTER, Stanley/OLBRICHT, Thomas H., Scripture and Theology, JSNTS 131; Sheffield 1996, 329–347.

ID., Hey Jude! Asking for the Original Situation and Message of a Catholic Epistle, in: NTS 43 (1997), 451–465.

ID., Was Paul Angry? Derhetorizing Galatians, in: STAMPS, Dennis L./PORTER, Stanley (eds.), The Rhetorical Interpretation of Scripture. Essays from the 1996 Malibu Conference, JSNTS 180; Sheffield 1999, 302–320.

Daria Pezzoli-Olgiati

Between Fascination and Destruction
Considerations on the Power of the Beast in Rev 13:1-10

Rev 13:3b contains a peculiar sentence I would like to quote to introduce the topic of this article: καὶ ἐθαυμάσθη ὅλη ἡ γῆ ὀπίσω τοῦ θηρίου. A literal translation could be: 'And the whole earth wondered behind the beast'.

In this sentence two points in particular need further investigation. First, there is a grammatical problem with the strange construction ἐθαυμάσθη ... ὀπίσω τοῦ θηρίου, which is neither Greek nor Hebrew.[1] Second, according to other passages in Revelation, it does not seem possible that the whole earth admires and honours the beast, since at the very least John's addressees know who it is and whence it comes. Or do they not? The quoted sentence presents an ambiguous, unclear scene of adoration, which is quite typical for Revelation.

This paper aims to analyse this ambiguity and to clarify the impressive presentation of the beast's power in Revelation. What kind of connotations are employed? How is this negative power interpreted and theologically situated? To approach these questions I have selected the vision of the beast emerging from the sea in Rev 13:1–10. First, I will examine the topic with a text-internal view of the beast's power. Second, I will present some reflections about the link between text and historical background. Third, I will briefly consider the historical context.

The Adoration of the First Beast (Rev 13:1-10)

To find a possible answer to the questions arising from Rev 13:3b it is necessary to consider the whole unit, Rev 13:1–10. For the first time the beast and its power are presented in full.[2] The vision can be structured as follows:

Description of the beast (vv. 1–3a)
1 And I saw a beast rising out of the sea, having ten horns and seven heads; and on its horns were ten diadems, and on its heads were blasphemous names. 2 And the beast that I saw was like a leopard, its feet were like a bear's, and its mouth was like a lion's mouth. And the dragon gave it his power and his throne and great

---

[1] This construction is without parallel in Greek and in Hebrew. See e.g. R.H. CHARLES, Revelation, 350–351, G.K. BEALE, The Book of Revelation, 693–694; F. BLASS/A. DEBRUNNER/F. REHKOPF, Grammatik, § 215.1, note 2.
[2] A similar, but not identical formula is found in the seven letters in Rev 2–3 (2:7.11.17.29; 3:6.13.22). About the hearing formula in Revelation see W. POPKES, Funktion; A.-M. ENROTH, Hearing Fomula.

authority. 3 And (I saw) one of its heads as slain to death, but its mortal wound had been healed.

Reaction of the inhabitants of the earth (vv. 3b–4)
And the whole earth wondered behind the beast. 4 And they worshipped the dragon, for he had given his authority to the beast, and they worshipped the beast, saying, 'Who is like the beast, and who can fight against it?'

Description of the beast's power (vv. 5–7)
5 And the beast was given a mouth uttering great and blasphemous words, and it was given power to act for forty two months. 6 And it opened its mouth to utter blasphemies against God, blaspheming his name and his dwelling, (and) those who dwell in heaven. 7 And it was given to make war on the saints and to conquer them and it was given power over every tribe and people and language and nation.

Reaction of the inhabitants of the earth (v. 8)
8 And all the inhabitants of the earth will worship it, everyone whose name has not been written from the foundation of the world in the book of life of the Lamb that was slaughtered.

Exhortation to endure (vv. 9–10)
9 Let anyone who has an ear listen:
10 If you are to be taken captive, into captivity you go; if you kill with the sword, with the sword you must be killed.
Here is the endurance and the faith of the saints.[3]

This structuring of the vision indicates three main parts: on the one hand two different descriptions of the beast – of its appearance and of its power – and, on the other, an exhortation addressed directly to the congregations in Asia Minor to whom John writes his letter.[4]

In the first description (13:1–3a) the beast is connoted by two different categories of attributes. Some describe its grandeur, while others point out its threatening and negative character. Its huge appearance and the evident symbols of royal authority such as horns and diadems[5] demonstrate an enormous power. The allusion to a mortal wound that has been healed shows that this huge power participated in authority over death and life. Beside these fascinating attributes, the description of the beast also includes absolute negative connotations. It comes from the sea: this part of the creation is seen negatively, as a domain of uncontrolled, destructive forces.[6] The repetition of the number ten (ten horns, ten diadems) alludes to an incomplete form of power.[7] The

---

[3] I have altered the NRSV at some points to show the problems of the Greek text.
[4] For an interesting interpretation of Revelation as a letter see M. KARRER, Johannesoffenbarung.
[5] For more details see D. PEZZOLI-OLGIATI, Täuschung, 125–126.
[6] D. PEZZOLI-OLGIATI, Täuschung, 124–25. In the new creation described in Rev 21:1 the sea does not appear any more.
[7] The number ten can be understood symbolically as opposition to seven, which is always related to perfection. See U. VANNI, L'Apocalisse, 54. According to this interpretation the beast has seven heads – it is a 'perfect', fully monstrous monster – but has a incomplete power (ten horns, ten diadems).

names of the beast are blasphemous and proclaim its antagonism to God.⁸ The beast is presented as a monster that looks like a leopard but with feet like a bear's and a mouth like a lion's: the monstrous animal concentrates characteristics of very dangerous beings.⁹ Finally, the aspect of danger and destruction is reiterated by the affirmation that the power of the beast originates entirely with the dragon.

Compared to the first, the second description of the beast (vv. 5–7) forms a climax. Here, the text focuses on the effects of the beast's power; again there is a list of asymmetrical features. On the one hand the negativity of this power is stressed: the beast speaks blasphemous words against God and his followers.¹⁰ The sole aim of the beast's power is self-realisation; its results are destruction and death. But, on the other hand, its power is represented as a great apparition: the beast speaks great words and has absolute authority over the whole earth (every tribe and people and language and nation). The recurrence of passive forms in expressions like ἐδόθη αὐτῷ στόμα (v. 5), ἐδόθη αὐτῷ ἐξουσία ποιῆσαι (v. 5), ἐδόθη αὐτῷ ποιῆσαι (v. 7), ἐδόθη αὐτῷ ἐξουσία (v. 7) brings a theologically problematic twist into the text: if understood as *passiva divina*, they can be interpreted as a limitation of the huge power of the beast and of the dragon. This assumption is reinforced by the limitation of the negative power to 42 months.¹¹ Nevertheless, even when the power of the destructive forces is strictly controlled by God, it appears as absolute, without any restrictions on earth.

The reaction of the earth's inhabitants draws on this ambiguous character of the negative power. In the first description (vv. 3b–4), quoted at the beginning of this paper, it is said that the whole earth, without exception,¹² worships the beast. The direct question in v. 4 τίς ὅμοιος τῷ θηρίῳ καὶ τίς δύναται πολεμῆσαι μετ' αὐτοῦ; stresses that all the earth's inhabitants recognise the authority of the beast (and the dragon) as absolute.¹³ In the second description (v. 8), however, there is a clear distinction between the followers of the beast

---

⁸ βλασφημία is repeated several times in Rev 13:1–10. Within Revelation this word is used of personages that show and declare an identity that does not correspond to their true name (cf. Rev 2:9). The beast presents itself as a divine power although it is (for John) evident that there is only one divine power in the world, the power of God and its lamb.

⁹ For the OT background see Dan 7:2–7; Hab 1:8; 2 Sam 17:8; Prov 17:12; Hos 13:7f. On the dependence of the description of the beast on Daniel see L.J. LIETAERT PEERBOLTE, Antecedents, 143ff.

¹⁰ See above, note 8.

¹¹ The idea that the time of the beast and the dragon is limited is often repeated: see Rev 11:2 (42 months); 11:3; 12:6 (1260 days), i.e. three and a half years, i.e. the half of seven, the perfect number.

¹² S. SEESEMANN, ὅλος, 175–176.

¹³ The vision of the beast is built as a parodistic parallelism to the vision of the lamb in Rev 5. In 5:2 a similar question is related to the lamb. Also the OT background (see as examples of parallel formulations Exod 15:11; Ps 89:7) emphasises the parodistic character of Rev 13:4.

and the followers of the Lamb:[14] the Christians, the victims of the beast, refuse to worship this destructive authority. In both passages, v. 3b–4 and v. 8, the adoration of the beast is described in typically religious terminology: the verb προσκυνέω is repeated several times.[15]

To summarise these observations: in the vision of the beast emerging from the sea there is an evolution, a dynamic description of the monstrous being. At the beginning, although it is clear that the beast belongs to the dragon, there are allusions to its imposing appearance, which justify the reaction of recognition and fascination by the inhabitants of the earth. The text introduces a sharp division between people worshipping the beast and the true followers of God and its lamb only after the presentation of the annihilating effects of the negative power.

The vision encompasses two different points of view. The inhabitants of the earth – including also the addressees of Revelation – look at the beast from a horizontal perspective: the greatness of the beast's power, who is even able to arise from death, can confuse even the Christians and induce them to accept its power. In contrast John, the seer, follows and describes the scene from a heavenly point of view. From this privileged perspective it is quite easy to recognise the clear contrast between the power of the beast and the power of God and its lamb.

Rev 13:9–10 interrupts the visionary character of the chapter: the narrative style is broken off by a direct exhortation to the readers. This last part of the text unit can be interpreted as an attempt to construct a coherent image of the discordant aspects of the power of the beast. Exhorting his addressees to endure the persecution caused from the destroying power, John admits on the one hand that the authority of the beast on earthly life is effective and absolute. In some cases it is not possible to escape prison or even a violent death. But on the other hand John encourages the followers of Christ to be patient[16] and to maintain the relationship with God in this time of suffering, since the power of the beast is in fact limited and represents only a terrible phase in God's plan which encompasses the whole world, from the first beginning until the new creation.

Many points I have briefly mentioned here become clearer within the context of the entire book of Revelation. For instance a comparison between Rev 13:1–10 and Rev 5 could point out many important details of the different quality of the beast's and the lamb's power. An accurate analysis of Rev 17–18 is necessary to fully understand how the negative forces and those co-operating with them are annihilated. A comparison of the letters to the seven congrega-

---

[14] The motif of the book where the names have been written since the foundation of the world is found also in Rev 17:8. To understand this motif a comparison with Rev 3:5 and 21:27 is important. See D. PEZZOLI-OLGIATI, Täuschung, 134–135.

[15] See H. GREEVEN, προσκυνέω, 759–767.

[16] ὑπομονή has an active meaning; see F. HAUCK, ὑπομονή, 585ff. According to Rev 1:9 ὑπομονή can be understood as the dimension where John's addressees experience the tension between persecution and salvation; see D. PEZZOLI-OLGIATI, Täuschung, 20ff.

tions in Asia Minor (Rev 2–3) to Rev 18 build the starting point for a reconstruction of the concrete manifestations of the negative power and the necessity for Christians to reject any kind of collaboration. The comparison between Rev 2–3 and 17–18 is also very important for understanding the urban dimension in which both the power of the beast and the divine power are acting. This list of topics can of course be further extended; for the purpose of this paper, however, we leave now the textual level and proceed to the question of its link to the historical context where it was written.

On the Link Between Visions and Historical Context

In the visions of Revelation, destructive power and authority are often connected with theoriomorphic beings such as the two beasts, the dragon, grasshoppers, and scorpions. There is no passage that explicitly relates these beings to a particular historical personage. Nevertheless it is fully clear that Revelation is written as a polemic and a condemnation of the Roman empire: the allusions and the employed imagery are quite evident even for modern readers.

However, any attempt to precisely relate the visions of Revelation to a particular personage in Roman history involves the use of accurate historical reconstruction and comparisons with extra-biblical documents. The text of Revelation itself operates on the level of allusion, and seems to resist a coherent identification with detailed historical facts.[17]

The fictional narration within the visions does not allow a precise identification: the images of Revelation are not conceived as allegories.[18] The link to the historical context is created differently; it is indicated by a different kind of markers such as 13:9, where the visionary narration is interrupted by a direct exhortation to the addressees. Another interesting example is found in Rev 17:7ff. At the sight of 'Babylon', presented as a woman sitting on a scarlet beast, John is greatly astonished. The following interpretation of the vision of this woman is introduced by the angel (Rev 17:7):

> But the angel said to me, 'Why are you so amazed? I will tell you the mystery of the woman, and of the beast with seven heads and ten horns that carries her'

The interpretation of the angel does not give a solution to the previous vision; it emphasises instead the necessity to interpret it. Also the very famous sentence in Rev 13:18 can be seen as such a link with the historical context:

> Here is wisdom: let anyone with understanding calculate the number of the beast, for it is the number of a person. Its number is six hundred and sixty-six.

---

[17] The controversy about dating Revelation following the allusions to the beast's heads in 17:9–14 illustrate very well this point. See A. STROBEL, Abfassung, 433; J.H. ULRICHSEN, Häupter.

[18] For a possible definition of allegory see K. KOCH, Visionsbericht, 437: 'Denn Allegorie meint eine bildliche Rede, für die Substitution vorausgesetzt werden kann; was bildlich gesagt wird, kann in eigentliche unbildliche Rede transponiert werden'.

The exhortation to guess the meaning of 666 can be understood as an invitation to the reader to become an interpreter. It is necessary to identify the beast in history, but this identification must be performed by the Christians living in the seven Asian cities.[19] Avoiding an explicit identification of the beast in contemporary history, the visions of Revelation seem to aim at a more radical criticism, a rejection of every form of such a negative power.[20]

The link between the visions and their historical context is given through the mediation of the reader: the addressees of Revelation are exhorted to interpret history, to recognise the signs of the grandiose but destructive power and to distinguish it from the true power, the power of life, the authority of God and its Lamb. This dynamic between text and history motivates the addressees to read their daily life in the flourishing cities of Asia Minor from a theological point of view.[21]

A Few Considerations on the Historical Background

As no comprehensive reconstruction of the historical background of Revelation can be attempted in this context, I only point out a few central points.[22]

Revelation was written towards the end of the reign of Domitian, that is, at the end of the first century C.E., in Asia Minor. Various non-biblical sources emphasise a negative image of this emperor, in particular toward the end of his reign. In this regard two elements in particular are often named: cruelty and religious ambitions. Also archaeological reconstruction reveals the wide presence of the emperor cult in the cities of the province of Asia. The religious centrality of the emperor is a fundamental aspect not only in the life of single Asian cities but also as a link between these flourishing but peripheral cities and the capital of the empire.

Although systematic repression of Christians is not attested for this time, membership in a Christian congregation may in some cases bring with it persecution. A further field of conflict lies in the necessity of the Christian to participate in the everyday life of the city (including also all the ceremonies and events related to the imperial cult) in order to pursue business.[23] Recent

---

[19] For the questions about the number of the beast see A.Y. COLLINS, Combat Myth, 174–176; J.H. ULRICHSEN, Häupter, 4; M. OBERWEIS, Bedeutung; R. BAUCKHAM, Climax, 384ff.; H. ULLAND, Vision, 299–300.

[20] See F. BOVON, Possession, particularly 233.

[21] For this approach to Revelation cf. U. VANNI, L'Apocalisse, 63–72, and D. PEZZOLI-OLGIATI, Täuschung.

[22] To deepen this aspect see P. PRIGENT, Temps, 55; A.Y. COLLINS, Crisis; F. BOVON, Possession; K. WENGST, Pax Romana; P.J.J. BOTHA, God; P. LAMPE, Christen; L.L. THOMPSON, Book of Revelation; R. PETRAGLIO, Obiezione, 317ff.; R. BAUCKHAM, Climax, 338ff.; D. PEZZOLI-OLGIATI, Täuschung, 215–246.

[23] On the discussion of persecution under the reign of Domitian cf. H.-J. KLAUCK, Sendschreiben, 153–182; on the subjective perception of social exclusion cf. A.Y. COLLINS, Persecution.

studies on the historical background of Revelation emphasise the centrality of economical activities and trade, particularly with Rome, for the cities of the province of Asia. This explains in a very plausible way also the wide use of economic and trade semantics particularly in Rev 2–3; 13:11–18 and 17–18.[24]

Between Fascination and Destruction

John, the seer, polemises against an attempt to mediate between the engagement in city life required by business and membership to the Christian community. He radically condemns any ambivalent attitude towards the fascination of power. Not all Christians refuse to fully participate in city life, which in John's eyes implies a general acceptance of the political-religious system. For them, however, the care of one's own business does not contradict membership in the Christian congregation and faith in God and Christ.[25] With the visions of the Apocalypse John depicts in a radical way the real quality, origin and effects of the authority on which the whole machinery is based.

Instead of a direct, polemical style, which is quite evident in the seven letters in Rev 2–3, Rev 13:1–10 expresses the necessity to resist the power of the beast and endure persecution through visionary means. Here the beast appears to all the inhabitants on earth as a fascinating, attractive power; nobody seems to be more powerful and great; nobody on earth can be compared with it. The beast and the dragon are presented as transcendent beings that require a religious adoration. But seen from heaven, from John's point of view, it is evident that whoever adores the beast does not really perceive the menace and perversion of such a power. Therefore, the strange grammatical construction quoted at the beginning, καὶ ἐθαυμάσθη ὅλη ἡ γῆ ὀπίσω τοῦ θηρίου, could be explained on a thematic level: the whole earth, adoring the beast, stands on the wrong side, the followers of the beast can not even see it straight on.

The description of the destructive power within Rev 13:1–10 aims to represent it in radical opposition to divine power, the transparent power of truth and life.[26] The narrative strategy in Rev 13:1–10, and I think in the whole series of visions, does not only aim to identify the negative power of the Roman empire, but it contains as well an exhortation to the addressees to interpret history, to recognise which power is really acting, to clearly discriminate life from death, salvation from perversion.

---

[24] See J.N. KRAYBILL, Imperial Cult.
[25] As an illustration see Rev 2:14.
[26] It can be of interest to observe that ὀπίσω is employed a few times within Revelation, in 1:10; 12:15 and 13:3. In the first two cases it can be translated as 'behind'. By contrast, the preposition with the opposite meaning, ἐνώπιον, is very frequent, and is used in the most cases in relation to God's and the Lamb's throne: the adoration of divine power is accomplished from face to face (see as examples Rev 4 and 5:8).

Bibliography

BAUCKHAM, Richard, The Climax of Prophecy. Studies on the Book of Revelation, Edinburgh 1993.

BEALE, Gregory K., The Book of Revelation, A Commentary to the Greek Text, NIGTC, Grand Rapids – Cambridge 1999.

BLASS, Friedrich/DEBRUNNER, Albert/REHKOPF, Friedrich, Grammatik des neutestamentlichen Griechischen, Göttingen ^{16}1984.

BOTHA, Pieter J.J., God, Emperor Worship and Society, Contemporary Experiences and the Book of Revelation, in: Neot. 22 (1988), 87–102.

BOVON, François, Possession ou enchantement, Les institutions romaines selon l'Apocalypse de Jean, in: CrSt 7 (1986), 221–238.

CHARLES, R.H., A Critical and Exegetical Commentary on the Revelation of St. John, Vol. I–II, ICC, Edinburgh 1920.

COLLINS, Adela Yarbro, The Combat Myth in the Book of Revelation, HDR 9, Montana 1976.

EAD., Persecution and Vengeance in the Book of Revelation, in: HELLHOLM, David (ed.), Apocalypticism in the Mediterranean World and the Near East, Proceedings of the International Colloquium on Apocalypticism, Uppsala, August 12–17, 1979, Tübingen ^{2}1989, 729–749.

EAD., Crisis and Catharsis, The Power of the Apocalypse, Philadelphia 1984.

ENROTH, Anne-Marit, The Hearing Formula in the Book of Revelation, in: NTS 36 (1990), 598–608.

GREEVEN, Heinrich, προσκυνέω, in: ThWNT VI (1959), 759–767.

HAUCK, Friedrich, ὑπομονή, in: ThWNT IV (1942), 585–593.

KARRER, Martin, Die Johannesoffenbarung als Brief. Studien zu ihrem literarischen, historischen und theologischen Ort, FRLANT 140, Göttingen 1986.

KLAUCK, Hans-Josef, Das Sendschreiben nach Pergamon und der Kaiserkult in der Johannesoffenbarung, in: Bib 73 (1992), 153–182.

KOCH, Klaus, Vom prophetischen zum apokalyptischen Visionsbericht, in: HELLHOLM, David (ed.), Apocalypticism in the Mediterranean World and the Near East, Proceedings of the International Colloquium on Apocalypticism, Uppsala, August 12–17, 1979, Tübingen ^{2}1989, 413–446.

KRAYBILL, J. Nelson, Imperial Cult and Commerce in John's Apocalypse, JSNTS 132, Sheffield 1996.

LAMPE, Peter, Die stadtrömischen Christen in den ersten beiden Jahrhunderten, WUNT II/18, Tübingen 1989.

LIETAERT PEERBOLTE, Lambertus J., The Antecedents of Antichrist: A Traditiohistorical Study of the Earliest Christian Views on Eschatological Opponents, JSJ.S 49, Leiden, New York, Köln 1996.

OBERWEIS, Michael, Die Bedeutung der neutestamentlichen „Rätselzahlen" 666 (Apk 13,18) und 153 (Joh 21,11), in: ZNW 77 (1986), 226–241.

PETRAGLIO, Renzo, Obiezione di coscienza, Il Nuovo Testamento provoca chi lo legge, Etica teologica oggi 1, Bologna ^{2}1992.

PEZZOLI-OLGIATI, Daria, Täuschung und Klarheit, Zur Wechselwirkung zwischen Vision und Geschichte in der Johannesoffenbarung, FRLANT 175, Göttingen 1997.

POPKES, Wiard, Die Funktion der Sendschreiben in der Johannes-Apokalypse, Zugleich ein Beitrag zur Spätgeschichte der neutestamentlichen Gleichnisse, in: ZNW 74 (1983), 90–107.

PRIGENT, Pierre, Au temps de l'Apocalypse, Le culte impérial au 1er siècle en Asie Mineure, in: RHPhR 55 (1975), 219–235.

SEESEMANN, Heinrich, ὅλος, ThWNT V (1954), 175f.

STROBEL, August, Abfassung und Geschichtstheologie der Apokalypse nach Kap. XVII. 9–12, in: NTS 10 (1964), 433–445.

THOMPSON, Leonard L., The Book of Revelation, Apocalypse and Empire, New York, Oxford 1990.

ULLAND, Harald, Die Vision als Radikalisierung der Wirklichkeit in der Apokalypse des Johannes, TANZ 21, Tübingen, Basel 1997.

ULRICHSEN, Jarl Henning, Die sieben Häupter und die zehn Hörner. Zur Datierung der Offenbarung des Johannes, in: StTh 39 (1985), 1–20.

VANNI, Ugo, L'Apocalisse, Ermeneutica, esegesi, teologia, Supplementi alla Rivista Biblica 17, Bologna 1988.

WENGST, Klaus, Pax Romana, Anspruch und Wirklichkeit, Erfahrungen und Wahrnehmung des Friedens bei Jesus und im Urchristentum, München 1986.

Bert Jan Lietaert Peerbolte

To Worship the Beast
The Revelation of John and the Imperial Cult in Asia Minor

Many interpreters see the book of Revelation as a virulent sectarian reaction of an early Christian apocalyptist to the predominance of the imperial cult in Asia Minor. A number of elements in the description of the forces of evil within the visions of this book clearly indicate that the author intended to describe this cult and its priesthood as an expression of Satan's reign on earth. For John the seer, the emperor and the worship he claimed formed the counterpart of Jesus Christ and the Almighty God. Reverence and worship should be directed at God, and, to a certain extent, his envoy Jesus Christ, not at the emperor of Rome. From the author's point of view his readers had a clear choice: either they would refuse to worship the emperor and be saved among the elect, or they would do as they were asked, perform their civic duties, and lose their place among the 144,000. An explicit description of the division of mankind John presupposes is found in 13:7–8: 'It (= the first Beast) was given authority over every tribe and people and language and nation, and all the inhabitants of the earth will worship it, everyone whose name has not been written from the foundation of the world in the book of life of the Lamb that was slaughtered' (NRSV).

The famous correspondence between Pliny the Younger and the emperor Trajan appears to underline that there was indeed a vehement enmity between the worship of Christ and that of the emperor. In his Ep. 10.96 Pliny asks the emperor on what grounds Christians should be punished: 'whether it is the mere name of Christian which is punishable, even if innocent of crime, or rather the crimes associated with the name.'[1] Pliny subsequently describes the procedure he used in order to determine whether the accused brought before him should be punished or not. If the accused confessed to being a Christian up to three times, Pliny had him or her taken away for execution. He continues his discussion of the problem by describing how some, who were anonymously accused, had already abstained from Christianity, showing this by revering the emperor's statue and the images of the gods as well as by reviling the name of Christ.[2] Pliny finally mentions his verdict on the Christians: 'I found nothing but a degenerate sort of cult carried to extravagant lengths.'[3]

---

[1] Ep 10.96.2, translation B. RADICE in Loeb Classical Library (LCL). For a discussion of Pliny's evidence on the Christians, see F.G. DOWNING, Pliny's Prosecutions. On the issue of the persecution of Christians see also F. MILLAR, The Imperial Cult.
[2] 'They all did reverence to your statue and the images of the gods in the same way as the others, and reviled the name of Christ' – Ep 10.96.6.
[3] Ep 10.96.8.

Trajan's reply to Pliny is rather moderate. According to the emperor there is no need for mass-persecutions aimed at Christians. Only when someone is accused of being a Christian and has subsequently, at the trial, confessed, he or she should be punished. The best way for an accused Christian to prove him- or herself innocent of the charges was apparently to pray to the Graeco-Roman gods: 'in the case of anyone who denies that he is a Christian, and makes it clear that he is not by offering prayers to our gods, he is to be pardoned as a result of his repentance however suspect his past conduct may be.'[4]

This correspondence between Pliny and Trajan points out a number of things. Firstly, there were clearly no mass persecutions aimed at Christians during or before Pliny's proconsulate.[5] Trajan's answer is revealing in this respect. Secondly, there was apparently no jurisprudence for Pliny to check the exact measure of the punishment he should apply to the people he found guilty. Thirdly, Pliny is not even sure of the exact nature of the crime he should find those people guilty of. Was being a Christian reason enough for them to be convicted or was it the active practice of their 'degenerate' Christian habits?

With regard to the influence of the imperial cult on Christians at the turn of the first and second centuries CE one more observation is to be made from Pliny's correspondence. The procedure that Pliny describes is plain and simple: he asks the accused whether they are Christians or not. Only after they have positively answered this question for the third time, they are sent away for execution. The worship of the emperor's statue and of the images of the gods is only mentioned as a final check for those who deny being a Christian. They should pay reverence to the emperor and the gods in order to substantiate their innocence. This element from Pliny's description of the justice procedures points out that (1) being a Christian was in itself enough to have the accused convicted, and (2) the best way for the accused to prove their non-Christian identity was to pay honour to the gods, and to the emperor. Since Trajan in his reply does not even mention his own statue, and merely speaks of the worship of the gods as civic duty, the focus in the conflict between the Christians and their surrounding Graeco-Roman society was not their refusal to take part in the imperial cult. It was their refusal to worship any Graeco-Roman gods at all.[6]

---

[4] Ep 10.97.

[5] Cf. F.G. DOWNING, Pliny's Prosecutions, 119, who describes the importance of Pliny's correspondence with Trajan: 'There was no official action taken against Christians in the courts in the provinces of Syria, Asia, Pontus, Bythinia, and around, before a conscientious governor attempted to establish on a firmer basis the order and efficiency and prosperity of the two provinces committed to his charge by an enlightened emperor.'

[6] The fact that Jews and Christians both refused to worship the Graeco-Roman deities is clearly expressed in early Christian apologetic literature. To mention but a few examples from an abundance of evidence: Aristides divides the human race into three groups, viz. 'those who worship what you call gods, Jews, and Christians' (τρία γένη εἰσιν ἐν ἀνθρώπων ἐν τῷδε τῷ κόσμῳ· ὧν εἰσὶν οἱ τῶν παρ' ὑμῖν λεγομένων θεῶν κροσκυνηταὶ καὶ Ἰουδαῖοι καὶ Χριστιανοί) – Arist Apol 2.1. Justin simply states: 'we do not worship

Pliny wrote his letter to Trajan only a short period after the book of Revelation was written. Furthermore, Pliny's territory was Bithynia and Pontus, a region that was situated to the northeast of the province of Asia, which is addressed in the book of Revelation. It may be therefore assumed that the situation described by Pliny cannot have been totally different from the context of the intended recipients of the Apocalypse of John. As a result the following question should be asked: why does the author of the book of Revelation so vehemently attack the imperial cult? It is this question that will be answered in the present article.

In order to find the answer, the course of the article will be the following. To begin with, a number of characteristic passages will be presented in which the author of the book of Revelation refers to the imperial cult in a negative way (section 1). Then the administrative organisation of cities in Asia Minor will be treated briefly (section 2), as well as the benefits brought by the imperial cult to the cities that implemented it (section 3). Finally, the literary polemic in the book of Revelation will be related to its religious and sociopolitical climate (section 4).

1. The Imperial Cult as Described in the Book of Revelation

In a recent study of the subject J. Nelson KRAYBILL has argued that the book of Revelation primarily takes a stand over against the economic power of Rome.[7] In KRAYBILL's words: 'John warned Christians to sever or to avoid economic and political ties with Rome because institutions and structures of the Roman Empire were saturated with unholy allegiance to an emperor who claimed to be divine (or was treated as such).'[8] Indeed John's rhetoric aims at unveiling what he perceived as the true identity of the Roman emperor and his empire. For John Rome was a rich harlot who seduced and ruled the kings of the earth (17:1–2,18), drank the blood of followers of Christ (17:6), and would wage a war against the Lamb (17:14). Of course, John presumes that the outcome of the war could be none other than victory for the Lamb and defeat for the harlot and the Beast (17:14; cf. 19:17–23).

The economic element in the description of the Beast is presented most clearly by the 'mark of the Beast' as mentioned in 13:16–17:[9] 'Also it causes all, both small and great, both rich and poor, both free and slave, to be marked

---

your (= Greek) gods' (μὴ τοὺς αὐτοὺς ὑμῖν σέβομεν θεούς) – Justin, Apol 24.2. Cf. also Dial 55.2, where Trypho quotes 1 Chr 16:26, and adds to it: οἱ θεοὶ τῶν ἐθνῶν, νομιζόμενοι θεοί, εἴδωλα δαιμονίων εἰσίν, ἀλλ' οὐ θεοί (italics: quotation from 1 Chron).

[7] J.N. KRAYBILL, Imperial Cult.
[8] J.N. KRAYBILL, Imperial Cult, 17. See for a discussion of the socio-economic situation of the Christian recipients of the Book of Revelation L.L.THOMPSON, Book, esp. 116–132 and 186–197.
[9] For further discussion, see L.J. LIETAERT PEERBOLTE, Antecedents, 148–149.

on the right hand or the forehead, so that no one can buy or sell who does not have the mark, that is, the name of the beast or the number of its name' (NRSV). Already Adolf DEISSMANN argued that χάραγμα was used in other contexts to describe the mark that slaves received from their master, but also for the stamp that was used by trade officials for drawing up a contract.[10] Evidence shows that these signs were marked with the name of the emperor.[11] Hence, no one could buy or sell anything without the approval of the allegedly divine emperor. By describing this economic power as the 'mark of the Beast' John obviously protested against the pervasion of economic life by the emperor worship.

J. Nelson KRAYBILL is correct in pointing out the economic element in John's description of Rome. And yet the true venom of John's polemics against Rome aims at the worship of the emperor as a divine being. According to John, only God is worthy of worship, not the emperor.

In the description of the heavenly throne in Revelation 4 John depicts the four creatures surrounding the throne as continually singing the praise of God by reciting the *trishagion* (4:8). He then describes the heavenly 'senate' of twenty-four elders who underline this doxology by worshipping God (4:10). After the portrayal of the Lamb in chapter five the elders are again mentioned as worshipping (5:14). Also in 7:11; 11:16 and 19:4 the heavenly worship of God is mentioned, as if to underline the fact that only 'the one seated on the throne' is to receive this honour. It is remarkable, by the way, that in none of these verses Christ or the Lamb is mentioned as the object of worship.[12] In fact, when John wants to worship Christ ('the angel') in 22:8 he is rebuked for this: 'You must not do that! I am a fellow servant with you and your comrades the prophets, and with those who keep the words of this book. Worship God!' (NRSV).

If, for John, God is the only one worthy of worship, the emperor's claim of divinity must have been a terrible blasphemy to him. It is no doubt for this reason that John includes references to the emperor in his description of the 'Beast from the sea' in Revelation 13.[13] In its physical appearance this Beast is described as a look-alike of both the Lamb and the Dragon (13:1–3a; cf. 5:6 and 12:3). The Beast combines elements from the description of all four terrible beasts of Daniel 7, and the Dragon hands over his authority to the Beast. The words used to describe this – δύναμις, θρόνος, and ἐξουσία – are also used in the book of Revelation as attributes of God and Christ.[14] By referring to the Beast so evidently as an envoy of Satan (cf. 12:9), John points out the origin of the Beast's power. And yet, 'the whole earth followed him in amazement' to

---

[10] See A. DEISSMANN, Licht, 289–290.
[11] See for instance the facsimile of the Augustan *charagma*, A. DEISSMANN, Licht, 290.
[12] The only verse in which the Lamb might be included in the worship is 5:14, but there it is not stated explicitly. In all other verses cited above only God is mentioned as object of worship.
[13] For a more detailed discussion, cf. L.J. LIETAERT PEERBOLTE, Antecedents, 141–156.
[14] L.J. LIETAERT PEERBOLTE, Antecedents, 142.

worship the Dragon and the Beast (13:3–4,8). The symbolism points out that the emperor received his power straight from Satan.

In his moulding of the old tradition of Leviathan and Behemoth John uses the former to symbolise the emperor.[15] The latter, however, is moulded with imagery depicting the priesthood that served the imperial cult. In Revelation 13 the priests are subsumed in the symbolism of 'another Beast', this time coming from the land (= Behemoth). Here the appearance of the creature as that of 'a lamb' is stated explicitly. The second Beast performs prophetic signs like causing fire to rain from heaven (13:13; cf. 1 Kgs 18:38), and deceives the inhabitants of the earth by these signs.[16] It is thus described as a false prophet, and it is by this exact same title that John mentions it again in 16:13; 19:20 and 20:10.

Rev 13:15 forms a remarkable element in the description of the two Beasts. Two characteristics of the imperial cult are mentioned in that verse that are difficult to trace in the evidence we have: the second Beast 'gives breath' to the statue of the first Beast so that it will speak, and it causes the death of those who do not worship the statue. The first element is probably a description of the way in which statues were made to 'speak'. If this is not intended as a description of some kind of trickery, the words of 13:15 should be taken as a metaphoric description of the fact that the priesthood functioned as the spokespersons for the imperial cult. Either way, the priests effectuate the power of the emperor within and by means of the cult. Furthermore, the second element in 13:15 points out that the priesthood could indeed have people killed for a refusal to worship the emperor – at least: from John's point of view. The persecution and even killing of Christians on behalf of the imperial cult is presupposed elsewhere in the Book of Revelation as well. The strongest reference to the death of Christians on behalf of their faith is found in 12:11: 'They (= 'our brothers', v. 10) have gained victory over him because of the blood of the lamb and because of the word of their testimony, and they did not cling to their lives unto death'.[17] The victory described here can be no other than the moral victory of martyrs who did not give in to repression.

From the above it may be clear that John argues against what he regarded as the satanic authority of the Roman emperor. The language he uses, however, is fierce of tone. Why did he and his fellow Christians take such an explicit stand over against the emperor and the Roman authorities? To find an answer

---

[15] For the use of the tradition of Leviathan and Behemoth, see L.J. LIETAERT PEERBOLTE, Antecedents, 153.

[16] The motif of 'deceit' (πλανᾶν) is an important feature in the traditional expectation of the coming of a false prophet. It is found throughout the corpus of early Christian and contemporary Jewish literature as an eschatological sign.

[17] The NRSV translates διὰ τὸ αἷμα τοῦ ἀρνίου καὶ διὰ τὸν λόγον τῆς μαρτυρίας αὐτῶν as 'by the blood of the Lamb and by the word of their testimony'. In combination with an accusative, however, διά means 'because of', not 'by'. The victory the 'brothers' gained therefore cannot be identified as the death of Christ. In stead the verb νικᾶν points at their own deaths.

we should consider a number of elements from the political and religious context of the Book of Revelation.

2. The Administrative Organisation of the Cities of Asia

The moment Alexander the Great headed east to defeat the Persians greatly changed the socio-political situation of Asia Minor. Cities that had previously been organised in small kingdoms with but a few contenders of their status to rival their position now became part of one great empire, though not for long. This change in the political situation brought about by Alexander marked the beginning of a period in which two systems rivalled each other. On the one hand, cities maintained a high degree of independence. On the other, the larger political context defined the boundaries to this independence in a strict manner. When the Romans eventually took control of the area the position of the *poleis* again changed. The Roman province of Asia came into existence in 133 BCE when king Attalus III of Pergamum handed over his kingdom to Rome. From then on the cities of Asia were incorporated in the Roman Empire.

In the early imperial period the political situation throughout the empire was redefined by Augustus (29 BCE). His reforms introduced a civil service to the Roman administration, which had become necessary because of the vast area then under Roman rule.[18] The prime task of this civil service was to implement the Roman system in the entire empire. Augustus developed a new tax system, and also a municipal system for the administration of the provinces.[19] Within this system cities were ranked after their status: the top ranking was that of a *colonia civium Romanorum*, to be followed by that of the *municipium* or *oppidum civium Romanorum*. The third and last category of especially privileged cities was that of the 'Latin' towns. These three categories of cities enjoyed special privileges such as partial (sometimes even total) immunity from taxation. Cities that were not reckoned among one of these three classes did not enjoy any privileges either.

The Augustan classification of cities more or less reflects the Roman class society as well as its patron-client structure. Cities came to strife after an improvement of their status in order to obtain privileges from Rome.[20] It was this administrative system that played an important part in the way in which the imperial cult was implemented in the province of Asia.

Life in the cities of Asia, as elsewhere, found its focus in the public domain: the *agora*, the *gymnasium*, the temples, the *bouleuterion* formed the areas where most of the activities within the town took place. It is important to note that a large part of these activities were, as we would label them in an

---

[18] For a general discussion of the influence of Augustus on the administration of the eastern provinces, see S.A. COOK *et al.* (eds.), History, Vol. X, 205–217.
[19] Cf. see S.A. COOK *et al.* (eds.), History, Vol. X, 191–193.
[20] See the description of 'the development of cities' in S. MITCHELL, Anatolia I, 198–226.

anachronistic distinction, cultural or religious in character – not political.[21] Civic life centred in a number of fields and one way of showing and supporting one's position was to partake in the religious duties of the town's citizens. Hence the numerous inscriptions that are witnesses to the frequency with which the ancients erected memorial shrines, gave votive offerings, and paid their respect to the gods.

Important as they must have been, political activities were probably only a minor part of the public life of towns in Asia. A procurator on behalf of the senate governed the province as a whole. This procurator for instance had to implement the imperial cult. To do this, procurators used the *koina*, gatherings of towns that collectively installed and kept the cult of the emperor. Important political decisions within a town were taken by the *boule*. It appears that 'the *demos* collectively, or private individuals other than magistrates, rarely initiated political action.'[22]

H.J. DE JONGE correctly draws attention to the fact that it was the *koinon* who took the lead in implementing the imperial cult.[23] This was probably a result of the competition between the various cities now having been brought into one political system. The competition as such remained, but the cooperation within the *koinon* could enhance the status of all cities included.

Although the *koinon* indeed played an important part in the implementation of the imperial cult, there is another side to the matter, which should not be underestimated. In his important monograph on the imperial cult in Asia Minor, Simon R.F. PRICE has argued that the imperial cult was implemented in this area quite differently than in the Latin West.[24] In Asia Minor the cult was not just imposed top-down in a hierarchic fashion. It was also implemented actively by the cities themselves. The prime reason for this, according to Price, was the fact that these towns were rooted in a long-standing tradition of cultic veneration of their rulers. But next to that, apparently, the cult brought special benefits to these cities, and it is to these special benefits we will turn in the next section.

3. The Benefits of the Imperial Cult

From its early stages on the imperial cult was used by Rome itself as a means to visualise and stress the emperor's presence throughout the *imperium Ro-*

---

[21] S. MITCHELL, Anatolia I, 198.
[22] S. MITCHELL, Anatolia I, 201.
[23] At the moment the present article was written, two important publications by H.J. DE JONGE on the imperial cult and the Book of Revelation were still forthcoming: H.J. DE JONGE, 'The Apocalypse of John and the Imperial Cult', and H.J. DE JONGE 'Function of Religious Polemics'. DE JONGE kindly gave me his typescripts to share his knowledge with me. I sincerely thank him for that. The description of the function of the *koinon* is given on the first pages of H.J. DE JONGE, Function.
[24] S.R.F. PRICE, Rituals, esp. 23–52.

manum.²⁵ In a period of history in which the representation of power could not be achieved by means of television broadcasts or newspapers the spread of statues portraying the emperor was an instrument for establishing his authority over against the inhabitants of the empire. It was apparently also for this reason that imperial statues were manufactured in three types: Price reconstructs the military, the divine, and the civilian portrait of emperors.²⁶ These statues were combined with busts, and all four types are found in imperial sanctuaries. Seen from the perspective of propaganda, it is not strange that the emperor was ranked among the gods: the emperor was ultimately in control of the earthly reality in which the inhabitants of his empire were living, and therefore the only reasonable position for his statue was among those of the gods.

As was already said above, Asia Minor knew a tradition in cultic veneration of rulers before the Roman period. Already during the Persian reign rulers of Asia Minor were honoured as deities, and so were e.g. civilian benefactors of a city.²⁷ Hellenism only brought a superficial change in this cultic veneration of rulers. Notwithstanding the pre-Roman history of ruler cults in Asia Minor, evidence shows that it was in the Roman period that most sanctuaries and shrines were erected.²⁸ The Roman republic inaugurated a comparable cult of the goddess of Roma, and under Julius Caesar and Augustus the cult was expanded with the worship of the *princeps*. Ever since this early beginning the cult of Roma and the emperor served as identity markers throughout the rapidly increasing area under Roman rule.

Seen from this perspective, it is clear why the Roman authorities took special interest in fostering the spread of the cult of Roma and her emperor. But what good was it to the cities of the province of Asia? What did they gain by their active participation in this cultic veneration of Roma and especially of the emperor?

For a revealing description of the balance of power within the relationship between Rome and the cities of Asia Minor we should turn to Tac Ann 3.60–63. Tacitus there describes how the cities were summoned by the senate of Rome to send a delegation to the imperial capital in order to have their privileges tested. The senate had heard that in several of the towns the sanctuary dedicated to Augustus had come to function as an asylum for refugees and even convicted criminals. In his typical Roman pride Tacitus praises this action: 'It was an impressive spectacle which that day afforded, when the senate scrutinised the benefactions of its predecessors, the constitutions of the prov-

---

[25] See e.g. one of the major conclusions of S.R.F. PRICE, Rituals, 248: 'The imperial cult, like the cults of the traditional gods, created a relationship of power between subject and ruler. It also enhanced the dominance of local élites over the populace, of cities over other cities, and of Greek over indigenous cultures. That is, the cult was a major part of the web of power that formed the fabric of society.'
[26] S.R.F. PRICE, Rituals, 181–188.
[27] S.R.F. PRICE, Rituals, 23–40.
[28] For an impression of the diffusion of the imperial cult in Asia Minor, see maps 2–5 in S.R.F. PRICE, Rituals.

inces, even the decrees of kings whose power antedated the arms of Rome, and the rites of the deities themselves, with full liberty as of old to confirm or change.'[29] One by one the delegations of the cities appeared before the senate: Ephesus, Magnesia, Aphrodisias, Stratonicea, Hierocaesarea, then delegations from Cyprus, and a number of others. Finally also the delegates from Pergamum, Smyrna, and Miletus are mentioned. Eventually the senate reduced the towns' possibilities for asylum, and ordered its decree to be published in bronze in all the sanctuaries used as a refuge (Ann 3.63).[30]

The episode referred to proves the degree to which the cities depended upon the central administration in Rome. Their public welfare was related to the privileges appointed to each of these cities by Rome, and if privileges were changed, this was surely felt throughout the town. It is obvious that a withdrawal of privileges could indeed happen. When Tiberius, for instance, found the inhabitants of Cyzicus negligent in their care for the cult of Augustus, he immediately withdrew their rights: 'The community of Cyzicus were charged with neglecting the cult of the deified Augustus; allegations were added of violence to Roman citizens; and they forfeited the freedom earned during the Mithridatic War, when the town was invested and they beat off the king as much by their own firmness as by the protection of Lucullus.'[31]

The examples from Tacitus underline that the Roman system worked on the basic principles of *divide et impera* and *do ut des*. PRICE describes the implementation of the imperial cult as a system of gift-exchange.[32] In this gift-exchange pattern both of the principles mentioned can be found. The cities intended to donate funds to the imperial cult by organising festivals and putting up sanctuaries. By this they hoped to gain respect from Rome in order to improve their status (*do ut des*). Rome on the other hand did not acknowledge each and every application for the building of a new sanctuary. By turning down some of the proposals to erect sanctuaries Rome, the emperor or the senate, kept the competition between the cities alive, thus preventing the formation of a large, unified opposition (*divide et impera*). 'It is necessary for gift-exchange to contain an element of uncertainty; an automatic exchange transforms gifts into purchases.'[33] By keeping the uncertainty alive Rome kept the competition alive.

It is thus clear that the various cities in Asia Minor hoped to improve their status and their privileges by positively supporting the imperial cult. Nevertheless, only three cities of the *koinon* of Asia were appointed *neokoros* before

---

[29] Tac Ann 3.60; translation J. JACKSON in LCL.
[30] The same function of imperial statues is described in Corp Herm 18.16: ἀλλὰ μὴν καὶ οἱ ἀνδριάντες οἱ τούτου τοῖς μάλιστα χειμαζομένοις ὅρμοι τυγχάνουσιν εἰρήνης· ἤδη δὲ καὶ μόνη εἰκὼν φανεῖσα βασιλέως ἐνήργησε τὴν νίκην ...
[31] Tac Ann 4.36; translation J. JACKSON in LCL.
[32] S.R.F. PRICE, Rituals, 65–77.
[33] S.R.F. PRICE, Rituals, 74.

the end of the first century CE: Pergamum, Smyrna, and Ephesus.[34] Temples, however, were not the only means to promote the imperial cult. Scattered throughout the region of Asia busts and smaller sanctuaries dedicated to the emperors have been found. For the cities and their inhabitants the dedication of, for instance, a statue to the emperor was a good opportunity to thank the Roman authorities for benefactions received for celebrating the divinity of the emperor. The way in which the emperor was honoured and venerated showed to Rome the loyalty of the worshippers. The cultic worship of the emperor as well as the games held in his honour could thus be used as a means to express gratitude and loyalty to the emperor and Rome. At the same time they created a possibility for both individual citizens as well as for the towns to improve their position in the *cursus honorum*.

4. Polemics in Context

Most cities in the Roman Empire were densely populated. In his reconstruction of the rise of early Christianity Rodney STARK calculates the density of for example Corinth in the period under discussion at 137 persons per acre. This is even somewhat higher than the density of Calcutta *anno* 2000.[35] After a description of the housing conditions and the problems delivered by sanitation, STARK simply observes: 'The Greco-Roman city was a pesthole of infectious disease.'[36]

The cities of Asia Minor addressed by John cannot have been much better places to live in than Rome or Corinth. Life in these cities must have been very difficult, given their dirty and overcrowded character. Only a strict observance of the common social system may have kept their inhabitants from fully becoming wolves to one another. In fact, Lucian of Samosata's dialogue *Charon* describes the situation in a telling metaphor: the 'cities resemble hives, in which everyone has a sting of his own and stings his neighbour, while some few, like wasps, harry and plunder the meaner sort.'[37]

The Roman social system with its total lack of upward mobility strongly focussed on *pietas* as the central virtue:[38] people should respect the gods, the

---

[34] According to S.R.F. PRICE, Rituals, 64–65, n. 47, the term *neokoros* ('temple warden') 'originally referred to a temple official or to a city, such as Ephesus, in connection with a prestigious cult. It was also soon applied informally to a city in connection with the imperial cult'. S.J. FRIESEN, Twice Neokoros, 2, argues that 'this term is only appropriate in reference to a province's imperial cult beginning in the late first century CE.' See also S.J. FRIESEN, Twice Neokoros, 50–75. In the above I have chosen to use *neokoros* as an informal designation in line with PRICE.

[35] R. STARK, Rise, 150.

[36] R. STARK, Rise, 155.

[37] Luc Charon 15.

[38] See e.g. Cic Planc 12.29: *pietas fundamentum est omnium virtutum*. This strong focus on *pietas* was brought to my attention by K. GALINSKY, 'Pietas and Piety in Roman Relig-

emperor, and each other. To fall short in respect was considered a serious vice. This strong focus on respect, virtue, and honour characterised the Graeco-Roman society to a high degree: the more a citizen deserved to be honoured, the more he was considered as an important member of society. The social context for the earliest Christians was therefore very much defined by the system of honour and praise. To participate in this social system one had to pay his respect (*pietas*) to those who ranked above him.

Within this system of honour and praise the religious attitudes of the inhabitants of the Roman Empire were considered of great importance. Polybius, for instance, describes the social cohesion brought about by the observance of the gods, by stating: 'But the quality in which the Roman commonwealth is most distinctly superior is in my opinion the nature of their religious convictions. I believe that it is the very thing which among other peoples is an object of reproach, I mean fear of the gods (δεισιδαιμονία), which maintains the cohesion of the Roman state'.[39]

The Christian refusal to worship the gods was indeed perceived by Graeco-Roman society as an anti-social act of atheism.[40] Jewish inhabitants of the empire had already been reproached and loathed for the same attitude,[41] and now this religious enmity obviously also befell the earliest Christians. The Book of Revelation makes clear that such a refusal to worship was indeed at stake as far as John was concerned. But why did he focus so much on the imperial cult?

The first part of the answer is to be found in the observation that John's criticism of the imperial cult is part of a Jewish-Christian tradition of polemic against idolatry. Already in the earliest extant description of a conversion of pagans to Christianity Paul describes the converts' pagan past as a worship of idols: '... you have turned toward God, away from the idols, to serve the living and true God' (1 Thess 1:9). The choice between a life with 'the living and true God' or a life of worshipping idols often recurs in Paul's letters. He explicitly warns the Corinthians to 'flee from all idol-worship' (1 Cor 10:14), and repeats the same warning in different terms elsewhere (see e.g. 2 Cor 6:16; Gal 5:20). In 1 Cor 12:2 Paul polemically refers to the Graeco-Roman pantheon as to the 'dumb idols' the Corinthians had served in their pre-Christian life.[42]

Idol worship appears to have been an important point of debate in the formative period of earliest Christianity. Whatever the historicity of the so-called apostolic decree, it is worth noting that Acts 15:29 describes abstinence from meat sacrificed to the idols as the first element of the apostolic compromise on

---

ion: The Impact of Augustus', a paper delivered at the annual meeting of the Society of Biblical Literature (Nashville, 2000).

[39] Polyb Hist 6.56.6–7; cf. also Cic Nat deor 1.3.
[40] Cf. the description offered by R. LANE FOX, Pagans, 425–428. See e.g. Julian, Contra Galilaeos 43b, and M. STERN (ed.), Greek and Latin Authors, vol. 2, 545.
[41] See among many other possible examples Philostr Vit Ap 5.33; Tac Hist 5.5.1–3.
[42] On the social dimensions of the early Christians' monotheistic visions, see W.A. MEEKS, First Urban Christians, 165–170.

dietary laws. Paul's discussion of exactly this problem in 1 Corinthians 8 shows that consumption of this kind of meat did indeed evoke discussions among the earliest Christians. His treatment of the subject shows us not only his pastoral attitude (esp. 8:9!), but also the different opinions on this problem that the earliest Christians held. Apparently some were troubled by the fact that others did eat from this meat. This problem, of course, has nothing to do with vegetarian preoccupations: it is all about the worship of the idols. Paul's answer is very clear: οὐδὲν εἴδωλον ἐν τῷ κόσμῳ καί (...) οὐδεὶς θεὸς εἰ μὴ εἷς. Here Paul denies the existence of other deities than God, but in v. 5 he does acknowledge the power that these non-existent deities held.

The polemic against idol worship was obviously no Christian invention. Many Old Testament texts warn against the worship of other gods than YHWH,[43] and Jewish Hellenistic literature frequently describes the same phenomenon in a critical way. Jub. 12:3–5 is an exemplary text in this respect. In that passage Abraham criticises his father Terah for his worship of statues: 'What profit or advantage do we gain from those idols that you worship and prostrate yourself in front of? For there is no spirit in them: dumb things they are that only lead us into error; so don't worship them.'[44] The picture *Jubilees* gives of Abraham is not exactly a neutral description. Abraham is depicted as a role model for Israel, and his faith in YHWH starts with this goodbye to the worship of idols.

Also in *Joseph and Aseneth* an important criticism of idolatry is found. Here, Aseneth is somehow pictured as a model for pagans who converted to Judaism. The crucial moment of her conversion is the moment in which Aseneth gets rid of her ancestral gods: 'And she took all her innumerable gold and silver gods and broke them up into little pieces, and threw them out of the window for the poor and the needy' (JosAs 10:13).[45] After Aseneth has cast all her luxury and her idols away, she starts a prayer to God. She asks for forgiveness for her sins, and describes those sins extensively. A short fragment may suffice to indicate the conception of idolatry that appears in this text: 'I have sinned, O Lord, I have sinned (...) My mouth, O Lord, has been defiled by things offered to idols and by the table of the gods of the Egyptians. I have sinned, O Lord, before thee; I have sinned and acted impiously, worshipping idols, dead and dumb, and I am not worth to open my mouth before thee (...)' (JosAs 12:5–6).

The same polemic can be found in the early Christian *Testaments of the Twelve Patriarchs*. Judah's farewell-speech contains an obvious allusion to the worship of other deities as a result of another serious vice, financial greed: 'the

---

[43] See e.g. Exod 20:3; Deut 5:7; 1 Kgs 18:27; Isa 43:10–13; Jer 2:26–28; 7:16–20; Ezek 8; 16; 23; Hos 1–3; 8:4–6; Zeph 1:4–5.

[44] Translation by R.H. CHARLES and C. RABIN in H.F.D. SPARKS, Apocryphal Old Testament.

[45] Translation by D. COOK in H.F.D. SPARKS, Apocryphal Old Testament.

love of money is a sure path to idolatry, because, when led astray by money, men call gods those that are no gods ...'[46]

To these examples many others could be added.[47] One specific text may, however, have influenced the imagery used in the Book of Revelation to a higher degree than other texts did, viz. Daniel 3. In this chapter king Nebuchadnezzar decides to have his statue (εἰκών in both LXX and Theod) erected throughout his empire so that 'all peoples, nations, and languages' should 'fall down and worship the golden statue that King Nebuchadnezzar has set up' (Dan 3:4–5; NRSV). The linguistic parallels between both the LXX and Theodotion of Daniel 3 on the one hand and Revelation 13 on the other are obvious.[48] It is very plausible therefore that Daniel 3 has influenced the description of Revelation 13. Probably even the use of the specific word εἰκών in the Book of Revelation has been evoked by Daniel 3. This word is used in distinction of the εἴδωλα of Rev 9:20.[49] The word εἰκών in the book of Revelation, no doubt, refers to a single image representing the Beast coming from the sea.[50] This Beast, in turn, represents a masculine person (the neuter being treated as a masculine in 13:8,14; 17:3,11).[51] The author of Revelation may well have borrowed this word from the description of Nebuchadnezzar's statue in Daniel 3, because he found it fitting for the context in which he himself wrote. It referred to a 'likeness' of the one worshipped, without specifying the exact form.[52] Seen against the danielic background of the terminology, however, it is likely that a statue is meant in Revelation 13.

The tradition of polemics against the worship of idols does define the religio-historical background of John's attack of the imperial cult, but the fierceness of that attack still has to be accounted for. In other words: there has to be a second part to the answer to the question asked above.

---

[46] TestXII Jud 23:1; translation by M. DE JONGE, in H.F.D. SPARKS, Apocryphal Old Testament.
[47] See among many other passages e.g. TestXII Levi 17:11; Wis 14:26–27; Sib 3:29–35; 4:7–8; LAB 44.
[48] In both Revelation 13 and Daniel 3 the issue at stake is the worship of the statue of a ruler: Nebuchadnezzar's εἰκών is mentioned in LXX and Theod Dan 3:1,5,10 (Theod 11), 12,18; cf. Rev 13:14,15; 14:9,11; 15:2; 16:2; 19:20; 20:4. The worship is described with προσκυνέω LXX and Theod Dan 3:6,7,10 (only LXX),11,12,15,18; cf. Rev 13:8,12, According to Rev 13:8 the Beast whose statue is to be worshipped has power over all inhabitants of the earth – πάντες οἱ κατοικοῦντες ἐπὶ τῆς γῆς – Rev 13:8,12; cf. LXX Dan 3:1 (πάντας τοὺς κατοικοῦντας ἐπὶ τῆς γῆς). In LXX Dan 3:4,7 the king's universal power is described as a power over all ἔθνη καὶ χῶραι, λαοὶ καὶ γλῶσσαι (Theod 3:4,7: λαοί, φυλαί, γλῶσσαι); cf. Rev 13:7 where the Beast is said to have power ἐπὶ πᾶσαν φυλὴν καὶ λαὸν καὶ γλῶσσαν καὶ ἔθνος.
[49] For the use of εἰκών, see the previous footnote.
[50] See G. BIGUZZI, Ephesus, 278.
[51] Ibid.
[52] For the use of the word εἰκών within the imperial cult, see S.R.F. PRICE, Rituals, 176–177: 'An *eikon*, whose semantic motivation as a "likeness", had a denotation as wide as the English term implies; out of context it is impossible to determine whether it refers to a statue, a bust, a tondo or a painting.'

Most likely, this second part of the answer is to be found in the circumstances to which the book of Revelation reacts. Recently arguments have been brought forward for a dating of the book under Trajan.⁵³ It is the present author's opinion, however, that the latter part of Domitian's reign is to be preferred as the date of the writing. Not only does this period fit the description of the Book of Revelation very well, as does the period of Trajan, but this date also corresponds to Irenaeus' testimony that the book was written under Domitian.⁵⁴

The traditional interpretation of the Book of Revelation refers to Domitian's claim of worship as 'our Lord and God'.⁵⁵ Suetonius' famous account of the life of Domitian describes how the emperor introduced *dominus et deus noster* as his formal title in a circular letter, and how this terminology was used from then on.⁵⁶ The evidence is not unproblematic, however. Suetonius clearly resented Domitian and his picture has been coloured by the *damnatio memoriae* that befell the emperor after his death. Writing under the *nouveau régime* Suetonius had reasons enough to discard the *ancien régime*.⁵⁷ And yet, other authors indicate that Suetonius did not invent Domitian's divine pretensions. A number of historians describe the same situation as Suetonius does. The common picture they give is that Domitian started his reign in a moderate way to change his course and proclaim himself divine soon after. The best summary is given by Eutropius: 'During the first years he held office in a moderate way, but soon he developed exorbitant vices (...) He issued that he be addressed as Lord and God.'⁵⁸ Most likely, however, Eutropius' account cannot be seen as independent from Suetonius'. The latter's treatment of Domitian has probably influenced those of Eusebius, Aurelius Victor, and Orosius as well. Nevertheless Eutropius' words are important, because they reflect the traditional verdict by Roman historians on Domitian. Furthermore, Martial, Pliny the Younger and Dio Chrysostomus appear to underline this verdict.⁵⁹

In one of his epigrams Martial refers to an edict by Domitian restoring the prime seats in the theatre to the knights as an 'edict of our Lord and God' (5.8.1). Although his description is put in ironic terms the terminology *domi-*

---

⁵³ A.o. D.E. AUNE, Revelation I, lvi–lxx (Aune distinguishes three redactional layers of Revelation and dates the last of these to the period of Trajan); H.J. DE JONGE, Apocalypse, typescript 1–2 ('The possibility cannot be ruled out that the founding of the temple in honour of Zeus Philios and Trajan in Pergamum in 114 CE formed the historical backcloth of the genesis of Revelation'); H.J. DE JONGE, Function.

⁵⁴ Iren, haer 5.30.3: *neque enim ante multum temporis visum est, sed pene sub nostro saeculo, ad finem Domitiani imperii.*

⁵⁵ On the worship of Domitian as a deity, see now M. CLAUSS, Kaiser, 119–132.

⁵⁶ Suet Dom 13.2: 'With no less arrogance he began as follows in dictating a circular letter in the name of his procurators, "Our Master and our God bids that this be done". And so the custom arose of henceforth addressing him in no other way even in writing or in conversation.' – translation J.C. ROLFE in LCL.

⁵⁷ See L.L. THOMPSON, Revelation, 111.

⁵⁸ *Primis tamen annis moderatus in imperio fuit, mox ad ingentia vitia progressus (...) dominum se et deum primus appelari iussit* – 7.23; translation mine.

⁵⁹ K. SCOTT, Imperial Cult, 102–112; Scott also mentions evidence from Statius.

nus et deus was evidently in use for Domitian.[60] It is clearly with great relief that Martial writes after Domitian's death: 'In vain, o ye flatteries, ye come to me, wretched creatures with your shameless lips; I think not to address any man as Master and God'.[61] Pliny the Younger, who wrote under Trajan, compares the latter's reign with that of Domitian: 'An open tribute to our emperor demands a new form, now that the wording of our private talk has changed. Times are different, and our speeches must show this; from the very nature of our thanks both the recipient and the occasion must be made clear to all. Nowhere should we flatter him as a divinity and a god; we are talking of a fellow-citizen, not a tyrant, one who is our father, not our over-lord'.[62] Statius, who probably did not even live to witness the tyrant's death, speaks of Domitian as the *forma dei praesens* (Silv 1.1.62), and *proximus ille deus* (Silv 5.2.170).[63]

Also Dio Chrystostomus gives evidence of the same manner of speaking as he describes Domitian 'who was called "Master and God" by all Greeks and barbarians, but who was really an evil daemon' (Or 45.1). Dio strongly disapproved of the *adulatio* that befell Domitian, and obviously he was not the only one. During his reign Domitian had tried to diminish the power of the Senate, and this was one of the reasons why the Senate immediately after his death decided to fully erase all that remembered of the deceased emperor: his statues were torn down, his name was carved out of all inscriptions, and Nerva was appointed as his successor. Domitian's death brought great relief for many inhabitants of the Empire – not just to Jews and Christians.

Strangely enough there is a discrepancy between Domitian's claims of divinity as described in literary sources and the archeological and epigraphical evidence. There is, for instance, no solid archeological evidence of a strong increase of activities in the imperial cult in Asia under Domitian's reign, although this increase has long been assumed. Steven J. FRIESEN has published a detailed reconstruction of the remnants of the imperial cult in Ephesus and the province of Asia as a whole.[64] His conclusions are that the imperial cult was present throughout the region, especially in Ephesus, but also that the cult did not focus too much on the single, reigning emperor. In stead, it promoted the worship of the *Sebastoi* as a dynasty: 'The Cult of the Sebastoi depended very little upon an individual emperor for its vitality.'[65] The way in which the cult was shaped in Ephesus meant a new step in the development of the imperial cult: '(...) in contrast to the cult of Rome and Augustus in Pergamum or the Cult of Tiberius, Livia, and the Senate in Smyrna, the imperial family appeared

---

[60] K. SCOTT, Imperial Cult, 105–108, mentions a number of other passages in which Martial uses the vocabulary of *dominus et deus* while referring to Domitian.
[61] Mart 10.72.1–3: ... *dicturus dominum deumque non sum* – translation by W.C.A. KER in LCL.
[62] *Nusquam ut deo, nusquam ut numini blandiamur; non enim de tyranno, sed de cive, non de domino, sed de parente loquimur* – Paneg 2.3; translation B. RADICE in LCL.
[63] K. SCOTT, Imperial Cult, 107.
[64] S.J. FRIESEN, Twice Neokoros.
[65] S.J. FRIESEN, Twice Neokoros, 166.

alone as the object of the province's worship without reference to other centers of Roman power.'[66]

FRIESEN and others have argued that the giant statue from Ephesus that has long been regarded as proof of Domitian's megalomania was in fact a portrait of his brother Titus.[67] Nevertheless, a 'series of dedications of numerous cities' does point at 'the establishment of the cult of Domitian at Ephesus, which involved the participation of the whole province'.[68] Furthermore, Ephesus was appointed *neokoros* of the imperial cult in 89/90 CE (for the second time, hence the Ephesian epithet *twice neokoros*).[69] Domitian was indeed worshipped as a divinity, but apparently not in the excessive way that was long assumed.

Epigraphic evidence does not substantiate the picture of Domitian as given by the literary sources mentioned.[70] The combination of *dominus et deus* is not found in inscriptions dedicated to Domitian, although there is ample evidence on the worship of Domitian as one of the gods. An inscription from Ephesus, for instance, describes him as ὁ θεῶν ἐμφανέστατος, whereas another one compares him to Ζεὺς Ἐλευθέριος.[71] Yet there is no conclusive indication of a strong increase of activities of the imperial cult under Domitian nor is there any proof that Domitian used stronger epitheta for his divine status than any of his predecessors.[72] The difference was probably the way in which Domitian himself perceived his divine status: he appears to have taken the whole thing rather seriously by using his cultic veneration as a means for establishing his power.

In the end, therefore, it is probably best to conclude that the polemics against the imperial cult in the book of Revelation did not result from some increase in the worship of Domitian as a divinity, but rather from an increased sensitivity on the part of the Christians. This sensitivity must have been evoked by the specific situation in which they lived: some Christians were killed because of their faith. The reason for their deaths should not be sought in a great change in the imperial cult, but in the tyrannic character of Domitian's reign.

This conclusion brings us to the second element within the picture the book of Revelation gives of the imperial cult: the polemic against the imperial priesthood, depicted as the second Beast or the 'false prophet'. In recent years the traditional consensus on a full scale persecution of Christians under Domitian has rightly been questioned.[73] There is in fact no other evidence for the persecution of Christians under Domitian than the Book of Revelation itself

---

[66] S.J. FRIESEN, Twice Neokoros, 167.
[67] S.J. FRIESEN, Twice Neokoros, 59–63.
[68] S.R.F. PRICE, Rituals, 198.
[69] S.J. FRIESEN, Twice Neokoros, 57.
[70] See A. MARTIN, Titulature, *passim*.
[71] A. MARTIN, Titulature, 195–196.
[72] A. MARTIN, Titulature, 196: 'Mais on a depuis longtemps souligné que, dès le règne d'Auguste, l'octroi au prince des titres qui lui donnent rang de divinité est un phénomène banal, particulièrement en Orient.'
[73] See e.g. H.-J. KLAUCK, Sendschreiben.

(see above, section 1). This observation inevitably leads to the conclusion that there were no mass-persecutions under Domitian.[74] The evidence from Pliny discussed above underlines this conclusion. Yet the fact that some Christians did die on behalf of their faith is relevant enough. John apparently responds to a situation which he perceived as one of crisis. It was this situation of 'perceived crisis' that led John to his attack of the imperial cult and its priesthood.

FRIESEN's study of the Cult of the Sebastoi in Ephesus shows that the imperial highpriests of the province, known as Asiarchs, held important social and administrative positions.[75] They stood in high esteem and functioned not only as the highpriests of the cult, but also had great political influence. The question whether or not these, and lower, imperial priests could put people to death at their refusal to worship the emperor is difficult to answer. In fact, the main evidence we have is, again, the picture given by the Book of Revelation itself. If this picture were the only one, we might have to reckon with the possibility of metaphoric language. Yet the apocryphal *Acts of Paul and Thecla* form an indication that imperial (high)priests did indeed have the authority to put people to death. Acts of Paul and Thecla 26 describes how Thecla committed a felony against an important man named Alexander. This Alexander is described in codex C as a συριάρχης, and in his 1891 edition LIPSIUS included this reading: συριάρχης τις 'Αλέξανδρος ὀνόματι. In many translations and in later editions the *varia lectio* σύρος has often been substituted for συριάρχης, but most likely the latter reading is the correct one.[76] If it is, the wealthy Alexander is depicted here as a highpriest in the imperial cult of Syria – a Syriach – in a way that forms a parallel to the Asiarchs discussed earlier.[77] If Alexander is indeed described as an imperial highpriest the charge against Thecla becomes comprehensible: she is sentenced to be killed by lions and a sign is put up describing her crime as that of sacrilege.[78] The sacrilege she had committed can be no other than her assault of Alexander. Thecla's dashing his (imperial) crown to the ground must have been perceived as sacrilegious. Alexander's

---

[74] U. RIEMER, Tier, 172, correctly argues against a full-scale persecution of Christians under Domitian. Unfortunately RIEMER fails to recognise the relevance of the description of the death of Christians given by the Book of Revelation itself. This is probably due to her failure to interpret the eschatological dimension of the Book of Revelation as a description of John's own present. RIEMER draws too strict a distinction between *Zeitgeschichte* and *Eschatologie* in her description of the Beast: 'Das "Tier" macht sich vielleicht in der Gegenwart bemerkbar, sein Wirken aber erweist sich erst in der Zukunft. Insofern ist es keine zeitgeschichtliche, sondern eine *eschatologische* Gestalt' (italics RIEMER) – Tier, 155. RIEMER unsufficiently takes into account that for John his present is an eschatological one.

[75] S.J. FRIESEN, Twice Neokoros, 97–112.

[76] *Pace* W. SCHNEEMELCHER II, 199. The reading συριάρχης solves a problem mentioned by J.N. BREMMER, viz. that it is difficult to understand why someone in a text that probably originated from Syria was explicitly mentioned as a Syrian. If σύρος is regarded as a later correction or mistake by a copyist, the matter is clear. See J. BREMMER, Apocryphal Acts, 50.

[77] S.R.R. PRICE, Rituals, 170.

[78] Ἡ δὲ αἰτία τῆς ἐπιγραφῆς αὐτῆς ἦν Ἱερόσυλος – Acts of Paul and Thecla 28.

authority as an imperial highpriest made it possible for him to have Thecla removed and executed at once – at least, that is what the intended readers in the second century will have understood. The Syriac version describes the charge against Thecla even more elaborately: 'Thecla they have called a violator of the temples, because she cast down the crown [of Caesar] from the head of Alexander, who wished to do uncleanness to her.'[79]

The description of Alexander in the Acts of Paul and Thecla does indicate that imperial highpriests could sentence people to death, but it does not point to Domitian's era. Other texts do, however, prove that under Domitian the act of lese majesty could lead to death: Cassius Dio narrates the story of a woman who undressed herself before a statue of Domitian and was killed for that reason,[80] and Philostratus mentions the story of a magistrate who 'was being prosecuted, because at a public sacrifice in Tarentum, where he held office, he had omitted to mention in the public prayers that Domitian was the son of Athene'.[81] This situation is also described by Suetonius: 'It was enough (sc. for anyone to be prosecuted) to accuse someone of any act or utterance against the emperor'.[82] This evidence points out that it was the repressive character of Domitian's reign rather than his divine pretensions that formed the danger for the Christians as well as for non-Christian inhabitants of the empire.

On the basis of the observation just made we should note that the imperial cult was, of course, an important instrument for establishing Domitian's power. Its priesthood may indeed have participated in the repression. It is true that the Acts of Paul and Thecla were written at a later date than the Book of Revelation and therefore primarily reflect the position of the priesthood at the end of the second century. The imperial cult was far more developed then than it was at the end of the first century. But still the description need not be totally anachronistic with regard to the power of the imperial priesthood at the end of the first century. The other literary evidence mentioned does indicate that any act against the emperor could lead to prosecution. The evidence may not be overwhelming, but still there is good reason to assume that the imperial priesthood was capable of forcing people's death. The description of Thecla's felony and Alexander's authority in the Acts of Paul and Thecla is indicative, the Book of Revelation clearly refers to the death of Christians who did not worship the emperor, and Pliny's correspondence with Trajan discussed in the introduction to this article points out the great ease with which Christians could be sentenced to death as a result merely of the fact that they confessed being a Christian. If a magistrate could be prosecuted merely because he forgot to mention the emperor in an official prayer, Christians could certainly be prosecuted for refusing to worship the emperor.

---

[79] Translation from W. WRIGHT, Apocryphal Acts, vol. 2.
[80] M. CLAUSS, Kaiser, 131; Cass Dio 67.12.2.
[81] Philostr Vit Ap 7,24; translation F.C. CONYBEARE in LCL.
[82] Suet Dom 12.

5. Conclusion

The book of Revelation was no doubt written for a number of reasons. The Christian apocalyptic John felt the need to describe his world in a manner that would point out the true nature of that world to his readers. In his writing he responded to a number of elements from his context, one of which was the death of some Christians who had died on behalf of their faith.

John fiercely reacted against the imperial cult. The emperor was present everywhere in the public areas of life. His statues stood in the market place, imperial sanctuaries were scattered throughout the province, and annual games were held to honour the emperor. His imperial priesthood was held in high esteem and excercised the power over life and death. Given the great importance of the imperial cult for the cities and their populations, it lies at hand that John the seer aimed his polemics at exactly this cult. The vehemence of his reaction must be explained from John's traditional background. Being a Jewish Christian the author of Revelation was familiar with the traditional Jewish polemics against idolatry. In his tradition idolatry was one of the main vices and the worship of a man as a deity was the worst kind of arrogance. Given the prominent social position held by the imperial cult and its priesthood, there was no better aim for John in his polemics against his cultural context. For him, the Roman empire brought economic and religious enslavement, and even the death of fellow-Christians.

By polemicising against the Roman imperial cult, John argued against his entire cultural and religious context and withdrew himself from that context. The religio-political propaganda by provincial authorities who wanted to improve their own position along with that of their towns could only work out in the proper manner if the inhabitants of their province would conform. By rejecting exactly the imperial cult, John and his fellow-Christians positioned themselves outside of the social system. By refusing to worship the gods and, most of all, the emperor they refuted the social system as such. Even though the Christians at the end of the first century must have formed a tiny minority, the Graeco-Roman authorities came to consider them as a serious threat to the stability brought about by the emperor and the gods. And indeed, so they turned out to be when, in due course, John's ideas appeared to be less those of a sectarian than many still consider them to have been.

Bibliography

AUNE, David E., Revelation. 3vols., Word Biblical Commentary 52A–C; Dallas 1997–1998.

BIGUZZI, Giancarlo, Ephesus, its Artemision, its Temple to the Flavian Emperors, and Idolatry in Revelation, in: NT 40 (1998), 276–290.

BREMMER, Jan N., Magic, Martyrdom and Women's Liberation in the Acts of Paul and Thecla, in: id. (ed.), The Apocryphal Acts of Paul and Thecla, Kampen 1996, 38–59.

CLAUSS, Manfred, Kaiser und Gott. Herrscherkult im römischen Reich, Stuttgart – Leipzig, 1999.

COOK, Stanley Arthur/ADCOCK, Frank E./CHARLESWORTH, Martin Percival (eds.), The Cambridge Ancient History, Vol. X: The Augustan Empire 44 B.C.–A.D.70, Cambridge 1934.

DE JONGE, Henk J., 'The Apocalypse of John and the Imperial Cult', in: F.T. VAN STRATEN/Johan H.M. STRUBBE et al. (eds.), Kykeon. FS H. VERSNEL, Leiden – New York – Köln, forthcoming.

ID., 'The Function of Religious Polemics. The Case of the Revelation of John versus the Imperial Cult', in: Arie VAN DER KOOIJ (ed.), Religious Polemics in Context, Leiderdorp, forthcoming.

DEISSMANN, Adolf, Licht vom Osten. Das Neue Testament und die neuentdeckten Texte der hellenistisch-römischen Welt, Tübingen ⁴1923.

DOWNING, F. Gerald, Pliny's Prosecutions of Christians: Revelation and 1 Peter, in: JSNT 34 (1988), 105–123

FRIESEN, Stephen J., Twice Neokoros. Ephesus, Asia and the Cult of the Flavian Imperial Family, RGRW 116 Leiden – New York – Köln 1993.

KLAUCK, Hans-Josef, Das Sendschreiben nach Pergamon und der Kaiserkult in der Johannesoffenbarung, in: Bib 73 (1992), 153–182.

KRAYBILL, J. Nelson, Imperial Cult and Commerce in John's Apocalypse, JSNTSS 132, Sheffield 1996.

LANE FOX, Robin, Pagans and Christians in the Mediterranean World from the Second Century AD to the Conversion of Constantine, London 1986.

LIETAERT PEERBOLTE, Lambertus J., The Antecedents of Antichrist. A Traditio-Historical Study of the Earliest Christian Views on Eschatological Opponents, SJSJ 49, Leiden – New York – Köln 1996.

MARTIN, Alain, La titulature épigraphique de Domitien, BKP 181, Frankfurt a.M., 1987.

MEEKS, Wayne A., The First Urban Christians. The Social World of the Apostle Paul, New Haven – London, 1983.

MILLAR, Fergus, 'The Imperial Cult and the Persecutions', in: DEN BOER, Willem (ed.), Le culte des souverains dans l'Empire Romain, Geneva 1973, 145–175.

MITCHELL, Stephen, Anatolia. Land, Men, and Gods in Asia Minor, Volume I: The Celts in Anatolia and the Impact of Roman Rule, Oxford 1993.

PRICE, Simon R.F., Rituals and Power. The Roman Imperial Cult in Asia Minor, Cambridge 1984.

RIEMER, Ulrike, Das Tier auf dem Kaiserthron? Eine Untersuchung zur Offenbarung des Johannes als historischer Quelle, BA 114, Stuttgart – Berlin, 1998.

SCHNEEMELCHER, Wilhelm (ed.), Neutestamentliche Apokryphen in deutscher Übersetzung, 2 vols., Tübingen ⁶1997.
SCOTT, Kenneth, The Imperial Cult under the Flavians, Stuttgart – Berlin 1936.
SPARKS, Hedley Frederick Davis (ed.), The Apocryphal Old Testament, Oxford 1984.
STARK, Rodney, The Rise of Christianity. A Sociologist Reconsiders History, Princeton 1996.
STERN, Menahem (ed.), Greek and Latin Authors on Jews and Judaism, 2 vols., Jerusalem 1976.
THOMPSON, Leonard L., The Book of Revelation. Apocalypse and Empire, New York – Oxford, 1990.
WRIGHT, William, Apocryphal Acts of the Apostles edited from Syriac Manuscripts in the British Museum and other Libraries, 2 vols., London – Edinburgh 1871.

Anhang

Liste der Mitarbeiterinnen und Mitarbeiter

Die Herausgeber:

Michael LABAHN

geb. 1964 in Braunschweig, Studium der Evangelischen Theologie in Oberursel/Ts., Tübingen und Göttingen, 1992–1995 Repetent, seit 1995 wiss. Assistent in Halle-Wittenberg, Mitarbeiter am Projekt Neuer Wettstein in Halle, 1998 Promotion in Göttingen, 1996–1998 berufsbegleitendes Vikariat. Forschungsschwerpunkte: Johannesevangelium, frühchristliche Wundergeschichten (Vorbereitung eines Bandes für die Reihe: ‚Erträge der Forschung'), Verhältnis des Neuen Testaments zu seiner Umwelt, Logienquelle (Habilitationsprojekt), Rezeption des Alten Testaments im Neuen Testament.
Email: AM.Labahn@t-online.de / Homepage: http://anu.theologie.uni-halle.de/NT/Labahn

Jürgen ZANGENBERG

geb. 1964 in Erlangen, Studium der Evangelischen Theologie in Erlangen, Heidelberg und Edinburgh. 1996 Promotion in Heidelberg (Frühes Christentum in Samarien, Tübingen 1998), 1995–1997 Vikariat in Nürnberg, Ernennung zum Pfarrer z.A und Ordination. Seit November 1997 Wissenschaftlicher Assistent an der Bergischen Universität Wuppertal. Intensive Ausgrabungstätigkeit in Israel und Jordanien, 1999 Gastprofessur am Bangor Theological Seminary in Bangor/Maine, 2000–2001 Stipendiat der Alexander-von-Humboldt Stiftung zur Forschungs- und Lehrtätigkeit an der Yale University Divinity School. Forschungsschwerpunkte: Johannesevangelium, Jesusforschung, Archäologie und Umwelt des NT (Qumran, Samaritaner), Bestattung im frühen Christentum (Habilitationsprojekt).
Email: zangenberg@t-online.de / Homepage http://www.uni-wuppertal.de/FB2/ev.theol/ (click on: Zangenberg)

Beiträgerinnen und Beiträger

Hannah M. COTTON

born 1946 in Jerusalem. D.Phil. Oxon. 1977. Professor of Ancient History and Classics at the Hebrew University of Jerusalem. Author of *Documentary Let-*

ters of Recommendation in Latin from the Roman Empire, Beiträge zur klassischen Philologie 132, 1982; *Masada II: The Latin and Greek Documents*, Jerusalem, 1989 (with J. Geiger); *Aramaic, Hebrew and Greek Texts from Nahal Hever and Other Sites (The Seiyâl Collection II)*. DJD XXVII, Oxford 1997 (with A. Yardeni), and many articles on judicial, administrative and social aspects of the papyrology of the Judaean Desert. Editor of *Scripta Classica Israelica (Yearbook of the Israel Society for the Promotion of Classical Studies)* since 1991. Coordinator since 1998 of the project *Corpus Inscriptionum Iudaeae/Palaestinae*, edited in Jerusalem-Tel Aviv-Koeln. Editor of *Rome, the Greek World and the East: Fergus Millar's Collected Papers* in three volumes (with Guy Rogers). Main interest: Roman provincial administration and jurisdiction with special emphasis on Judaea/Syria Palaestina. Currently writing together with Werner Eck the Roman *Fasti* of Judaea/Syria-Palaestinae from 6 to 324 CE.
Email: Cotton@h2.hum.huji.ac.il

Richard E. DEMARIS

born 1953, M.Div. in Biblical Studies from Princeton Theological Seminary (1980), M.Phil. and Ph.D. in Religion (New Testament) from Columbia University (1986, 1990), since 1995 Associate Professor of New Testament at Valparaiso University (Indiana/USA). Visiting Senior Associate, American School (Athens), 1992 and 1994; Catholic Biblical Association Young Scholar 1995-1996; affiliate of the Ohio State University Excavations at Isthmia. Primary research interests: archaeology and the New Testament world (Corinth); social-scientific interpretation (early Christian ritual).
Email: richard.demaris@valpo.edu / Homepage: www.valpo.edu/theology/demaris.html

Werner ECK

geb. 1939. Promotion 1968 an der Universität Erlangen-Nürnberg, Habilitation 1974/5 an der Universität zu Köln. 1975–1979 Professor an der Universität des Saarlandes, seit 1979 in Köln. Arbeitsschwerpunkte: Geschichte der römischen Kaiserzeit, Sozialgeschichte, Administration. Geschichte des frühen Christentums. Römische Epigraphik. Seit 1999 zusammen mit Kollegen in Israel Vorbereitung eines Corpus Inscriptionum Iudaeae/Palaestinae. Mitherausgeber der Zeitschrift für Papyrologie und Epigraphik; Projektleiter der Prosopographia Imperii Romani an der Berlin-Brandenburgischen Akademie der Wissenschaften.
Email: werner.eck@uni-koeln.de / Homepage: http://www.uni-koeln.de/philfak/ifa/altg/eck/index.html

Marco FRENSCHKOWSKI

geb. 1960, Promotion: 1994, Habilitation: 2001. Publikationen zum Neuen Testament und seiner religiösen Umwelt (Offenbarung und Epiphanie, 2 Bände 1995–1997; demnächst: Q-Studien), zur Alten Kirche, zum antiken Judentum, daneben zu neuen religiösen Bewegungen. Mitarbeiter bei TRE, RAC, BBKL, RGG 4. Aufl., TBLNT 2. Aufl., HWbPh u.a. Nachschlagewerken. Auch literaturwissenschaftliche und volkskundliche Arbeiten (etwa in EM); Hrsg. der kommentierten H.P. Lovecraft-Gesamtausgabe (bisher 5 Bände).

Gudrun GUTTENBERGER

studied at the Universities of Bonn, Tübingen, Heidelberg, Mainz and Rome; she studied under G. Theißen and was awarded a doctorate from Heidelberg University (1998). She taught Gender Studies at Mainz (1998–2001) and is currently Professor of Biblical Theology and Religious Education at the Evangelische Fachhochschule Hannover. Current research focus: Gospel of Mark. Email: Info@gu-gu.de / Homepage: http://www.gu-gu.de

Outi LEHTIPUU

born 1967 in Espoo, Finland. She is Researcher at the Department of Biblical Studies in the University of Helsinki. Master of Theology 1994 (Univ. of Helsinki.) BA in History 1999. Licenciate of Theology 1999. Member of the research project "Early Jewish Christianity". Academic interests: the Gospel of Luke, Concepts of afterlife in antiquity, early Jewish Christianity.

Bert Jan LIETHAERT PEERBOLTE

born 1963 in Den Haag/The Hague, NL. Studied Theology in Groningen and Leiden; PhD Leiden 1995 (The Antecedents of Antichrist); held administrative positions in the Dutch Reformed Church 1995–1998; post-doctoral scholarship granted by Kampen Theological University 1996–1998 (Paul the Missionary, forthcoming); subsequently Lecturer for New Testament at Utrecht University 1999–2000; since 2000 Lecturer for New Testament at Kampen Theological University. Research areas: Apocalypticism, the Book of Revelation, Paul and Paulinism.
Email: litaertpeerbolte@planet.nl.

Martin MEISER

geb. 1957 in Bamberg, Studium der Evangelischen Theologie in Neuendettelsau, Hamburg, Tübingen, München, 1983–1991 Vorbereitungsdienst und Pfarrdienst in der Evang.-Luth. Kirche in Bayern, 1991–2001 Assistent in Erlangen, seit 2001 Assistent in Mainz. Forschungsschwerpunkte: altkirchliche

Rezeption des Neuen Testaments, das frühe Christentum in seiner jüdischen und pagan-antiken Umwelt.
Email: mnmeiser@theologie.uni-erlangen.de

Markus ÖHLER

geb. 1967, Studium der Evangelischen Theologie in Wien, 1992–1996 Vertragsassistent, 1996–1999 Universitätsassistent, seit 2001 Ao. Prof. am Institut für Neutestamentliche Wissenschaft an der Evangelisch-theologischen Fakultät der Universität Wien, 1996–1999 Mitarbeiter am *Novum Testamentum Patristicum*, 1996 Promotion in Wien, 2001 Habilitation, 1999–2001 Forschungsaufenthalt an der Universität Tübingen. Forschungsschwerpunkte: Biblische Theologie, Sozialgeschichte des frühen Christentums (Projekt: Antikes Vereinswesen und frühes Christentum), moderne hermeneutische Ansätze.
e-mail: markus.oehler@unvie.ac.at.

Daria PEZZOLI-OLGIATI

geb. 1966 in Locarno / CH, Studium der Theologie in Freiburg i.Ue. und Zürich, 1996 Promotion in Zürich, 1997 Forschungsaufenthalt in Rom, 1998–1999 in Oxford. Seit 1995 Assistentin am Lehrstuhl für allgemeine Religionsgeschichte und Religionswissenschaft an der Theologischen Fakultät in Zürich, 2000 Oberassistentin. Forschungsschwerpunkte: Johannesoffenbarung und Apokalyptik, Probleme des religionsgeschichtlichen Vergleichs, religiöse Interpretation von Raum. Habilitationsprojekt zur religiösen Interpretation der Stadt in der Antike.

Lauri THURÉN

born 1961 in Turku, Finland. ThD 1990 in Åbo Academy University. Studies in Åbo, Berkeley, and Uppsala. Professor of Exegesis in Joensuu University, Finland. Author of Derhetorizing Paul (2000), Argument and Theology in 1 Peter (1995), and The Rhetorical Strategy of 1 Peter (1990).
Email: lauri.thuren@joensuu.fi / Homepage: http://www.abo.fi/fak/tf/personal/thuren.htm

François P VILJOEN

born 1960. Study at Potchefstroomse Universiteit vir Christelike Hoër Onderwys (RSA) 1979–1990. Promotion at Potchefstroom 1990. Practical ministry in Gereformeerde Kerke in Suid-Afrika 1998–1990 (Gobabis, Namibia); 1990–1994 (Oudtshoorn, RSA); 1994–1998 (George, RSA). Associate Professor in New Testament at Potchefstroomse Universiteit vir Christelike Hoër

Onderwys since 1998. Research: Synoptic Gospels and Church Music in the early Christian communities.
E-mail: sbbfpv@puknet.puk.ac.za   /   Homepage: http://www.puk.ac.za/theology/sbb.html

Stellenregister

I. Altes Testament

Genesis
4,21	*196*
22,1–2	*108*
22,11	*108*
46,2	*108*

Exodus
3,4	*108*
15	*196*
15,1–19	*198*
15,11	*231*
18,3	*188*
20,3	*250*

Numeri
20,15LXX	*188*
24,17	*127*

Deuteronomium
5,7	*250*
32,1–42	*198*
32,43	*203, 204*

Richter
3,9	*152*
3,15	*152*

1Samuel
2,1–10	*198*
3,4(LXX)	*108*
16,14–23	*198*
18,10	*198*
24,9	*97*
26,17	*97*
26,19	*97*
29,8	*97*

2Samuel
3,21	*97*
4,8	*97*
4,16	*231*
9,11	*97*
22,50	*203, 204*

1Könige
1,2	*97*
1,43	*97*
2,38	*97*
18,27	*250*
18,38	*243*
19,35	*186*
20,4	*97*
20,9	*97*

2Könige
2,12	*108*
3,15	*198*

Jesaja
11,10	*204*
11,20	*203*
26,9–20	*198*
35,5	*163*
42,7	*163*
43,10–13	*250*
45,15	*152*
61,1	*163*

Jeremia
2,26–28	*250*
5,22	*161*
7,16–20	*250*
27	*215, 220, 221, 222, 224, 225, 226*
27,8	*221*
27,12	*221*

Hesekiel
8	*250*
16	*250*
23	*250*

Hosea			Sprüche		
1–3	250		8,28f	161	
8,4–6	250		17,12	231	
13,7f	231		24,21	219, 220	

Jona			Daniel		
2,3–10	198		1–3	251	
			1,10	97	
Habakuk			2,21	220	
1,8	231		3	251	
			3,1	251	
			3,4f	251	
Zephania			3,4θ'	251	
1,4f	250		3,5	251	
			3,6	251	
Psalmen			3,7	251	
18,50	203, 204		3,10	251	
24,5LXX	152		3,11	251	
24	197		3,12	251	
26,1LXX	152		3,15	251	
26,9LXX	152		3,18	251	
30	197		3,26–83	198	
34,23LXX	159		4,16	97, 231	
35,15LXX	159		7	242	
48	197				
61,2LXX	152		Nehemia		
61,6LXX	152		9,27	152	
64,5LXX	152				
69,10	164		1Chronik		
74,12ff	161		6,31	196	
81	197		16,5–7	196	
82	197		16,26	240	
87,2LXX	159		21,3	97	
89,7	231		21,23	97	
89,10	161		23,5	196	
92	197				
93	197		2Chronik		
93,3	161		5,11–13	196	
94	197				
103	198				
104,6f	161				
110,1	104				
114,7	110				
117,1	203, 204				
118	198				
136	198				

II. Apokryphen und Pseudepigraphen des Alten Testaments

Ester-Zusätze

D 2 (ad 5,1)	151
E 13 (ad 8,12)	152

Hiob		
26,12f	161	
38,4–11	161	

1Makkabäer

4,30	152

2Makkabäer

5,21	*160*
7,9	*152*
7,19	*185*
9,9	*186*
9,11f	*168*
9,12	*220*
13,23	*220*

3Makkabäer

6,32	*152*
7,16	*152*

Psalmen Salomos

2,25–29	*168*

Sapientia Salomonis

14,26f	*251*
16,7	*152*

Sirach

10,7	*110*

Baruch

4,22	*152*

Apokalypse Abrahams

8,1	*108*
9,1	*108*

Apokalypse Adams und Evas

41	*108*

2Baruch (syr. Baruchapokalypse)

22,2	*108*

4Esra

4–5	*142*
14,2	*108*

1Henoch

17–19	*142*

Jakobsleiter

1,8	*108*

Joseph und Aseneth

10,13	*250*
12,5f	*250*
14,4	*108*
14,6	*108*

Jubiläenbuch

12,3–5	*250*
18,1–2,10	*108*
44,5	*108*

Liber Antiquitatum Biblicarum

44	*251*

Oracula Sibyllina

1,10	*142*
1,101	*142*
3,29–35	*251*
3,337f	*142*
4,7f	*251*
4,76–78	*160*
5,143	*222*
5,159	*222*
5,485	*142*

Armen. Paenitentia Adami

48 (41) Stone	*108*

Testamenta XII Patriarcharum

Juda

23,1	*251*

Levi

17,11	*251*

Testamentum Iobi

3,1	*108*

Testamentum Salomonis

prol 1,5	*108*
6,3	*142*

Vita Adae et Evae

37,3	*142*

III. Qumran

4Q 521

Frgm. 2 II
8　　　　　　*163*

4QEn^b ar = 4Q 202

1 IV, 5 a. o.　　*110*

11QTgJob (11Q 10)

24,6f　　　　*110*

IV. Jüdisch-hellenistische Literatur

Epistula Aristeae

187–300　　　*219*

Josephus

Antiquitates Judaicae
2,172　　　*108*
14,185–267　*24*
14,213–216　*53*
14,215　　　*53*
14,235　　　*24*
15,336　　　*33*
16,23　　　*197*
16,162ff　　*55*
17,227　　　*16*
17,300　　　*16*
17,303　　　*16*
17,314　　　*16*
18,31　　　*34*
18,33　　　*180*
18,35　　　*180*
18,55ff　　　*29*
18,66ff　　　*56*
18,250　　　*127*
18,261–288　*186*
19,4　　　　*168*
19,6　　　　*160*
19,338　　　*127*
20,113　　　*34*
20,182f　　　*185*
Contra Apionem
2,41　　　　*99*
3,216　　　*197*
De Bello Judaico
1,403　　　*154*
1,412　　　*33*
2,22　　　　*16*
2,80　　　　*16*
2,91　　　　*16*
2,118　　　*99*
2,169ff　　　*29*
2,247　　　*180*
2,389　　　*127*
2,433　　　*220*
3,289ff　　　*36*
3,350f　　　*124*
3,443–461　*126*
3,444f　　　*124*
3,445　　　*124*
3,479　　　*151*
4,112f　　　*152*
4,175–180　*220*
5,194　　　*31*
6,125f　　　*31*
6,310　　　*124*
6,312f　　　*126, 127*
7,70f　　　*152*
7,100–115　*152*
7,418　　　*99*
Vita
52　　　　*124, 125*

Philo

De Abrahamo
176　　　　*108*
De Ebrietate
20f　　　　*56*
De Fuga et Inventione
162　　　　*152*
De Sobrietate
53　　　　*152*
De Specialibus Legibus
II 198　　　*152*
De Vita Mosis
3,216　　　*197*
In Flaccum
4　　　　　*56, 61*
36–39　　　*110*
103　　　　*180*
136ff　　　*56*
136　　　　*65*
163　　　　*180*
Legatio ad Gaium
114　　　　*168*
118　　　　*168*
155　　　　*181*
157　　　　*29, 181*
162　　　　*168*
317　　　　*29*
Quis Rerum Divinarum Heres sit
22　　　　*98*
Quod Deus sit Immutabilis
156　　　　*152*

Pseudo-Philo

  De Jona
    2,7   *152*
    39,155   *152*
    52,214   *152*

Pseudo-Phocylides
    60,3   *142*

V. Neues Testament

Logienquelle
3,4	*103*
4,1–13	*107*
4,8	*103, 104*
4,12	*103, 104*
6,20–49	*105, 107, 108*
6,36	*103*
6,40	*106*
6,46	*95, 105, 107, 108, 111*
7,1–10	*105, 112*
7,6	*105*
7,22	*163*
9,59–60	*105*
9,59	*105*
10,2	*103*
10,21	*103*
10,22	*107*
11,2	*103*
11,13	*103*
11,25	*106*
12,6	*103*
12,30	*103*
12,39–40	*104*
12,39	*106*
12,42–46	*104*
12,43	*104*
12,45	*104*
12,46	*104*
12,53	*103*
13,5	*104*
13,25–27	*106*
13,25	*104, 105*
13,34	*108*
13,35	*103*
14,16–23	*104*
14,21	*104, 106*
16,13	*103, 104, 106*
17,?–35	*106*
17,23–35	*104*
19,12–27	*104*
19,12–26	*106*
19,15–16	*104*
19,18	*104*
19,20	*104*
22,8	*112*
22,30	*112*

Matthäus
5,16	*65*
5,41	*113*
7,21	*107*
8,11	*133*
8,12	*133*
9,27–31	*163*
10,24	*106*
13,40–42	*133*
13,42	*133*
14,22ff	*160*
22,21	*189*
24,9	*63*
24,51	*133*
25,30	*133*
25,31–46	*133*
27,37	*30*

Markus
2,1ffparr	*163*
2,17	*120*
3,6	*128*
4,35ffparr	*160*
5,1	*120*
6,6	*120*
6,14	*180*
6,15	*119*
6,27	*128*
6,45ff	*160*
6,45	*120*
7,24	*120, 121*
8,13	*120*
8,22–26	*120, 128, 163*
8,27	*120, 121*
8,28	*120*
8,29	*120*
8,33	*120*
9,7	*129*
9,13	*128*
10,46ffparr	*163*
10,46	*120*
10,52	*120, 121*
11,1	*120*
11,11	*120*

12,13–17	*128, 218, 223*
13	*128, 129*
13,13	*63*
14,1f	*120*
14,3	*120*
14,61	*119*
14,62	*129*
15,26	*30*
15,39	*129, 167*

Lukas

1–2	*136*
1,1–4	*180*
1,53	*135*
2,1	*43*
2,11	*150, 187*
2,14	*187*
3,1	*180*
3,14	*176*
3,19	*180, 184*
4,6	*187*
4,28–30	*187*
4,31–44	*187*
6,9	*66*
6,21	*135*
6,33	*66*
6,35	*66*
7,1–10	*176*
8,14	*180*
9,7	*180*
11,37–52	*180*
13,1–5	*184, 185, 189, 190*
13,9	*180*
13,28f	*133*
13,31	*189*
14,1–24	*180*
14,1–6	*180*
16,19–31	*133*
16,23	*143*
16,24	*143*
20,20	*187*
20,26	*187*
21,12	*180*
21,24	*186*
22,25	*178, 181*
22,31	*108*
23,1–25	*176, 185, 187*
23,38	*30*

Johannes

1,1	*168*
1,9f	*166*
1,12	*149*
1,18	*168*
1,19ff	*164*
1,29	*149, 153*
1,36	*153*
1,47	*154*
1,49	*154, 164*
2,1–4,54	*148, 149, 154*
2,1–11	*164*
2,11	*149*
2,13ff	*164*
2,17	*164*
3	*166*
3,11ff	*149*
3,16f	*149, 153*
3,16	*153*
3,19	*166*
4,1–42	*149*
4,4ff	*149*
4,10	*149*
4,13f	*149*
4,21	*149*
4,22	*153, 156*
4,23	*149*
4,41f	*149*
4,42	*148, 151, 152, 153, 154, 155, 156, 167*
4,46–54	*148, 149, 155*
4,46–53	*112*
4,47–49	*156*
4,53	*156*
5,1ff	*162*
5,18	*163, 168*
5,26	*147*
6,1–25	*160*
6,14	*154, 161*
6,15	*154, 157, 161, 166*
6,16–21	*160, 166*
6,18	*160*
6,32ff	*147*
6,57	*147*
7,1	*163*
7,19ff	*163*
7,25	*154*
8,31	*154*
8,37ff	*163*
9,1–10,21	*164*
9,1ff	*161*
9,1	*162*
9,6f	*161, 162*

9,39–41	*164*
10	*163*
10,1ff	*163*
11,52	*153*
11,53	*163*
12,23–28	*166*
12,31	*166*
13,34f	*167*
13,34	*167*
15,4	*167*
15,12f	*167*
15,12	*167*
15,16f	*167*
15,17	*167*
15,18f	*167*
15,21	*63*
18,4–12	*166*
18,33	*156*
18,36	*165, 166*
18,37	*156*
18,38	*167*
18,39	*156*
19,3	*156*
19,10f	*166*
19,11	*168*
19,14	*157*
19,15	*157, 167*
19,19	*30, 153, 156*
19,21	*156*
20,28	*99, 148, 157, 159*
20,29	*157*
20,30f	*157, 160, 167*

Apostelgeschichte

1,1f	*180*
2,10	*176*
4	*185*
4,19	*187*
4,20	*187*
4,25–29	*187*
4,27	*176, 184, 185, 189*
5	*185*
5,29	*176, 185, 187, 188, 189, 190, 223*
5,37	*185*
5,38f	*185*
5,41	*185*
5,42	*187*
9	*187*
9,4	*108*
9,23f	*176*
10	*176*
11,26	*62*
12	*180, 185, 186*
12,20–24	*186*
12,20–23	*186*
12,20	*180*
12,21–24	*187*
12,21–23	*187, 189*
12,24f	*186*
13,7ff	*66*
14,19f	*187*
14,22	*187*
15,29	*249*
16,12	*180*
16,16	*106*
16,19	*179*
16,21	*176, 179*
16,22–24	*181*
16,35–40	*187*
16,37	*223*
16,39	*176*
17,4	*66*
17,5	*176*
17,6f	*179*
17,6	*180*
17,7	*179*
17,8	*180*
17,9	*181*
17,12	*66*
17,22–31	*136*
17,28	*180*
18,12–17	*189*
18,12–16	*184*
18,12	*179*
18,13	*179*
18,17	*184*
19,23–27	*179*
19,31	*175*
19,37–39	*187*
19,37	*175, 179*
19,38f	*187*
21–26	*177, 178, 180*
22,3	*197*
22,7	*108*
21,13	*187*
22,25	*187*
23,1	*187*
23,29	*175, 187*
24,2–4	*176*
24,2	*18, 187*
24,5	*179*
24,6	*179*

24,13	*187*		4,5	*111*
24,16	*187*		5,1–8	*74*
24,22–27	*176, 189, 190*		6,9–11	*74*
24,22	*175*		6,15–18	*74*
24,27	*176*		6,15	*73*
25,4	*175*		6,18	*74*
25,5	*180*		7,10	*111*
25,8	*179, 187*		7,12	*111*
25,9	*176*		8	*250*
25,10f	*187*		8,5f	*112*
25,10	*187*		8,5	*97*
25,16	*175, 180*		8,9	*250*
25,25	*175, 187*		9,5	*111*
25,26	*99, 100, 112*		10,14	*249*
26,14	*108*		11,17–34	*84*
26,22	*187*		11,23	*111*
26,28	*62*		11,26	*84, 111*
26,32	*175*		12,2	*249*
27	*176*		12,12–26	*76*
28,17–19	*175*		13–15	*195, 205*
28,30f	*183*		13–14	*205*
			13,1	*205*
Römer			13,12	*75*
1,1–17	*203*		14,3–9	*205*
1,3–4	*96*		14,3	*207*
1,7	*203*		14,7	*205*
1,15	*203*		14,8	*206*
1,18–21	*203*		14,15–17	*206*
6,18	*67*		14,16	*207*
6,22	*67*		14,17	*207*
12,1	*203*		14,26	*207*
13	*189, 215, 219, 223, 224*		15	*207*
			15,26	*84*
13,1–7	*175, 189*		15,29	*60*
13,3	*66*		15,52	*207*
14,3	*203*		16,22	*110*
14,10	*203*			
15,1–13	*203*		2Korinther	
15,1–3	*203*		3,18	*75*
15,5–6	*203*		4,7	*76*
15,6	*203*		5,10	*133*
15,8–9	*203, 205*		6,16	*249*
15,9–12	*195, 203*		11,23f	*176*
15,9	*204*		11,32	*110*
15,10	*204*			
15,11	*204*		Galater	
15,12	*204*		1,18f	*109*
			1,19	*111*
1Korinther			5,13	*67*
1,21–25	*84*		5,20	*249*
2,2	*84*		6,7–10	*133*
3,10–15	*75*			

Epheser

4,5	*112*
5,3–14	*208*
5,15–20	*208*
5,15	*208*
5,16	*208*
5,17	*208*
5,18ff	*209*
5,18–19	*210*
5,18	*208, 210*
5,19	*195, 208*
5,20	*208*
5,21ff	*208*

Kolosser

3,5–15	*210*
3,16	*195, 210*
3,17	*210*

1Thessalonicher

1,9	*249*
2,14	*176*
4,15	*111*
5,15ff	*111*

Philipper

2,6–11	*156*
2,11	*96, 107*
4,5	*111*

1Timotheus

2	*189*
2,1f	*167, 189*

Titus

2,12	*167*
3,1	*215, 219*

1Petrus

1,1–2,10	*216*
1,1	*216*
1,3	*216*
1,14	*66, 216*
1,15f	*65*
1,18	*216*
1,23	*216*
2–3	*215*
2	*189, 219*
2,5	*65*
2,7–8	*216*
2,9	*65*
2,11–17	*65*
2,11f	*65*
2,11	*66*
2,13–17	*65, 66, 225*
2,13–14	*217*
2,13	*224, 225*
2,15	*67*
2,17	*65, 67, 189, 217*
2,18–3,7	*225*
2,18–20	*225*
2,18	*224, 225*
2,20	*66*
2,21–25	*225*
2,21–24	*224*
2,25	*66, 216*
3,6	*66*
3,11	*66*
3,12	*217*
3,16	*216*
3,17	*66*
3,18–22	*216*
4,2–6	*216*
4,3	*65, 66*
4,5	*217*
4,16	*62, 63*
4,17–18	*216*
4,18	*217*
4,19	*66*
5	*225*
5,2–5	*225*
5,2	*225*
5,3	*225*
5,5	*225*
5,9	*65, 222*
5,13	*65, 222*

1Johannes

4,14	*152, 156*

3Johannes

11	*66*

Apokalypse

1,9	*232*
1,10	*235*
2–3	*229, 233, 235*
2,3	*63*
2,7	*229*
2,9	*231*
2,11	*229*

2,14	235	17–18	218, 232, 233, 235
2,17	229	17,1f	241
2,29	229	17,3	251
3,5	232	17,6	241
3,6	229	17,7ff	233
3,13	229	17,7	233
3,22	229	17,8	232
4	235, 242	17,9–14	233
4,8	242	17,11	251
4,10	242	17,14	241
5	231, 232	17,18	222, 241
5,2	231	18	233
5,6	242	19,4	242
5,8	235	19,17–23	241
5,14	242	19,20	243, 251
7,11	242	20,4	251
9,20	251	20,10	243
11,2	231	20,11–21,4	133
11,3	231	21,1	230
11,16	242	21,27	232
12,3	242	22,8	242
12,6	231	22,20	110
12,9	242		
12,10	243		
12,11	243		
12,15	235		
13	242, 243, 251		
13,1–10	229, 231, 232, 235		
13,1–3	229, 230, 242		
13,3–4	230, 231, 232, 243		
13,3	229, 235		
13,4	231		
13,5–7	230, 231		
13,7–8	239		
13,7	251		
13,8	230, 232, 243, 251		
13,9	233		
13,9–10	230, 232		
13,11–18	235		
13,12	251		
13,13	243		
13,14	251		
13,15	243, 251		
13,16f	241		
13,18	233		
14,9	251		
14,11	251		
15,2	251		
16,2	251		
16,13	243		

VI. Apostolische Väter

1 Clemens

59–61	189

Didache

10,6	110, 111

An Diognet

5	188, 219
5,10	188
5,16	67
7,1f	188

Polycarp

Epistulae

12,3	188
2,3	188

VII. Neutestamentliche Apokryphen

Acta Pauli et Theclae

26	255
28	256

Acta Thomae
  6,55–57   *134*

Oracula Sibyllina
  2,252–310   *134*
  2,303   *142*

Paulus-Apokalypse
  31–42   *134*

Petrus-Apokalypse
  7–12   *134*

VIII. Altkirchliche Schriften und Autoren

Acta Apollonii
  37   *189*

Acta Carpi et Papylae (lat. Text)
  7   *112*

Acta Cypriani
  6   *112*

Acta Felicitatis
  15   *189*

Acta Irenaei
  6   *112*

Acta S. Maximi
  Schlusssatz   *112*

Acta Polycarpi
  8,2   *112*
  10,2   *189*
  21,1   *188*

Acta Scilitanorum
  9   *189*

Aristides
  Apologia
    2,1   *240*

  15,8   *179*

Athenagoras
  Legatio pro Christianis
    2   *179*
    37   *189*

Basilius
  Moralia
    11,3   *189*
    59,1   *189*

Ps.-Cyprian
  Ad Novatianum
    15,4   *189*
  De Singularitate Clericorum
    5   *189*

Epiphanius
  Haereses
    42,11,15   *189*

Eusebius
  Historia Ecclesiastica
    1,7,14 (Julius Africanus)
                  111
    2,10,1   *189*
    6,14,7   *168*
    7,11,5   *189*
  Praeparatio Evangelica
    13,10,13   *189*

Hippolyt von Rom
  Refutatio Omnium Haeresium
    IX 12,9   *99*

Irenaeus
  Adversus Haereses
    3,8,1   *189*
    5,24   *189*
    5,30,3   *252*

Justinus
  1 Apologia
    4   *179*
    11   *188*
    12   *188*
    17,3   *188*
    24,2   *240*

2 Apologia
    2,15   *183*
Dialogus
    55,2   *240*

Lactantius
  De Mortibus Persecutorum
    3   *158*

Minucius Felix
  Octavius
    8,4   *62, 64*

Origenes
  Ad Africanum de Historia Susannae
    14   *25*
  Commentarii in Epistulam ad Romanos
    9,27   *189*
  Contra Celsum
    1,1   *62, 64*

Hermae Pastor
    5,3(=56,3f)   *67*

Tertullianus
  Apologeticum
    2,8   *183*
    30,4   *189*
    39   *64*
  De Fuga in Persecutione
    12,6   *189*
    12,8,9   *189*
  Scorpiace
    14,2f   *189*

Theophilus von Antiochien
  An Autolycus
    1,11,1   *188, 189*
    3,8   *188*
    3,14   *189*

IX. Gnostica

Corpus Hermenticum
    18,16   *247*

X. Rabbinische Literatur/Judaica

Talmud Babli
    Hullin 139b   *109*
    Ketubbot 103b *108*
    Makkot 24a   *108*
    Sanhedrin 139b *109*

Talmud Yerushalmi
    Megillah 3,3 74a *21*

Genesis Rabba
    8,10   *100*

Qohelet Rabba
    6,10   *100*

XI. Außerchristliche antike Literatur

Apollonius Rhodius
  Argonautica
    2,704   *109*

Appianus
  Bellum Civile
    2,21,149f *160*

Archilochos
    Fragmenta 88 *109*

Aelius Aristides
  Orationes
    43,1   *149*
    43,30   *149*
    45,20   *149*
    45,25   *149*
    47,66   *149*

Aristophanes
  Fragmenta
    370   *73*
  Thesmophoriazusae
    295   *109*

Aristoteles
   Poetica
      I 1447,28   *200*
   Politica
      5–7   *201*

Arrianus
   Anabasis
      1,26,2   *160*

Artemidorus
   Oneirocritus
      2,39   *149*

Athenaeus
   Deipnosophistae
      XIII 559a   *73*

Aurelius Victor
   Liber de Caesaribus
      11,2   *157*

Callimachus
   Hymni
      1,91ff   *109*

Cicero
   De Natura Deorum
      I,3   *249*
   Epistulae ad Atticum
      6.1.15   *17*
   Epistulae ad Quintum Fratrem
      1,3,1–10   *108*
      2,3,5   *52, 61*
   In L. Pisonem
      9   *51, 52*
   Post Reditum in Senatu
      13,33   *52*
   Post Reditum ad Quirites
      5,13   *52*
   Pro Cnaeo Plancio
      12,29   *248*
      15,36   *52*
      18,45   *52*
   Pro P. Sextio
      34,55   *52*
   Tusculanae Disputationes
      1,16   *144*
      3,22   *83*

Codex Theodosianus
   2,1,10   *21*

Demosthenes
   Orationes
      18,43   *149*

Digesta Iustiniani
   3,4,1   *60*
   4,8   *20*
   47,22,1,1   *60*
   47,22,1,2   *61*
   47,22,2   *61*
   47,22,3   *61*
   47,22,3,2   *61*
   47,22,4   *51, 60*
   48,4   *61*
   50,1,28   *20*
   50,6,6,12   *60*

Dio Cassius
   Historiae Romanae
      21 (=Zonaras 9,31)
          83
      38,13,1f   *52*
      48,39,2   *164*
      52,36,1f   *55*
      57,8,2   *98*
      60,6,6   *56*
      60,17,5   *181*
      60,35,4   *184*
      61,20,1   *184*
      64,8,1   *127*
      64,93   *126*
      66,8,1   *161*
      67,4,75   *157*
      67,12,2   *256*
      67,13,4   *157*

Dio Chrysostomus
   Orationes
      1,84   *149*
      3,31   *160*
      37,11   *103*
      45,1   *157, 253*

Diodorus Siculus
   Bibliotheca Historica
      3,61,4   *103*
      3,61,6   *99*

Stellenregister

20,100,3	*149*
37,26,1	*149*

Diogenes Laertius

Vitae Philosophorum
5,16	*149*

Dionysius Harlicarnassensis

Antiquitates Romanae
1,3,3	*150*
4,32,1	*150*
4,43,2	*51*

Euripides

Bacchae
45–48	*185*
83	*109*
152	*109*

Ion
125f	*109*

Phoenissae
1604ff	*143*

Eutropius

Breviarium ab Urbe Condita
7,23	*252*

Florus

Epitoma Bellorum Omnium Annorum DCC
1,6,3	*51*

Gellius

Noctes Atticae
16,13,9	*42*

Herodotus

Historiae
7,35	*160*
7,65	*160*

Hesiodus

Opera et Dies
167–173	*141*

Theogonia
713–735	*138*
740	*143*

Historia Augusta

Hadrianus
25	*161*

Homer

Ilias
5,31	*109*
8,13–15	*138*
23,99–101	*137*

Odyssee
4,561–569	*141*
10,491	*137*
11,14–19	*137*
11,38–41	*137, 139*
11,51–83	*137, 139*
11,152–224	*139*
11,204–208	*137*
11,218–222	*137*
11,225–332	*137, 139*
11,385–566	*137, 139*
11,489–491	*137*
11,541–566	*139*
11,576–600	*137*
11,576–581	*139*
11,582–600	*139*
11,582–592	*135*
12,1–15	*137*
24,1–10	*143*

Q. Horatius Flaccus

Carmina
2,19,7–8	*109*

Homerische Hymnen
22,5	*149*

Isocrates

Panegyricus
88f	*160*

Julianus Imperator

Contra Galilaeos
43b	*249*

Livius

Ab Urbe Condita
39,8,3ff	*51*
39,15,11	*51*
39,18,3–6	*61*

Lucanus
> De Bello Civili
>> 5   *160*

Lucianus
> Alexander
>> 4   *149*
>
> Charon sive Contemplantes
>> 15   *248*
>
> De Peregrini Morte
>> 11   *62*
>
> Dialogi Mortuorum
>> 12   *186*
>> 14   *186*
>> 16   *186*
>
> Philopseudes sive Incredulus
>> 25   *143*

Lysias
> Orationes
>> 2,29   *160*

Marcellus Empiricus
> De Medicamentis
>> 36,70   *109*

Martialis
> Epigrammata
>> 2,91,1   *151*
>> 4,1,10   *182*
>> 5,1,7   *151*
>> 5,5,2   *182*
>> 5,8,1   *157, 182, 252*
>> 7,2,6   *182*
>> 7,8,2   *182*
>> 7,34,8   *157*
>> 8,2,6   *157*
>> 8,66,6   *151*
>> 9,66,3   *157*
>> 10,72   *158*
>> 10,72,1–3   *157, 253*
>> 10,72,3   *182*
>> 12,6,3f   *182*

Menander
> Fragmenta 924K *160*

Ovidius
> Ars Amatoria
>> 2,1   *109*
>
> Ex Ponto
>> 8,26   *98*
>
> Fasti
>> 2,142   *98*
>
> Tristia
>> 4,10,7f   *181*

Ps-Ovidius
> Nux
>> 145f   *151*

Parmenides
> 1,18   *143*

Pausanias
> Graeciae Descriptio
>> 1,8,5   *149*
>> 2,1,9   *149*
>> 2,2,3   *77*
>> 2,2,6–8   *81*
>> 2,3,1   *82*
>> 2,3,6–11   *78*
>> 2,3,6   *77, 79*
>> 10,29,1   *135*

Philostratos
> Vita Apollonii
>> 5,33   *249*
>> 7,24   *256*
>> 8,4   *157*

Pindarus
> Isthmia
>> 5,53   *97*
>
> Olympia
>> 5,17   *149*

Platon
> Apologia
>> 29d   *185*
>
> Gorgias
>> 523a–527e   *142*
>> 523a–b   *142*
>> 524a   *140*
>> 524c–525a   *143*
>> 525b–526b   *142*
>
> Leges
>> VII 812e   *201*
>
> Phaedo
>> 112a–114c   *142*

Stellenregister

113a–114a *142*
113d–114c *142*
114b–c *142*
Phaedrus
   248e–249b *142*
Politicus
   267e *163*
   275b–c *163*
Respublica
   345b–e *163*
   398ff *201*
   404d *73*
   614b–621d *142*
   614c–d *143*
   615e–616b *142*

Plinius d.Ä.
  Naturalis Historia
   5,15,71 *122*
   5,16,18 *122*
   27,106,131 *109*
   34,1,1 *51*
   35,46,159 *51*

Plinius d.J.
  Epistulae
   10,33 *58, 61*
   10,34 *58*
   10,92f *58*
   10,93 *58*
   10,96–97 *183, 218*
   10,96 *59, 62, 239*
   10,96,2–4 *63*
   10,96,2 *239*
   10,96,4 *63*
   10,96,5f *63*
   10,96,6 *239*
   10,96,7 *63, 64*
   10,96,8 *63, 239*
   10,96,9 *66*
   10,97 *64, 240*
  Panegyricus
   2,3 *157, 253*
   5,6 *150*
   6,1 *150*
   6,2 *150*
   8,1 *150*
   22,3 *150, 161*
   30,5 *150*
   42,3 *150*
   52,2 *157*
   52,3 *157*

   67,6 *150*

Plutarchus
  Alexander
   17 *160*
  Antonius
   24,4 *164*
  Brutus
   30,3f *98*
  Caesar
   37,7 *160*
   38,5 *160*
  Camillus
   10,6 *150*
  De Defectu Oraculorum
   7 (413c) *103*
  De Fortuna Alexandri
   329c *150*
  De Genio Socratis
   21f *142*
  De Iside et Osiride
   12 (355e) *103*
   35 (365a) *103*
  De Sera Numinis Vindicta
   22–33 *142*
   27f *143*
  Dion
   46,1 *150*
  Numa
   17,1ff *51*

Polybius
  Historiae
   6,56,6f *249*
   16,18,2 *121*

Q. Asconius Pedianus
  Commentationes in Aliquot Orationes M. Tullii Ciceronis
   In L. Pisonem 8
     52
   Pro L. Cornelio Balbo 67
     52

Claudius Ptolemaeus
  Geographia
   5.15.21 *122*
   8.20.12 *122*

Quintilianus
   Institutio Oratoria
      3,7,9   *186*

Seneca
   Naturales Quaestiones
      4 praef 10f *184*
   Oedipus Rex
      567   *109*
      622   *109*

Sophokles
   Aiax
      695   *109*

Statius
   Silvae
      1,1,62   *253*
      1,61ff   *182*
      2,7,32   *184*
      5,2,170   *253*

Strabon
   Geographica
      8,6,20   *73*
      10,5,3   *73*

Suetonius
   De Vita Caesarum
     Augustus
       31,4   *52*
       32,1   *54*
       53   *105*
       53,1   *98, 158*
     Caligula
       19,3   *160*
     Claudius
       25,4   *57*
     Domitianus
       8,2   *182*
       12   *256*
       13,2   *158, 159, 182, 252*
     Iulius Caesar
       42,3   *53*
       84,5   *66*
     Nero
       16   *218*
       57   *126*
       57,2   *126*
     Tiberius
       27   *98, 158*
       36   *56*
     Titus
       5   *125*
     Vespasianus
       1   *127*
       4,5   *126, 127*
       7   *127, 129*
       7,2   *161, 162*

Tabula Irnitana
   84   *20*
   89   *20*

Tabulae duodecim
   8,27   *51*

Tacitus
   Annales
      2,85   *56*
      2,87   *98*
      3,60–63 *246*
      3,60   *247*
      3,63   *247*
      4,36   *247*
      12,54,1 *184*
      14,17   *57*
      15,44   *218*
      15,73   *184*
   Historiae
      2,8,1   *126*
      4,81,1–3 *161*
      4,81–82 *127, 129*
      5,5,1–3 *249*
      5,9,3   *184*
      5,13   *127*
      5,13,2   *126*

Vergilius
   Aeneis
      6,236–901 *136*
      6,272–312 *139*
      6,337–383 *139*
      6,413   *143*
      6,440–476 *139*
      6,477–534 *139*
      6,548–627 *139*
      6,608–614 *139*
      6,700–702 *139*
      6,679–892 *139*

7,1–20   *137*

Xenophon

  Anabasis
  1,8,16   *149*

XII. Antike Inschriften

AE

  1902, 230 (= 1926,136)
                44
  1971, 477 (= Pilatus-Inschrift)
                32–34

CIG

  2349   *151*
  4335   *151*
  4336   *151*
  4337   *151*
  4339   *151*

CIL

  I² 581   *51, 55, 61*
  III 13587   *44*
  III 6813 (= DESSAU 1038)
                40
  VI 2193   *55*
  VI 4416   *55*
  XIV 2112 p.I l.10–13
                60
  XIV 2112 p.I *l*.10–13
                59
  XVI 33   *44*

GIBM

  600   *164*

I.Eph

  27   *99*
  271F   *151*
  II 459   *29*
  VII 2 3501   *29*
  VII 2 3502   *29*

I.Mil

  VI,2 940f   *66*
  VI,2 940g   *66*
  VI,2 940h   *66*

I.Smyr

  519   *151*

IBM

  IV/1 894   *151*

IG

  V/1 380   *151*
  VIII 1840   *151*
  XII/1 978   *151*
  XII/5 557   *151*

IG²

  II 3284   *151*
  III/1 3273   *151*
  III/1 3293   *151*
  III/1 3384   *151*
  III/1 3385   *151*

IGR

  III 209   *164*
  III 210   *164*
  III 609   *151*
  III 610   *151*
  III 718   *151*
  III 719   *151*
  III 721   *151*
  III 729   *151*
  IV 305   *151*

ILS

  4966   *55*
  II/2 7212   *59, 60*

ISM

  68,28–38   *154*

Le Bas

  1342   *151*

OGIS

  415   *110*
  418,1   *110*
  423,2   *110*
  425,3   *110*
  426,3   *110*
  458,32ff   *151*
  458,35   *151*

489,1	*97*		63,10	*23*
606	*97*		63,11	*23*
607,2	*97*			
669	*100*		P.Jericho	

RÉS 1919

    2117 *110*

SEG

    31,1405–1407 *35*
    I 329,29–39 *154*

SIG³

    760   *151*
    814   *150*

Syll³

    408,6f   *149*
    814,32   *99*
    814   *100*

XIII. Papyri

BGU

    IV 1074   *55*
    V 1,108   *61*

P.Agon

    1   *55*
    6   *55*

P.Euphr

    1   *20*

P.Fouad

    266   *101*

P.Hever

    13   *21, 23*
    61   *23*
    63   *21, 22*
    63,4   *23*
    63,6f   *23*
    63,8   *23*

P.Jericho

    16   *14*

P.Lond

    III 1178   *55*

P.Mur

    29   *19*
    30   *19*
    114   *16*

P.Oxy

    1021   *150*
    1029   *58*

P.Tebtunis

    2,248,6   *99*

P.Yadin

    9   *21, 23*
    13   *14*
    15   *14*
    15,10f   *18*
    15,26f   *18*
    21   *16*
    24   *14*
    26,2–11   *14*

PGM

    13,201f   *103*

RDGE

    22   *15*
    58,53–6   *15*

XIV. Samaritanische Literatur

Memar Marqah

    1,1   *108*

TANZ – Texte und Arbeiten zum Neutestamentlichen Zeitalter

Markus Sasse
Der Menschensohn im Evangelium nach Johannes

TANZ 35, 2000, XIV, 336 Seiten, div. Tab.,
€ 43,–/SFr 77,–
ISBN 3-7720-2827-6

Das Johannesevangelium ist von einer christologischen Intention geleitet – Ziel ist die theologische Integration von ausgestoßenen Judenchristen in eine johanneische Gemeinde. Die Menschensohnchristologie beantwortet die Fragen, die für die theologisch orientierungslos gewordene Gemeinde am wichtigsten sind: "Ist Jesus der Messias?" und "Warum mußte Jesus sterben?". Diese beiden Fragen vermag keine andere christologische Konzeption im Johannesevangelium zusammen zu beantworten. Nach einer Einführung in die Kommunikationssituation des Johannesevangeliums bietet Markus Sasses Untersuchung ausführliche Auslegungen der Jesus-reden, in denen der Menschensohnbegriff eine wichtige Rolle spielt. Neben einer traditionsgeschichtlichen Herleitung der verwendeten Motive geht es v.a. um die Bestimmung der argumentativen Funktion des Menschensohnbegriffs in der Jesus-Biographie des Johannesevangeliums.

Holger Sonntag
ΝΟΜΟΣ ΣΩΤΗΡ
Zur politischen Theologie des Gesetzes bei Paulus und im antiken Kontext

TANZ 34, 2000, XII, 376 Seiten,
€ 48,–/SFr 86,–
ISBN 3-7720-2826-8

Wie wird ein Mensch gerecht, wie kann er ein sicheres, kultiviert-menschliches, kurz: lebenswertes Leben führen und – für den jüdisch-christlichen Bereich: über den Tod hinaus – bewahren? In dieser philologisch-thematisch aufgebauten Untersuchung wird herausgearbeitet, daß nach gemein-antiker Auffassung das Gesetz eine zentrale Rolle bei der Erlangung und Bewahrung von Gerechtigkeit und gutem Leben spielt. Die paulinische Kritik an diesem Konsens paganer, jüdischer und christlicher Autoren verdankt sich der Offenbarung des einen Evangeliums Jesu Christi. Denn dieses stellt als verbindliche Äußerung des einen Gottes nicht nur den Weg zur Beseitigung vergangener und gegenwärtiger Schuld dar; darüber hinaus ist es auch die Weisung für richtiges Handeln gegenüber Gott und den Mitmenschen. Auf Grund dieses Doppelcharakters steht das Evangelium des Paulus aber im Konflikt mit allen anderen Normen, seien sie jüdischer oder paganer Provenienz.

Gabriele Faßbeck
Der Tempel der Christen
Traditionsgeschichtliche Untersuchungen zur Aufnahme des Tempelkonzepts im frühen Christentum

TANZ 33, 2000, XII, 317 Seiten,
€ 48,–/SFr 86,–
ISBN 3-7720-2825-X

In der neutestamentlichen Forschung war die Beschäftigung mit Tempel und Kult des Frühjudentums lange von Vorbehalten geprägt, die eher die theologischen Präferenzen der Wissenschaftler widerspiegelten als die historischen Sachverhalte in der Zeit des frühen Christentums. Neuere Arbeiten haben die Bedeutung des Tempels auch für die ersten christlichen Generationen erkannt. Diese Untersuchung zeigt auf, wie interessiert frühchristliche Autoren an der Übernahme tempeltheologischer Konzepte waren und welche Wege sie beschritten, um diese für ihre eigenen Aussageabsichten fruchtbar zu machen.

A. Francke Verlag Tübingen und Basel